STATISTICAL HANDBOOK ON THE AMERICAN FAMILY
Second Edition

Edited by
Bruce A. Chadwick and Tim B. Heaton

Oryx Press
1999

The rare Arabian Oryx is believed to have inspired the myth of the unicorn. This desert antelope became virtually extinct in the early 1960s. At that time, several groups of international conservationists arranged to have nine animals sent to the Phoenix Zoo to be the nucleus of a captive breeding herd. Today, the Oryx population is over 1,000, and over 500 have been returned to the Middle East.

© 1999 The Oryx Press
4041 North Central at Indian School Road
Phoenix, Arizona 85012-3397

Published simultaneously in Canada
Printed and bound in the United States of America

∞ The paper used in this publication meets the minimum requirements of American National Standard for Information Science—Permanence of Paper for Printed Library Materials, ANSI Z39.48, 1984.

Library of Congress Cataloging-in-Publication Data

Statistical handbook on the American family/[compiled] by Bruce A. Chadwick and Tim B. Heaton.—2nd ed.
    p. cm.
Includes bibliographical references and index.
ISBN 1-57356-169-X (alk. paper)
    1. Family—United States—Statistics.   2. United States—Statistics, Vital.   I. Chadwick, Bruce A.   II. Heaton, Tim B.
HQ536.S727   1999
306.85'0973'021—dc21   98-42669
                                         CIP

Contents

List of Tables and Figures

Preface

Today, many Americans appear convinced that the family continues to be in the throes of a series of crises. A rather high national rate of divorce and the subsequent effects on children, the neglect of children by working parents, teenage pregnancy, out-of-wedlock births, changing family roles, and family violence continue to be topics of discussion, debate, and, occasionally, legislation related to the American family. These trends in various aspects of family life provide mixed evidence about the current state of the American family. On the one hand, the vast majority of Americans are still marrying and the divorce rate has actually declined a little. On the other hand, young people are delaying marriage, many are cohabiting before marriage, out-of-wedlock births continue to increase, and fertility has dropped to near replacement level.

This new statistical handbook has been prepared so that interested individuals will have the latest information, enabling them to make their own informed evaluations about the American family at the end of the 20th century and the beginning of the 21st. The 340 tables, charts, and illustrations presented in these pages contain the most recent family data available. They document substantial change in some dimensions of family life and remarkable stability in others. The perception of overall family decline or improvement is left to the reader.

All of the tables, figures, and illustrations contained in this second edition are new. A few tables from the original *Statistical Handbook on the American Family* have been extended to include information from 1996 or 1997. In addition, a new section on family demographics and economic context has been added. Information about family income, assets, and debts is presented, as well as home ownership, health insurance, and consumer patterns. Also, statistics concerning poverty and public assistance are reported. These demographics, along with the economic context, enhance the readers' understanding of the contemporary American family.

We have searched the many public domain national databases for information about the family. All of the tables and figures in this book report national data, with the exception of a few that contain material about the 50 individual states. The *Statistical Abstract of the United States* was a source of valuable demographic information (*Statistical Abstract of the United States, 1997*. U.S. Department of Commerce. Bureau of the Census, 1997). It provides statistical data from a variety of publications, produced by both government agencies and private entities.

The second wave of the *National Survey of Families and Households*, a public-use national sample of over 13,000 households, was conducted in 1993 and 1994 (*National Survey of Families and Households, 1995* [machine-readable data file], James Sweet and Larry Bumpass, principal investigators. Distributed by the Center for Demography and Ecology, University of Wisconsin–Madison). We computed a large number of insightful tables about family processes and feelings about family life using these data. These tables included information about the nation as a whole, for men and women, and for those with different marital status, different levels of education, and belonging to different racial/ethnic groups.

The *General Social Survey* conducted by the National Opinion Research Center over a 25-year period (1972-1997) allowed the computation of tables presenting significant information about family attitudes and how such attitudes have changed over the years. Approximately 1,500 interviews with adults over the age of 18 have been obtained each year, which have included a sizable number of questions about the family (Davis, James Allan and Smith, Tom W. *General Social Surveys, 1972-1997* [machine-readable data file]. NORC ed. Chicago: National Opinion Research Center, producer, 1997; Storrs, CT: The Roper Center for Public Opinion Research, University of Connecticut, distributor).

Demographic information on family formation, sexual activity, and fertility was obtained from the *1995*

National Survey of Family Growth. Interviews about their family lives were obtained from 10,847 women between 15 and 44 years of age (Abma J., Chadra A., Mosher W., Peterson L., and Piccinio L. *Fertility, Family Planning and Women's Health: New Data from the 1995 National Survey of Family Growth*. National Center for Health Statistics. Vital Health Stat 23(19) 1997).

Nearly all of the tables and figures have been created especially for this volume. The only exceptions are a few tables previously published by the Gallup organization. This previously unpublished material, along with some relevant published material, provides a rich cache of current information regarding the status of contemporary American families.

Acknowledgements

The word processing skillls of Jo Scofield are greatly acknowledged,
as is the secretarial assistance of Rachel Orme and Danna Judd.
The Center for Studies of the Family, Brigham Young University,
generously supported this project.

We thank The Gallup Report for permission to reprint from their pages.

List of Abbreviations

The following abbreviations are used throughout the book.

CPS   Current Population Survey
GSS-NORC   General Social Surveys conducted by the National Opinion Research Center
NSFG   National Survey of Family Growth
NSFH   National Survey of Families and Households
NSYW   National Survey of Young Women

A. Marriage

1. TRENDS

The marriage rate has been declining since the 1970s (see Figure A1-1 and Table A1-2). Correspondingly, the average age at marriage has steadily increased (Figure A1-5). Men now marry for the first time at age 26 on average, and women at age 24. Likewise, the proportion of people who remarry has declined. Among those who dissolved their marriage in the late 1960s, 73 percent had remarried within five years (Table A1-6). Now this figure has declined to 50 percent. As the rate of marital dissolution increased, an increasing proportion of marriages involved a remarriage for the bride, groom, or both (Figure A1-9). As the divorce rate has leveled off, and even declined, the mix of marriages has not changed as much in the last decade. There has been a gradual but steady increase in the number of interracial marriages (Figure A1-10).

2. MARITAL STATUS

As marriage rates have declined and divorce rates have increased, the percentage of the population that is married has declined (Figure A2-1). Forty percent of women aged 15-44 are in their first marriage and almost 40 percent have never married. Blacks and Hispanics are more likely to have never married than whites (Figure A2-2). Projections suggest that the marital status of the adult population will not change much over the next 10 to 15 years (Table A2-6). Women with moderate levels of education and who lived with two parents from birth are most likely to be married (Table A2-7).

3. ATTITUDES

People's attitudes about marriage and about gender roles within marriage are rather divided (Table A3-1). Sixty-three percent say a woman can have a fully satisfying life without getting married, while 18 percent disagree. Men apparently are more dependent on marriage in order to have fulfilling lives. A slight majority believes that both parents should contribute to family income. There is general disapproval for childbearing outside of marriage. There is support for commitment to make marriage work out and for fathers to pay child support even if they can't see their children frequently.

Nearly half of the population thinks that a man considers looks to be more important than brains when he thinks about marrying a woman (Table A3-2). This pattern was virtually the same in 1949 and 1997. Men are much more likely to propose than women, and this pattern also remained fairly stable since 1952 (Table A3-3).

Unmarried people tend to think their lives would be about the same or better if they were married (Table A3-4). Aspects of their lives that would benefit most from marriage include their standard of living, economic security, sex, and overall happiness. Leisure time would suffer the most if singles were to marry.

1.TRENDS

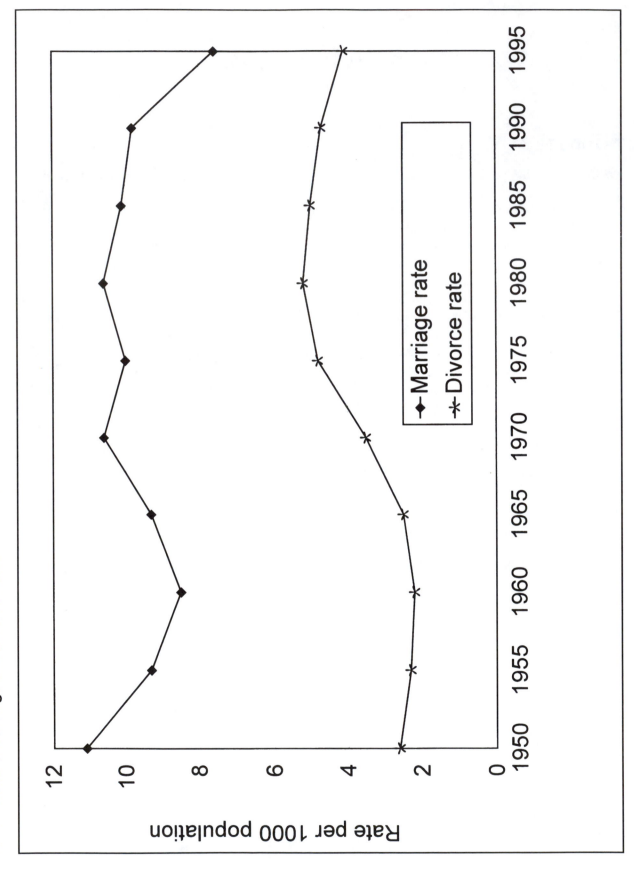

A1-1   **Trend in Marriage and Divorce Rates**

A1-2 Marriages and Divorces: 1970–1995

YEAR	NUMBER (1,000)	MARRIAGES						DIVORCES AND ANNULMENTS		
			Rate per 1,000 population					NUMBER (1,000)	Rate per 1,000 population	
		Total	Men, 15 yrs. old and over[2]	Women, 15 yrs. old and over [2]	Unmarried women				Total[2]	Married women,15 yrs. old and over
					15 yrs. old and over	15 to 44 yrs. old				
1970	2,159	10.6	31.1	28.4	76.5	140.2		708	3.5	14.9
1975	2,153	10.0	27.9	25.6	66.9	118.5		1,036	48.8	20.3
1980	2,390	10.6	28.5	26.1	61.4	102.6		1,189	5.2	22.6
1983	2,446	10.5	28.0	25.7	59.9	99.3		1,158	5.0	21.6
1984	2,477	10.5	28.0	25.8	59.5	99.0		1,169	5.0	21.5
1985	2,413	10.1	27.0	24.9	57.0	94.9		1,190	5.0	21.7
1986	2,407	10.0	26.6	24.5	56.2	93.9		1,178	4.9	21.2
1987	2,403	9.9	26.3	24.3	55.7	92.4		1,166	4.8	20.8
1988	2,396	9.8	26.0	24.0	54.6	91.0		1,167	4.8	20.7
1989	2,403	9.7	25.8	23.9	54.2	91.2		1,157	4.7	20.4
1990	2,443	9.8	26.8	24.1	54.5	91.3		1,182	4.7	20.9
1991	2,371	9.4	(NA)	(NA)	54.2	86.8		1,189	4.7	20.9
1992	2,362	9.3	(NA)	(NA)	53.3	88.2		1,215	4.8	21.2
1993	2,334	9.0	(NA)	(NA)	52.3	86.8		1,187	4.6	20.5
1994	2,362	9.1	(NA)	(NA)	51.5	84.0		1,191	4.6	20.5
1995 provisional.	2,336	8.9	(NA)	(NA)	50.8	83.0		1,169	4.4	19.8

NA Not available. [1] Beginning 1980, includes nonlicensed marriages registered in California. [2] Rates for 1981-88 are revised and may differ from rates published.

A1-3 Percent Distribution of Marriages, by Marriage Order: 1970–1988

MARRIAGE ORDER	1970	1980	1981	1982	1983	1984	1985	1986	1987	1988
Total	100.0	100.0	100.0	100.0	100.0	100.0	100.0	100.0	100.0	100.0
First marriage of bride and groom	68.6	56.2	54.7	54.8	64.4	54.4	54.3	53.9	53.9	54.1
First marriage of bride, remarriage of groom	7.6	11.3	11.8	11.6	11.6	11.5	11.5	11.3	11.3	11.1
Remarriage of bride, first marriage of groom	7.3	9.8	10.1	103.	10.5	10.7	10.9	11.2	11.3	11.4
Remarriage of bride and groom	16.5	22.7	23.4	23.3	23.5	23.4	23.4	23.6	23.5	23.4

Vital Statistics Report; and unpublished data.

A1-4   Marriages and Divorces—Number and Rate, by State: 1980–1995

[By place of occurrence]

DIVISION AND STATE	MARRIAGES [1]						DIVORCES [3]					
	Number (1,000)			Rate per 1,000 population [2]			Number (1,000)			Rate per 1,000 population [2]		
	1980	1990	1995	1980	1990	1995	1980	1990	1995	1980	1990	1995
U.S.	2,390.3	2,443.0	2,336.0	10.6	9.8	8.9	1,189.0	1,182.0	1,169.0	5.2	4.7	4.4
New England	106.3	112.2	99.5	8.6	8.5	7.5	49.0	44.0	39.8	4.0	3.4	3.0
Maine	12.0	11.8	10.8	10.7	9.7	8.7	6.2	5.3	5.5	5.5	4.3	4.4
New Hampshire . .	9.3	10.6	9.6	10.0	9.5	8.4	5.3	5.3	4.9	5.7	4.7	4.2
Vermont	5.2	6.1	6.1	10.2	10.9	10.3	2.6	2.6	2.8	5.1	4.5	4.8
Massachusetts . . .	46.3	47.8	43.6	8.1	7.9	7.2	17.9	16.8	13.5	3.1	2.8	2.2
Rhode Island	7.5	8.1	7.4	7.9	8.1	7.5	3.6	3.8	3.7	3.8	3.7	3.7
Connecticut	26.0	27.8	22.0	8.4	7.9	6.7	13.5	10.3	9.6	4.3	3.2	2.9
Middle Atlantic	294.0	314.1	276.1	8.0	8.3	7.2	124.7	121.6	119.7	3.4	3.2	3.1
New York	144.5	169.3	147.4	8.2	8.6	8.1	62.0	57.9	56.0	3.5	3.2	3.1
New Jersey	55.8	58.0	52.9	7.6	7.6	6.7	27.8	23.6	24.3	3.8	3.0	3.1
Pennsylvania	93.7	86.8	75.8	7.9	7.1	6.3	34.9	40.1	39.4	2.9	3.3	3.3
East North Central .	395.5	364.5	331.0	9.5	8.6	7.6	212.4	[4]153.3	[4]144.9	5.1	[4]4.2	[4]3.3
Ohio	99.8	95.8	90.1	9.2	9.0	8.1	58.8	51.0	48.7	5.4	4.7	4.4
Indiana	57.9	54.3	50.4	10.5	9.6	8.7	40.0	(NA)	(NA)	7.3	(NA)	(NA)
Illinois	109.8	97.1	83.2	9.6	8.8	7.0	51.0	44.3	38.8	4.5	3.8	3.3
Michigan	86.9	76.1	71.0	9.4	8.2	7.4	45.0	40.2	39.9	4.9	4.3	4.2
Wisconsin	41.1	41.2	36.3	8.7	7.9	7.1	17.5	17.8	17.5	3.7	3.6	3.4
West North Central .	173.7	156.1	145.8	10.1	8.7	7.9	79.6	76.9	75.3	4.6	4.3	4.1
Minnesota	37.6	33.7	32.8	9.2	7.7	7.1	15.4	15.4	15.8	3.8	3.5	3.4
Iowa	27.5	24.8	22.0	9.4	9.0	7.8	11.9	11.1	10.5	4.1	3.9	3.7
Missouri	54.6	49.3	44.9	11.1	9.6	8.4	27.6	26.4	26.8	5.6	5.1	5.0
North Dakota	6.1	4.8	4.6	9.3	7.5	7.2	2.1	2.3	2.2	3.3	3.6	3.4
South Dakota	8.8	7.7	7.3	12.7	11.1	10.0	2.8	2.6	2.9	4.1	3.7	4.0
Nebraska	14.2	12.5	12.1	9.1	8.0	7.4	6.4	6.5	6.3	4.1	4.0	3.8
Kansas	24.8	23.4	22.1	10.5	9.2	8.6	13.4	12.6	10.7	5.7	5.0	4.2
South Atlantic	413.1	455.4	442.9	11.2	10.4	9.4	206.3	226.1	227.3	5.6	5.2	4.8
Delaware	4.4	5.6	5.4	7.5	8.4	7.5	2.3	3.0	3.7	3.9	4.4	5.1
Maryland	46.3	46.1	42.8	11.0	9.7	8.5	17.5	16.1	15.0	4.1	3.4	3.0
Dist. of Columbia .	5.2	4.7	3.5	8.1	8.2	6.4	4.7	2.7	1.9	7.3	4.5	3.4
Virginia	60.2	71.3	67.9	11.3	11.4	10.3	23.6	27.3	28.9	4.4	4.4	4.4
West Virginia	17.4	13.2	11.2	8.9	7.2	6.1	10.3	9.7	9.4	5.3	5.3	5.1
North Carolina . . .	46.7	52.1	61.6	7.9	7.8	8.6	28.1	34.0	37.0	4.8	5.1	5.1
South Carolina . . .	53.9	55.8	44.6	17.3	15.9	12.1	13.6	16.1	14.8	4.4	4.5	4.0
Georgia	70.6	64.4	61.5	12.9	10.3	8.5	34.7	35.7	37.2	6.4	5.5	5.2
Florida	108.3	142.3	144.3	11.1	10.9	10.2	71.6	81.7	79.5	7.3	6.3	5.6
East South Central .	168.8	185.5	193.4	11.5	12.0	12.0	87.5	93.8	95.0	6.0	6.1	5.9
Kentucky	32.7	51.3	47.6	8.9	13.5	12.3	16.7	21.8	22.9	4.6	5.8	5.9
Tennessee	59.2	66.6	82.3	12.9	13.9	15.7	30.2	32.3	33.1	6.6	6.5	6.3
Alabama	49.0	43.3	42.0	12.6	10.6	9.9	26.7	25.3	26.0	6.9	6.1	6.1
Mississippi	27.9	24.3	21.5	11.1	9.4	8.0	13.8	14.4	13.1	5.5	5.5	4.8
West South Central .	298.2	292.9	294.5	12.6	10.8	10.2	155.0	[4]135.7	[4]136.2	6.5	[4]6.0	[4]4.7
Arkansas	26.5	35.7	36.6	11.6	15.3	14.7	15.9	16.8	16.0	6.9	6.9	6.5
Louisiana	43.5	41.2	40.8	10.3	9.6	9.4	18.1	(NA)	(NA)	4.3	(NA)	(NA)
Oklahoma	46.5	33.2	28.5	15.4	10.6	8.7	24.2	24.9	21.8	8.0	7.7	6.7
Texas	181.8	182.8	188.5	12.8	10.5	10.1	96.8	94.0	98.4	6.8	5.5	5.3
Mountain	241.7	250.9	272.0	21.3	18.3	17.4	86.1	87.0	[4]74.3	7.6	6.3	[4]4.7
Montana	8.3	7.0	6.6	10.6	8.6	7.6	4.9	4.1	4.2	6.3	5.1	4.8
Idaho	13.4	15.0	15.5	14.2	13.9	13.3	6.6	6.6	6.8	7.0	6.5	5.8
Wyoming	6.9	4.8	5.2	14.6	10.7	10.7	4.0	3.1	3.2	8.5	6.6	6.7
Colorado	34.9	31.5	34.3	12.1	9.8	9.2	18.6	18.4	(NA)	6.4	5.5	(NA)
New Mexico	16.6	13.2	15.1	12.8	8.8	9.0	10.4	7.7	11.3	8.0	4.9	6.7
Arizona	30.2	37.0	38.9	11.1	10.0	9.2	19.9	25.1	27.6	7.3	6.9	6.6
Utah	17.0	19.0	21.6	11.6	11.2	11.1	7.8	8.8	8.9	5.3	5.1	4.6
Nevada	114.3	123.4	134.8	142.8	99.0	88.1	13.8	13.3	12.4	17.3	11.4	8.1
Pacific	298.8	334.4	291.5	9.4	8.5	6.9	187.9	180.7	[4]53.2	5.9	4.6	[4]1.3
Washington	47.7	48.6	42.0	11.6	9.5	7.7	28.6	28.8	29.7	6.9	5.9	5.5
Oregon	23.0	25.2	25.7	8.7	8.9	8.2	17.8	15.9	15.0	6.7	5.5	4.8
California [5]	210.9	236.7	199.6	8.9	7.9	6.3	133.5	128.0	(NA)	5.6	4.3	(NA)
Alaska	5.4	5.7	5.5	13.3	10.2	9.0	3.5	2.9	3.0	8.8	5.5	5.0
Hawaii	11.9	18.1	18.8	12.3	16.4	15.8	4.4	5.2	5.5	4.6	4.6	4.6

NA Not available.   [1] Data are counts of marriages performed, except as noted.   [2] Based on total population residing in area; population enumerated as of April 1 for 1980; estimated as of July 1 for all other years.   [3] Includes annulments.   [4] Excludes data for states shown below as not available.   [5] Marriage data include nonlicensed marriages registered.

A1-5   Median Age at First Marriage

A1-6   First Marriage Dissolution and Years Until Remarriage for Women, by Race and Hispanic Origin, 1988

[For women 15 to 44 years old. Based on 1988 National Survey of Family Growth; see Appendix III. Marriage dissolution includes death of spouse, separation because of marital discord, and divorce]

ITEM	Number (1,000)	YEARS UNTIL REMARRIAGE (cumulative percent)					
		All	1	2	3	4	5
ALL RACES [1]							
Year of dissolution of first marriage:							
All years	11,577	56.8	20.6	32.8	40.7	46.2	49.7
1980-84	3,504	47.5	16.3	28.1	36.4	[2]41.1	[2]45.4
1975-79	3,235	65.3	21.9	36.0	44.7	52.7	55.4
1970-74	1,887	83.2	24.9	38.6	47.9	56.4	61.2
1965-69	1,013	89.9	32.6	48.7	60.2	65.0	72.8
WHITE							
Year of dissolution of first marriage:							
All years	10,103	59.9	21.9	35.2	43.5	49.4	53.0
1980-84	3,030	51.4	18.2	31.1	40.3	[2]45.2	[2]49.8
1975-79	2,839	69.5	23.2	38.5	46.9	55.6	58.4
1970-74	1,622	87.5	24.9	39.8	49.8	59.3	64.3
1965-69	893	91.0	34.7	52.3	64.9	69.3	76.9
BLACK							
Year of dissolution of first marriage:							
All years	1,166	34.0	10.9	16.5	19.6	22.7	25.0
1980-84	380	19.7	[3]4.7	[3]10.6	[3]12.9	[2]14.8	[2]14.8
1975-79	301	32.3	[3]11.4	[3]15.6	18.5	22.2	24.9
1970-74	227	59.0	22.3	29.4	35.3	38.7	42.3
1965-69	98	81.2	[3]20.9	[3]27.3	[3]31.3	40.8	52.1
Hispanic, [4] all years	942	44.7	12.5	16.6	22.7	27.8	29.9

[1] Includes other races.   [2] The percent having remarried is biased downward because the women had not completed the indicated number of years since dissolution of first marriage at the time of the survey.   [3] Figure does not meet standard of reliability or precision.   [4] Hispanic persons may be of any race.

A1-7 Percent Distribution of Marriages, by Age, Sex, and Previous Marital Status: 1980 and 1990

[Data cover marriage registration area; see text, section 2. Based on a sample and subject to sampling variability; for details, see source]

SEX AND PREVIOUS MARITAL STATUS	Total	Under 20 years old	20-24 years old	25-29 years old	30-34 years old	35-44 years old	45-64 years old	65 years old and over
WOMEN								
All marriages: [1]								
1980	100.0	21.1	37.1	18.7	9.3	7.8	5.0	1.0
1990	100.0	10.6	29.3	24.6	14.2	13.9	6.1	1.0
First marriages: [2]								
1980	100.0	30.4	47.3	16.0	4.0	1.6	0.6	0.1
1990	100.0	16.6	40.8	27.2	10.1	4.5	0.7	0.1
Remarriages: [2][3]								
1980	100.0	1.7	15.3	24.4	20.6	20.8	14.3	2.9
1990	100.0	0.6	8.0	19.9	21.7	31.3	16.0	2.7
Previously divorced: [4] 1980	100.0	1.7	16.7	26.7	22.5	21.6	10.0	0.6
1990	100.0	0.6	8.6	20.9	23.0	32.5	13.6	0.6
MEN								
All marriages: [1]								
1980	100.0	8.5	35.7	23.8	12.3	10.5	7.4	1.8
1990	100.0	4.3	24.7	27.1	16.6	16.4	9.1	1.9
First marriages: [2]								
1980	100.0	12.7	50.0	25.7	7.5	2.9	1.1	0.1
1990	100.0	6.6	36.0	34.3	14.8	7.1	1.1	0.1
Remarriages: [2][3]								
1980	100.0	0.2	7.2	20.1	21.9	25.6	20.0	5.1
1990	100.0	0.1	3.6	13.8	19.9	33.8	23.8	5.1
Previously divorced: [4] 1980	100.0	0.2	7.7	21.7	24.1	27.7	17.3	1.4
1990	100.0	0.1	3.8	14.8	21.2	35.8	22.6	1.7

[1] Includes marriage order not stated. [2] Excludes data for Iowa. [3] Includes remarriages of previously widowed.
[4] Excludes remarriages in Michigan, Ohio, and South Carolina.

A1-8   Marriage Rates and Median Age of Bride and Groom, by Previous Marital Status: 1970–1990

[Data cover marriage registration area; see text, section 2. Figures for previously divorced and previously widowed exclude data for Michigan and Ohio for all years, for South Carolina beginning 1975, and for the District of Columbia for 1970. Based on a sample and subject to sampling variability; for details, see source. For definition of median, see Guide to Tabular Presentation]

YEAR	MARRIAGE RATES [1]						MEDIAN AGE AT MARRIAGE (years)					
	Women			Men			Women			Men		
	Single	Divorced	Wid-owed	Single	Divorced	Wid-owed	First mar-riage	Remarriage		First mar-riage	Remarriage	
								Divorced	Widowed		Divorced	Widowed
1970	93.4	123.3	10.2	80.4	204.5	40.6	20.6	30.1	51.2	22.5	34.5	58.7
1975	75.9	117.2	8.3	61.5	189.8	40.4	20.8	30.2	52.4	22.7	33.6	59.4
1980	66.0	91.3	6.7	54.7	142.1	32.2	21.8	31.0	53.6	23.6	34.0	61.2
1985	61.5	81.8	5.7	50.1	121.6	27.7	23.0	32.8	54.6	24.8	36.1	62.7
1986	59.7	79.5	5.5	49.1	117.8	26.8	23.3	33.1	54.3	25.1	36.6	62.9
1987	58.9	80.7	5.4	48.8	115.7	26.1	23.6	33.3	53.9	25.3	36.7	62.8
1988	58.4	78.6	5.3	48.3	109.7	25.1	23.7	33.6	53.9	25.5	37.0	63.0
1989	58.7	75.6	5.1	48.2	105.6	24.5	23.9	34.0	53.8	25.9	37.3	62.9
1990	57.7	76.2	5.2	47.0	105.9	23.8	24.0	34.2	54.0	25.9	37.4	63.1

[1] Rate per 1,000 population 15 years old and over in specified group.

A1-9   Percent Distribution of Marriages by Marriage Order

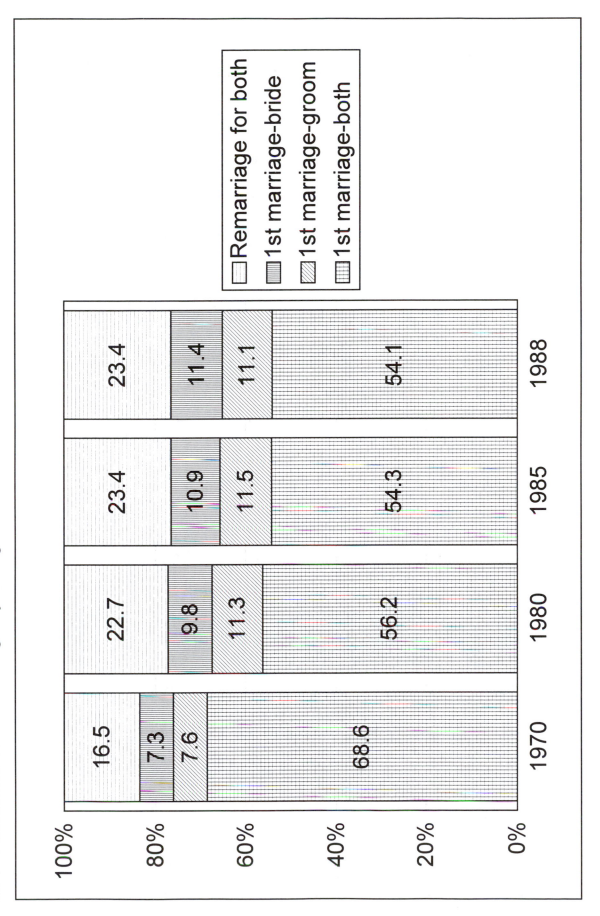

A1-10   Trend in Interracial and Interethnic Marriage

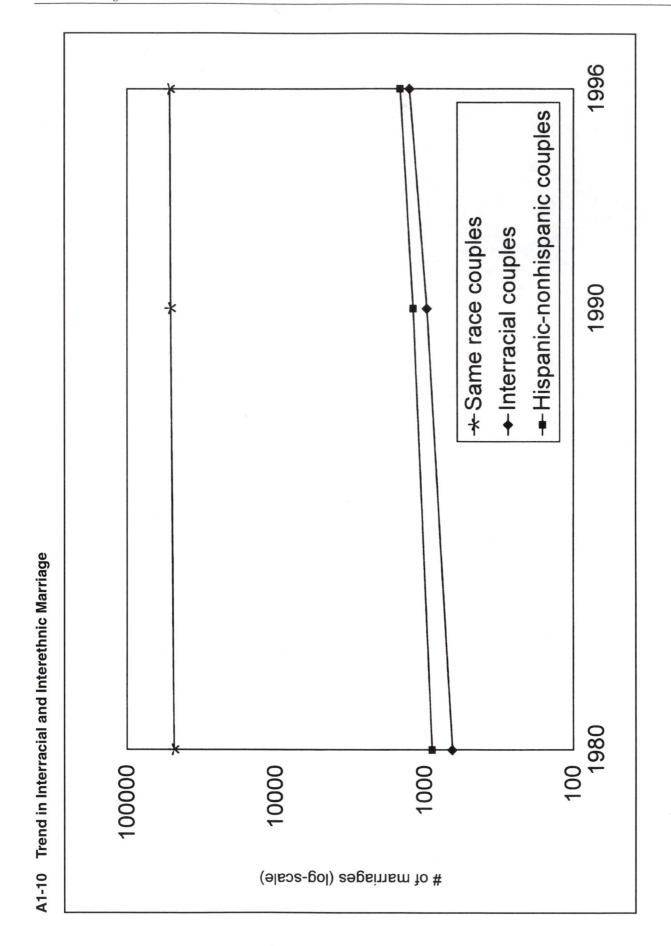

A1-11 Unmarried Couples, by Selected Characteristics: 1980–1996

[In thousands. As of **March**. An "unmarried couple" is two unrelated adults of the opposite sex sharing the same household. See headnote, table 66]

PRESENCE OF CHILDREN AND AGE OF HOUSEHOLDER	1980	1985	1990	1995	1996
Unmarried couples, total..................	1,589	1,983	2,856	3,668	3,958
No children under 15 years old.................	1,159	1,380	1,966	2,349	2,516
Some children under 15 years old..............	431	603	891	1,319	1,442
Under 25 years old......................	411	425	596	742	816
25 to 44 years old	837	1,203	1,775	2,188	2,315
45 to 64 years old	221	239	358	558	606
65 years old and over.....................	119	116	127	180	221

A1-12 Married Couples of Same or Mixed Races and Origins: 1980–1996

[In thousands. As of **March**. **Persons 15 years old and over.** Persons of Hispanic origin may be of any race. Except as noted, based on Current Population Survey; see headnote, table 66]

RACE AND ORIGIN OF SPOUSES	1980	1990	1995	1996
Married couples, total	**49,714**	**53,256**	**54,937**	**54,664**
RACE				
Same race couples	48,264	50,889	51,733	51,616
White/White...........................	44,910	47,202	48,030	48,056
Black/Black...........................	3,354	3,687	3,703	3,560
Interracial couples	651	964	1,392	1,260
Black/White...........................	167	211	328	337
Black husband/White wife..............	122	150	206	220
White husband/Black wife..............	45	61	122	117
White/other race [1]	450	720	988	884
Black/other race [1]	34	33	76	39
All other couples [1]	799	1,401	1,811	1,789
HISPANIC ORIGIN				
Hispanic/Hispanic	1,906	3,085	3,857	3,888
Hispanic/other origin (not Hispanic)..............	891	1,193	1,434	1,464
All other couples (not of Hispanic origin)	46,917	48,979	49,646	49,312

[1] Excluding White and Black.

2. MARITAL STATUS

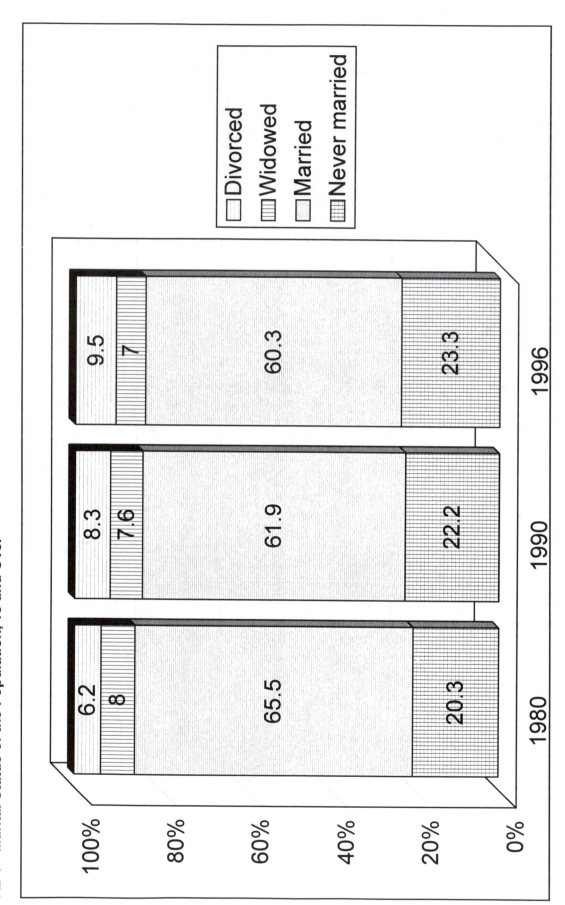

A2-1   Marital Status of the Population, 18 and Over

A2-2   Marital Status of the Population, 18 and Over, by Race

Legend:
- Divorced
- Widowed
- Married
- Never Married

White: Divorced 9.3, Widowed 7.1, Married 62.8, Never Married 20.7

Black: Divorced 11.5, Widowed 7.2, Married 42.2, Never Married 39.2

Hispanic: Divorced 7.7, Widowed 3.9, Married 58.3, Never Married 30.2

A2-3   Marital Status of Women Aged 15–44

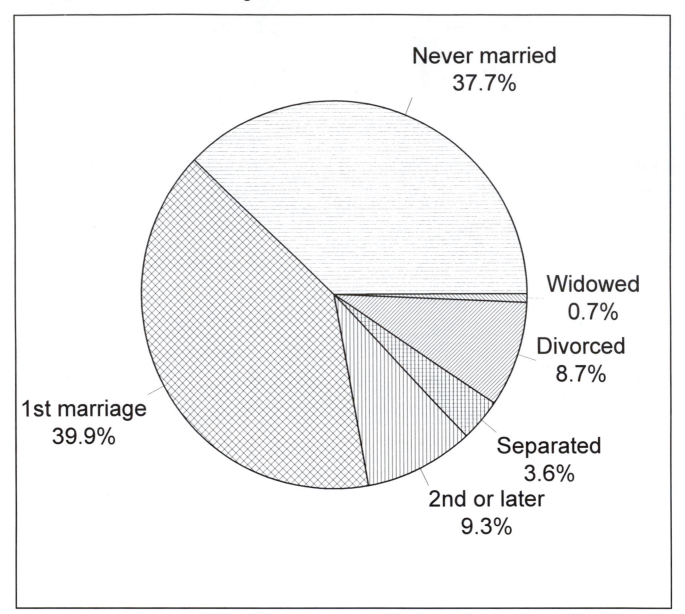

A2-4 Marital Status of the Population by Race and Hispanic Origin, 1996

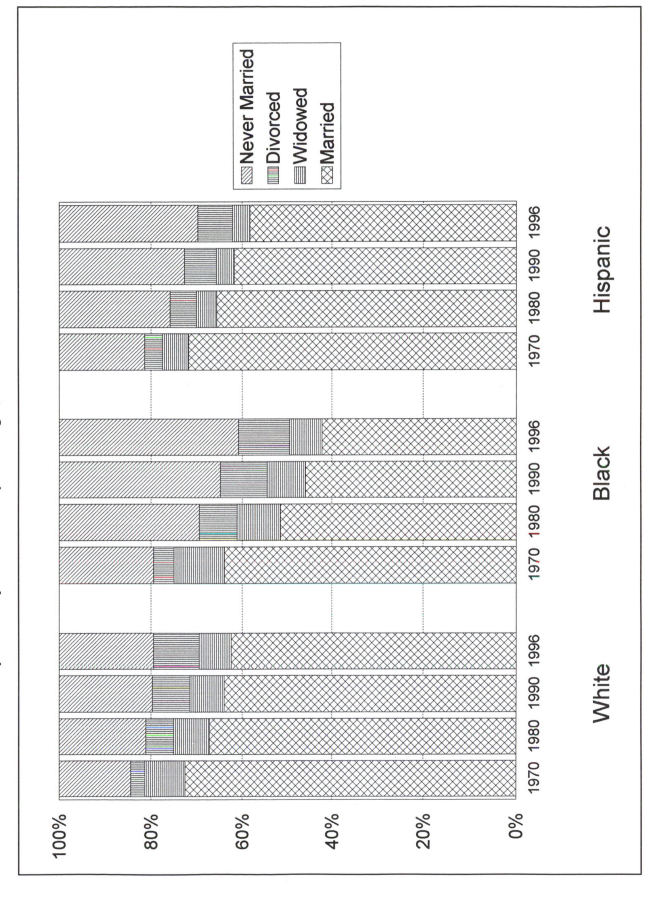

A2-5   Marital Status of the Population, by Sex, Race, and Hispanic Origin: 1980–1996

[In millions, except percent. As of March. Persons 18 years old and over. Excludes members of Armed Forces except those living off post or with their families on post. Based on Current Population Survey, see text, section 1, and Appendix III]

MARITAL STATUS, RACE, AND HISPANIC ORIGIN	TOTAL				MALE				FEMALE			
	1980	1990	1995	1996	1980	1990	1995	1996	1980	1990	1995	1996
Total [1]	159.5	181.8	191.6	193.2	75.7	86.9	92.0	92.7	83.8	95.0	99.6	100.4
Never married	32.3	40.4	43.9	44.9	18.0	22.4	24.6	24.9	14.3	17.9	19.3	20.0
Married.	104.6	112.6	116.7	116.4	51.8	55.8	57.7	57.6	52.8	56.7	58.9	58.8
Widowed.	12.7	13.8	13.4	13.5	2.0	2.3	2.3	2.5	10.8	11.5	11.1	11.1
Divorced	9.9	15.1	17.6	18.2	3.9	6.3	7.4	7.8	6.0	8.8	10.3	10.5
Percent of total	100.0	100.0	100.0	100.0	100.0	100.0	100.0	100.0	100.0	100.0	100.0	100.0
Never married	20.3	22.2	22.9	23.3	23.8	25.8	26.8	26.8	17.1	18.9	19.4	19.9
Married.	65.5	61.9	60.9	60.3	68.4	64.3	62.7	62.1	63.0	59.7	59.2	58.6
Widowed.	8.0	7.6	7.0	7.0	2.6	2.7	2.5	2.7	12.8	12.1	11.1	11.0
Divorced	6.2	8.3	9.2	9.5	5.2	7.2	8.0	8.4	7.1	9.3	10.3	10.5
White, total.	139.5	155.5	161.3	162.6	66.7	74.8	78.1	78.8	72.8	80.6	83.2	83.8
Never married	26.4	31.6	33.2	33.7	15.0	18.0	19.2	19.3	11.4	13.6	14.0	14.4
Married.	93.8	99.5	102.0	102.2	46.7	49.5	50.6	50.9	47.1	49.9	51.3	51.3
Widowed.	10.9	11.7	11.3	11.5	1.6	1.9	1.9	2.1	9.3	9.8	9.4	9.4
Divorced	8.3	12.6	14.8	15.2	3.4	5.4	6.3	6.5	5.0	7.3	8.4	8.7
Percent of total	100.0	100.0	100.0	100.0	100.0	100.0	100.0	100.0	100.0	100.0	100.0	100.0
Never married	18.9	20.3	20.6	20.7	22.5	24.1	24.6	24.5	15.7	16.9	16.9	17.2
Married.	67.2	64.0	63.2	62.8	70.0	66.2	64.9	64.5	64.7	61.9	61.7	61.3
Widowed.	7.8	7.5	7.0	7.1	2.5	2.6	2.5	2.7	12.8	12.2	11.3	11.2
Divorced	6.0	8.1	9.1	9.3	5.0	7.2	8.1	8.3	6.8	9.0	10.1	10.3
Black, total	16.6	20.3	22.1	22.3	7.4	9.1	9.9	10.0	9.2	11.2	12.2	12.4
Never married	5.1	7.1	8.5	8.8	2.5	3.5	4.1	4.2	2.5	3.6	4.4	4.6
Married.	8.5	9.3	9.6	9.4	4.1	4.5	4.6	4.5	4.5	4.8	4.9	4.9
Widowed.	1.6	1.7	1.7	1.6	0.3	0.3	0.3	0.3	1.3	1.4	1.4	1.3
Divorced	1.4	2.1	2.4	2.6	0.5	0.8	0.8	1.0	0.9	1.3	1.5	1.6
Percent of total	100.0	100.0	100.0	100.0	100.0	100.0	100.0	100.0	100.0	100.0	100.0	100.0
Never married	30.5	35.1	38.4	39.2	34.3	38.4	41.7	42.1	27.4	32.5	35.8	36.8
Married.	51.4	45.8	43.2	42.2	54.6	49.2	46.7	45.0	48.7	43.0	40.4	39.9
Widowed.	9.8	8.5	7.6	7.2	4.2	3.7	3.1	2.8	14.3	12.4	11.3	10.7
Divorced	8.4	10.6	10.7	11.5	7.0	8.8	8.5	10.2	9.5	12.0	12.5	12.6
Hispanic, [2] total	7.9	13.6	17.6	18.1	3.8	6.7	8.8	9.1	4.1	6.8	8.8	9.0
Never married	1.9	3.7	5.0	5.5	1.0	2.2	3.0	3.3	0.9	1.5	2.1	2.2
Married.	5.2	8.4	10.4	10.6	2.5	4.1	5.1	5.1	2.6	4.3	5.3	5.5
Widowed.	0.4	0.5	0.7	0.7	0.1	0.1	0.2	0.1	0.3	0.4	0.6	0.6
Divorced	0.5	1.0	1.4	1.4	0.2	0.4	0.6	0.6	0.3	0.6	0.8	0.8
Percent of total	100.0	100.0	100.0	100.0	100.0	100.0	100.0	100.0	100.0	100.0	100.0	100.0
Never married	24.1	27.2	28.6	30.2	27.3	32.1	33.8	36.0	21.1	22.5	23.5	24.3
Married.	65.6	61.7	59.3	58.3	67.1	60.9	57.9	56.3	64.3	62.4	60.7	60.3
Widowed.	4.4	4.0	4.2	3.9	1.6	1.5	1.8	1.4	7.1	6.5	6.6	6.4
Divorced	5.8	7.0	7.9	7.7	4.0	5.5	6.6	6.3	7.6	8.5	9.2	9.0

[1] Includes persons of other races, not shown separately.   [2] Hispanic persons may be of any race.

A2-6   Marital Status of the Population, by Sex and Age, 1996

[As of **March. Persons 18 years old and over.** Excludes members of Armed Forces except those living off post or with their families on post. Based on Current Population Survey; see text, section 1, and Appendix III]

SEX AND AGE	NUMBER OF PERSONS (1,000)					PERCENT DISTRIBUTION				
	Total	Never married	Mar-ried	Wid-owed	Di-vorced	Total	Never married	Mar-ried	Wid-owed	Di-vorced
Male	**92,741**	**24,893**	**57,617**	**2,476**	**7,755**	**100.0**	**26.8**	**62.1**	**2.7**	**8.4**
18 to 19 years old	3,610	3,525	77	-	8	100.0	97.6	2.1	-	0.2
20 to 24 years old	8,792	7,126	1,561	-	106	100.0	81.0	17.8	-	1.2
25 to 29 years old	9,752	5,075	4,264	12	402	100.0	52.0	43.7	0.1	4.1
30 to 34 years old	10,638	3,147	6,565	32	895	100.0	29.6	61.7	0.3	8.4
35 to 39 years old	11,091	2,303	7,611	19	1,159	100.0	20.8	68.6	0.2	10.4
40 to 44 years old	10,182	1,443	7,320	47	1,372	100.0	14.2	71.9	0.5	13.5
45 to 54 years old	15,324	1,247	11,889	124	2,064	100.0	8.1	77.6	0.8	13.6
55 to 64 years old	10,092	501	8,315	299	976	100.0	5.0	82.4	3.0	9.7
65 to 74 years old	8,213	359	6,494	788	571	100.0	4.4	79.1	9.6	7.0
75 years old and over	5,048	167	3,521	1,156	203	100.0	3.3	69.8	22.9	4.0
Female	**100,425**	**20,023**	**58,822**	**11,070**	**10,511**	**100.0**	**19.9**	**58.6**	**11.0**	**10.5**
18 to 19 years old	3,580	3,300	273	1	6	100.0	92.2	7.6	-	0.1
20 to 24 years old	8,861	6,070	2,529	10	252	100.0	68.5	28.5	0.1	2.8
25 to 29 years old	9,709	3,650	5,426	26	607	100.0	37.6	55.9	0.2	6.3
30 to 34 years old	10,819	2,215	7,481	58	1,066	100.0	20.5	69.1	0.5	9.9
35 to 39 years old	11,388	1,487	8,262	122	1,518	100.0	13.1	72.6	1.0	13.3
40 to 44 years old	10,417	1,009	7,566	157	1,685	100.0	9.7	72.6	1.5	16.2
45 to 54 years old	16,260	1,025	11,869	699	2,667	100.0	6.3	73.0	4.3	16.4
55 to 64 years old	10,992	512	7,617	1,390	1,474	100.0	4.7	69.3	12.6	13.4
65 to 74 years old	10,057	384	5,514	3,301	858	100.0	3.8	54.8	32.8	8.5
75 years old and over	8,341	370	2,285	5,306	379	100.0	4.4	27.4	63.6	4.5

- Represents or rounds to zero.

A2-7   Marital Status of the Population—Projections, by Age and Sex: 2000 and 2010

[These numbers are based on the 1990 census, as enumerated, with modifications for age and race, and household estimates from 1991 to 1994, and are projected forward using alternative marital status and household-type proportions. Series 1, shown here, is based on a time series model and is the preferred projection. For series 1, assumptions about future changes in family and household situation extend trends of the past 30 years]

CHARACTERISTIC	NUMBER (1,000)		PERCENT DISTRIBU- TION		CHARACTERISTIC	NUMBER (1,000)		PERCENT DISTRIBU- TION	
	2000	2010	2000	2010		2000	2010	2000	2010
Population 18 years and over	203,852	225,206	100.0	100.0	55 to 64 years old	23,962	35,283	100.0	100.0
					Never married (single)	1,254	1,905	5.2	5.4
Never married (single)	44,459	50,747	21.8	22.5	Ever married	22,707	33,379	94.8	94.6
Ever married	159,393	174,459	78.2	77.5	Married, spouse present	16,424	23,360	68.5	66.2
Married, spouse present	111,408	119,016	54.7	52.8	Other	6,283	10,019	26.2	28.4
Other	47,985	55,443	23.5	24.6	65 to 74 years old	18,136	21,057	100.0	100.0
18 to 24 years old	26,258	30,138	100.0	100.0	Never married (single)	825	899	4.5	4.3
Never married (single)	20,917	24,429	79.7	81.1	Ever married	17,311	20,159	95.5	95.7
Ever married	5,341	5,708	20.3	18.9	Married, spouse present	11,309	13,305	62.4	63.2
Married, spouse present	3,750	4,003	14.3	13.3	Other	6,002	6,854	33.1	32.5
Other	1,591	1,705	6.1	5.7	75 years and over	16,574	18,351	100.0	100.0
25 to 34 years old	37,233	38,292	100.0	100.0	Never married (single)	943	1,012	5.7	5.5
Never married (single)	12,288	14,006	33.0	36.6	Ever married	15,631	17,339	94.3	94.5
Ever married	24,946	24,286	67.0	63.4	Married, spouse present	6,293	7,394	38.0	40.3
Married, spouse present	18,967	18,115	50.9	47.3	Other	9,338	9,944	56.3	54.2
Other	5,979	6,171	16.1	16.1					
35 to 44 years old	44,659	38,521	100.0	100.0	Females, 18 years and over	105,927	116,776	100.0	100.0
Never married (single)	5,886	5,660	13.2	14.7	Never married (single)	19,955	22,904	18.8	19.6
Ever married	38,774	32,860	86.8	85.3	Ever married	85,972	93,872	81.2	80.4
Married, spouse present	28,930	23,628	64.8	61.3	Married, spouse present	55,682	59,485	52.6	50.9
Other	9,844	9,233	22.0	24.0	Other	30,290	34,387	28.6	29.4
45 to 54 years old	37,030	43,564	100.0	100.0	Males, 18 years and over	97,925	108,430	100.0	100.0
Never married (single)	2,346	2,836	6.3	6.5	Never married (single)	24,504	27,843	25.0	25.7
Ever married	34,684	40,729	93.7	93.5	Ever married	73,421	80,587	75.0	74.3
Married, spouse present	25,736	29,212	69.5	67.1	Married, spouse present	55,726	59,531	56.9	54.9
Other	8,948	11,517	24.2	26.4	Other	17,695	21,056	18.1	19.4

A2-8   Number of Women 15–44 Years of Age and Percent Distribution by Current Marital Status, According to Selected Characteristics: United States, 1995

Characteristic	Number In thousands	Total	Never married	Currently Married First	Currently Married Second or later	Formerly married Separated	Formerly married Divorced	Formerly married Widowed
			Percent distribution					
All women	60,201	100.0	37.7	39.9	9.3	3.6	8.7	0.7
Age at interview								
15-19 years	8,961	100.0	95.5	3.8	–	0.5	0.1	–
20-24 years	9,041	100.0	65.7	26.6	0.7	2.7	4.2	0.1
25-29 years	9,693	100.0	35.7	48.8	3.7	4.2	7.1	0.6
30-34 years	11,065	100.0	20.1	52.4	12.2	4.7	10.1	0.5
35-39 years	11,211	100.0	13.5	52.1	15.8	4.7	12.8	1.1
40-44 years	10,230	100.0	9.6	48.1	20.5	4.3	15.8	1.6
Family background								
Both parents from birth[1]	37,233	100.0	32.9	45.0	9.7	3.2	8.6	0.6
Single parent from birth	2,093	100.0	59.0	21.0	4.8	5.0	9.2	1.0
Both parents, then 1 parent	8,003	100.0	47.2	32.6	8.2	4.1	7.0	0.9
Stepparent[2]	8,378	100.0	41.8	33.6	10.3	3.8	9.9	0.6
Other	4,493	100.0	43.1	31.7	8.9	4.9	10.2	1.2
Parity								
0 births	25,242	100.0	71.7	20.0	2.5	1.1	4.5	0.2
1 birth	10,706	100.0	23.1	48.1	11.5	3.6	12.6	1.1
2 births	13,875	100.0	8.7	60.5	14.5	4.9	10.8	0.6
3 or more births	10,377	100.0	8.8	52.5	16.9	8.1	12.1	1.6
Education at interview[3]								
No high school diploma or GED[4]	5,424	100.0	23.2	38.9	12.9	9.6	13.2	2.4
High school diploma or GED	18,169	100.0	18.1	48.3	15.2	5.2	12.3	1.0
Some college, no bachelor's degree	12,399	100.0	27.2	46.8	10.9	3.5	10.9	0.6
Bachelor's degree or higher	11,748	100.0	29.5	54.1	6.8	1.6	7.7	0.4
Poverty level income at interview[3]								
0-149 percent	10,072	100.0	32.6	29.8	8.7	11.0	16.0	1.8
0-99 percent	5,992	100.0	36.0	25.6	7.0	13.7	16.3	1.4
150-299 percent	14,932	100.0	23.2	48.2	11.4	4.0	12.3	1.0
300 percent or higher	22,736	100.0	20.4	56.5	13.4	1.7	7.7	0.4
Race and Hispanic origin								
Hispanic	6,702	100.0	38.6	40.1	7.3	5.5	7.6	0.9
Non-Hispanic white	42,522	100.0	33.6	43.2	11.1	2.7	9.0	0.4
Non-Hispanic black	8,210	100.0	56.9	21.9	3.3	6.9	9.4	1.6
Non-Hispanic other	2,767	100.0	41.5	43.1	5.7	3.2	5.3	1.3

– Quantity zero.
[1]Includes women who lived with either both biological or both adoptive parents until they left home.
[2]Parents separated or divorced, then custodial parent remarried.
[3] Limited to women 22-44 years of age at time of interview.
[4]GED is general equivalency diploma
NOTE: Percents may not add to 100 due to rounding.

3. ATTITUDES

A3-1   Beliefs about Marriage and Gender Roles

	Strongly Agree	Agree	Neither Agree nor Disagree	Disagree	Strongly Disagree
A woman can have a fully satisfying life without getting married.	11.7	41.7	30.4	12.0	4.2
Both the husband and wife should contribute to family income.	15.3	43.7	33.3	6.4	1.4
It is all right for a woman to have a child without being married.	3.9	20.4	26.4	26.9	22.3
It is much better for everyone if the man earns the main living and the woman takes care of the home and family.	18.4	23.8	26.4	20.9	10.5
A man can have a fully satisfying life without getting married.	8.2	29.5	32.1	21.4	8.8
Marriage is a lifetime relationship and should never be ended except under extreme circumstances.	36.8	39.2	12.9	8.3	2.9
It is all right for a man to have a child without being married.	3.1	16.5	24.3	29.9	26.1
It is all right for a couple with an unhappy marriage to get a divorce when their youngest child is under age 5.	7.6	31.0	34.8	17.3	9.4
A husband whose wife is working full-time should spend just as many hours doing housework as his wife.	21.9	45.6	20.7	9.6	2.2
Parents ought to let their adult children live with them when the children are having problems.	5.9	33.7	41.1	16.0	3.3
A father who doesn't live with his children should pay child support even if he cannot see the children frequently.	29.1	50.8	13.8	5.1	1.2
When a marriage is troubled and unhappy, it is generally better for the children if the couple stays together.	4.6	16.9	34.1	35.4	9.0
The partner who earns the most money should have the most say in family decisions.	1.8	4.0	18.4	51.4	24.4

A3-2 Are Looks or Brains More Important?

	Looks	Brains	Both (vol.)	Neither (vol.)/ no opinion
1997				
Average	47%	36%	11%	6%
Husbands	44%	36%	14%	6%
Wives	50%	35%	8%	7%
1949				
Average	47%	39%	3%	11%
Husbands	42%	43%	4%	11%
Wives	53%	34%	2%	11%

A3-3 Who Makes the Marriage Proposal?

	Husband	Wife	Both (vol.)	Other (vol.)	No opinion
Average					
1997	82%	9	5	2	2
1952	76%	12	4	8	0

1997, by Gender

	Husband	Wife	Both (vol.)	Other (vol.)	No opinion
Husbands	82%	9	4	2	3
Wives	83%	8	6	2	1

A3-4   How Would Your Life Be Different If You Were Married: Unmarried People 18–35 Who Are Not Cohabiting

	Much Worse	Worse	Same	Better	Much Better
Standard of Living					
Men	4	13	38	37	10
Women	4	8	35	38	15
Average	4	10	36	38	13
Job Opportunities					
Men	3	8	70	15	4
Women	8	7	75	11	4
Average	4	7	73	12	4
Economic Security					
Men	3	15	39	34	10
Women	3	6	32	40	19
Average	3	9	35	38	16
Friendships					
Men	1	10	55	27	8
Women	3	6	64	21	7
Average	2	8	60	23	7
Sex Life					
Men	2	6	27	37	28
Women	5	5	27	36	27
Average	4	5	27	36	28
Leisure Time					
Men	5	28	41	21	6
Women	5	19	41	25	9
Average	5	23	41	23	8
Overall Happiness					
Men	3	8	28	38	24
Women	4	7	33	36	20
Average	4	7	31	37	22

B. Quality of Marriage and Family Life

1. MARITAL AND FAMILY SATISFACTION

One of the best kept secrets of the last 25 years is how much American women and men enjoy being married. A high divorce rate, accounts of spouse abuse, anti-family rhetoric, praise of cohabitation, and a delay in age-at-marriage have created a public perception that marriage has become a rather dreary affair. The data about marital happiness or satisfaction paint a different picture. Each year for the past 25 years, the National Opinion Research Center (NORC) has requested their national samples of married adults to rate their marriages (see Table B1-1). The question asked is "Taking things all together, how would you describe your marriage? Would you say your marriage is 'very happy,' 'pretty happy,' 'or not too happy'." The level of marital happiness has varied little over the years as from 62 to 68 percent of both men and women have reported their marriages as "very happy." An additional 30 to 40 percent have answered "pretty happy" while less than five percent described their marriages as "not too happy." (Obviously, some of the "not too happy" marriages have ended in divorce, thus reducing this number.) Nevertheless, the percentages of married men and women who experience happiness or satisfaction from their marriages are remarkable and speak to a high level of marital quality.

Strong evidence of high marital satisfaction is also revealed when NORC asked the married men and women in their samples to rate the happiness they derive from various aspects of their lives (Table B1-7). American women and men reported they receive higher satisfaction from their family life than from their work, their friendships, where they live, their health, their financial situation, or their leisure time. Family life is broader than marriage since it also includes relationships with children. When the results of marital and parental happiness are combined, it appears most married Americans derive considerable satisfaction from their family lives.

When asked to compare the happiness of their marriage to that of friends' marriages, Americans are

pleasantly surprised with the happiness they experience in their marriages. They observe family and friends divorce, watch marital conflict in the media, listen to anti-family discussion, and come to believe that most couples are unhappy in their marriages, and they feel rather lucky that they enjoy theirs.

Modern society has reduced some demands on the family, such as economic production. Few families produce the food they eat and the goods they consume as they did in the not-too-distant past. At the same time, modern society has increased other demands on the contemporary family. For example, the family has become the major source of acceptance and emotional support, and the major haven from the impersonal relationships that dominate modern life. The efforts of couples to enhance the quality of their family life are apparent in the success of "how to have a happy marriage" books and in the popularity of marital rejuvenation seminars and retreats. A cursory examination of the titles of articles in magazines displayed at the check-out counters in supermarkets reveals an abundance of material focusing on strengthening family relations and keeping the excitement in a marriage. Overall, the evidence indicates that most Americans are satisfied with their marriages and are willing to devote some attention to preserving and perhaps enhancing the quality of their family life.

2. FAMILY ROLES AND DIVISION OF LABOR

The "traditional" division of family roles had the husband as the primary breadwinner, the family automobile mechanic, and the family gardener. Traditionally, the wife was responsible for the home (especially keeping it clean), the preparation of meals, the laundering of clothes, and the care of the children. As more and more married women have entered the labor force, a movement towards a more egalitarian division of family roles has emerged. Although attitudes have changed and more husbands agree they should help around the house, research has found they are slower in increasing their actual helping behavior. For example, Arlie Hochschild[1] observed in her book, *The Second Shift: Working Parents and the Revolution at Home.* (New York: Viking, 1989) that working married women continue to work two 40-hour a week shifts, one in the workplace and the other at home.

As can be seen in Tables B2-1 and B2-2, wives spend an average of 33 hours per week performing the nine major family activities. The total number of hours would be higher, perhaps Hochschild's 40 hours, if childcare activities had been included. Husbands reported they spend 20 hours each week doing the same family activities. Not only do husbands devote fewer hours to family tasks, but they also spend most of their time doing traditionally masculine activities. Outdoor tasks occupy more of husbands' time than any other task. Husbands also spend more time than their wives maintaining the family automobiles, but it is important to note that they spend three hours a week cooking and over two hours doing dishes and cleaning the house. Not surprisingly, husbands claim they devote more time to household tasks than their wives given them credit for (Table B2-4).

Although it appears husbands are helping with household activities more than in the past (Table B2-5), the responsibility to see that everything gets done still seems to reside with the wife/mother. She can ask for help from other family members, but she is still responsible. It is suspected that some wives refuse help from their husbands because of their acceptance of traditional family roles. Research has discovered that many of these wives somehow feel they are a failure as a wife and/or mother if they don't mange the household, even though they work full time outside the home.

3. MARITAL AND FAMILY CONFLICT

Couples reported in the National Survey of Family and Households that they argue about money and children most often (Table B3-1). Disagreement over household tasks and spending time together follow closely behind. Arguments about sex occur less frequently. Reports of disagreements from wives are very similar to those of their husbands.

Calmly discussing a disagreement is the strategy most frequently employed to resolve family conflict, followed by keeping the difference of opinion to one's self (Table B3-2). On the average, husbands and wives admitted that a heated argument emerges from disagreements only "seldom." Physical violence as a means of conflict resolution was rarely acknowledged. Additional information about spouse and child abuse is presented in Section D.5, Physical Punishment and Child Abuse and in Section E.4, Involuntary Intercourse and Rape.

1. MARITAL AND FAMILY SATISFACTION

B1-1   Marital Happiness of Married Individuals

Survey Question: Taking things all together, how would you describe your marriage? Would you say that your marriage is very happy, pretty happy, or not too happy?

Year	N	Happiness			
		Very Happy	Pretty Happy	Not too Happy	Total
1973	1072	68%	30%	3%	100%
1974	1054	69	27	4	100
1975	995	67	30	3	100
1976	973	67	31	2	100
1977	965	66	31	4	100
1978	954	65	32	3	100
1980	882	64	33	3	100
1982	981	62	34	3	100
1983	961	66	31	3	100
1984	825	57	40	3	100
1985	863	63	34	3	100
1986	819	63	34	3	100
1987	904	62	34	3	100
1988	787	61	37	3	100
1989	840	65	33	2	100
1990	724	63	34	3	100
1991	800	62	35	3	100
1993	853	61	36	3	100
1994	1529	62	36	2	100
1996	1379	62	36	2	100
Total	**19165**				
Average		**64**	**33**	**3**	**100**

B1-2   Happiness with Aspects of Marriage, by Age, Education, Race, and Sex

Survey Question: How happy are you with each of the following aspects of your relationship? (Rated on a scale from 1 for very unhappy to 7 for very happy)

	Relation-ship	Under-standing from Spouse	Love and Affection	Time with Spouse	Demands from Spouse	Sexual Relationship	Way Spouse Spends Money	House-work Spouse Does	Spouse as Parent
Average	6.0	5.5	5.8	5.2	5.4	5.3	5.5	5.6	6.1
Age of Respondent									
18-24	6.3	5.5	6.0	4.6	5.4	5.9	5.3	5.5	6.4
25-34	6.0	5.5	5.8	4.8	5.3	5.5	5.3	5.5	6.1
35-44	5.8	5.4	5.7	4.8	5.2	5.3	5.3	5.3	6.0
45-64	5.9	5.5	5.7	5.4	5.4	5.2	5.5	5.6	6.1
65 +	6.2	6.0	6.1	6.2	5.8	5.1	5.7	6.0	6.4
Highest Year in School									
Less than h.s.	6.0	5.7	5.8	5.6	5.4	5.3	5.5	5.6	6.1
High school	6.0	5.5	5.8	5.3	5.4	5.4	5.4	5.5	6.1
Some college	6.0	5.5	5.8	5.1	5.4	5.3	5.5	5.6	6.1
16 + years	5.8	5.6	5.8	5.1	5.4	5.2	5.5	5.6	6.1
Race of Respondent									
Black	5.8	5.5	5.6	5.2	5.1	5.3	5.1	5.3	6.0
White	6.0	5.5	5.8	5.2	5.4	5.3	5.5	5.6	6.1
Hispanic	6.0	5.7	5.9	5.5	5.2	5.5	5.4	5.6	6.2
Other	5.9	5.7	5.9	5.3	5.3	5.7	5.7	5.5	5.9
Sex of Respondent									
Male	6.0	5.7	5.9	5.3	5.4	5.3	5.5	6.0	6.3
Female	5.9	5.4	5.7	5.2	5.3	5.3	5.4	5.1	5.9

B1-3   Happiness with Various Aspects of Marriage Reported by Married Individuals

Survey Questions: How happy are you with each of the following aspects of your relationship? How do you feel about the fairness in your relationship in each of the following areas? Would you like to spend more time with your spouse than you do nowadays, less time, or about the same?

Characteristic of Marriage	Male	Female	Average
Percent saying their relationship is "very happy"	45	43	44
Percent saying they are "very" happy with:			
Understanding from partner	35	30	33
Love and affection	45	43	44
Time with partner	28	28	28
Demands partner places on you	26	27	26
Sexual relationship	31	32	32
Way partner spends money	34	33	34
Work partner does around the house	47	30	39
Partner as a parent	59	48	54
Percent saying that relationship is "fair":			
Household chores	69	63	66
Working for pay	82	79	81
Spending money	85	83	84
Child care	59	54	57
Percent saying they would like to spend more time with spouse	53	50	51

B1-4 Assessments of Various Aspects of Family Life by Married Individuals, by Age, Education, Race, and Sex

Survey Question: Please indicate how much you agree or disagree with each of the following statements:

	PERCENT WHO "AGREE"				
	Our Family Has Fun Together	Things are Tense and Stressful in Our Family	Family Members Show Concern and Love for Each Other	Family Members Feel Distant and Apart From Each Other	Our Family Works Well Together As a Team
Average	89	14	92	7	76
Age of Respondent					
18-24	91	13	99	5	71
25-34	92	13	93	7	79
35-44	88	14	90	7	76
45-64	84	15	92	8	70
Highest Year in School					
Less than h. s.	86	21	89	13	76
High school	87	14	90	7	76
Some college	90	13	94	5	75
16 + years	91	10	94	5	77
Race of Respondent					
Black	91	11	92	9	82
White	88	13	92	6	73
Hispanic	91	17	90	14	82
Other	91	8	95	8	85
Sex of Respondent					
Male	88	11	92	5	74
Female	89	16	92	8	77

B1-5   Frequency of Interaction with Spouse, by Age, Education, Race, and Sex

Survey Question: During the past month, about how OFTEN did you and your husband/wife spend time alone with each other, talking or sharing an activity? . . . time together in social activities with either friends or relatives?

	Spend Time Alone	Spend Time in Social Activities
	1=never, 2=once a month, 3=2 or 3 times a month, 4=once a week, 5= 2 or 3 times a week, 6=almost every day	
Average (percent)	4.8	3.2
Age of Respondent		
18-24	4.6	3.4
25-34	4.4	3.2
35-44	4.3	3.0
45-64	4.9	3.2
65 +	5.5	3.6
Highest Year in School		
Less than h. s.	4.8	3.1
High school	4.7	3.2
Some college	4.7	3.3
16 + years	4.8	3.3
Race of Respondent		
Black	4.3	2.9
White	4.8	3.3
Hispanic	4.7	3.0
Other	4.4	3.2
Sex of Respondent		
Male	4.8	3.3
Female	4.7	3.2

B1-6 Family Dining Together, by Age, Education, Race, and Sex

Survey Question: How many evenings last week did you eat dinner with at least one of your children? How many evenings did your whole family living here eat dinner together?

	Average Number of Evenings Last Week	
	Eating Dinner with at Least One of the Children	**Eating Dinner with the Whole Family**
Average (percent)	5.6	4.5
Age of Respondent		
18-24	5.8	5.0
25-34	5.0	4.9
35-44	5.6	4.4
45-64	5.2	4.3
Highest Year in School		
Less than h. s.	5.7	4.7
High school	5.6	4.5
Some college	5.4	4.4
16 + years	5.7	4.6
Race of Respondent		
Black	5.1	4.1
White	5.6	4.5
Hispanic	5.7	5.0
Other	5.5	5.1
Sex of Respondent		
Male	5.3	4.5
Female	5.8	4.6

B1-7   Average Level of Satisfaction with Various Aspects of Lives, by Age, Education, Marital Status, Race, and Sex

Survey Question: Overall, how satisfied are you with . . . ?

	Home	Neighborhood	City or Town	Financial Situation	Leisure Time	Health	Appearance	Friendships	Family Life	Present Job
				(scale of 1 for very dissatisfied to 7 for very satisfied)						
Average	5.5	5.4	5.2	4.7	4.7	5.4	5.2	5.7	5.8	5.2
Age of Respondent										
18-24	5.4	5.3	5.2	4.1	4.4	6.0	5.3	5.7	5.9	5.1
25-34	5.2	5.2	5.2	4.3	4.2	5.7	5.3	5.6	5.8	5.1
35-44	5.4	5.3	5.3	4.4	4.1	5.5	5.1	5.5	5.6	5.1
45-64	5.7	5.5	5.3	4.7	4.7	5.2	5.0	5.7	5.7	5.3
65 +	6.1	6.0	5.8	5.3	5.8	5.2	5.4	6.0	6.1	5.8
Highest Year in School	5.8	5.6	5.5	4.5	5.1	5.2	5.4	5.9	6.0	5.2
Less than h.s.	5.5	5.4	5.4	4.6	4.7	5.5	5.1	5.7	5.8	5.2
Some college	5.4	5.4	5.2	4.5	4.4	5.5	5.1	5.6	5.7	5.1
16 + years	5.6	5.6	5.3	5.0	4.5	5.5	5.2	5.6	5.6	5.3
Marital Status										
Married	5.7	5.6	5.4	4.9	4.6	5.5	5.2	5.7	5.9	5.4
Separated	4.8	4.9	5.0	3.5	4.3	5.2	5.1	5.5	4.9	4.8
Divorced	5.2	5.2	5.2	4.0	4.4	5.3	5.1	5.6	5.3	5.1
Widowed	5.9	5.9	5.7	4.8	5.6	5.1	5.2	6.0	5.9	5.1
Never married	5.2	5.2	5.1	4.2	4.6	5.6	5.3	5.6	5.6	4.8
Race of Respondent										
Black	5.5	5.1	5.1	4.1	4.7	5.5	5.6	5.8	5.9	5.0
White	5.6	5.6	5.4	4.8	4.7	5.4	5.1	5.7	5.8	5.2
Hispanic	5.6	5.3	5.4	4.4	4.6	5.5	5.4	5.8	6.0	5.3
Other	5.4	5.2	5.1	4.7	4.5	5.3	5.3	5.8	5.7	5.3
Sex of Respondent										
Male	5.5	5.4	5.3	4.7	4.7	5.5	5.4	5.6	5.8	5.2
Female	5.6	5.5	5.5	4.6	4.7	5.4	5.0	5.8	5.8	5.3

B1-8 **Perception of Whether Men or Women Have Better Lives, by Sex, Age, Region, Race, Education, Income, and Employment**

Survey Question: All things considered, who have better lives in this country—men or women?

	Men	Women	Same (vol.)	No opinion	No. of interviews
			Percent who agree		
National	60%	21%	15%	4%	1065
Sex					
Male	50	26	18	6	531
Female	69	16	12	3	534
Age					
18-29 years	66	21	12	1	213
30-49 years	67	18	11	4	473
50-64 years	48	28	20	4	197
65 & older	48	20	22	10	173
Region					
East	63	18	16	3	262
Midwest	65	18	12	5	268
South	54	27	13	6	374
West	57	20	19	4	161
Race					
White	60	19	16	5	725
Non-white	54	38	7	1	307
Education					
College postgraduate	61	15	14	10	137
College graduate	64	14	13	9	283
Some college	66	17	14	3	281
No college	65	25	16	4	498
Income					
$50,000 & over	61	18	16	5	261
$30,000-49,999	66	15	13	6	252
$20,000-29,999	65	23	9	3	181
Under $20,000	54	26	17	3	315
Employment Status					
Full time	62	21	13	4	599
Part time	63	22	12	3	110
Not employed	65	20	12	3	145
Retired	50	20	22	8	194

B1-9   Perceptions of Whether Men or Women Have Better Lives: 1975–1993

Question: All things considered, who have better lives in this country—men or women?

	Percent who agree		
	1975	1989	1993
Men	32%	49%	60%
Women	28	22	21
Same (vol.)	31	21	15
No opinion	9	8	4

B1-10   Husbands and Wives Report of Whose Lives are More Difficult: 1952–1997

Generally speaking, whose life is more difficult—a man's or a woman's?

	More Difficult Life					
	1952			1997		
	Men	No difference	Women	Men	No difference	Women
Husbands	30%	23%	47%	19%	29%	52%
Wives	18	21	61	16	22	62
Average	24	22	54	17	26	57

2. FAMILY ROLES AND DIVISION OF LABOR

B2-1 Average Hours Per Week Wives Spend Doing Household Tasks, by Age, Education, Marital Status, and Race

Survey Question: Write in the approximate number of hours per week that you normally spend doing th following things:

	Hours per Week								
	Preparing Meals	Washing Dishes	Cleaning House	Outdoor Tasks	Shop-ping	Washing/ Ironing	Paying Bills	Auto Maintenance	Driving
Average	8.6	5.9	7.3	2.2	3.3	4.3	2.0	.3	1.6
Age of Respondent									
18-24	6.3	5.0	6.7	1.2	2.7	3.7	1.8	.3	1.1
25-34	8.2	5.9	7.8	3.1	3.1	4.5	2.0	.3	2.1
35-44	9.0	5.9	7.8	3.4	3.4	4.8	2.0	.3	2.7
45-64	8.8	5.7	6.9	3.3	3.3	4.1	1.9	.3	1.1
65 +	10.5	6.7	7.0	3.5	3.5	3.6	2.0	.2	.6
Highest Year in School									
Less than h.s.	10.3	7.1	8.6	2.2	3.5	4.6	2.2	.3	1.5
High school	9.3	6.4	8.0	2.5	3.5	4.5	2.2	.3	1.6
Some colleg	8.1	5.3	6.6	2.1	3.1	4.0	1.8	.3	1.7
16 + years	8.2	4.8	5.6	1.8	2.9	3.8	1.6	.2	1.7
Marital Status									
Married	10.0	6.2	7.8	2.3	3.4	4.6	2.0	.2	1.7
Separated	8.2	5.9	6.8	1.5	3.3	4.3	2.4	.6	1.9
Divorced	7.5	5.2	6.5	2.3	3.3	3.9	2.2	.6	2.1
Widowed	8.4	5.6	6.2	2.5	2.8	2.9	1.8	.4	.6
Never married	6.6	4.7	5.4	1.5	3.0	3.3	1.8	.4	1.0
Race of Respondent									
Black	9.3	6.2	7.6	1.7	4.2	4.5	2.6	.4	2.0
White	8.8	5.8	7.1	2.3	3.1	4.2	1.8	.2	1.5
Hispanic	11.0	7.4	8.8	2.1	4.1	4.9	2.5	.4	2.2
Other	8.7	6.1	6.9	1.8	3.2	3.7	1.8	.3	2.2

B2-2   Average Hours Per Week Husbands Spend Doing Household Tasks, by Age, Education, Marital Status, and Race

Survey Question: Write in the approximate number of hours per week that you normally spend doing the following things:

	Hours per Week								
	Preparing Meals	Washing Dishes	Cleaning House	Outdoor Tasks	Shopping	Washing/ Ironing	Paying Bills	Auto Maintenance	Driving
Average	3.0	2.4	2.2	4.8	1.8	1.1	1.5	1.6	1.7
Age of Respondent									
18-24	2.7	2.4	2.3	3.7	1.4	1.6	1.6	2.6	1.7
25-34	3.2	2.3	2.5	4.0	1.6	1.4	1.5	1.6	1.3
35-44	2.9	2.3	2.1	4.5	1.6	1.2	1.5	1.8	1.7
45-64	2.9	2.2	1.9	5.0	1.8	.8	1.4	1.5	1.0
65 +	3.5	2.9	2.3	6.2	2.5	.7	1.8	1.2	1.1
Highest Year in School									
Less than h.s.	3.3	2.5	2.6	4.9	1.9	1.1	1.4	2.2	1.7
High school	2.8	2.3	2.2	5.4	1.8	1.0	1.5	1.8	1.3
Some college	3.3	2.3	2.2	4.5	1.7	1.2	1.6	1.5	1.2
16 + years	3.1	2.5	1.8	3.8	1.7	.9	1.7	1.1	1.1
Marital Status									
Married	2.7	2.3	2.0	5.1	1.7	.9	1.5	1.6	1.3
Separated	5.1	3.0	3.2	2.7	2.2	1.8	1.9	1.5	1.4
Divorced	4.5	2.9	2.9	3.9	1.9	1.6	1.7	1.4	1.4
Widowed	4.8	3.2	3.2	3.9	2.1	1.6	1.7	1.0	.5
Never married	3.8	2.5	2.8	3.0	1.9	1.9	1.5	1.7	1.1
Race of Respondent									
Black	4.1	3.0	3.2	4.3	2.2	1.7	2.0	2.3	2.1
White	2.9	2.3	2.0	4.8	1.7	1.0	1.5	1.4	1.1
Hispanic	3.0	2.3	2.2	4.5	2.3	1.3	1.7	2.8	2.4
Other	3.4	2.5	2.3	4.1	1.6	1.2	1.7	1.5	1.9

B2-3   Husbands' and Wives' Report of Husbands Doing Housework, Cooking, and Dishes, 1997

Survey Question: (Men) Do you help with the housework, cooking, and dishes in your home? (Women) Does your husband help with housework, cooking, and dishes in your home?

	Husbands (N=592)			Wives (N=593)		
Activity	Yes	No	No opinion	Yes	No	No opinion
Housework	97%	3%	0%	75%	24%	1%
Cooking	83%	16%	1%	63%	13%	0%
Dishes	93%	7%	0%	79%	21%	0%

B2-4   Percent of Husbands and Wives Who Report that Husbands Do Housework, Cooking, and Dishes: 1949–1997

Survey Question: (Men) Do you help with the housework, cooking, and dishes in your home? (Women) Does your husband help with housework, cooking, and dishes in your home?

	Husbands (N-592)		Wives (N-Unknown)	
Activity	Yes	No	Yes	No
Housework	85%	15%	62%	38%
Cooking	73%	27%	40%	60%
Dishes	86%	14%	62%	38%

B2-5   Husbands' and Wives' Perceptions of Who Dominates Marriage, by Sex, Age, Region, Race, Education, and Income

Survey Question: In general, do you think American women dominate their husbands—or do you think husbands dominate their wives?

| | Who Dominates | | | |
	Wives	Husbands	Equally	No opinion
National	26%	39%	26%	9%
Sex				
Male	27%	39%	25%	9%
Female	25%	40%	26%	9%
Age				
18-29 years	20%	53%	23%	4%
30-49 years	27%	43%	23%	7%
50-64 years	30%	33%	26%	11%
65 & older	28%	22%	36%	14%
Region				
East	28%	7%	26%	9%
Midwest	27%	40%	24%	9%
South	26%	40%	24%	10%
West	23%	40%	29%	8%
Race				
White	26%	39%	26%	9%
Non-white	30%	43%	22%	5%
Education				
College postgraduate	25%	47%	21%	7%
Bachelor's degree only	23%	50%	20%	7%
Some college	26%	36%	28%	10%
High school or less	27%	38%	27%	8%
Income				
$75,000 & over	26%	39%	24%	11%
$50,000 & over	23%	41%	27%	9%
$30,000-49,999	31%	42%	22%	5%
$20,000-29,999	26%	42%	23%	9%
Under $20,000	24%	38%	32%	6%

B2-6   Perceptions of Whether Wives Dominate Husbands: 1952–1997

Survey Question: In general, do you think American women dominate their husbands—or do you think husbands dominate their wives?

| | *1952* | | | | *1997* | | | |
	Wives	Husband	Equally	No opinion	Wives	Husband	Equally	No opinion
Average	32%	19%	45%	5%	26%	39%	26%	9%
Husband	34%	16%	45%	5%	26%	37%	27%	10%
Wives	26%	22%	49%	3%	27%	37%	28%	8%

B2-7   Men's and Women's Perceptions of Who Is More Often Irritating, by Sex, Age, Region, Race, Education, Income, and Employment

Survey Question: How often would you say you feel resentful specifically toward women because of something they do—or perhaps something they don't do—that you find irritating and just typically female: very often, often, occasionally, rarely, or never? How often would you say you feel resentful specifically toward men because of something they do—or perhaps something they don't do—that you find irritating and just typically male: very often, often, occasionally, rarely, or never?

	Very Often		Often		Occasionally		Rarely		Never		No Opinion	
	Women	Men	Women	Men	Women	Men	Women	Men	Women	Men	Women	Men
National	7%	14%	13%	26%	44%	40%	25%	14%	9%	5%	2%	1%
Sex												
Male	6%	13%	7%	19%	40%	40%	33%	19%	12%	7%	2%	2%
Female	8%	15%	18%	32%	47%	40%	20%	9%	6%	4%	1%	•
Age												
18-29 years	6%	16%	14%	31%	40%	32%	28%	16%	11%	4%	1%	1%
30-49 years	8%	17%	13%	29%	46%	36%	26%	13%	7%	5%	•	•
50-64 years	7%	15%	10%	23%	46%	46%	27%	14%	8%	1%	2%	1%
65 & older	7%	7%	14%	15%	42%	51%	21%	13%	13%	13%	3%	1%
Region												
East	4%	11%	14%	26%	47%	41%	25%	13%	9%	8%	1%	1%
Midwest	5%	14%	10%	28%	45%	39%	29%	13%	10%	6%	1%	•
South	10%	18%	12%	26%	44%	36%	22%	14%	11%	5%	1%	1%
West	8%	12%	18%	25%	38%	45%	28%	15%	6%	2%	2%	1%
Race												
White	7%	13%	13%	26%	43%	40%	27%	15%	9%	6%	1%	•
Black	11%	26%	15%	26%	46%	35%	17%	8%	10%	4%	1%	1%
Education												
College post-graduate	2%	4%	10%	22%	50%	51%	31%	19%	7%	4%	0%	0%
College graduate	5%	8%	10%	23%	44%	46%	31%	18%	9%	4%	1%	1%
Some college	6%	12%	12%	27%	47%	41%	26%	17%	9%	3%	•	•
No college	9%	17%	15%	27%	42%	37%	24%	11%	9%	7%	1%	1%
Income												
$50,000 & over	7%	10%	10%	25%	43%	44%	32%	17%	7%	4%	1%	•
$30,000-49,999	5%	11%	12%	27%	47%	40%	30%	18%	6%	4%	0%	0%
$20,000-29,999	5%	10%	17%	27%	40%	41%	24%	14%	12%	6%	2%	2%
Under $20,000	9%	21%	14%	25%	46%	38%	21%	9%	9%	7%	1%	•
Employment Status												
Full time	6%	13%	13%	29%	46%	40%	27%	14%	8%	4%	•	•
Part time	11%	14%	10%	21%	44%	41%	26%	17%	8%	6%	1%	1%
Not employed	8%	26%	17%	31%	39%	32%	23%	7%	11%	2%	2%	2%
Retired	7%	9%	13%	18%	44%	47%	23%	15%	11%	10%	2%	1%

• Less than one percent

B2-8 Attitude Toward Women's Roles, by Age, Education, Marital Status, Race, and Sex, 1996

Survey Questions: It is all right for mothers to work full time when their youngest child is under three. It is much better for everyone if the man earns the main living and the woman takes care of the home and family. Preschool children are likely to suffer if their mother is employed. Both the husband and wife should contribute to family income.

	Percent who agree that			
	mother working doesn't hurt child	better for man to work, woman to tend home	preschool kids suffer if mother works	both husband and wife should work
Average	67	38	46	83
Age of Respondent				
18-24	78	24	34	86
25-34	71	26	34	85
35-44	71	34	45	86
45-64	64	39	49	84
65 +	50	70	67	73
Highest Year in School				
Less than h.s.	58	56	53	72
High school	66	44	46	80
Some college	70	34	43	86
16 + years	69	26	45	91
Marital Status				
Married	63	41	51	85
Widowed	53	65	60	70
Divorced	68	37	42	84
Separated	75	35	41	85
Never married	76	24	35	84
Race of Respondent				
White	65	39	49	84
Black	78	35	30	76
Other	63	45	50	85
Sex of Respondent				
Male	57	41	54	84
Female	74	36	40	83

B2-9   Attitudes Toward Women's Roles, 1996

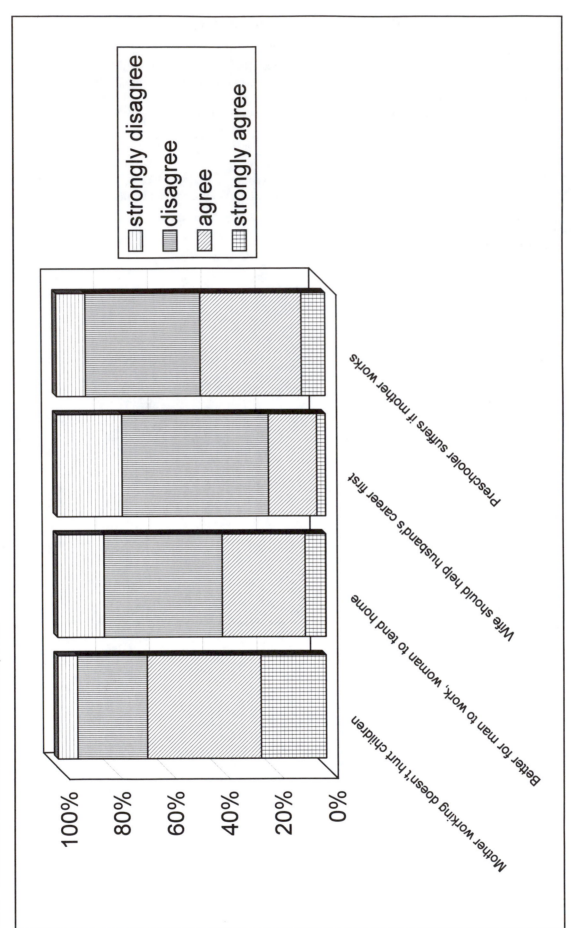

Legend: strongly disagree, disagree, agree, strongly agree

Categories: Mother working doesn't hurt children; Better for man to work, woman to tend home; Wife should help husband's career first; Preschooler suffers if mother works

B2-10 Trend in Attitudes Toward Female Roles

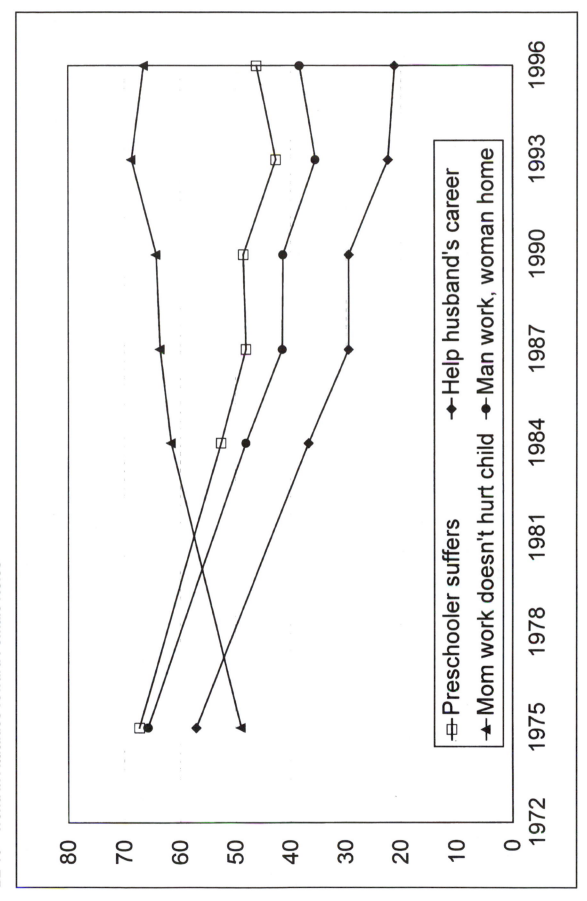

B2-11   Attitudes Toward Women's Political Roles, by Age, Education, Marital Status, Race, and Sex, 1996

Survey Questions: Women should take care of running their homes and leave running the country up to men. Most men are better suited emotionally for politics than are most women. If your party nominated a woman for President, would you vote for her if she were qualified for the job?

	Percent who agree that		
	women should take care of the home, not the country	women are not suited for politics	they would vote for a female president
Average	16	22	93
Age of Respondent			
18-24	12	20	94
25-34	11	15	94
35-44	12	18	95
45-64	16	22	94
65 +	36	39	86
Highest Year in School			
Less than h.s.	33	33	86
High school	19	24	92
Some college	13	18	95
16 + years	7	17	97
Marital Status			
Married	16	21	93
Widowed	41	36	85
Divorced	15	25	93
Separated	14	21	93
Never married	9	15	96
Race of Respondent			
White	16	22	92
Black	18	20	97
Other	22	27	92
Sex of Respondent			
Male	17	23	92
Female	16	21	94

B2-12   Support for Attitude that Women Should Take Care of Home and Family, 1993

Survey Question: Is it better for society if men are the achievers outside the home and women take care of the home and family?

Attitude	Men	Women	Total
Strongly Agree	22%	29%	26%
Moderately Agree	18%	16%	17%
Moderately Disagree	23%	15%	19%
Strongly Disagree	36%	38%	37%
No Opinion	1%	2%	1%

B2-13   Perceived Differences Between Men and Women in Personality, Interests, or Ability: 1989–1993

Survey Question: Now I'd like you to think about men's and women's personalities, interests, and abilities. Not including purely physical differences, do you think men and women are basically similar or basically different?

Respondents	1989			1993		
	Similar	Different	No opinion	Similar	Different	No opinion
Total	40%	58%	2%	34%	65%	1%
Men	--	--	--	43%	56%	1%
Women	--	--	--	26%	73%	1%

B2-14   Reported Reasons for Perceived Differences Between Men and Women: 1989–1993

Survey Question: What do you think is the main reason men and women are different? Is it mainly because of the way men and women are raised, or are the differences part of their biological make-up?

	1989					1993				
	Raised	Genetics	Both	Other	No opinion	Raised	Genetics	Both	Other	No opinion
Average	40%	45%	13%	1%	1%	36%	50%	11%	2%	1%
Men	--	--	--	--	--	32%	52%	10%	4%	2%
Women	--	--	--	--	--	39%	48%	11%	1%	1%

B2-15   Approval of Woman Working Outside the Home, If Her Husband Is Able to Support Her: 1938–1993

Survey Question: Do you approve of a married woman holding a job in business or industry if her husband is able to support her?

Year	Approve	Disapprove	No opinion
1938	22%	78%	0%
1970	60%	36%	4%
1975	68%	29%	3%
1993	86%	13%	1%

B2-16   Approval for Paying Women Same Salary as Men for Doing Same Work: 1954–1993

Survey Question: Do you approve or disapprove of paying women the same salary as men, if they are doing the same work?

Year	Approve	Disapprove	No opinion
1954	87%	13%	0%
1962	88%	10%	2%
1993	99%	1%	0%

B2-17 Effect of Women's Movement on Lives of Men and Women, 1989 and 1993

Survey Question: How has the women's movement affected your life? Has it made it easier, harder, no change, or no opinion at all?

| | Lives of Men | | | | | | | | Lives of Women | | | | | | | |
| | 1989 | | | | 1993 | | | | 1989 | | | | 1993 | | | |
Respondents	Easier	Harder	No change	No opinion	Easier	Harder	No change	No opinion	Easier	Harder	No change	No opinion	Easier	Harder	No change	No opinion
Average	36%	43%	15%	6%	33%	54%	8%	5%	50%	36%	5%	5%	50%	45%	2%	3%
Men	36%	42%	15%	7%	36%	47%	11%	6%	55%	38%	3%	4%	55%	41%	1%	3%
Women	36%	43%	15%	6%	30%	60%	6%	4%	47%	35%	6%	6%	47%	48%	3%	2%

B2-18   Pressure Men and Women Feel from Society Concerning Their Sex Roles, 1993

Survey Question: Do you ever resent the expectation that society places on you as a woman (man)?

Feeling of person	Pressured as a woman	Pressured as a man
Strongly yes	25%	13%
Moderately yes	20%	15%
No	53%	68%
No opinion	2%	4%

3. MARITAL AND FAMILY CONFLICT

B3-1   Disagreement on Selected Topics Among Married Couples, by Age, Education, Race, and Sex

Survey questions: The following is a list of subjects on which couples often have disagreements. How often, if at all, in the past year have you had open disagreements about each of the following: (1=never, 2=once a month, 3=several times a month, 4=about once a week, 5= several times a week, 6=almost every day)?

	Household Tasks	Money	Spending Time Together	Sex	In-laws	Children
Average	2.0	2.1	2.0	1.8	1.5	2.1
Age of Respondent						
18-24	2.2	2.8	2.8	2.2	2.2	2.1
25-34	2.3	2.4	2.2	2.0	1.8	2.3
35-44	2.2	2.3	2.1	1.9	1.6	2.4
45-64	1.9	1.9	1.8	1.6	1.4	2.0
65 +	1.6	1.5	1.6	1.3	1.2	1.5
Highest Year in School						
Less than h. s.	1.9	2.0	2.1	1.7	1.5	2.0
High school	2.0	2.1	2.0	1.8	1.5	2.1
Some college	2.1	2.2	2.0	1.8	1.6	2.2
16 + years	2.0	2.0	1.8	1.7	1.5	2.1
Race of Respondent						
Black	2.3	2.4	2.3	2.0	1.6	2.2
White	2.0	2.0	1.9	1.7	1.5	2.1
Hispanic	2.2	2.3	2.3	2.0	1.6	2.1
Other	2.1	1.9	1.9	1.7	1.5	2.1
Sex of Respondent						
Male	2.0	2.0	2.0	1.8	1.6	2.0
Female	2.0	2.1	1.9	1.7	1.5	2.2

B3-2 How Married Couples Deal with Disagreements, by Age, Education, Race, and Sex

Survey questions: There are various ways that couples deal with serious disagreements. When you have a serious disagreement with your husband/wife, how often do you: (1=never, 2=seldom, 3=sometimes, 4=often, 5=always)

	Keep Opinions to Self	Discuss Disagreements Calmly	Argue Heatedly or Shout	End up Hitting or Throwing Things
Average	2.5	3.3	2.1	1.1
Age of Respondent				
18-24	2.3	3.3	2.3	1.1
25-34	2.3	3.4	2.2	1.1
35-44	2.5	3.3	2.2	1.1
45-64	2.6	3.4	2.0	1.1
65 +	2.6	3.4	1.7	1.0
Highest Year in School				
Less than h. s.	2.6	3.2	2.0	1.1
High school	2.6	3.3	2.0	1.1
Some college	2.5	3.4	2.1	1.1
16 + years	2.5	3.5	2.1	1.1
Race of Respondent				
Black	2.6	3.4	2.1	1.1
White	2.5	3.4	2.1	1.1
Hispanic	2.4	3.3	2.1	1.1
Other	2.4	3.5	2.2	1.2
Sex of Respondent				
Male	2.6	3.4	2.0	1.1
Female	2.5	3.4	2.1	1.1

C. Divorce and Separation

1. TRENDS

After a long period of rising divorce rates, the trend reversed in the mid-1980s and divorce rates started to decline (see Tables C1-1 and C1-2). At first, scholars were skeptical about this reversal, thinking it was due to the decline in marriage or some other temporary phenomenon. Results from life histories, however, indicate that the decline is real (Figure C1-3). Still, divorce and marital separation rates remain higher than they have been throughout most of this century.

Marital dissolution is higher among those who marry before age 20 (Figure C1-4). Indeed, at least part of the reason dissolution rates are declining is because age at marriage is increasing. Marital dissolution is also higher among blacks, those who were not raised by two biological parents, premarital cohabitors, and the least educated (Table C1-6).

About one-fifth of married people say they have felt their marriage might be in trouble, but only two percent say they have a high or very high chance of breaking up (Table C1-10). Women perceive their marriages as a little less stable than do men.

2. ASPECTS OF MARRIAGE BEFORE AND AFTER SEPARATION

People who are currently divorced or separated rate understanding from their ex-spouse as quite low before the separation (Table C2-1). There were also problems because of lack of love and affection, demands from the spouse, not enough time spent together, sex, and money. Former spouses do not give their ex-partners low ratings as parents. Those from dissolved marriages also report that their relationship was stressful and lacked love (Table C2-2). Wives are more likely than husbands to want the marriage to end (Table C2-3).

Most ex-spouses have contact with each other, some on a weekly basis (Table C2-4). A majority of people begin dating others with a few months after the separation, and the children tend to be indifferent toward their dating. About 40 percent of ex-spouses say their spouse was already involved with someone else just before they ended their marriage, but that they themselves were not.

3. ATTITUDES

The percentage who favor easy divorce declined somewhat in the 1980s, but then increased slightly in the 1990s (Figure C3-1). Younger people, those with less education, and those who have already divorced think it should be easier to get a divorce (Table C3-2). Currently married people generally think their lives would be worse if they were divorced (Table C3-3). In particular, their sex lives, economic situation, and overall happiness would be most affected.

4. CHILD SUPPORT

Mothers generally gain custody of the children and over half of custodial parents are supposed to receive child support (Table C4-1). Only 68 percent of those who are supposed to receive payments actually do and only about 40 percent receive a full payment. In 1995, child support enforcement agencies had nearly 20 million cases and collected over 10 billion dollars (Table C4-3).

1. TRENDS

C1-1 Divorces and Annulments—Duration of Marriage, Age at Divorce, and Children Involved: 1970–1990

(Data cover divorce-registration area; see text, section 2. Based on a sample and subject to sampling variability; for details, see source. Median age computed on data by single years of age)

DURATION OF MARRIAGE, AGE AT DIVORCE, AND CHILDREN INVOLVED	1970	1975	1980	1983	1984	1985	1986	1987	1988	1989	1990
Median duration of marriage (years)	6.7	6.5	6.8	7.0	6.9	6.8	6.9	7.0	7.1	7.2	7.2
Median age at divorce:											
Men (years)	32.9	32.2	32.7	34.0	34.3	34.4	34.6	34.9	35.1	35.4	35.6
Women (years)	29.8	29.5	30.3	31.5	31.7	31.9	32.1	32.5	32.6	32.9	33.2
Estimated number of children involved in divorce (1,000)	870	1,123	1,174	1,091	1,081	1,091	1,064	1,038	1,044	1,063	1,075
Avg. number of children per decree	1.22	1.08	0.98	0.94	0.92	0.92	0.90	0.89	0.89	0.91	0.90
Rate per 1,000 children under 18 years of age	12.5	16.7	17.3	17.4	17.2	17.3	16.8	16.3	16.4	16.8	16.8

Source: U.S. National Center for Health Statistics of the United States, Vital Statistics of the United States, annual, Monthly Vital Statistics Report; and unpublished data.

C1-2 Marriages and Divorces: 1970–1995

YEAR	MARRIAGES[1]						DIVORCES AND ANNULMENTS		
	Total [Number] (1,000)	Rate per 1,000 population					Total [Number] (1,000)	Rate per 1,000 population	
		Total [Percent]	Men 15 years old and over[2]	Women 15 years old and over[2]	Unmarried women			Total[2] [Percent]	Married women 15 yrs old and over
					15 years old and over	15–44 years old			
1970	2,159	10.6	31.1	28.4	76.5	140.2	708	3.5	14.9
1975	2,153	10.0	27.9	25.6	66.9	118.5	1,036	4.8	20.3
1980	2,390	10.6	28.5	26.1	61.4	102.6	1,189	5.2	22.6
1983	2,446	10.5	28.0	25.7	59.9	99.3	1,158	5.0	21.3
1984	2,477	10.5	28.0	25.8	59.5	99.0	1,169	5.0	21.5
1985	2,413	10.1	27.0	24.9	57.0	94.9	1,190	5.0	21.7
1986	2,407	10.0	26.6	24.5	56.2	93.9	1,178	4.9	21.2
1987	2,403	9.9	26.3	24.3	55.7	92.4	1,166	4.8	20.8
1988	2,396	9.8	26.0	24.0	54.6	91.0	1,167	4.8	20.7
1989	2,403	9.7	25.8	23.9	54.2	91.2	1,157	4.7	20.4
1990	2,443	9.8	26.0	24.1	54.5	91.3	1,182	4.7	20.9
1991	2,371	9.4	(NA)	(NA)	54.2	86.8	1,189	4.7	20.9
1992	2,362	9.3	(NA)	(NA)	53.3	88.2	1,215	4.8	21.2
1993	2,334	9.0	(NA)	(NA)	52.3	86.8	1,187	4.6	20.5
1994	2,362	9.1	(NA)	(NA)	51.5	84.0	1,191	4.6	20.5
1995 provisional	2,336	8.9	(NA)	(NA)	50.8	83.0	1,169	4.4	19.8

NA Not available.
[1]Beginning 1980, includes nonlicensed marriages registered in California.
[2]Rates for 1981-88 are revised and may differ from rates published previously.

Source: U.S. National Center for Health Statistics, Vital Statistics of the United States, annual; Monthly Vital Statistics Report; and unpublished data.

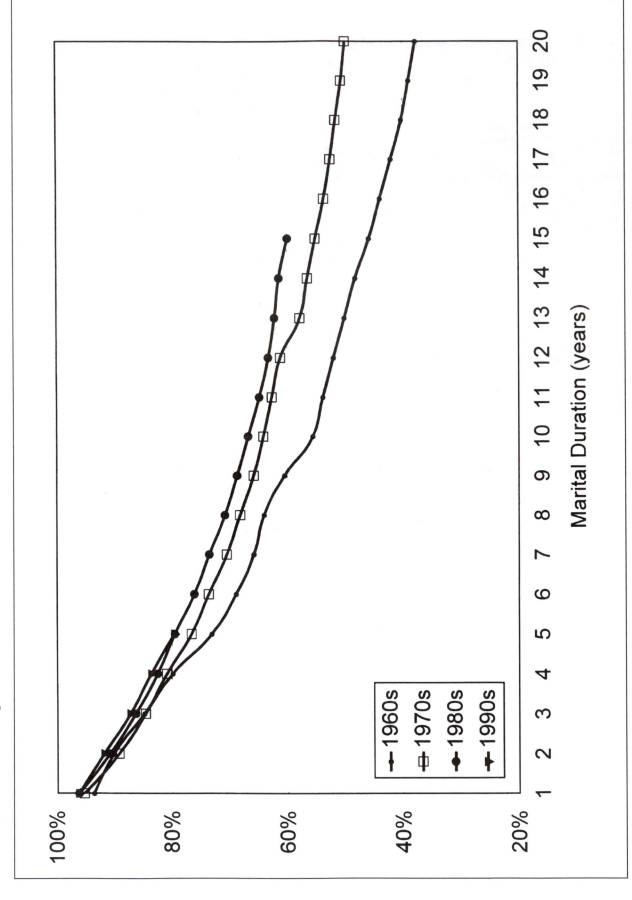

C1-3   Percent of Marriages That Have Not Dissolved

C1-4   Percent of Marriages That Have Not Dissolved, by Year Married and Age at Marriage

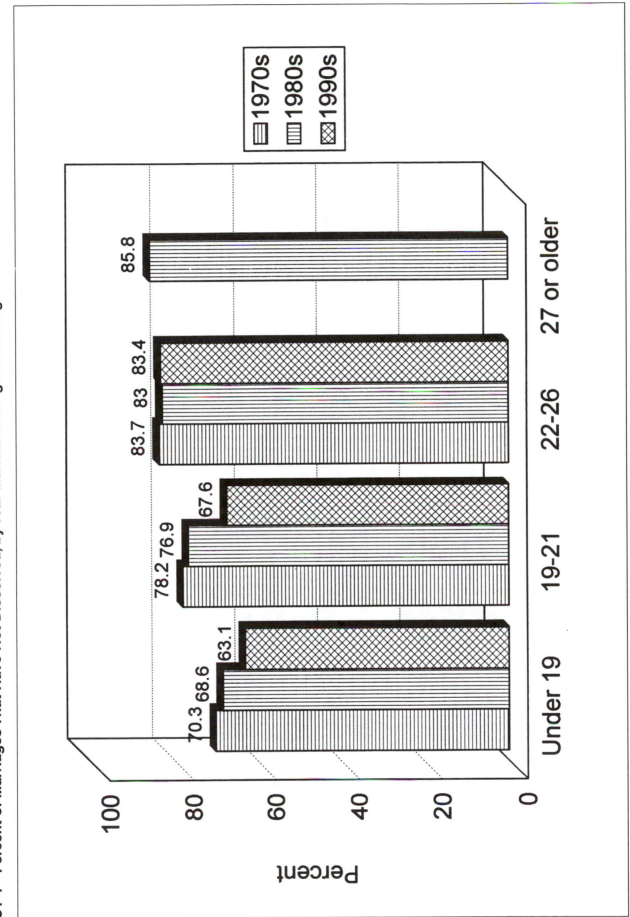

C1-5   Percent of Marriages That Have Not Dissolved by Bride's Age at Marriage

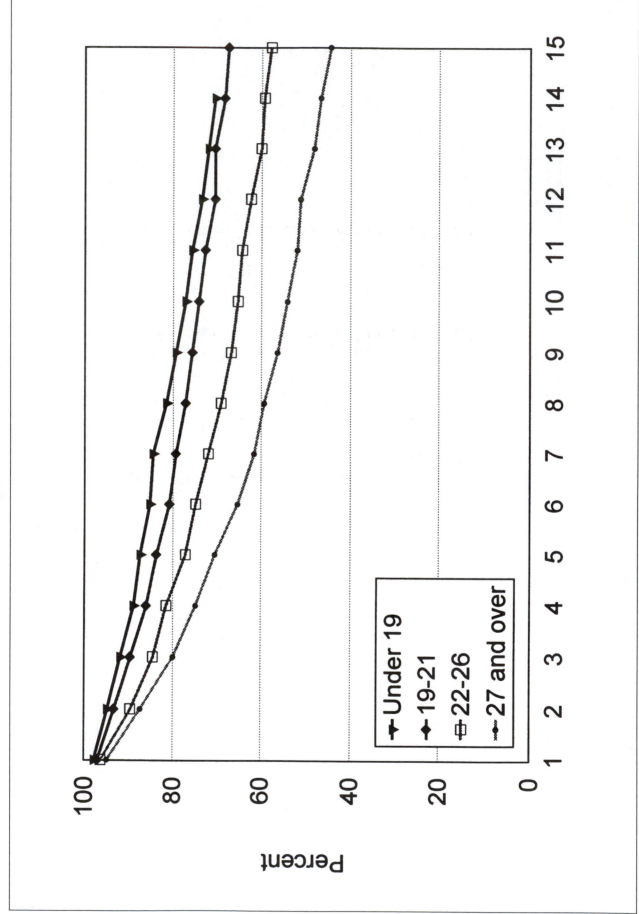

C1-6 Number of Ever-Married Women 15–44 Years of Age and Cumulative Percent Whose First Marriage Was Dissolved by Separation, Divorce, or Annulment, by Years Since First Marriage and Selected Characteristics: United States, 1995

Characteristic	Number in thousands	All marital durations	Years since first marriage			
			1	3	5	10
			Cumulative percent dissolved at interview			
All women	37,521	34.5	4.6	13.8	20.2	28.6
Age at first marriage						
Under 18 years	4,533	59.1	7.4	21.5	33.1	46.8
18-19 years	8,687	47.2	6.8	18.3	25.6	37.8
20-22 years	11,034	30.8	3.6	13.0	18.7	25.8
23 years and over	13,267	20.9	3.0	8.9	13.5	18.6
Year of first marriage						
1990-95	8,240	13.4	3.8	10.8	13.4	NA
1985-89	7,753	27.8	3.8	13.6	19.7	27.8
1980-84	7,747	36.6	4.7	14.1	21.3	32.8
Before 1980	13,782	49.7	5.5	15.6	23.9	35.7
Family background						
Both parents from birth[1]	25,000	31.8	4.2	12.1	17.6	25.5
Single parent from birth	859	44.1	6.1	17.3	26.4	35.8
Both parents, then 1 parent	4,227	35.9	5.8	16.4	23.4	31.4
Stepparent[2]	4,878	41.0	6.4	19.6	27.9	36.4
Other	2,557	43.2	2.9	14.4	23.7	36.2
Cohabitation before first marriage						
No, never cohabited at all	18,901	20.4	2.0	6.4	9.5	14.5
No, but cohabited after first marriage	4,420	96.1	13.6	40.0	58.0	83.2
Yes, with first husband	13,443	34.1	4.8	15.3	22.4	30.1
Yes, with someone else	757	34.5	13.3	20.0	26.9	33.1
Education at interview[3]						
No high school diploma or GED[4]	4,168	45.9	7.5	17.9	26.9	37.8
High school diploma or GED	14,881	39.3	5.3	15.6	22.6	32.4
Some college, no bachelor's degree	9,025	34.9	4.4	14.4	21.0	29.1
Bachelors degree or higher	8,288	22.8	2.1	8.1	12.6	18.5
Poverty level income at interview[3]						
0-149 percent	6,788	53.1	8.4	21.3	31.0	44.4
0-99 percent	3,832	57.9	9.9	23.0	33.7	49.7
150–299 percent	11,473	35.7	4.3	13.9	19.9	29.2
300 percent or higher	18,102	28.1	3.3	11.0	16.7	23.2
Race and Hispanic origin						
Hispanic	4,116	33.2	4.2	12.4	17.9	27.9
Non-Hispanic white	28,260	33.9	4.6	13.8	20.0	27.8
Non-Hispanic black	3,536	45.3	6.5	17.9	28.0	39.6
Non-Hispanic other	1,619	24.3	2.2	8.7	12.3	20.2

NA Category not applicable.
[1]Includes women who lived with either both biological or both adoptive parents until they left home.
[2]Parents separated or divorced, or custodial parent remarried.
[3]Limited to women 22-44 years of age at time of interview.
[4]GED is general equivalency diploma.

C1-7   **Median Duration of Marriages and Average Number of Children Involved in Divorce**

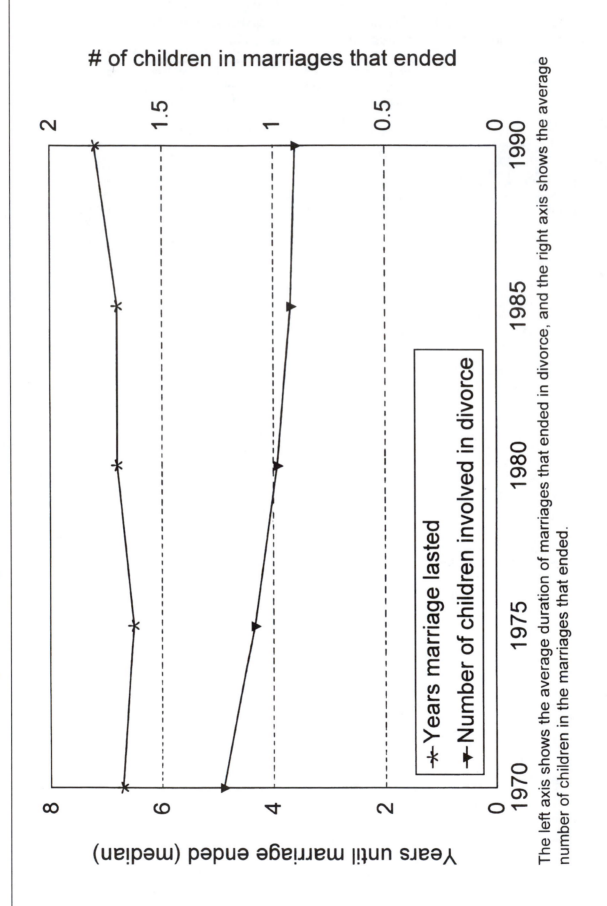

# of children in marriages that ended

Years until marriage ended (median)

The left axis shows the average duration of marriages that ended in divorce, and the right axis shows the average number of children in the marriages that ended.

Legend:
- Years marriage lasted
- Number of children involved in divorce

C1-8 First Marriage Dissolution and Years Until Remarriage for Women, by Race and Hispanic Origin, 1988

[for women 15 to 44 years old. Based on 1988 National Survey of Family Growth. Marriage dissolution includes death of spouse, separation because of marital discord, and divorce]

ITEM	Number (1,000)	All	1	2	3	4	5
ALL RACES[1]							
Year of dissolution of first marriage:							
All years	11,577	56.8	20.6	32.8	40.7	46.2	49.7
1980-84	3,504	47.5	16.3	28.1	36.4	41.1[2]	45.4[2]
1975-79	3,235	65.3	21.9	36.0	44.7	52.7	55.4
1970-74	1,887	83.2	24.9	38.6	47.9	56.4	61.2
1965-69	1,013	89.9	32.6	48.7	60.2	65.0	72.8
WHITE							
Year of dissolution of first marriage:							
All years	10,103	59.9	21.9	35.2	43.5	49.4	53.0
1980-84	3,030	51.4	18.2	31.1	40.3	45.2[2]	49.8[2]
1975-79	2,839	69.5	23.2	38.5	46.9	55.6	58.4
1970-74	1,622	87.5	24.9	39.8	49.8	59.3	64.3
1965-69	893	91.0	34.7	52.3	64.9	69.3	76.9
BLACK							
Year of dissolution of first marriage:							
All years	1,166	34.0	10.9	16.5	19.6	22.7	25.0
1980-84	380	19.7	4.7[3]	10.6[3]	12.9[3]	14.8[2]	14.8[2]
1975-79	301	32.3	11.4[3]	15.6[3]	18.5	22.2	24.9
1970-74	227	59.0	22.3	29.4	35.3	38.7	42.3
1965-69	98	81.2	20.9[3]	27.3[3]	31.3[3]	40.8	52.1
Hispanic,[4] all years	942	44.7	12.5	16.6	22.7	27.8	29.9

[1]Includes other races.

[2]The percent having remarried is biased downward because the women had not completed the indicated number of years since dissolution of first marriage at the time of the survey.

[3]Figure does not meet standard of reliability or precision.

[4]Hispanic persons may be of any race.

Source: National Center for Health Statistics, Advance Data from Vital and Health Statistics, No. 194.

C1-9   Marriage Experience for Women, by Age and Race: 1980 and 1990

[In percent. As of June. Based on Current Population Survey; see text, section]

MARITAL STATUS AND AGE	ALL RACES		WHITE		BLACK		HISPANIC[1]	
	1980	1990	1980	1990	1980	1990	1980	1990
EVER MARRIED								
20 to 24 years old	49.5	38.5	52.2	41.3	33.3	23.5	55.4	45.8
25 to 29 years old	78.6	69.0	81.0	73.2	62.3	45.0	80.2	69.6
30 to 34 years old	89.9	82.2	91.6	85.6	77.9	61.1	88.3	83.0
35 to 39 years old	94.3	89.4	95.3	91.4	87.4	74.9	91.2	88.9
40 to 44 years old	95.1	92.0	95.8	93.4	89.7	82.1	94.2	92.8
45 to 49 years old	95.9	94.4	96.4	95.1	92.5	89.7	94.4	91.7
50 to 54 years old	95.3	95.5	95.8	96.1	92.1	91.9	95.0	91.8
DIVORCED AFTER FIRST MARRIAGE								
20 to 24 years old	14.2	12.5	14.7	12.8	10.5	9.6	9.4	6.8
25 to 29 years old	20.7	19.2	21.0	19.8	20.2	17.8	13.9	13.5
30 to 34 years old	26.2	28.1	25.8	28.6	31.4	26.6	21.1	19.9
35 to 39 years old	27.2	34.1	26.7	34.6	32.9	35.8	21.9	29.7
40 to 44 years old	26.1	35.8	25.5	35.2	33.7	45.1	19.7	26.6
45 to 49 years old	23.1	35.2	22.7	35.5	29.0	39.8	23.9	24.6
50 to 54 years old	21.8	29.5	21.0	28.5	29.0	39.2	22.5	22.9
REMARRIED AFTER DIVORCE								
20 to 24 years old	45.5	38.1	47.0	39.3	(B)	(B)	(B)	(B)
25 to 29 years old	53.4	51.8	56.4	52.8	27.9	44.4	(B)	49.5
30 to 34 years old	60.9	59.6	63.3	61.4	42.0	42.0	58.3	45.9
35 to 39 years old	64.9	65.0	66.9	66.5	50.6	54.0	45.2	51.2
40 to 44 years old	67.4	67.1	68.6	69.5	58.4	50.3	(B)	53.9
45 to 49 years old	69.2	65.9	70.4	67.2	62.7	55.0	(B)	51.0
50 to 54 years old	72.0	63.0	72.6	65.4	72.7	50.2	(B)	62.2
REDIVORCED AFTER REMARRIAGE								
20 to 24 years old	8.5	13.1	(NA)	(NA)	(NA)	(NA)	(NA)	(NA)
25 to 29 years old	15.6	17.8	(NA)	(NA)	(NA)	(NA)	(NA)	(NA)
30 to 34 years old	19.1	22.7	(NA)	(NA)	(NA)	(NA)	(NA)	(NA)
35 to 39 years old	24.7	28.5	(NA)	(NA)	(NA)	(NA)	(NA)	(NA)
40 to 44 years old	28.4	30.6	(NA)	(NA)	(NA)	(NA)	(NA)	(NA)
45 to 49 years old	25.1	36.4	(NA)	(NA)	(NA)	(NA)	(NA)	(NA)
50 to 54 years old	29.0	34.5	(NA)	(NA)	(NA)	(NA)	(NA)	(NA)

B Base is less than 75,000.
NA Not available.
[1]Persons of Hispanic origin may be of any race.

Source: U.S. Bureau of the Census, Current Population Reports, P23-180.

C1-10   Perceived Marital Stability: Married Respondents

	Male	Female	Total
During the past year, have you ever thought that your marriage might be in trouble (% saying yes)	19.8	23.6	21.6
What do you think the chances are that you and your husband/wife will eventually separate or divorce?			
Very low	75.7	76.3	76.0
Low	16.2	14.5	15.4
About even	6.3	6.6	6.4
High	1.0	1.4	1.2
Very high	.8	1.2	1.0

2. ASPECTS OF MARRIAGE BEFORE AND AFTER SEPARATION

C2-1   Aspects of Marriage Before Separation: Respondents Who Experienced a Marital Separation in the Last Six Years

In the months before you separated, how happy were you with: (rated on a 7-point scale where 1=very unhappy and 7=very happy)

	Understanding from Spouse	Love and Affection	Time with Spouse	Demands Spouse Placed on You	Sexual Relationship	Way Spouse Spent Money	Work You and Spouse Did Around the House	Your Spouse as Parent
Average	2.2	2.4	2.7	2.6	2.6	2.7	3.1	3.7
Age of Respondent								
18-24	1.7	2.3	2.5	2.1	2.3	1.9	2.4	3.2
25-34	2.4	2.5	2.8	2.6	3.0	2.7	3.1	3.9
35-44	2.2	2.3	2.5	2.5	2.5	2.7	3.0	3.5
45-64	2.3	2.3	2.9	2.8	2.5	2.9	3.4	3.7
65+	2.3	2.6	3.1	2.4	2.4	2.7	3.4	4.7
Highest Year in School								
Less than h. s.	2.4	2.6	3.0	2.4	3.0	2.7	3.2	3.8
High school	2.2	2.3	2.5	2.5	2.7	2.6	2.9	3.6
Some college	2.3	2.5	2.6	2.7	2.5	2.7	3.0	3.6
16+ years	2.2	2.2	2.9	2.7	2.3	3.0	3.5	4.0
Race of Respondent								
Black	2.6	2.8	2.7	2.8	3.2	2.7	3.1	3.8
White	2.1	2.3	2.6	2.5	2.5	2.7	3.0	3.7
Hispanic	2.9	3.1	3.4	2.8	3.3	3.0	3.4	3.9
Sex of Respondent								
Male	2.5	2.6	3.0	2.7	2.9	2.9	3.7	4.3
Female	2.0	2.2	2.4	2.4	2.4	2.5	2.6	3.2

C2-2   Relationship with Spouse Before Separation: Respondents Who Experienced a Marital Separation in the Last Six Years

How well does each of these statements describe your relationship in the months before you separated (rated on a 7-point scale where 1=not at all true and 7=very true)?

	Relationship was boring	Relationship was stressful	I didn't love him/her anymore	He/she didn't love me anymore
Average	4.4	2.4	2.7	2.6
Age of Respondent				
18-24	4.8	2.3	2.5	2.1
25-34	4.3	2.5	2.8	2.6
35-44	4.5	2.3	2.5	2.5
45-64	4.4	2.3	2.9	2.8
65 +	4.1	2.6	3.1	2.4
Highest Year in School				
Less than h.s.	4.7	2.6	3.0	2.4
High school	4.5	2.3	2.5	2.5
Some college	4.1	2.5	2.6	2.7
16+ years	4.4	2.2	2.9	2.7
Race of Respondent				
Black	4.4	2.8	2.7	2.8
White	4.5	2.3	2.6	2.5
Hispanic	3.9	3.1	3.4	2.8
Sex of Respondent				
Male	4.2	2.6	3.0	2.7
Female	4.6	2.2	2.4	2.4

C2-3   Who Wanted the Marriage to End?: Respondents Who Experienced a Marital Separation in the Last Six Years

	I did . . . partner did not	I did . . . more than partner	Both of us wanted it	Partner wanted it more	Partner did . . . I did not
Average (percent)	26	18	23	13	20
Age of Respondent					
18-24	51	20	15	5	10
25-34	27	24	23	10	16
35-44	26	16	21	15	21
45-64	18	12	28	17	25
65 +					
Highest Year in School					
Less than h.s.	34	18	24	9	16
High school	26	20	23	14	18
Some college	26	17	22	11	25
16 + years	20	15	26	18	21
Race of Respondent					
Black	29	18	21	8	24
White	26	18	23	14	20
Hispanic	28	13	26	15	20
Sex of Respondent					
Male	14	14	27	15	31
Female	37	21	20	11	10

C2-4 Contact with Ex-Spouse: Respondents Who Separated in the Last Six Years

	Male	Female	Average
During the past year, how often have you had any contact with your former husband or wife (by phone, mail, visits, etc.)?			
Not at all	23	22	23
About once a year	7	8	8
Several times a year	17	18	17
One to three times a month	18	21	19
About once a week	17	16	17
More that once a week	18	15	17
How would you describe your CURRENT relationship with your former husband/wife?			
Very unfriendly	21	19	20
Somewhat unfriendly	10	17	14
Neither unfriendly nor friendly	32	29	30
Somewhat friendly	21	21	21
Very friendly	16	14	15

C2-5   Experiences Related to Marital Separation: Respondents Who Separated in the Last Six Years

	Male	Female	Average
In the last year before your separation, how often did you and your husband/wife argue?			
Hardly ever or not at all	15	16	15
A couple times a month	16	14	15
About once a week	17	11	14
Several times a week	33	31	32
At least every day	16	19	18
Many times a day	4	10	7
Did those arguments ever become physical?			
Yes	17	33	26
No	83	67	74
Were you ever cut, bruised, or seriously injured in a fight with him/her?			
Yes	52	64	60
No	48	36	40
Was your husband/wife ever cut, bruised, or seriously injured in a fight with you?			
Yes	30	15	20
No	70	85	80
How soon after your separation did you begin dating?			
Within a month	21	21	21
One to six months after	28	29	28
Six months to a year after	18	13	15
Over a year later	19	17	18
I have not dated since our separation	16	20	18
How did your children feel about you dating after your marriage ended?			
Strongly opposed you dating	4	7	6
Opposed you dating	8	10	9
Did not care one way or the other	44	34	39
Encouraged you to date	8	15	12
Strongly encouraged you to date	4	8	6
I did not have any children or they were too young to care	31	27	29
After your marriage ended, how did your children feel about whether you should remarry? Did your child/children:			
Strongly oppose you remarrying	6	9	8
Oppose you remarrying	7	12	10
Not care one way or the other	46	33	39
Encourage you to remarry	9	13	11
Strongly encourage you to remarry	2	7	5
I did not have any children or they were too young to care	30	26	28
Was your husband/wife involved with someone else just before your marriage ended?			
Yes	42	39	41
No	40	42	41
Don't know	18	19	19
Were you involved with someone else just before your marriage ended?			
Yes	17	18	18
No	83	82	82

3. ATTITUDES

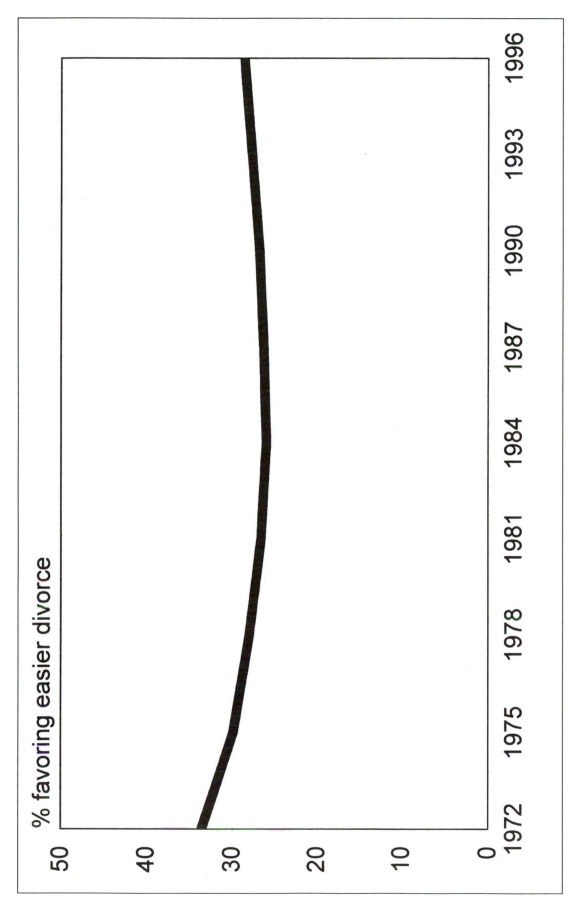

C3-1   Trend in Attitudes Toward Divorce

C3-2   Attitudes Toward Divorce Laws, 1996

Percent who say it should be easier to obtain a divorce:

Average	28.6
Age of Respondent	
18-24	46.1
25-34	29.1
35-44	29.2
45-64	25.8
65 +	20.3
Highest Year in School	
Less than h.s.	37.1
High school	30.5
Some college	28.3
16+ years	21.5
Marital Status	
Married	19.0
Separated	25.9
Divorced	35.4
Widowed	52.3
Never married	39.9
Race of Respondent	
White	24.1
Black	53.2
Other	29.9
Sex of Respondent	
Male	30.5
Female	27.1

C3-3   How Would Your Life Be Different If You Were to Separate?:   Married Respondents

(1=much worse, 2=worse, 3=same, 4=better, 5=much better)

	Standard of Living	Job Opportunities	Economic Security	Friend-ships	Sex Life	Leisure Time	Overall Happiness	Being a Parent
Average	2.3	2.9	2.3	2.8	2.1	2.7	1.9	2.4
Age of Respondent								
18-24	2.7	3.1	2.5	3.2	2.0	3.1	1.9	2.7
25-34	2.4	3.0	2.4	2.9	2.0	2.8	1.9	2.3
35-44	2.3	3.0	2.3	2.8	2.0	2.7	1.9	2.2
45-64	2.2	2.8	2.3	2.7	2.1	2.7	2.0	2.5
65+	2.1	2.5	2.3	2.5	2.2	2.6	1.9	2.4
Highest Year in School								
Less than h.s.	2.3	2.7	2.4	2.8	2.2	2.7	2.2	2.7
High school	2.2	2.8	2.3	2.8	2.1	2.7	2.0	2.5
Some college	2.3	2.9	2.3	2.8	2.0	2.7	1.8	2.3
16 + years	2.3	3.0	2.4	2.7	2.1	2.7	1.9	2.0
Race of Respondent								
Black	2.7	3.1	2.7	3.0	2.5	3.0	2.5	2.9
White	2.2	2.8	2.3	2.7	2.0	2.7	1.8	2.3
Hispanic	2.4	2.9	2.5	3.0	2.4	2.6	2.3	2.6
Other	2.5	3.0	2.6	2.8	2.4	2.8	2.1	2.6
Sex of Respondent								
Male	2.4	2.9	2.6	2.7	2.3	2.9	1.9	2.2
Female	2.1	2.5	2.0	2.8	1.9	2.5	1.9	2.5

4. CHILD SUPPORT

C4-1 Child Support—Award and Recipiency Status of Custodial Parent, 1991

[In thousands except as noted. Custodial parents 15 years and older with own children under 21 years of age present from absent parents as of spring 1992. Covers civilian noninstitutional population. Based on Current Population Survey]

AWARD AND RECIPIENCY STATUS	ALL CUSTODIAL PARENTS				CUSTODIAL PARENTS BELOW THE POVERTY LEVEL			
	Total		Mothers	Fathers	Total		Mothers	Fathers
	Number	Percent distri-bution			Number	Percent distri-bution		
Total	11,502	(X)	9,918	1,584	3,720	(X)	3,513	207
With child support agreement or award	6,190	(X)	5,542	648	1,438	(X)	1,368	71
Supposed to receive payments in 1991	5,326	100.0	4,883	443	1,257	100.0	1,200	57
Actually received payments in 1991	4,006	75.2	3,728	278	859	68.3	845	14
Received full amount.	2,742	51.5	2,552	189	499	39.7	497	2
Received partial payments	1,265	23.8	1,176	89	360	28.6	348	12
Did not receive payments in 1991	1,320	24.8	1,156	164	398	31.7	355	43
Child support not awarded.	5,312	(X)	4,376	936	2,282	(X)	2,145	136
MEAN INCOME AND CHILD SUPPORT								
Received child support payments in 1991:								
Mean total money income (dol.)	19,217	(X)	18,144	33,579	5,734	(X)	5,687	(B)
Mean child support received (dol.)	2,961	(X)	3,011	2,292	1,910	(X)	1,922	(B)
Received the full amount due:								
Mean total money income (dol.)	20,050	(X)	19,310	30,012	5,980	(X)	6,004	(B)
Mean child support received (dol.)	3,543	(X)	3,618	2,536	2,670	(X)	2,660	(B)
Received partial payments:								
Mean total money income (dol.)	17,411	(X)	15,611	41,163	5,392	(X)	5,235	(B)
Mean child support received (dol.)	1,699	(X)	1,694	1,773	857	(X)	871	(B)
Received no payments in 1991:								
Mean total money income (dol.)	15,919	(X)	14,602	25,184	5,399	(X)	5,525	(B)
Without child support agreement or award:								
Mean total money income (dol.)	13,283	(X)	10,226	27,578	4,979	(X)	4,942	5,560

B Base too small to meet statistical standards for reliability. X Not applicable.

C4-2 Child Support—Selected Characteristics of Custodial Parents, 1991

CHARACTERISTIC	ALL CUSTODIAL PARENTS				CUSTODIAL PARENTS BELOW THE POVERTY LEVEL			
	Total				Total			
	Number	Percent distri-bution	Mothers	Fathers	Number	Percent distri-bution	Mothers	Fathers
Total[1]	11,502	100.0	9,918	1,584	3,720	100.0	3,513	207
Age:								
15 to 17 years old	92	0.8	88	5	61	1.6	58	3
18 to 29 years old	3,197	27.8	3,022	175	1,529	41.1	1,472	57
30 to 39 years old	5,058	44.0	4,379	679	1,555	41.8	1,455	100
40 years old and over	3,154	27.4	2,429	725	575	15.5	528	47
Race and Hispanic origin:								
White	8,319	72.3	6,966	1,352	2,134	57.4	1,979	154
White, non-Hispanic	7,227	62.8	5,993	1,235	1,582	42.5	1,455	126
Black	2,886	25.1	2,698	188	1,478	39.7	1,433	45
Hispanic origin[2]	1,160	10.1	1,043	118	591	15.9	563	28
Current marital status:								
Married	3,428	29.8	2,707	721	410	11.0	338	73
First marriage	955	8.3	740	214	193	5.2	168	25
Divorced, remarried	2,474	21.5	1,967	507	217	5.8	170	47
Divorced	3,599	31.3	3,052	546	935	25.1	877	58
Separated	1,705	14.8	1,514	191	874	23.5	836	38
Widowed[3]	85	0.7	80	5	14	0.4	14	0
Never married	2,685	23.3	2,565	120	1,487	40.0	1,449	38
Educational attainment:								
Less than high school diploma	2,559	22.2	2,272	286	1,549	41.6	1,452	98
High school graduate	4,695	40.8	4,092	603	1,489	40.0	1,419	70
Some college, no degree	2,250	19.6	1,931	319	468	12.6	449	19
Associate degree	729	6.3	649	80	117	3.1	109	8
Bachelor's degree or more	1,269	11.0	974	295	97	2.6	84	13
Number of own children present from an absent parent:								
One	6,036	52.5	5,090	946	1,422	38.2	1,308	113
Two	3,565	31.0	3,085	480	1,152	31.0	1,097	55
Three	1,290	11.2	1,166	123	701	18.8	679	22
Four or more	612	5.3	577	35	445	12.0	429	17

[1]Includes other items, not shown separately.
[2]Hispanic persons may be of any race.
[3]Includes widowed persons whose previous marriage ended in divorce.

C4-3   Child Support Enforcement Program–Caseload and Collections: 1980–1995

[For years ending Sept. 30. Includes Puerto Rico, Guam, and the Virgin Islands. The Child Support Enforcement program locates absent parents, establishes paternity of children born out-of-wedlock, and establishes and enforces support orders. By law, these services are available to all families that need them. The program is operated at the State and local government level but 68 percent of administrative costs are paid by the Federal government. Child support collected for families not receiving Aid to Families with Dependent Children (AFDC) goes to the family to help it remain self-sufficient. Most of the child support collected on behalf of AFDC families goes to Federal and State governments to offset AFDC payments. Based on data reported by State agencies. Minus sign (-) indicates net outlay]

ITEM	Unit	1980	1985	1990	1991	1992	1993	1994	1995
Total cases	1,000	5,432	8,401	12,796	13,423	15,158	17,125	18,610	19,162
AFDC and AFDC arrears only caseload	1,000	(NA)	(NA)	7,953	8,034	8,717	9,638	10,420	10,379
AFDC cases	1,000	4,583	6,242	5,872	6,166	6,752	7,472	7,986	7,880
AFDC arrears only cases[1]	1,000	(NA)	(NA)	2,082	1,868	1,965	2,166	2,434	2,499
Non-AFDC cases	1,000	849	2,159	4,843	5,389	6,441	7,487	8,190	8,783
Cases for which a collection was made:									
AFDC cases	1,000	503	684	701	755	837	879	926	976
AFDC arrears only cases[1]	1,000	(NA)	(NA)	224	278	255	289	308	342
Non-AFDC cases	1,000	243	654	1,363	1,555	1,749	1,958	2,169	2,406
Percentage of cases with collections:									
AFDC cases	Percent	11.0	11.0	11.9	12.2	12.4	11.8	11.6	12.4
AFDC arrears only cases[1]	Percent	(NA)	(NA)	10.8	14.9	13.0	13.4	12.7	13.7
Non-AFDC cases	Percent	28.7	30.3	28.1	28.9	27.2	26.1	26.5	27.4
Absent parents located, total	1,000	643	878	2,062	2,387	3,152	3,777	4,204	4,950
Paternities established, total	1,000	144	232	393	472	512	554	592	659
Support orders established, total[2]	1,000	374	669	1,022	821	879	1,026	1,025	1,051
FINANCES									
Collections, total	Mil. dol	1,478	2,694	6,010	6,885	7,964	8,907	9,850	10,828
AFDC collections[3]	Mil. dol	603	1,090	1,750	1,984	2,259	2,416	2,550	2,690
State share	Mil. dol	274	415	620	700	787	847	891	939
Incentive payments to States	Mil. dol	72	145	264	278	299	339	407	400
Federal share	Mil. dol	246	341	533	626	738	777	762	822
Payments to AFDC families[4]	Mil. dol	10	189	334	381	435	446	457	474
Non-AFDC collections	Mil. dol	874	1,604	4,260	4,902	5,705	6,491	7,300	8,138
Administrative expenditures, total	Mil. dol	466	814	1,606	1,804	1,995	2,241	2,556	3,012
State share	Mil. dol	117	243	545	593	652	724	816	917
Federal share	Mil. dol	349	571	1,061	1,212	1,343	1,517	1,741	2,095
Program savings, total	Mil. dol	127	86	-190	-201	-170	-278	-496	-852
State share	Mil. dol	230	317	338	385	434	462	482	422
Federal share	Mil. dol	-103	-231	-528	-586	-605	-740	-978	-1,273
Total fees and costs recovered for non-AFDC cases	Mil. dol	5	3	22	34	29	31	33	33
Percentage of AFDC payments recovered	Percent	5.2	7.3	10.3	10.7	11.4	12.0	12.5	13.6

NA Not available.

[1] Reflects cases that are no longer receiving AFDC but still have outstanding child support due.

[2] Through 1990 includes modifications to orders.

[3] Beginning 1993 includes medical support payments not shown separately.

[4] Beginning 1985, States were required to pass along to the family the first $50 of any current child support collected each month.

D. Children

1. CHILDBEARING AND ADOPTION

After the post-World War II baby boom, birth rates have remained relatively stable throughout the late 1970s and 1980s (see Figure D1-1). Since 1990, the birth rate has declined. The actual number of births has generally increased as the population has grown, but even the number of births dropped off in the 1990s. By 1994, the average woman gave birth to approximately two children, just enough to replace the population (Figure D1-2). Younger women expect to have more than two children, but it remains to be seen whether they will actually have as many as they expect to have (Table D1-8). Expected fertility is higher for women with less education, the poor, and minorities. One-third of women age 15 to 44 have had no pregnancies, and over a third have had one or two pregnancies (Table D1-9).

An increasing percentage of births occur before marriage (Figure D1-17). Since 1990, about one-third of first births occur before the mother is married. This trend is not the result of a large increase in teenage mothers; rather, people are delaying marriage longer than in the past.

Despite wide use of contraceptives (reported in Section E), 28 percent of women aged 15-44 report they have had an unintended birth (Figure D1-26). Unintended births are more likely among women who are not currently married, who are poor, and minorities (Table D1-27). Still, a majority of women were happy when they became pregnant (Table D1-28).

Most women in the childbearing ages are fecund (biologically capable of having children). About one-fourth have been sterilized, and 10 percent have difficulty getting pregnant (Table D1-29). A majority of women have received family planning services and most have received a medical service in the last year (Table D1-30 and D1-31). Only 14 percent, however, have sought treatment or services for infertility. Slightly over half of mothers breastfeed their infants (Table D1-35). About one percent of women in the childbearing ages are seeking to adopt a child (Table D1-37).

2. INTERACTION WITH CHILDREN

Parents report fairly frequent activity with children—playing together, having private talks, helping with homework, and watching TV or videos (Table D2-1). Parents say they do each of these activities about once a week. Because patterns of interaction change when children reach school age (5–17), information about children in this age group is reported separately. Parents spend a fair amount of time alone with each child in this age group (Table D2-2). Parents spend about four hours a week checking homework, talking about school work, and talking about things learned in school. Almost half, however, report that they do not eat meals with children very frequently (Table D2-3). Parents also spend time talking about things that worry or excite the child (Table D2-4). A large majority of parents give their children hugs or kisses (Table D2-5). They also share enjoyable times together, laugh with children, and find that children are easy to love (Table D2-6).

Parents report knowing most of their children's friends, and friends are frequent visitors in the home (Table D2-8). Frequency of visits by friends and parents' knowledge of friends is comparable across education levels and race or ethnic identity.

There is not clear consensus on beliefs about children and parental responsibilities (Table D2-9). There is some sense that older children and parents are obligated to help each other, but this belief is not shared by all. There is also disagreement about whether one can have a satisfying life without having children and the consequences if children are cared for by someone other than the parent.

About half of parents pay children allowance (Table D2-10). An even greater percentage pay children for doing work around the house.

Adults tend to believe that their mother had a greater influence on them than did their father (Table D2-11). About half of parents would give themselves a grade of B as parents and another third feel they merit an A (Table D2-12).

3. CHILDREN'S PROBLEM BEHAVIORS AND DISAGREEMENT

One-fifth of parents say they have a child that is difficult to raise (Table D3-1). Fifteen percent of the children have seen a therapist. The most common school problem reported by parents is that children had to repeat a grade (Table D3-2). Some parents have had to meet with a teacher or the principal and about 10 percent of the children have been expelled at some point. A smaller percentage (5.5%) have been in trouble with the police (Table D3-3).

It is not uncommon for children to be at home alone after school, but parents are less likely to leave them at home alone in the evenings or overnight (Table D3-4). Parents also restrict TV viewing, but are more likely to restrict the type of program than the amount of time spent viewing (Table D3-5). The most common form of discipline is talking to children, followed by taking away privileges (Table D3-6). Yelling at children is not unusual for about half of the parents, but only about a fifth of the parents spank children very often.

The most common sources of disagreement reported by parents are about helping around the house and getting along with other family members (Tables D3-7 through D3-10). Dress and school issues also cause some disagreement. Money, staying out late, sexual behavior, smoking, drinking or drug use, friends, and a boy or girl friend are less common sources of disagreement. Parents are often able to have a calm discussion about disagreements, but sometimes end up refusing to talk about the issue, or letting the children have their own way (Table D3-11). Parents report that they generally do not argue and shout over disagreements.

4. CHILDREN OF DIVORCE AND SEPARATION

As the divorce rate has risen, increased concern has been expressed over the well-being of children with divorced or separated parents. About one-third of non-resident parents say they see their child and talk with their child almost weekly, but an even larger percentage say they only have contact about once per year (Table D4-1). About 70 percent of custodial parents say they receive little help and over 80 percent say they receive little interference from the other parent (Table D4-2). Help is more common than interference.

The most common source of conflict between divorced or separated parents is over financial support (Table D4-3). Living arrangements and where and how the child spends time are also problematic on a regular basis. Problems also arise over visitation because a parent does not show up or because of last-minute changes in schedule (Table D4-4). Parents generally do try to hide conflict from their children (Table D4-5). Finally, most nonresidential parents do not have a major role in important decisions affecting the child (Table D4-6).

5. PHYSICAL PUNISHMENT AND CHILD ABUSE

Although most parents agree than spanking is sometimes necessary, only 10 percent of parents say they spanked their child in the last week (Table D5-1). Most people have fairly positive evaluations of the way in which the government and society deal with child abuse (Table D5-4).

The number of substantiated cases of child abuse increased steadily in the first half of the 1990s, but declined somewhat in 1995 (Figure D5-5). Neglect is the most common form of confirmed abuse, followed by physical abuse. Sexual abuse is a distant third, with emotional maltreatment and medical neglect being less frequent (Table D5-6). About half of the victims in these cases are between the ages of two and nine. Twelve percent of adults say they were punched, kicked, or choked as a child, and 5 percent report even more serious abuse.

1. CHILDBEARING AND ADOPTION

D1-1 Trend in Number of Live Births and Birth Rates

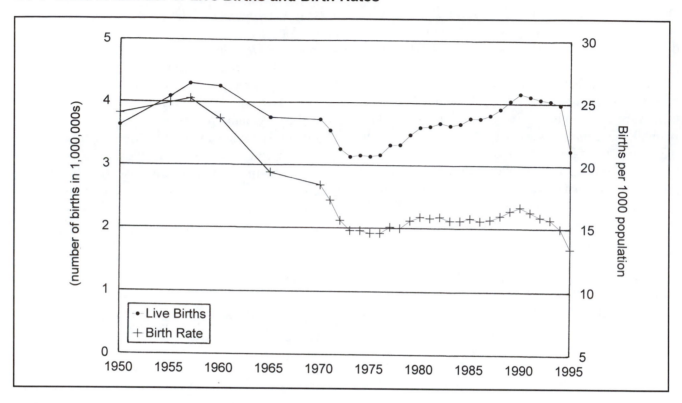

D1-2 Trend in Fertility: Total Fertility Rate

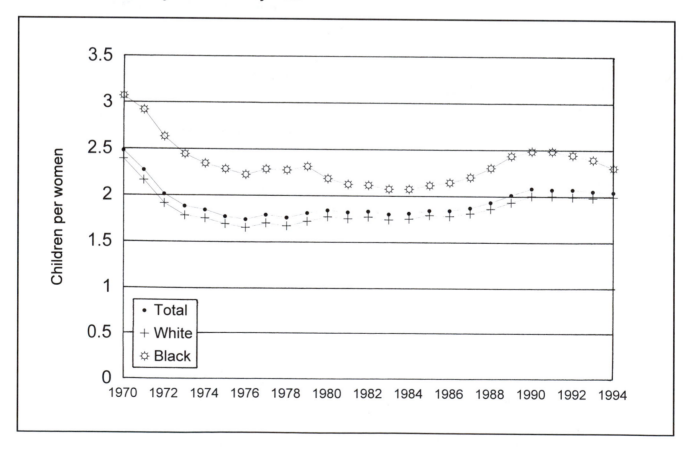

D1-3 Live Births, Deaths, Marriages, and Divorces: 1950–1995

YEAR	NUMBER (1,000)					RATE PER 1,000 POPULATION				
	Births [1]	Deaths		Marriages [3]	Divorces [4]	Births [1]	Deaths		Marriages [3]	Divorces [4]
		Total	Infant [2]				Total	Infant [2]		
1950	3,632	1,452	104	1,667	385	24.1	9.6	29.2	11.1	2.6
1955	4,097	1,529	107	1,531	377	25.0	9.3	26.4	9.3	2.3
1957	4,300	1,633	112	1,518	381	25.3	9.6	26.3	8.9	2.2
1960	4,258	1,712	111	1,523	393	23.7	9.5	26.0	8.5	2.2
1965	3,760	1,828	93	1,800	479	19.4	9.4	24.7	9.3	2.5
1970	3,731	1,921	75	2,159	708	18.4	9.5	20.0	10.6	3.5
1971	3,556	1,928	68	2,190	773	17.2	9.3	19.1	10.6	3.7
1972	3,258	1,964	60	2,282	845	15.6	9.4	18.5	10.9	4.0
1973	3,137	1,973	56	2,284	915	14.8	9.3	17.7	10.8	4.3
1974	3,160	1,934	53	2,230	977	14.8	9.1	16.7	10.5	4.6
1975	3,144	1,893	51	2,153	1,036	14.6	8.8	16.1	10.0	4.8
1976	3,168	1,909	48	2,155	1,083	14.6	8.8	15.2	9.9	5.0
1977	3,327	1,900	47	2,178	1,091	15.1	8.6	14.1	9.9	5.0
1978	3,333	1,928	46	2,282	1,130	15.0	8.7	13.8	10.3	5.1
1979	3,494	1,914	46	2,331	1,181	15.6	8.5	13.1	10.4	5.3
1980	3,612	1,990	46	2,390	1,189	15.9	8.8	12.6	10.6	5.2
1981	3,629	1,978	43	2,422	1,213	15.8	8.6	11.9	10.6	5.3
1982	3,681	1,975	42	2,456	1,170	15.9	8.5	11.5	10.6	5.1
1983	3,639	2,019	41	2,446	1,158	15.6	8.6	11.2	10.5	5.0
1984	3,669	2,039	40	2,477	1,169	15.6	8.6	10.8	10.5	5.0
1985	3,761	2,086	40	2,413	1,190	15.8	8.8	10.6	10.1	5.0
1986	3,757	2,105	39	2,407	1,178	15.6	8.8	10.4	10.0	4.9
1987	3,809	2,123	38	2,403	1,166	15.7	8.8	10.1	9.9	4.8
1988	3,910	2,168	39	2,396	1,167	16.0	8.9	10.0	9.8	4.8
1989	4,041	2,150	40	2,403	1,157	16.4	8.7	9.8	9.7	4.7
1990	4,158	2,148	38	2,443	1,182	16.7	8.6	9.2	9.8	4.7
1991	4,111	2,170	37	2,371	1,187	16.3	8.6	8.9	9.4	4.7
1992	4,065	2,176	35	2,362	1,215	15.9	8.5	8.5	9.3	4.8
1993	4,000	2,269	33	2,334	1,187	15.5	8.8	8.4	9.0	4.6
1994 prel.	3,979	2,286	31	2,362	1,191	15.0	8.8	7.9	9.1	4.6
1995 prel. [5]	3,244	1,926	24	1,954	973	13.4	8.8	7.7	7.6	4.1

[1] Prior to 1960, data adjusted for underregistration. [2] Infants under 1 year, excluding fetal deaths; rates per 1,000 registered live births. [3] Includes estimates for some States through 1965 and also for 1976 and 1977 and marriage licenses for some States for all years except 1973 and 1975. Beginning 1978, includes nonlicensed marriages in California. [4] Includes reported annulments and some estimated State figures for all years. [5] Rates are for the month of December 1995 only.

D1-4 Live Births, by Race and Type of Hispanic Origin—Selected Characteristics: 1990 and 1994

[Represents registered births. Excludes births to nonresidents of the United States. Data are based on race of mother]

RACE AND HISPANIC ORIGIN	NUMBER OF BIRTHS (1,000)		BIRTHS TO TEENAGE MOTHERS, PERCENT OF TOTAL		BIRTHS TO UNMARRIED MOTHERS, PERCENT OF TOTAL		PERCENT OF MOTHERS BEGINNING PRENATAL CARE DURING—				PERCENT OF BIRTHS WITH LOW BIRTH WEIGHT [1]	
							First trimester		Third trimester or no care			
	1990	1994	1990	1994	1990	1994	1990	1994	1990	1994	1990	1994
Total	4,158	3,953	12.8	13.1	26.6	32.6	74.2	80.2	6.0	4.4	7.0	7.3
White	3,290	3,121	10.9	11.3	16.9	25.4	77.7	82.8	4.9	3.6	5.7	6.1
Black	684	636	23.1	23.2	66.7	70.4	60.7	68.3	10.9	8.2	13.3	13.2
American Indian, Eskimo, Aleut .	39	38	19.5	21.0	53.6	57.0	57.9	65.2	12.9	9.8	6.1	6.4
Asian and Pacific Islander [2] . . .	142	158	5.7	5.7	(NA)	16.2	(NA)	79.7	(NA)	4.1	(NA)	6.8
Filipino	26	30	6.1	6.0	15.9	18.5	77.1	81.3	4.5	3.6	7.3	7.8
Chinese	23	27	1.2	1.0	5.0	7.2	81.3	86.2	3.4	2.7	4.7	4.8
Japanese	9	9	2.9	2.8	9.6	11.2	87.0	89.2	2.9	1.9	6.2	6.9
Hawaiian	6	6	18.4	19.6	45.0	48.6	65.8	77.0	8.7	4.7	7.2	7.2
Hispanic origin [3]	595	665	16.8	17.8	36.7	43.1	60.2	68.9	12.0	7.6	6.1	6.2
Mexican	386	455	17.7	18.6	33.3	40.8	57.8	67.3	13.2	8.3	5.5	5.8
Puerto Rican	59	57	21.7	23.2	55.9	60.2	63.5	71.7	10.6	6.5	9.0	9.1
Cuban	11	12	7.7	7.3	18.2	22.9	84.8	90.1	2.8	1.6	5.7	6.3
Central and South American .	83	93	9.0	10.4	41.2	45.9	61.5	71.2	10.9	6.5	5.8	6.0
Other and unknown Hispanic .	(NA)	48	(NA)	20.8	(NA)	43.5	(NA)	72.1	(NA)	6.2	(NA)	7.5

NA Not available.   [1] Births less than 2,500 grams (5 lb.-8 oz.).   [2] Includes other races not shown separately.   [3] Hispanic persons may be of any race. Includes other types, not shown separately.

D1-5 Births and Birth Rates: 1980–1994

ITEM	1980	1985	1986	1987	1988	1989	1990	1991	1992	1993	1994
Live births [1]	3,612	3,761	3,757	3,809	3,910	4,041	4,158	4,111	4,065	4,000	3,953
White	2,936	3,038	3,019	3,044	3,102	3,192	3,290	3,241	3,202	3,150	3,121
Black	568	582	593	611	639	673	684	683	674	659	636
American Indian	29	34	34	35	37	39	39	39	39	39	38
Asian or Pacific Islander	74	105	108	117	129	133	142	145	150	153	158
Male	1,853	1,928	1,925	1,951	2,002	2,069	2,129	2,102	2,082	2,049	2,023
Female	1,760	1,833	1,832	1,858	1,907	1,971	2,029	2,009	1,983	1,951	1,930
Males per 100 females	105	105	105	105	105	105	105	105	105	105	105
Age of mother:											
Under 20 years old	562	478	472	473	489	518	533	532	518	501	518
20 to 24 years old	1,226	1,141	1,102	1,076	1,067	1,078	1,094	1,090	1,070	1,038	1,001
25 to 29 years old	1,108	1,201	1,200	1,216	1,239	1,263	1,277	1,220	1,179	1,129	1,089
30 to 34 years old	550	696	721	761	804	842	886	885	895	901	906
35 to 39 years old	141	214	230	248	270	294	318	331	345	357	372
40 years old or more	24	29	31	36	41	46	50	54	58	61	66
Birth rate per 1,000 population	15.9	15.8	15.6	15.7	16.0	16.4	16.7	16.3	15.9	15.5	15.2
White	15.1	15.0	14.8	14.9	15.0	15.4	15.8	15.4	15.0	14.7	14.4
Black	21.3	20.4	20.5	20.8	21.5	22.3	22.4	21.9	21.3	20.5	19.5
American Indian	20.7	19.8	19.2	19.1	19.3	19.7	18.9	18.3	18.4	17.8	17.1
Asian or Pacific Islander	19.9	18.7	18.0	18.4	19.2	18.7	19.0	18.2	18.0	17.7	17.5
Male	16.8	16.7	16.5	16.5	16.8	17.2	17.6	17.1	16.7	(NA)	(NA)
Female	15.1	15.0	14.9	14.9	15.2	15.6	15.9	15.6	15.2	(NA)	(NA)
Plural birth ratio [2]	19.3	21.0	21.6	22.0	22.4	23.0	23.3	23.9	24.4	25.2	25.7
White	18.5	20.4	21.2	21.6	22.0	22.5	22.9	23.4	24.0	24.9	25.5
Black	24.1	25.3	24.9	25.4	25.8	26.9	27.0	27.8	28.2	28.7	29.4
Fertility rate per 1,000 women [3]	68.4	66.2	65.4	65.7	67.2	69.2	70.9	69.6	68.9	67.6	66.7
White [3]	64.8	64.1	63.1	63.3	64.5	66.4	68.3	67.0	66.5	65.4	64.9
Black [3]	84.7	78.8	78.9	80.1	82.6	86.2	86.8	85.2	83.2	80.5	76.9
American Indian [3]	82.7	78.6	75.9	75.6	76.8	79.0	76.2	75.1	75.4	73.4	70.9
Asian or Pacific Islander [3]	73.2	68.4	66.0	67.1	70.2	68.2	69.6	67.6	67.2	66.7	66.8
Age of mother:											
10 to 14 years old	1.1	1.2	1.3	1.3	1.3	1.4	1.4	1.4	1.4	1.4	1.4
15 to 19 years old	53.0	51.0	50.2	50.6	53.0	57.3	59.9	62.1	60.7	59.6	58.9
20 to 24 years old	115.1	108.3	107.4	107.9	110.2	113.8	116.5	115.7	114.6	112.6	111.1
25 to 29 years old	112.9	111.0	109.8	111.6	114.4	117.6	120.2	118.2	117.4	115.5	113.9
30 to 34 years old	61.9	69.1	70.1	72.1	74.8	77.4	80.8	79.5	80.2	80.8	81.5
35 to 39 years old	19.8	24.0	24.4	26.3	28.1	29.9	31.7	32.0	32.5	32.9	33.7
40 to 44 years old	3.9	4.0	4.1	4.4	4.8	5.2	5.5	5.5	5.9	6.1	6.4
45 to 49 years old	0.2	0.2	0.2	0.2	0.2	0.2	0.2	0.2	0.3	0.3	0.3

NA Not available.   [1] Includes other races not shown separately.   [2] Number of multiple births per 1,000 live births.   [3] Per 1,000 women, 15 to 44 years old in specified group. The rate for *age of mother 45 to 49 years old* computed by relating births to mothers 45 years old and over to women 45 to 49 years old.

D1-6 Total Fertility Rate and Intrinsic Rate of Natural Increase: 1960–1994

[Based on race of child and registered births only, thru 1979. Beginning 1980, based on race of mother. Beginning 1970, excludes births to nonresidents of United States. The *total fertility rate* is the number of births that 1,000 women would have in their lifetime if, at each year of age, they experienced the birth rates occurring in the specified year. A total fertility rate of 2,110 represents "replacement level" fertility for the total population under current mortality conditions (assuming no net immigration). The *intrinsic rate of natural increase* is the rate that would eventually prevail if a population were to experience, at each year of age, the birth rates and death rates occurring in the specified year and if those rates remained unchanged over a long period of time. Minus sign (-) indicates decrease.

ANNUAL AVERAGE AND YEAR	TOTAL FERTILITY RATE			INTRINSIC RATE OF NATURAL INCREASE			ANNUAL AVERAGE AND YEAR	TOTAL FERTILITY RATE			INTRINSIC RATE OF NATURAL INCREASE		
	Total	White	Black and other	Total	White	Black and other		Total	White	Black and other	Total	White	Black and other
1960-64 . . .	3,449	3,326	4,326	18.6	17.1	27.7	1979	1,808	1,716	2,310	-5.7	-7.7	3.8
1965-69 . . .	2,622	2,512	3,362	8.2	6.4	18.6	1980	1,840	1,773	2,177	-5.1	-7.0	4.0
1970-74 . . .	2,094	1,997	2,680	-0.7	-2.5	9.1	1981	1,812	1,748	2,118	-5.6	-7.4	3.0
1975-79 . . .	1,774	1,685	2,270	-6.6	-8.5	3.0	1982	1,828	1,767	2,107	-5.2	-7.0	3.0
1980-84 . . .	1,819	1,731	2,262	-5.4	-7.3	3.0	1983	1,799	1,741	2,066	-5.8	-7.5	2.2
1985-88 . . .	1,870	1,769	2,339	-4.2	-6.3	4.3	1984	1,807	1,749	2,071	-5.6	-7.3	2.1
							1985	1,844	1,787	2,109	-4.8	-6.5	2.7
1970	2,480	2,385	3,067	6.0	4.5	14.4	1986	1,838	1,776	2,136	-4.9	-6.7	2.8
1971	2,267	2,161	2,920	2.6	0.8	12.6	1987	1,872	1,805	2,198	-4.1	-6.1	4.0
1972	2,010	1,907	2,628	-2.0	-3.9	8.6	1988	1,934	1,857	2,298	-2.9	-5.1	5.7
1973	1,879	1,783	2,443	-4.5	-6.5	5.7	1989	2,014	1,931	2,433	-1.4	-3.6	7.4
1974	1,835	1,749	2,339	-5.4	-7.2	4.0	1990	2,081	2,003	2,480	-0.1	-2.3	8.3
1975	1,774	1,686	2,276	-6.7	-8.6	3.0	1991	2,073	1,996	2,480	-0.2	-2.4	8.2
1976	1,738	1,652	2,223	-7.4	-9.3	2.1	1992	2,065	1,994	2,442	-0.4	-2.5	7.5
1977	1,790	1,703	2,279	-6.2	-8.1	3.2	1993	2,046	1,982	2,385	-0.7	-1.9	3.7
1978	1,760	1,668	2,265	-6.8	-8.8	2.9	1994	2,036	1,985	2,300	(NA)	(NA)	(NA)

NA Not available.

D1-7 Projected Fertility Rates, by Race and Age Group: 1996 and 2010

AGE GROUP	ALL RACES [1]		WHITE		BLACK		AMERICAN INDIAN, ESKIMO, ALEUT		ASIAN AND PACIFIC ISLANDERS		HISPANIC [2]	
	1996	2010	1996	2010	1996	2010	1996	2010	1996	2010	1996	2010
Total fertility rate . .	2,059	2,108	1,988	2,046	2,428	2,438	2,152	2,159	1,952	1,954	2,977	2,977
Birth rates:												
10 to 14 years old. . . .	1.4	1.6	0.8	0.9	4.8	4.8	1.7	1.7	0.9	0.8	2.6	2.6
15 to 19 years old. . . .	59.4	63.6	50.7	56.0	109.7	111.5	78.2	81.8	28.2	28.7	103.7	103.7
20 to 24 years old. . . .	115.7	118.2	109.2	112.6	157.4	158.7	143.3	143.7	80.3	79.5	184.1	184.1
25 to 29 years old. . . .	117.9	119.5	118.8	120.7	112.4	113.1	108.7	109.0	121.5	121.7	152.4	152.4
30 to 34 years old. . . .	78.8	81.0	79.9	82.0	66.6	67.8	61.7	62.9	100.8	101.1	96.7	96.7
35 to 39 years old. . . .	31.6	32.1	31.5	31.7	27.8	27.7	27.4	27.4	48.0	47.3	45.3	45.3
40 to 44 years old. . . .	5.6	5.9	5.4	5.6	5.4	5.3	6.0	6.0	10.4	10.3	10.8	10.8
45 to 49 years old. . . .	0.3	0.3	0.2	0.2	0.3	0.2	0.3	0.3	1.0	1.0	0.6	0.6

[1] Includes other races not shown separately.   [2] Persons of Hispanic origin may be of any race.

D1-8 Number of Women 15–44 Years of Age, and Mean Number of Children Ever Born, Additional Births Expected, and Total Births Expected, by Selected Characteristics: United States, 1995

Characteristic	Number in thousands	Children ever born	Additional births expected	Total births expected
			Mean	
All women	60,201	1.242	0.973	2.214
Age at interview				
15-19 years	8,961	0.094	2.147	2.240
20-24 years	9,041	0.546	1.771	2.316
25-29 years	9,693	1.082	1.262	2.344
30-34 years	11,065	1.590	0.670	2.260
35-39 years	11,211	1.859	0.256	2.115
40-44 years	10,230	1.961	0.077	2.038
Marital status				
Never married	22,679	0.368	1.695	2.063
Ever married	37,522	1.770	0.536	2.306
Currently married	29,673	1.752	0.579	2.331
Formerly married	7,849	1.838	0.374	2.212
Fecundity status				
Contraceptively sterile	14,565	2.463	0.001	2.464
Noncontraceptively sterile	1,855	1.665	0.003	1.668
Impaired fecundity	6,156	1.009	0.934	1.943
Fecund	37,625	0.786	1.403	2.189
Education at interview[1]				
No high school diploma or GED[2]	5,424	2.509	0.395	2.904
High school diploma or GED	18,169	1.732	0.472	2.204
Some college, no bachelors degree	12,399	1.299	0.813	2.112
Bachelors degree or higher	11,748	0.977	1.003	1.980
Poverty level income at interview[1]				
0-149 percent	10,072	2.190	0.559	2.749
0-99 percent	5,992	2.346	0.541	2.887
150-299 percent	14,932	1.639	0.644	2.283
300 percent or more	22,736	1.145	0.763	1.907
Race and Hispanic origin				
Hispanic	6,702	1.569	1.093	2.663
Non-Hispanic white	42,522	1.163	0.951	2.114
Non-Hispanic black	8,210	1.425	0.867	2.292
Non-Hispanic other	2,766	1.123	0.316	2.440

[1]Limited to women 22-44 years of age at time of interview.

[2]GED is general equivalency diploma.

D1-9 Number of Women 15–44 Years of Age and Percent Distribution by Number of Pregnancies, According to Selected Characteristics: United States, 1995

Characteristic	Number in thousands	Number of pregnancies[1] Total	None	1	2	3	4 or more
		Percent distribution					
All women	60,201	100.0	33.4	16.4	20.3	14.2	15.7
Age at interview							
15-19 years	8,961	100.0	84.0	12.3	3.2	0.6	0.1
20—24 years	9,041	100.0	55.2	20.2	14.0	5.0	5.6
25-29 years	9,693	100.0	31.1	24.1	19.4	13.1	12.3
30-34 years	11,065	100.0	17.4	16.8	26.3	18.9	20.07
35-39 years	11,211	100.0	12.5	12.6	27.6	22.4	24.8
40-44 years	10,230	100.0	12.1	13.4	26.9	21.3	26.3
Family background							
Both parents from birth[2]	37,233	100.0	33.4	15.6	21.2	14.8	14.9
Single parent from birth	2,093	100.0	28.6	17.3	19.4	14.4	20.4
Both parents, then 1 parent	8,003	100.0	37.7	18.6	16.6	12.3	14.7
Stepparent[3]	8,378	100.0	33.0	18.0	19.7	12.7	16.5
Other	4,493	100.0	28.7	15.9	20.0	15.0	20.4
Residence at interview							
Metropolitan, central city	18,550	100.0	35.0	16.9	18.4	12.7	17.0
Metropolitan, suburban	29,303	100.0	33.2	16.3	20.4	15.1	14.9
Nonmetropolitan	12,347	100.0	31.5	15.9	22.5	14.2	15.7
Education at interview[4]							
No high school diploma or GED[5]	5,424	100.0	3.2	10.7	22.8	23.3	40.0
High school diploma or GED	18,169	100.0	13.9	17.6	27.4	20.2	21.0
Some college, no bachelor's degree	12,399	100.0	25.7	17.6	22.9	15.9	17.9
Bachelor's degree or higher	11,748	100.0	37.9	18.1	21.1	12.7	10.2
Poverty level income at interview[4]							
0-149 percent	10,072	100.0	12.1	11.9	22.1	19.8	34.2
0-99 percent	5,992	100.0	10.6	11.4	21.0	20.4	36.6
150—299 percent	14,932	100.0	18.1	17.6	24.9	19.2	20.2
300 percent or higher	22,736	100.0	28.3	18.8	24.5	15.5	12.9
Race and Hispanic origin							
Hispanic	6,702	100.0	26.8	16.6	19.1	15.2	22.2
Non-Hispanic white	42,522	100.0	34.9	16.2	21.0	14.1	13.7
Non-Hispanic black	8,210	100.0	28.1	17.8	18.1	14.8	21.2
Non-Hispanic other	2,767	100.0	41.2	15.2	17.7	11.2	14.8

[1]Based on interviewer-administered portion of the survey.
[2]Includes women who lived with either both biological or both adoptive parents until they left home.
[3]Parents separated or divorced, then custodial parent remarried.
[4]Limited to women 22-44 years of age at time of interview.
[5]GED is general equivalency diploma.

NOTE: Percents may not add to 100 due to rounding

D1-10 Number of Women 15–44 Years of Age and Percent Distribution by Number of Children Ever Born, According to Selected Characteristics: United States, 1995

Characteristic	Number in thousands	Total	Number of children ever born				
			None	1	2	3	4 or more
			Percent Distribution				
All Women	60,201	100.0	41.9	17.8	23.0	11.6	5.7
Age at interview							
15-19 years	8,961	100.0	91.6	7.6	0.5	0.2	—
20-24 years	9,041	100.0	65.3	20.2	10.2	3.6	0.8
25-29 years	9,693	100.0	43.5	23.2	20.2	9.0	4.1
30-34 years	11,065	100.0	26.4	21.0	30.4	15.1	7.1
35-39 years	11,211	100.0	19.6	16.8	35.5	19.0	9.1
40-44 years	10,230	100.0	17.5	17.0	35.2	19.0	11.2
Marital status							
Never married	22,679	100.0	79.8	10.9	5.3	2.3	1.7
Currently married	29,673	100.0	19.2	21.5	35.1	17.0	7.3
Formerly married	7,849	100.0	18.7	23.6	28.9	17.7	11.1
Residence at interview							
Metropolitan, central city	18,550	100.0	44.7	18.2	20.0	11.0	6.0
Metropolitan, suburban	29,303	100.0	41.7	17.6	24.0	11.7	4.9
Nonmetropolitan	12,347	100.0	38.2	17.6	25.3	12.0	6.9
Education at interview[1]							
No high school diploma or GED[2]	5,424	100.0	7.9	15.3	29.2	27.2	20.6
High school diploma or GED	18,169	100.0	21.1	21.4	32.6	16.8	8.1
Some college, no bachelor's degree	12,399	100.0	35.6	21.0	27.6	11.4	4.5
Bachelor's degree or higher	11,748	100.0	49.1	17.6	22.9	8.1	2.4
Poverty level income at interview[1]							
0-149 percent	10,072	100.0	15.7	15.6	29.6	21.4	17.7
0-99 percent	5,992	100.0	14.0	14.4	28.2	23.7	19.7
150-299 percent	14,932	100.0	24.6	21.5	30.4	16.1	7.4
300 percent or higher	22,736	100.0	40.5	20.2	26.8	1.0	2.3
Race and Hispanic origin							
Hispanic	6,702	100.0	34.8	17.9	20.3	16.3	10.7
Non-Hispanic white	42,522	100.0	43.5	17.2	24.2	10.9	4.1
Non-Hispanic black	8,210	100.0	37.3	20.7	20.5	12.3	9.2
Non-Hispanic other	2,767	100.0	48.4	17.2	19.5	8.3	6.7

— Quantity zero.
[1] Limited to women 22-44 years of age at time of interview.
[2] GED is general equivalency diploma.
NOTE: Percents may not add to 100 due to rounding.

D1-11 Women Who Have Had a Child in the Last Year, by Age: 1980–1994

AGE OF MOTHER	WOMEN WHO HAD A CHILD IN LAST YEAR (1,000)			TOTAL BIRTHS PER 1,000 WOMEN			FIRST BIRTHS PER 1,000 WOMEN		
	1980	1990	1994	1980	1990	1994	1980	1990	1994
Total	3,247	3,913	3,890	71.1	67.0	64.7	28.5	26.4	27.4
15 to 29 years old [1] . . .	2,476	2,568	2,389	103.7	90.8	85.6	48.6	43.2	46.3
15 to 19 years old . .	(NA)	338	397	(NA)	39.8	45.2	(NA)	30.1	36.3
20 to 24 years old [2] .	1,396	1,038	938	96.6	113.4	100.7	(NA)	51.8	58.4
25 to 29 years old . .	1,081	1,192	1,054	114.8	112.1	107.7	(NA)	46.2	43.9
30 to 44 years old. . . .	770	1,346	1,501	35.4	44.7	46.6	6.3	10.6	11.0
30 to 34 years old . .	519	892	1,006	60.0	80.4	90.4	(NA)	21.9	23.0
35 to 39 years old . .	192	377	399	26.9	37.3	36.0	(NA)	6.5	7.3
40 to 44 years old . .	59	77	95	9.9	8.6	9.6	(NA)	1.2	1.8

NA Not available.   [1] For 1980-88, 18 to 29 years old.   [2] For 1980-88, 18 to 24 years old.

D1-12 Characteristics of Women Who Have Had a Child in the Last Year, 1995

[As of June. Covers civilian noninstitutional population. Since the number of women who had a birth during the 12-month period was tabulated and not the actual numbers of births, some small underestimation of fertility for this period may exist due to the omission of: (1) Multiple births, (2) Two or more live births spaced within the 12-month period (the woman is counted only once), (3) Women who had births in the period and who did not survive to the survey date, (4) Women who were in institutions and therefore not in the survey universe. These losses may be somewhat offset by the inclusion in the CPS of births to immigrants who did not have their children born in the United States and births to nonresident women. These births would not have been recorded in the vital registration system. Based on Current Population Survey (CPS);

CHARACTERISTIC	TOTAL, 15 TO 44 YEARS OLD			15 TO 29 YEARS OLD			30 TO 44 YEARS OLD		
	Number of women (1,000)	Women who have had a child in the last year		Number of women (1,000)	Women who have had a child in the last year		Number of women (1,000)	Women who have had a child in the last year	
		Total births per 1,000 women	First births per 1,000 women		Total births per 1,000 women	First births per 1,000 women		Total births per 1,000 women	First births per 1,000 women
Total [1]	60,225	61.4	23.2	27,742	81.2	38.1	32,483	44.4	10.4
White	48,603	59.2	22.6	22,001	76.6	36.5	26,602	44.8	11.1
Black	8,617	70.6	26.4	4,276	109.0	49.6	4,342	32.7	3.7
Hispanic [2]	6,632	79.6	25.0	3,511	99.9	40.6	3,120	56.8	7.5
Currently married	31,616	85.5	30.3	8,445	168.2	76.1	23,171	55.3	13.6
Married, spouse present	29,202	87.2	31.4	7,720	172.4	78.9	21,482	56.6	14.3
Married, spouse absent [3]	2,414	64.5	17.4	725	123.4	46.6	1,689	39.3	4.9
Widowed or divorced	5,762	28.4	4.1	1,015	65.2	11.8	4,748	20.6	2.5
Never married	22,846	36.3	18.0	18,282	41.9	22.0	4,564	14.0	2.1
Educational attainment:									
Less than high school	12,629	57.3	19.6	9,005	65.6	26.2	3,624	36.9	3.1
High school, 4 years	18,404	67.4	25.5	7,050	119.6	56.6	11,354	35.0	6.2
College: 1 or more years	29,192	59.3	23.2	11,687	70.0	36.2	17,505	52.2	14.6
No degree	12,724	56.1	21.2	6,578	71.1	34.3	6,147	40.0	7.2
Associate degree	4,663	56.9	19.2	1,451	102.6	47.1	3,213	36.2	6.7
Bachelor's degree	8,884	65.3	27.0	3,149	56.2	34.2	5,735	70.2	23.1
Grad. or prof. degree	2,921	59.2	26.8	510	48.8	41.7	2,411	61.4	23.7
Labor force status:									
Employed	39,989	46.5	20.9	16,596	61.8	35.4	23,393	35.6	10.6
Unemployed	3,287	53.5	22.8	2,086	59.8	30.4	1,202	42.6	9.6
Not in labor force	16,949	98.1	28.5	9,060	121.7	44.8	7,889	71.0	9.8
Occupation of employed women:									
Managerial-professional	11,059	46.2	22.3	3,148	65.3	40.2	7,911	38.6	15.2
Tech., sales, admin. support	16,997	48.6	21.5	7,754	63.8	36.6	9,243	35.9	8.8
Service workers	7,612	44.0	16.6	4,001	53.0	25.6	3,611	34.0	6.6
Farming, forestry, and fishing	501	41.0	27.9	235	40.7	40.7	266	41.3	16.5
Precision prod., craft, repair	813	56.6	37.5	272	87.4	70.4	541	41.1	21.0
Operators, fabricators, laborers	3,007	39.5	17.8	1,186	67.3	39.1	1,821	21.5	3.8
Family income: Under $10,000	6,957	91.0	32.8	4,081	124.1	49.7	2,875	44.1	8.8
$10,000 to $19,999	8,159	64.3	25.8	4,358	93.1	44.5	3,801	31.4	4.3
$20,000 to $24,999	4,542	60.6	20.3	2,355	83.5	37.6	2,188	36.0	1.7
$25,000 to $29,999	4,364	57.0	18.9	2,104	77.8	34.1	2,259	37.7	4.7
$30,000 to $34,999	4,076	60.6	24.3	1,840	75.6	43.4	2,236	48.2	8.6
$35,000 to $49,999	9,949	59.1	20.8	4,160	80.8	32.9	5,789	43.5	12.2
$50,000 to $74,999	9,720	52.5	23.3	3,735	62.8	41.0	5,985	46.0	12.3
$75,000 and over	7,088	53.1	19.2	2,765	34.8	13.6	4,323	64.8	22.8

[1] Includes women of other races and women with family income not reported, not shown separately.   [2] Persons of Hispanic origin may be of any race.   [3] Includes separated women.

D1-13 Families, by Number of Own Children Under 18 Years Old: 1980–1996

RACE, HISPANIC ORIGIN, AND YEAR	NUMBER OF FAMILIES (1,000)					PERCENT DISTRIBUTION				
	Total	No children	One child	Two children	Three or more children	Total	No children	One child	Two children	Three or more children
ALL FAMILIES [1]										
1980	59,550	28,528	12,443	11,470	7,109	100	48	21	19	12
1985	62,706	31,594	13,108	11,645	6,359	100	50	21	19	10
1990	66,090	33,801	13,530	12,263	6,496	100	51	20	19	10
1995	69,305	35,009	14,088	13,213	6,995	100	51	20	19	10
1996	69,594	35,391	14,041	13,206	6,957	100	51	20	19	10
Married couple	53,567	28,647	9,352	10,278	5,290	100	53	17	19	10
Male householder [2]	3,513	1,885	1,005	471	152	100	54	29	13	4
Female householder [2]	12,514	4,859	3,683	2,457	1,514	100	39	29	20	12
WHITE FAMILIES										
1980	52,243	25,769	10,727	9,977	5,769	100	49	21	19	11
1985	54,400	28,169	11,174	9,937	5,120	100	52	21	18	9
1990	56,590	29,872	11,186	10,342	5,191	100	53	20	18	9
1995	58,437	30,486	11,491	10,983	5,478	100	52	20	19	9
1996	58,869	30,783	11,455	11,110	5,521	100	52	19	19	9
BLACK FAMILIES										
1980	6,184	2,364	1,449	1,235	1,136	100	38	23	20	18
1985	6,778	2,887	1,579	1,330	982	100	43	23	20	15
1990	7,470	3,093	1,894	1,433	1,049	100	41	25	19	14
1995	8,093	3,411	1,971	1,593	1,117	100	42	24	20	14
1996	8,055	3,472	1,958	1,485	1,140	100	43	24	18	14
HISPANIC FAMILIES [3]										
1980	3,029	946	680	698	706	100	31	22	23	23
1985	3,939	1,337	904	865	833	100	34	23	22	21
1990	4,840	1,790	1,095	1,036	919	100	37	23	21	19
1995	6,200	2,216	1,408	1,406	1,171	100	36	23	23	19
1996	6,287	2,238	1,450	1,437	1,160	100	36	23	23	18

[1] Includes other races, not shown separately.   [2] No spouse present.   [3] Hispanic persons may be of any race.

D1-14 Live Births, by State, 1994

DIVISION AND STATE	All races [1]	WHITE		BLACK		Hispanic [2]	Birth rate [3]	Fertility rate [4]
		Total	Non-Hispanic	Total	Non-Hispanic			
United States............	3,952,767	3,121,004	3,245,115	636.391	619,198	665,026	15.2	66.7
Northeast.................	732,796	581.627	620,498	120.632	110,287	93,274	(NA)	(NA)
New England	179,832	158.687	158.544	15.149	12,630	15,687	(NA)	(NA)
Maine	14,441	14,118	14,124	77	69	107	11.6	51.4
New Hampshire...........	15,106	14,840	14,090	104	87	187	13.3	56.2
Vermont................	7,377	7,263	6,864	27	25	38	12.7	54.6
Massachusetts	83,787	72,107	75,033	8,121	6,667	8,435	13.9	59.3
Rhode Island	13,466	11,839	10,682	1,085	946	1,623	13.5	59.6
Connecticut	45,655	38,520	37,751	5,735	4,836	5,297	13.9	62.1
Middle Atlantic	552,964	422,940	461,954	105,483	97,657	77,587	43.2	192.3
New York................	278,392	204,271	212,247	58,901	53,155	53,216	15.3	66.8
New Jersey	117,501	88,343	99,215	23,185	21,546	18,083	14.9	65.9
Pennsylvania	157,071	130,326	150,492	23,397	22,956	6,288	13.0	59.6
Midwest..................	888,659	736,071	825.305	128,086	126,858	50,507	(NA)	(NA)
East North Central..........	634,106	511,934	584,800	107,582	106,934	42,246	(NA)	(NA)
Ohio	155,944	130,279	152,952	23,615	23,505	2,717	14.0	61.8
Indiana	82,595	72,711	80,004	8,978	8,941	2,324	14.4	62.4
Illinois	189,257	142,348	158,799	40,971	40,798	30,350	16.1	70.5
Michigan	138,028	107,783	127,222	27,175	26,876	4,454	14.5	63.1
Wisconsin	68,282	58,813	65,823	6,843	6,814	2,401	13.4	59.9
West North Central	254,553	224,137	240,505	20.504	19,924	8,261	(NA)	(NA)
Minnesota	64,305	57,617	57,784	3,015	2,554	1,661	14.1	61.9
Iowa	37,079	35,226	35,985	1,055	1,047	1,060	13.1	60.8
Missouri................	73,543	60,489	72,253	11,875	11,813	1,224	13.9	62.6
North Dakota	8,584	7,700	8,392	68	67	116	13.5	62.6
South Dakota	10,507	8,777	10,377	76	76	124	14.6	68.6
Nebraska	23,156	21,148	21,393	1,273	1,265	1,382	14.3	64.9
Kansas	37,379	33,180	34,321	3,142	3,102	2,694	14.6	66.7
South	1,364,273	997,827	1,172.373	331,428	327,781	189,869	(NA)	(NA)
South Atlantic............	665,854	460,919	614,469	187,800	184,882	50,217	(NA)	(NA)
Delaware	10,411	7,774	9,870	2,396	2,315	526	14.7	62.7
Maryland	73,971	46,497	70,319	24,615	23,641	3,090	14.8	61.9
Dist. of Columbia...........	9,930	1,481	9,040	8,032	7,618	850	17.4	68.5
Virginia	95,039	69,315	90,323	22,331	22,176	4,609	14.5	60.5
West Virginia	21,375	20,451	21,260	798	794	106	11.7	53.3
North Carolina............	101,420	70,295	98,260	27,882	27,807	3,135	14.3	62.1
South Carolina	52,043	32,016	51,357	19,409	19,380	643	14.2	60.6
Georgia	111,011	69,641	106,400	39,070	38,852	4,363	15.7	64.9
Florida................	190,654	143,449	157,640	43,267	42,299	32,895	13.7	65.8
East South Central	229,067	164,485	226,875	62,102	62,020	2,072	(NA)	(NA)
Kentucky	52,983	47,641	52,479	4,895	4,876	466	13.8	60.1
Tennessee	73,191	55,613	72,319	16,603	16,576	845	14.1	61.4
Alabama	60,939	39,690	60,320	20,649	20,615	579	14.4	62.9
Mississippi	41,954	21,541	41,757	19,955	19,953	182	15.7	68.2
West South Central	469,352	372,423	331,029	81,526	80,879	137,580	(NA)	(NA)
Arkansas	34,718	26,378	33,893	7,836	7,806	782	14.2	64.9
Louisiana	67,817	37,925	66,340	28,645	28,432	1,413	15.7	67.6
Oklahoma	45,703	35,812	43,381	4,769	4,734	2,260	14.0	64.6
Texas	321,114	272,308	187,415	40,276	39,907	133,125	17.5	75.0
West	967,039	805.479	626.939	56,245	54,272	331,376	(NA)	(NA)
Mountain	249,719	223.466	189.216	8,300	7,889	58,405	(NA)	(NA)
Montana	11,067	9,733	10,457	32	24	250	12.9	60.9
Idaho	17,526	16,952	15,512	62	59	1,978	15.5	70.3
Wyoming	6,428	6,104	5,963	61	57	460	13.5	61.2
Colorado	54,071	49,292	43,391	2,773	2,679	10,667	14.8	63.3
New Mexico	27,591	23,053	14,601	521	505	12,984	16.7	74.8
Arizona................	70,846	61,570	45,135	2,485	2,322	24,135	17.4	79.7
Utah..................	38,279	36,333	35,538	287	201	2,704	20.1	85.9
Nevada	23,911	20,429	18,619	2,079	2,042	5,227	16.4	74.5
Pacific..................	717,320	582.013	437.723	47.945	46,383	272,971	(NA)	(NA)
Washington	77,358	67,600	66,599	3,065	2,880	8,108	14.5	62.9
Oregon	41,837	38,819	37,450	947	931	4,357	13.6	61.3
California................	567,930	462,719	306,435	42,807	41,510	257,750	18.1	78.3
Alaska.................	10,678	7,440	9,905	499	461	580	17.6	75.2
Hawaii.................	19,517	5,435	17,334	627	601	2,176	16.6	74.7

NA Not available.   [1] Includes other races not shown separately.   [2] Persons of Hispanic origin may be of any race. Births by Hispanic origin of mother.   [3] Per 1,000 estimated population.   [4] Per 1,000 women aged 15-44 years estimated.

D1-15 Women Who Have Had a Child in the Last Year, by Age and Labor Force Status: 1980–1995

YEAR	TOTAL, 18 TO 44 YEARS OLD			18 TO 29 YEARS OLD			30 TO 44 YEARS OLD		
	Number (1,000)	In the labor force		Number (1,000)	In the labor force		Number (1,000)	In the labor force	
		Number (1,000)	Percent		Number (1,000)	Percent		Number (1,000)	Percent
1980	3,247	1,233	38	2,476	947	38	770	287	37
1981	3,381	1,411	42	2,499	1,004	40	881	407	46
1982	3,433	1,508	44	2,445	1,040	43	988	469	48
1983	3,625	1,563	43	2,682	1,138	42	942	425	45
1984	3,311	1,547	47	2,375	1,058	45	936	489	52
1985	3,497	1,691	48	2,512	1,204	48	984	488	50
1986	3,625	1,805	50	2,452	1,185	48	1,174	620	53
1987	3,701	1,881	51	2,521	1,258	50	1,180	623	53
1988 [1]	3,667	1,866	51	2,384	1,177	49	1,283	688	54
1990 [1]	3,913	2,068	53	2,568	1,275	50	1,346	793	59
1992 [1]	3,688	1,985	54	2,346	1,182	50	1,342	802	60
1994 [1]	3,890	2,066	53	2,389	1,209	51	1,501	857	57
1995 [1]	3,696	2,034	55	2,252	1,150	51	1,444	884	61

[1] Lower age limit is 15 years old.

D1-16 Childless Women and Children Ever Born, by Race, Age, and Marital Status, 1995

CHARACTERISTIC	Total number of women (1,000)	WOMEN BY NUMBER OF CHILDREN EVER BORN (percent)				CHILDREN EVER BORN	
		Total	None	One	Two or more	Total number (1,000)	Per 1,000 women
ALL RACES [1]							
Women ever married.	37,378	100	19.0	22.3	58.7	65,948	1,764
15 to 19 years old.	319	100	43.9	45.5	10.6	218	684
20 to 24 years old.	3,036	100	36.7	34.4	28.9	3,096	1,020
25 to 29 years old.	6,105	100	28.8	29.2	42.0	8,112	1,329
30 to 34 years old.	9,006	100	18.7	23.0	58.4	15,634	1,736
35 to 39 years old.	9,660	100	13.2	16.9	69.8	19,578	2,027
40 to 44 years old.	9,252	100	12.3	17.9	69.8	19,310	2,087
Women never married.	22,846	100	79.1	10.8	10.2	8,886	389
15 to 19 years old.	8,701	100	92.4	6.3	1.3	826	95
20 to 24 years old.	6,018	100	78.3	12.6	9.1	2,106	350
25 to 29 years old.	3,564	100	69.6	13.4	17.0	2,181	612
30 to 34 years old.	2,050	100	61.7	14.9	23.4	1,684	821
35 to 39 years old.	1,523	100	60.5	15.4	24.1	1,315	863
40 to 44 years old.	992	100	65.9	14.6	19.5	775	782
WHITE							
Women ever married.	31,819	100	19.6	22.3	58.1	55,113	1,732
15 to 19 years old.	269	100	40.1	48.6	11.3	197	732
20 to 24 years old.	2,651	100	37.5	34.3	28.3	2,636	994
25 to 29 years old.	5,243	100	29.7	29.6	40.7	6,758	1,289
30 to 34 years old.	7,652	100	19.3	22.8	58.1	12,958	1,693
35 to 39 years old.	8,233	100	13.6	16.6	69.9	16,519	2,006
40 to 44 years old.	7,771	100	12.5	17.9	69.6	16,045	2,065
Women never married.	16,784	100	87.0	8.0	5.0	3,597	214
15 to 19 years old.	6,806	100	94.6	4.5	0.9	456	67
20 to 24 years old.	4,516	100	84.1	10.2	6.7	1,075	238
25 to 29 years old.	2,517	100	80.5	10.6	8.8	872	346
30 to 34 years old.	1,306	100	77.0	9.9	13.0	605	463
35 to 39 years old.	946	100	81.3	10.9	7.8	312	329
40 to 44 years old.	693	100	80.4	11.8	7.9	277	400
BLACK							
Women ever married.	3,746	100	14.1	22.8	63.1	7,417	1,980
15 to 19 years old.	23	(B)	(B)	(B)	(B)	13	(B)
20 to 24 years old.	235	100	29.4	36.7	33.9	297	1,263
25 to 29 years old.	568	100	16.4	29.1	54.9	951	1,676
30 to 34 years old.	888	100	13.9	24.3	61.7	1,841	2,073
35 to 39 years old.	986	100	10.7	18.0	71.4	2,079	2,109
40 to 44 years old.	1,046	100	11.7	19.4	69.0	2,236	2,137
Women never married.	4,872	100	52.1	20.6	27.4	4,773	980
15 to 19 years old.	1,439	100	82.9	14.6	2.5	302	210
20 to 24 years old.	1,160	100	54.7	22.3	23.0	933	804
25 to 29 years old.	851	100	37.4	22.2	40.4	1,166	1,370
30 to 34 years old.	641	100	30.9	26.0	43.1	974	1,519
35 to 39 years old.	521	100	22.9	23.1	54.0	953	1,831
40 to 44 years old.	260	100	28.8	22.5	48.8	444	1,711

B Base figure too small to meet statistical standards for reliability. [1] Includes other races, not shown separately.

D1-17 Timing of First Birth in Relation to First Marriage

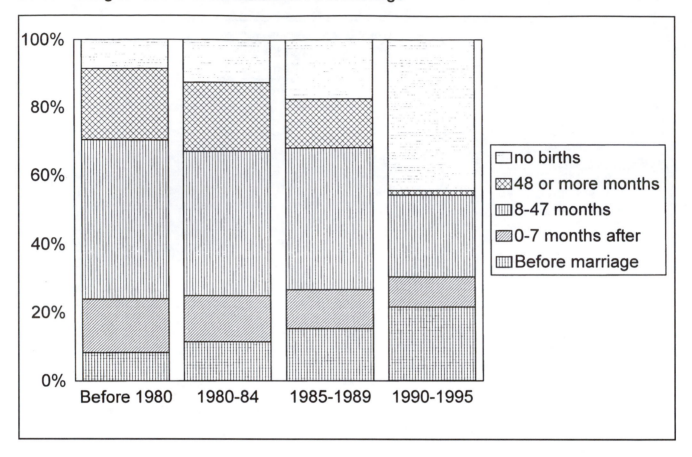

D1-18 Number of Women 15–44 Years of Age and Percent Distribution by Timing of First Birth in Relation to First Marriage, According to Selected Characteristics: United States, 1995

Characteristic	Number in thousands	Total	Timing of first birth in relation to first marriage				
			Before marriage	0-7 months after	8-47 months after	48 or more months after	No births
			Percent distribution				
All women	60,201	100.0	16.9	8.0	24.7	9.4	41.9
Never married	22,679	100.0	20.2	(NA)	(NA)	(NA)	79.8
Ever married[1]	37,621	100.0	13.3	12.9	39.6	15.1	19.1
Age at first marriage:							
Under 18 years	4,533	100.0	7.7	32.9	46.3	8.2	5.8
18-19 years	8,687	100.0	10.2	17.0	45.7	16.2	10.9
20-22 years	11,034	100.0	12.4	9.8	40.7	19.3	17.8
23 years or older	13,267	100.0	17.9	5.9	32.8	13.4	30.0
Year of first marriage:							
1990-95	8,240	100.0	21.6	8.8	23.9	1.3	44.4
1985-89	7,7.53	100.0	15.3	11.4	41.4	14.4	17.5
1980—84	7,747	100.0	11.4	13.5	42.3	20.3	12.5
Before 1980	13,782	100.0	8.3	15.7	46.5	21.0	8.5
Year of first birth							
1990-95	8,469	100.0	31.0	9.6	37.3	22.2	(NA)
1985-89	8,243	100.0	29.0	10.3	40.7	20.0	(NA)
1980-84	7,489	100.0	24.6	14.4	42.0	19.0	(NA)
Before 1980	10,757	100.0	25.3	19.5	48.4	6.8	(NA)
Family background							
Both parents from birth[2]	37,233	100.0	11.5	8.0	28.0	11.8	40.7
Single parent from birth	2,093	100.0	42.2	6.2	10.2	2.9	38.5
Both parents, then 1 parent	8,003	100.0	20.6	5.9	19.6	5.4	48.4
Stepparent[3]	8,378	100.0	19.3	10.7	20.4	5.9	43.7
Other	4,493	100.0	25.6	8.0	21.2	6.4	38.7
Race and Hispanic origin							
Hispanic	6,702	100.0	21.6	9.2	30.5	3.9	34.8
Non-Hispanic white	42,522	100.0	9.7	8.4	26.5	11.9	43.5
Non-Hispanic black	8,210	100.0	44.7	6.0	9.7	2.3	37.3
Non-Hispanic other	2,767	100.0	11.6	5.9	27.3	6.8	48.4

NA Category not applicable.

[1]The "Before marriage" category includes both premarital and nonmarital births because some women were never married. The exception is in the panels for "ever married" women, in which the "Before marriage" category includes only premarital births.

[2]Includes women who lived with either both biological or both adoptive parents until they left home.

[3]Parents separated or divorced, then custodial parent remarried.

NOTE: Percents may not add to 100 due to rounding.

D1-19 Percent of Births to Unmarried Mothers, by Race

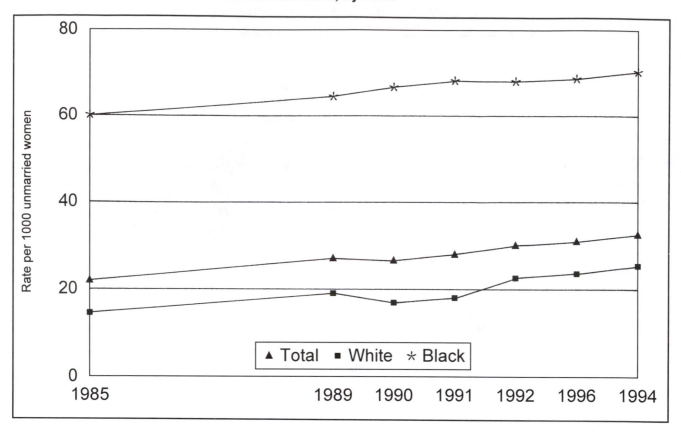

D1-20 Percent of Births to Unmarried Mothers

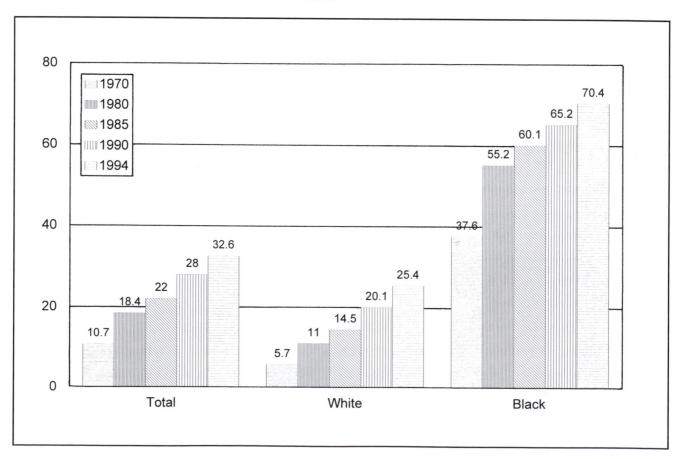

D1-21 Births to Unmarried Women, by Race of Child and Age of Mother: 1980–1994

RACE OF CHILD AND AGE OF MOTHER	1980	1990	1992	1993	1994	RACE OF CHILD AND AGE OF MOTHER	1980	1990	1992	1993	1994
NUMBER (1,000)						25 to 29 years	15.0	19.7	19.1	18.9	18.4
Total live births [1] .	666	1,165	1,225	1,240	1,290	30 to 34 years	6.2	10.1	10.4	10.7	10.6
White	320	647	722	742	794	35 years and over.	2.4	4.5	5.1	5.4	5.6
Black	326	473	459	452	448						
Under 15 years old	9	11	11	11	12	AS PERCENT OF ALL BIRTHS IN RACIAL GROUPS					
15 to 19 years old.	263	350	354	357	381						
20 to 24 years old.	237	404	436	439	449						
25 to 29 years old.	100	230	233	234	238	Total [1]	18.4	28.0	30.1	31.0	32.6
30 to 34 years old.	41	118	128	132	137	White	11.0	20.1	22.6	23.6	25.4
35 years old and over . .	16	53	63	67	72	Black	55.2	65.2	68.1	68.7	70.4
PERCENT DISTRIBUTION						BIRTH RATE [2]					
						Total [1] [3]	29.4	43.8	45.2	45.3	46.9
Total [1]	100.0	100.0	100.0	100.0	100.0	White [3]	17.6	31.8	35.2	35.9	38.3
White	48.1	55.6	58.9	59.8	61.6	Black [3]	82.9	93.9	86.5	84.0	82.1
Black	48.9	40.6	37.5	36.5	34.8	15 to 19 years	27.6	42.5	44.6	44.5	46.4
Under 15 years	1.4	0.9	0.9	0.9	0.9	20 to 24 years	40.9	65.1	68.5	69.2	72.2
15 to 19 years	39.5	30.0	28.9	28.8	29.6	25 to 29 years	34.0	56.0	56.5	57.1	59.0
20 to 24 years	35.6	34.7	35.6	35.4	34.8	30 to 34 years	21.1	37.6	37.9	38.5	40.1

[1] Includes other races not shown separately.   [2] Rate per 1,000 unmarried women (never-married, widowed, and divorced) estimated as of July 1.   [3] Covers women aged 15 to 44 years.

D1-22 Low Birth Weight and Births to Teenage Mothers and to Unmarried Women—States: 1990 and 1995

DIVISION AND STATE	PERCENT OF BIRTHS WITH LOW BIRTH WEIGHT[1]		BIRTHS TO TEENAGE MOTHERS, PERCENT OF TOTAL		BIRTHS TO UNMARRIED WOMEN, PERCENT OF TOTAL	
	1990	1995	1990	1995	1990	1995
U.S.	7.0	7.3	12.8	13.2	28.0	32.0
N.E.	5.9	(NA)	8.4	(NA)	24.2	(NA)
ME	5.1	6.3	10.8	10.6	22.6	27.8
NH	4.9	5.3	7.2	7.6	16.9	22.4
VT	5.3	5.4	8.5	8.1	20.1	24.8
MA	5.9	6.0	8.0	7.5	24.7	25.6
RI	6.2	6.7	10.5	9.7	26.3	29.2
CT	6.6	6.9	8.2	8.5	[2]26.6	29.9
M.A.	7.3	(NA)	9.5	(NA)	29.9	(NA)
NY	7.6	7.6	9.1	9.3	[2]33.0	37.9
NJ	7.0	7.4	8.4	8.0	24.3	27.0
PA	7.1	7.4	10.9	10.8	28.6	32.3
E.N.C.	7.1	(NA)	13.2	(NA)	28.3	(NA)
OH	7.1	7.5	13.8	13.7	[2]28.9	32.9
IN	6.6	7.5	14.5	14.6	26.2	31.7
IL	7.6	7.8	13.1	12.8	31.7	33.6
MI	7.6	7.5	13.5	12.4	[2]26.2	0.0
WI	5.9	6.0	10.2	10.5	24.2	27.3
W.N.C.	5.9	(NA)	11.1	(NA)	23.2	(NA)
MN	5.1	5.7	8.0	8.4	20.9	23.7
IA	5.4	6.0	10.2	11.0	21.0	25.2
MO	7.1	7.6	14.4	14.4	28.6	32.0
ND	5.5	5.2	8.6	9.6	18.4	23.5
SD	5.1	5.5	10.8	11.9	22.9	28.4
NE	5.3	6.4	9.8	10.0	20.7	24.3
KS	6.2	6.4	12.3	13.3	21.5	26.4
S.A.	7.9	(NA)	14.4	(NA)	30.9	(NA)
DE	7.6	8.4	11.9	13.2	29.0	35.0
MD	7.8	8.5	10.5	10.3	[2]29.6	33.4
DC	15.1	13.2	17.8	16.2	64.9	66.0
VA	7.2	7.6	11.7	11.4	26.0	29.2
WV	7.1	7.9	17.8	17.2	25.4	30.5
NC	8.0	8.7	16.2	15.2	29.4	31.4
SC	8.7	9.3	17.1	17.3	32.7	37.3
GA	8.7	8.7	16.7	16.3	32.8	35.2
FL	7.4	7.7	13.9	13.7	31.7	35.8
E.S.C.	8.2	(NA)	18.4	(NA)	30.6	(NA)
KY	7.1	7.6	17.5	17.1	23.6	28.6
TN	8.2	8.6	17.6	16.9	30.2	32.8
AL	8.4	9.0	18.2	18.5	30.1	34.5
MS	9.6	9.8	21.3	22.2	40.5	45.3
W.S.C.	7.3	(NA)	16.3	(NA)	22.2	(NA)
AR	8.2	8.2	19.7	19.6	29.4	32.9
LA	9.2	9.5	17.6	19.2	36.8	42.6
OK	6.6	6.9	16.2	17.0	25.2	30.4
TX	6.9	7.1	15.6	16.6	[2]17.5	30.0
Mountain	6.8	(NA)	12.8	(NA)	25.1	(NA)
MT	6.2	5.8	11.5	12.6	[2]23.7	26.3
ID	5.7	5.9	12.3	14.1	16.7	19.9
WY	7.4	7.4	13.6	15.2	19.8	26.5
CO	8.0	8.4	11.3	12.2	21.2	24.9
NM	7.4	7.5	16.3	18.4	35.4	42.6
AZ	6.4	6.8	14.2	15.2	32.7	38.2
UT	5.7	6.3	10.3	10.8	13.5	15.7
NV	7.2	7.4	12.6	13.7	[2]25.4	42.0
Pacific	5.7	(NA)	11.5	(NA)	30.2	(NA)
WA	5.3	5.5	10.8	11.5	23.7	26.7
OR	5.0	5.5	12.0	13.0	25.7	28.9
CA	5.8	6.0	11.6	12.4	[2]31.6	31.9
AK	4.8	5.4	9.7	11.2	26.2	29.9
HI	7.1	7.0	10.5	10.1	24.8	29.2

NA Not available.   [1] Less than 2,500 grams (5 pounds-8 ounces).   [2] Marital status of mother is inferred.

D1-23 Trend in the Teenage Birth Rate

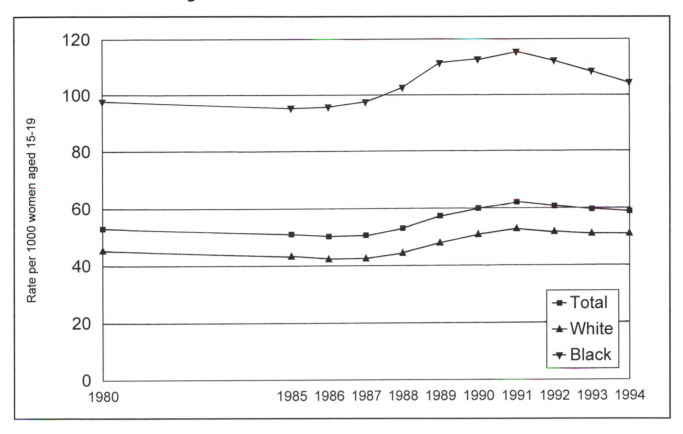

D1-24 Teenagers—Births and Birth Rates, by Race, Age, and Sex: 1980–1994

ITEM	1980	1985	1986	1987	1988	1989	1990	1991	1992	1993	1994
NUMBER OF BIRTHS											
All races, total [1]...	552,161	467,485	461,905	462,312	478,353	506,503	521,826	519,577	505,415	501,093	505,488
15-17 years	198,222	167,789	168,572	172,591	176,624	181,044	183,327	188,226	187,549	190,535	195,169
18-19 years	353,939	299,696	293,333	289,721	301,729	325,459	338,499	331,351	317,866	310,558	310,319
White...........	393,564	324,590	317,970	315,464	323,830	340,472	354,482	352,359	342,739	341,817	348,081
15-17 years	129,341	107,993	107,177	108,592	109,739	111,736	114,934	118,809	118,786	121,309	126,388
18-19 years	264,223	216,597	210,793	206,872	214,091	228,736	239,548	233,550	223,953	220,508	221,693
Black...........	147,378	130,857	131,594	134,050	140,608	150,699	151,613	150,956	146,800	143,153	140,968
15-17 years	65,069	55,656	57,003	59,361	61,856	63,832	62,881	63,571	63,002	63,156	62,563
18-19 years	82,309	75,201	74,591	74,689	78,752	86,867	88,732	87,385	83,798	79,997	78,405
BIRTH RATE											
All races, total [1]...	53.0	51.0	50.2	50.6	53.0	57.3	59.9	62.1	60.7	59.6	58.9
15-17 years	32.5	31.0	30.5	31.7	33.6	36.4	37.5	38.7	37.8	37.8	37.6
18-19 years	82.1	79.6	79.6	78.5	79.9	84.2	88.6	94.4	94.5	92.1	91.5
White...........	45.4	43.3	42.3	42.5	44.4	47.9	50.8	52.8	51.8	51.1	51.1
15-17 years	25.5	24.4	23.8	24.6	26.0	28.1	29.5	30.7	30.1	30.3	30.7
18-19 years	73.2	70.4	70.1	68.9	69.6	72.9	78.0	83.5	83.8	82.1	82.1
Black...........	97.8	95.4	95.8	97.6	102.7	111.5	112.8	115.5	112.4	108.6	104.5
15-17 years	72.5	69.3	69.3	72.1	75.7	81.9	82.3	84.1	81.3	79.8	76.3
18-19 years	135.1	132.4	135.1	135.8	142.7	151.9	152.9	158.6	157.9	151.9	148.3

[1] Includes races other than white and black.

D1-25 Births to Teens, Unmarried Mothers, and Prenatal Care: 1985–1994

CHARACTERISTIC	1985	1989	1990	1991	1992	1993	1994
Births to teenage mothers, total	12.7	12.8	12.8	12.9	12.7	12.8	13.1
White	10.8	10.7	10.9	11.0	10.9	11.0	11.3
Black	23.0	23.1	23.1	23.1	22.7	22.7	23.2
American Indian, Eskimo, Aleut	19.1	18.8	19.5	20.3	20.0	20.3	21.0
Asian and Pacific Islander [1]	5.5	6.1	5.7	5.8	5.6	5.7	5.7
Filipino	5.8	6.4	6.1	6.1	5.6	5.8	6.0
Chinese	1.1	1.2	1.2	1.1	1.0	1.0	1.0
Japanese	2.9	2.9	2.9	2.7	2.6	2.7	2.8
Hawaiian	15.9	16.4	18.4	18.1	18.4	18.5	19.6
Other	(NA)	(NA)	(NA)	(NA)	(NA)	6.5	6.4
Hispanic origin [2]	16.5	16.7	16.8	17.2	17.1	17.4	17.8
Mexican	17.5	17.4	17.7	18.1	18.0	18.2	18.6
Puerto Rican	20.9	21.9	21.7	21.7	21.4	22.3	23.2
Cuban	7.1	7.0	7.7	7.1	7.1	6.8	7.3
Central and South American	8.2	8.6	9.0	9.4	9.6	9.9	10.4
Other and unknown Hispanic	(NA)	(NA)	(NA)	(NA)	(NA)	21.0	20.8
Percent births to unmarried mothers	22.0	27.1	26.6	28.0	30.1	31.0	32.6
White	14.5	19.0	16.9	18.0	22.6	23.6	25.4
Black	60.1	64.5	66.7	68.2	68.1	68.7	70.4
American Indian, Eskimo, Aleut	40.7	NA	53.6	55.3	55.3	55.8	57.0
Asian and Pacific Islander [1]	10.1	NA	(NA)	(NA)	14.7	15.7	16.2
Filipino	12.1	NA	15.9	16.8	16.8	17.7	18.5
Chinese	3.7	NA	5.0	5.5	6.1	6.7	7.2
Japanese	7.9	NA	9.6	9.8	9.8	10.0	11.2
Hawaiian	(NA)	NA	45.0	45.0	45.7	47.8	48.6
Hispanic origin [2]	29.5	35.5	36.7	38.5	39.1	40.0	43.1
Mexican	25.7	31.7	33.3	35.3	36.3	37.0	40.8
Puerto Rican	51.1	55.2	55.9	57.5	57.5	59.4	60.2
Cuban	16.1	17.5	18.2	19.5	20.2	21.0	22.9
Central and South American	34.9	38.9	41.2	43.1	43.9	45.2	45.9
Percent of mothers beginning prenatal care 1st trimester	76.2	75.5	74.2	76.2	77.7	78.9	80.2
White	79.4	79.0	77.7	79.5	80.8	81.8	82.8
Black	61.8	60.4	60.7	61.9	63.9	66.0	68.3
American Indian, Eskimo, Aleut	60.3	60.5	57.9	59.9	62.1	63.4	65.2
Asian and Pacific Islander [1]	75.0	75.6	(NA)	(NA)	76.6	77.6	79.7
Filipino	77.2	78.0	77.1	77.1	78.7	79.3	81.3
Chinese	82.4	81.9	81.3	82.3	83.8	84.6	86.2
Japanese	85.8	86.7	87.0	87.7	88.2	87.2	89.2
Hawaiian	(NA)	69.7	65.8	68.1	69.9	70.6	77.0
Hispanic origin [2]	61.2	59.5	60.2	61.0	64.2	66.6	68.9
Mexican	59.9	56.7	57.8	58.7	62.1	64.8	67.3
Puerto Rican	58.3	62.7	63.5	65.0	67.8	70.0	71.7
Cuban	82.5	83.2	84.8	85.4	86.8	88.9	90.1
Central and South American	60.6	60.8	61.5	63.4	66.8	68.7	71.2
Percent of mothers beginning prenatal care 3d trimester or no care	5.7	6.4	6.0	5.8	5.2	4.8	4.4
White	4.7	5.2	4.9	4.7	4.2	3.9	3.6
Black	10.0	11.7	10.9	10.7	9.9	9.0	8.2
American Indian, Eskimo, Aleut	11.5	11.9	12.9	12.2	11.0	10.3	9.8
Asian and Pacific Islander [1]	6.1	5.8	(NA)	(NA)	4.9	4.6	4.1
Filipino	4.6	4.6	4.5	5.0	4.3	4.0	3.6
Chinese	4.2	3.5	3.4	3.4	2.9	2.9	2.7
Japanese	2.6	2.6	2.9	2.5	2.4	2.8	1.9
Hawaiian	(NA)	7.6	8.7	7.5	7.0	6.7	4.7
Hispanic origin [2]	12.5	13.0	12.0	11.0	9.5	8.8	7.6
Mexican	12.9	14.6	13.2	12.2	10.5	9.7	8.3
Puerto Rican	15.5	11.3	10.6	9.1	8.0	7.1	6.5
Cuban	3.7	4.0	2.8	2.4	2.1	1.8	1.6
Central and South American	12.5	11.9	10.9	9.5	7.9	7.3	6.5
Percent of births with low birth weight [3]	6.8	7.0	7.0	7.1	7.1	7.2	7.3
White	5.6	5.7	5.7	5.8	5.8	6.0	6.1
Black	12.4	13.2	13.3	13.6	13.3	13.3	13.2
American Indian, Eskimo, Aleut	5.9	6.4	6.1	6.2	6.2	6.4	6.4
Asian and Pacific Islander [1]	6.1	6.9	(NA)	(NA)	6.6	6.6	6.8
Filipino	6.9	7.3	7.3	7.3	7.4	7.0	7.8
Chinese	5.0	5.0	4.7	5.1	5.0	4.9	4.8
Japanese	5.9	6.4	6.2	5.9	7.0	6.5	6.9
Hawaiian	6.4	7.2	7.2	6.7	6.9	6.8	7.2
Hispanic origin [2]	6.2	6.2	6.1	6.1	6.1	6.2	6.2
Mexican	5.8	5.6	5.5	5.6	5.6	5.8	5.8
Puerto Rican	8.7	9.5	9.0	9.4	9.2	9.2	9.1
Cuban	6.0	5.8	5.7	5.6	6.1	6.2	6.3
Central and South American	5.7	5.8	5.8	5.9	5.8	5.9	6.0

NA Not available.   [1] Includes other races not shown separately.   [2] Hispanic persons may be of any race. Includes other types, not shown separately.   [3] Births less than 2,500 grams (5 lb.-8 oz.).

D1-26 Percent of Women 15–44 Who Ever Had an Unintended Birth

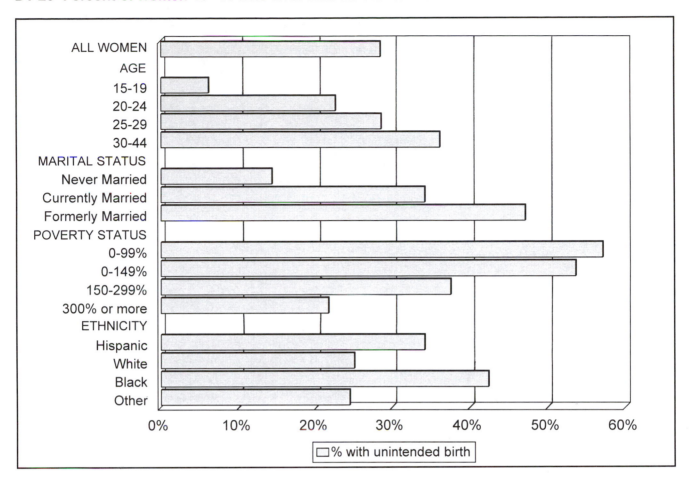

D1-27 Number of Women 15–44 Years of Age and Percent Who Ever Had an Unintended Birth, by Selected Characteristics: United States, 1995

Characteristic	Number in thousands	Percent who ever had an unintended birth[1]
All women	60,201	28.4
Age at interview		
16-19 years	8,961	6.1
20-24 years	9,041	22.5
25-29 years	9,693	28.5
30-44 years	32,506	36.1
Marital status		
Never married	22,679	14.2
Currently married	29,673	34.2
Formerly married	7,849	47.0
Parity		
1 birth	10,706	33.8
2 births	13,875	44.0
3 or more births	10,377	70.8
Poverty level income at interview[2]		
0-149 percent	10,072	53.5
0-99 percent	5,992	57.0
150-299 percent	14,932	37.5
300 percent or more	22,736	21.6
Race and Hispanic origin		
Hispanic	6,702	34.2
Non-Hispanic white	42,522	25.0
Non-Hispanic black	8,210	42.3
Non-Hispanic other	2,767	24.4

[1]Based on "traditional" version (comparable to Cycle 4 and previous cycles) of wantedness status.
[2]Limited to women 22-44 years of age at time of interview.

D1-28 Number of Pregnancies in 1991–95 to Women 15–44 Years of Age at Interview, Percent Distribution by Value on the Scale of How Happy She Was to Be Pregnant, and Mean Scale Value, According to Selected Characteristics: United States, 1995

Characteristic	Number in thousands	Total	Scale value[1]				Mean scale value
			1-3	4-6	6-7	8-10	
			Percent distribution				
All pregnancies[2]	25,666	100.0	18.8	11.6	8.0	61.6	7.3
Wantedness status at conception[3]							
Intended	16,666	100.0	2.0	4.1	5.4	88.5	9.2
Mistimed	6,281	100.0	32.8	25.3	15.5	26.4	5.2
Unwanted	3,622	100.0	67.3	20.2	5.5	7.1	2.9
Age at outcome and wantedness							
15-19 years	2,952	100.0	32.7	22.2	8.8	36.3	5.6
Intended	758	100.0	1.7	6.6	8.4	83.3	9.0
Mistimed	1,692	100.0	36.5	29.3	10.4	23.8	4.8
Unwanted	492	100.0	68.0	21.2	3.4	7.5	2.9
20-29 years	12,668	100.0	19.2	10.8	8.7	61.4	7.3
Intended	7,786	100.0	2.1	3.5	6.7	87.7	9.2
Mistimed	3,253	100.0	34.1	24.8	15.6	25.5	5.1
Unwanted	7,584	100.0	72.8	17.4	4.2	5.6	2.6
30-44 years	7,652	100.0	14.5	10.0	6.1	69.4	7.8
Intended	5,541	100.0	2.1	4.7	3.6	89.7	9.2
Mistimed	773	100.0	26.9	24.1	21.1	27.9	5.5
Unwanted	1,309	100.0	60.3	23.7	7.1	8.9	3.2
Marital status at outcome and wantedness							
Married	15,012	100.0	10.6	7.8	6.8	74.8	8.3
Intended	11,327	100.0	1.7	2.8	4.4	91.2	9.4
Mistimed	2,170	100.0	24.5	22.4	18.7	34.5	5.9
Unwanted	1,480	100.0	58.9	25.0	6.7	9.4	3.3
Unmarried	8,332	100.0	35.4	19.5	9.9	35.2	6.4
Intended	2,769	100.0	3.7	9.9	10.6	75.8	8.5
Mistimed	3,584	100.0	39.7	28.0	12.5	19.8	4.6
Unwanted	1,930	100.0	73.6	17.0	4.0	5.4	2.5
Race and Hispanic origin and wantedness							
Hispanic	3,924	100.0	18.3	11.4	7.1	63.2	7.4
Intended	2,333	100.0	2.6	5.2	4.4	87.9	9.2
Mistimed	856	100.0	28.6	17.9	12.8	40.7	5.9
Unwanted	732	100.0	56.5	23.5	9.0	11.1	3.6
Non-Hispanic white	16,626	100.0	15.2	10.3	7.5	67.0	7.7
Intended	10,982	100.0	1.6	3.0	4.6	90.8	9.4
Mistimed	3,898	100.0	31.6	26.0	16.5	25.9	5.2
Unwanted	1,683	100.0	66.1	21.6	5.1	7.2	3.0
Non-Hispanic black	3,944	100.0	32.8	19.0	10.9	37.4	5.6
Intended	1,602	100.0	3.8	11.0	12.3	72.9	8.5
Mistimed	1,278	100.0	35.2	30.3	14.1	20.4	4.8
Unwanted	1,032	100.0	75.7	17.1	3.9	3.3	2.3

[1]Based on women's response to a 1-10 scale, with 1 being "very unhappy to be pregnant,"' and 10 being "very happy to be pregnant"
[2]Includes pregnancies with wantedness status reported as "don't know" and pregnancies to women of other race and origin groups not shown separately.
[3]Based on "traditional" version (comparable to Cycle 4 and previous cycles) of wantedness status. See "Definitions of Terms."

D1-29 Number of Women 15–44 Years of Age and Percent Distribution by Fecundity Status, According to Selected Characteristics: United States, 1995

| | Number | | Surgically sterile | | | |
Characteristic	in thousands	Total	Contra-ceptive	Noncontra-ceptive	Impaired fecundity	Fecund
			Percent distribution			
All women	60,201	100.0	24.2	3.1	10.2	62.5
Age at interview						
15-24 years	18,002	100.0	1.6	0.1	6.1	92.2
25-34 years	20,758	100.0	22.0	1.2	11.2	65.6
35-44 years	21,440	100.0	45.3	7.4	12.8	34.6
Marital status						
Never married	22,679	100.0	4.5	0.9	6.7	87.9
Currently married	29,673	100.0	36.6	4.1	12.9	46.3
Formerly married	7,849	100.0	34.1	5.8	10.2	50.0
Parity 0						
15-44 years	25,242	100.0	2.8	1.5	11.0	84.7
15-24 years	14,113	100.0	0.2	0.1	5.5	94.3
25-34 years	7,139	100.0	2.9	0.7	13.9	82.5
35-44 years	3,991	100.0	11.9	8.1	25.7	54.3
Parity 1 or more						
15-44 years	34,958	100.0	39.7	4.2	9.6	46.5
15-24 years	3,889	100.0	6.7	0.3	8.4	84.6
25-34 years	13,620	100.0	32.1	1.5	9.8	56.7
35-44 years	17,449	100.0	52.9	7.2	9.8	30.1
Education at interview[1]						
No high school diploma or GED[2]	5,424	100.0	44.1	5.1	12.9	37.9
High school diploma or GED	18,169	100.0	38.0	5.0	12.3	44.8
Some college, no bachelor's degree	12,399	100.0	26.3	3.5	10.7	59.5
Bachelor's degree or higher	11,748	100.0	17.0	2.0	10.7	70.3
Race and Hispanic origin						
Hispanic	6,702	100.0	22.9	2.3	10.8	64.0
Non-Hispanic white	42,522	100.0	24.7	3.2	10.0	62.2
Non-Hispanic black	8,210	100.0	25.5	3.7	10.1	60.7
Non-Hispanic other	2,767	100.0	15.6	2.3	13.1	69.1

[1]Limited to women 22-44 years of age at time of interview.
[2]GED is general equivalency diploma.
NOTE: Percents may not add to 100 due to rounding.

D1-30 Number of Women 15–24 Years of Age, Percent Who Ever Received Family Planning Services, and Percent Who Received the Specified Services at First Family Planning Visit, by Selected Characteristics: United States, 1995

Characteristic	Number in thousands	Ever received family planning services[1]	Services received at first visit[1]		
			Birth control method	Birth control counseling	Birth control checkup or test
			Percent		
All women[2]	18,002	58.6	50.8	39.9	40.2
Never had intercourse	5,538	11.6	7.7	7.3	6.1
Ever had intercourse[3]	12,464	79.5	69.9	54.4	55.4
Age at first visit:					
Under 18 years	5,929	100.0	87.3	70.2	70.5
18-19 years	2,501	100.0	89.8	69.1	71.5
20-24 years	1,480	100.0	86.9	60.3	62.8
Timing of first visit:					
Before first intercourse	2,855	100.0	87.6	69.5	71.1
After first intercourse	7,008	100.0	87.9	68.4	69.2
Provider for first visit:					
Clinic	4,536	100.0	89.0	74.9	74.0
Private doctor or HMO[4]	4,814	100.0	89.6	63.6	68.7
Other place	475	100.0	75.2	67.3	49.6
Poverty level income at interview:[5]					
0-149 percent	2,502	85.7	74.9	58.6	59.3
150-299 percent	2,815	89.2	81.1	60.4	62.6
300 percent or more	2,651	88.7	80.5	59.3	65.3
Race and Hispanic origin:					
Hispanic	1,644	74.4	60.9	48.5	47.4
Non-Hispanic white	8,269	79.9	71.5	54.1	58.2
Non-Hispanic black	2,074	83.1	73.1	58.7	53.4

[1]First family planning visit refers to first receipt of any of the following family planning services from a medical care provider: sterilization operation, birth control method, check up or medical test for birth control, counseling about birth control, or counseling about getting sterilized.
[2]Includes women of other race and origin groups not shown separately.
[3]Ever had (voluntary) sexual intercourse after first menstrual period.
[4]HMO is health maintenance organization.
[5]Limited to women 20-24 years of age at time of interview.
NOTE: Percents do not add to 100 because women could report more than 1 service at first visit.

D1-31 Number of Women 15–44 Years of Age and Percent Who Received the Specified Medical Services from a Medical Care Provider in the 12 Months Prior to Interview, by Selected Characteristics: United States, 1995

Characteristic	Number in thousands	Pregnancy test	Pap smear	Pelvic exam	HIV test[1]	Other STD[2] test or treatment	Test or treatment for infection[3]
				Percent			
All women	60,201	16.0	61.9	61.3	17.3	7.6	21.0
Age at interview							
15-19 years	8,961	16.1	33.5	32.4	14.6	9.4	16.9
15-17 years	5,452	11.4	23.0	23.4	12.1	7.1	12.2
18-19 years	3,508	23.3	49.9	46.4	18.5	13.0	24.2
20-24 years	9,041	27.4	68.7	66.5	23.7	14.0	28.1
25-29 years	9,693	25.3	70.9	69.3	23.6	10.3	25.7
30-34 years	11,065	17.4	69.5	70.3	18.5	6.5	21.8
35-39 years	11,211	8.1	62.9	62.6	14.2	4.7	19.2
40-44 years	10,230	4.3	62.7	63.2	10.0	2.2	15.1
Marital status							
Never married	22,679	15.5	52.1	49.8	18.9	10.7	20.1
Currently married	29,673	17.3	68.5	69.0	14.5	4.7	20.9
Formerly married	7,849	12.4	64.8	65.3	23.1	9.7	24.2
Poverty level income at interview[4]							
0-149 percent	10,072	18.6	57.6	57.5	23.1	9.9	23.9
0-99 percent	5,992	19.8	56.6	56.0	25.8	11.7	25.6
150-299 percent	14,932	13.7	62.6	62.6	16.1	6.8	20.7
300 percent or more	22,736	14.6	74.1	73.6	15.7	5.4	20.5
Race and Hispanic origin							
Hispanic	6,702	19.8	52.2	52.6	21.9	7.2	20.4
Non-Hispanic white	42,522	14.8	63.2	63.2	14.5	7.1	20.9
Non-Hispanic black	8,210	19.8	67.6	63.0	28.7	11.4	24.8
Non-Hispanic other	2,767	14.3	47.7	47.7	14.7	*	13.6

*Figure does not meet standard of reliability or precision.
[1]Excludes HIV (human immunodeficiency virus) tests done as part of blood donation.
[2]STD is sexually transmitted disease.
[3]Refers to vaginal, urinary tract, and pelvic infections.
[4]Limited to women 22-44 years of age at time of interview.
NOTE: Percents do not add to 100 because women could report more than 1 medical service in the 12 months prior to interview.

D1-32 Number of Women 15-44 Years of Age, Percent Who Received at Least One Family Planning Service in the 12 Months Prior to Interview from a Medical Care Provider, and Percent Reporting the Specified Method of Payment, by Selected Characteristics: United States, 1995

Characteristic	Number in thousands	At least 1 family planning service[1]	Method of payment				
			Medicaid at all	Insurance alone	Own income alone	Own income and insurance	Other public assistance or free[2]
			Percent				
All women[3]	60,201	32.9	4.6	9.2	11.3	7.7	1.3
Age at interview							
15-19 years	8,961	28.5	4.8	7.4	8.8	3.4	3.2
15-17 years	5,452	21.9	4.1	5.4	5.6	*	*
18-19 years	3,508	38.6	6.0	10.5	13.7	*	*
20-24 years	9,041	54.7	10.1	14.1	21.7	7.9	2.5
25-29 years	9,693	49.8	7.5	14.2	17.3	12.9	*
30-34 years	11,065	36.3	3.7	10.2	12.0	10.9	*
35-39 years	11,211	20.1	2.2	6.3	5.9	6.2	*
40-44 years	10,230	12.0	*	3.6	3.6	4.2	*
Marital status							
Never married	22,679	36.6	6.2	9.4	13.5	5.8	2.1
Currently married	29,673	31.0	2.7	9.6	10.2	9.2	0.7
Formerly married	7,849	29.8	7.4	6.7	8.7	7.2	*
Education at interview[4]							
No high school diploma or GED[5]	5,424	23.6	11.0	5.1	4.4	*	*
High school diploma or GED	18,169	29.7	5.6	7.8	9.7	7.1	0.8
Some college, no bachelor's degree	12,399	34.1	2.9	9.9	13.4	8.6	*
Bachelor's degree or higher	11,748	38.3	*	12.1	13.6	13.7	*
Poverty level income at interview[4]							
0-1 49 percent	10,072	31.3	14.6	5.2	8.5	2.3	1.9
0-99 percent	5,992	32.4	17.7	4.5	7.8	*	*
150-299 percent	14,932	30.2	2.8	8.4	11.5	7.6	*
300 percent or more	22,736	34.0	*	11.3	11.9	11.8	*
Race and Hispanic origin							
Hispanic	6,702	32.7	8.5	8.6	10.6	3.4	*
Non-Hispanic white	42,522	33.7	2.8	9.3	12.4	9.3	1.0
Non-Hispanic black	8,210	33.3	10.8	10.1	7.5	4.0	1.8

*Figure does not meet standard of reliability or precision.
[1]Family planning services include sterilizing operation, birth control method, checkup or medical test for birth control, counseling about birth control, or counseling about getting sterilized.
[2]Respondents spontaneously mentioned another form of public assistance or that the service was free.
[3]Includes women of other race and origin groups not shown separately.
[4]Limited to women 22-44 years of age at time of interview.
[5]GED is general equivalency diploma.
NOTE: Percents do not add to total who received "at least 1 family planning service" because women may have received more than 1 service and used more than 1 payment method.

D1-33 Number of Women 15-44 Years of Age, Percent Who Received at Least One Medical Service in the 12 Months Prior to Interview from a Medical Care Provider, and Percent Reporting the Specified Method of Payment, by Selected Characteristics, United States, 1995

Characteristic	Number in thousands	At least 1 medical service[1]	Medicaid at all	Insurance alone	Own income alone	Own income and insurance	Other public assistance or free[2]
				Percent			
All women[3]	60,201	70.6	9.2	24.1	21.2	17.4	3.0
Age at interview							
15-19 years	8,961	43.9	8.9	15.5	13.6	5.8	5.4
15-17 years	5,452	32.2	6.9	12.0	8.7	4.0	4.1
18-19 years	3,508	62.1	12.1	21.1	21.2	8.6	7.4
20-24 years	9,041	78.9	16.6	25.0	28.5	12.6	4.7
25-29 years	9,693	80.1	13.1	26.5	23.1	20.1	2.7
30-34 years	11,065	78.6	8.3	26.4	23.3	22.0	2.7
35-39 years	11,211	70.5	6.0	24.1	20.7	20.7	1.4
40-44 years	10,230	69.2	4.0	26.0	17.9	20.9	1.8
Marital status							
Never married	22,679	61.3	12.0	19.2	19.8	10.3	4.3
Currently married	29,673	76.6	4.8	28.8	22.1	23.5	1.8
Formerly married	7,849	75.2	18.1	20.4	21.7	15.2	3.7
Education at interview[4]							
No high school diploma or GED[5]	5,424	66.7	27.5	15.0	15.8	5.3	5.2
High school diploma or GED	18,169	73.7	10.2	24.2	22.4	18.0	2.2
Some college, no bachelor's degree	12,399	76.8	5.8	28.1	23.4	21.5	1.9
Bachelor's degree or higher	11,748	80.1	*	29.9	23.6	28.5	2.0
Poverty level income at interview[4]							
0-149 percent	10,072	70.4	31.1	13.3	17.2	6.3	5.0
0-99 percent	5,992	70.0	38.9	9.8	15.1	3.6	5.5
150-299 percent	14,932	71.5	5.3	24.6	24.2	18.5	2.4
300 percent or more	22,736	80.0	1.1	31.6	23.2	27.2	1.3
Race and Hispanic origin							
Hispanic	6,702	67.5	17.5	21.6	18.9	8.6	5.0
Non-Hispanic white	42,522	70.8	5.5	24.0	22.9	20.6	2.4
Non-Hispanic black	8,210	76.3	22.6	26.9	16.9	10.0	4.2

*Figure does not meet standard of reliability or precision.

[1]Medical services include Pap smear; pelvic exam; prenatal care; postpartum care; HIV test; testing or treatment for other sexually transmitted diseases; testing or treatment for vaginal, urinary or pelvic infection; abortion; or pregnancy test.

[2]Respondents spontaneously mentioned another form of public assistance or that the service was free.

[3]Includes women of other race and origin groups not shown separately.

[4]Limited to women 22-44 years of age at time of interview.

[5]GED is general equivalency diploma.

NOTE: Percents may not add to total who received "at least 1 medical service" because women may have received more than 1 service and used more than 1 payment method.

D1-34 Number of Women 15-44 Years of Age, Percent Who Have Ever Received Any Infertility Services, and Percent Who Have Ever Received the Specified Infertility Services, by Selected Characteristics: United States, 1995

Characteristic	Number in thousands	Any services[1]	Advice	Tests on woman or man	Ovulation drugs	Surgery or treatment for blocked tubes	Assisted reproductive technology[2]
				Percent			
All women	60,201	15.4	6.4	4.2	3.0	1.5	1.0
Age at interview							
15-24 years	18,002	4.4	1.1	0.2	0.3	0.1	0.0
25-34 years	20,758	17.1	6.3	3.7	3.1	1.2	0.8
35-44 years	21,440	22.9	10.9	8.1	5.2	2.9	2.1
Parity, age, and marital status							
0 births	25,242	6.4	4.6	3.7	2.2	1.1	1.2
15-24 years	14,113	1.2	0.5	0.2	0.2	0.1	0.1
25-34 years	7,139	8.7	6.5	4.6	3.0	1.0	1.1
35-44 years	3,991	20.7	15.5	14.5	8.0	4.8	5.3
Married	5,685	20.9	16.0	13.6	8.3	4.1	4.7
Unmarried	19,558	2.2	1.2	0.8	0.4	0.2	0.1
1 or more births	34,968	21.8	7.7	4.6	3.6	1.8	0.9
15–24 years	3,889	16.1	3.3	0.3	0.6	0.5	–
25-34 years	13,620	21.5	6.2	3.1	3.1	1.3	0.6
35-44 years	17,449	23.4	9.8	6.7	4.6	2.4	1.4
Married	23,988	24.1	9.2	6.0	4.6	2.1	1.1
Unmarried	10,970	16.8	4.3	1.6	1.3	0.9	0.5
Education at interview[3]							
No high school diploma or GED[4]	5,424	14.9	3.3	2.0	1.2	0.7	0.2
High school diploma or GED	18,169	20.0	7.8	4.9	3.9	2.0	1.1
Some college, no bachelor's degree	12,399	19.4	7.8	5.6	3.3	2.0	1.2
Bachelor's degree or higher	11,748	18.0	10.3	7.1	5.3	1.9	2.2
Poverty level income at interview[3]							
0-149 percent	10,072	16.6	4.8	2.1	1.5	0.9	0.2
0-99 percent	5,992	14.2	4.0	1.7	0.9	0.5	0.1
150-299 percent	14,932	17.9	6.3	3.9	3.1	1.4	0.6
300 percent or higher	22,736	20.3	10.3	7.6	5.3	2.5	2.2
Race and Hispanic origin							
Hispanic	6,702	13.4	4.9	2.4	1.7	0.9	0.6
Non-Hispanic white	42,522	16.3	7.2	4.9	3.5	1.6	1.2
Non-Hispanic black	8,210	13.0	3.8	2.2	1.4	0.9	0.3
Non-Hispanic other	2,767	12.3	5.0	3.9	2.9	1.9	1.4

– Quantity zero.
0.0 Quantity more than zero but less than 0.05.
[1]Includes services to help get pregnant as well as to help prevent miscarriage.
[2]Includes artificial insemination, In vitro fertilization, gamete intrafallopian transfer (GIFT), and other techniques not shown separately.
[3]Limited to women 22-44 years of age at time of interview.
[4]GED is general equivalency diploma.
NOTE: Percents do not add to total ever receiving "any services" because some women reported more than 1 service. Also "any services" includes services to help prevent miscarriage and other infertility services, not shown separately.

D1-35 Percent of Singleton Babies Born in 1990–93 Who Were Ever Breastfed, Percent Distribution by Duration of Breastfeeding, and Mean Duration of Breastfeeding in Weeks, According to Selected Characteristics of the Mother: United States, 1995

Characteristic	Percent breastfed at all	Total	Duration of breastfeeding			Mean duration in weeks
			0-2 months	3-4 months	5 or more months	
			Percent distribution			
All babies[1]	55.2	100.0	40.3	8.6	51.1	28.7
Age at time of birth						
Under 20 years	36.0	100.0	69.7	4.5	25.8	17.5
20-24 years	46.4	100.0	46.6	12.4	41.0	24.1
25 years and over	63.0	100.0	35.0	7.8	57.3	31.5
25-29 years	56.4	100.0	39.8	8.7	51.5	28.2
30-44 years	69.1	100.0	31.3	7.1	61.6	34.0
Marital status at time of birth						
Never married	31.4	100.0	54.8	8.3	36.8	20.8
Married	63.4	100.0	37.7	8.5	53.8	30.1
Formerly married	50.2	100.0	45.3	11.3	43.4	26.4
Wantedness status at conception						
Intended	60.4	100.0	38.1	9.4	52.6	29.7
Mistimed	46.3	100.0	50.7	6.7	42.6	23.3
Unwanted	36.9	100.0	38.1	4.7	57.3	31.6
Region of residence at interview						
Northeast	54.5	100.0	31.7	7.9	60.3	32.6
Midwest	50.8	100.0	38.6	8.1	53.3	27.9
South	45.5	100.0	48.3	7.9	43.7	26.6
West	73.0	100.0	40.2	9.9	49.9	28.7
Education at interview[2]						
No high school diploma or GED[3]	38.9	100.0	44.9	8.8	46.4	26.8
High school diploma or GED	49.0	100.0	44.0	9.8	46.2	27.2
Some college, no bachelor's degree	63.0	100.0	43.9	7.1	49.1	26.5
Bachelor's degree or higher	81.1	100.0	28.7	8.5	62.8	35.2
Poverty level income at interview[2]						
0-149 percent	42.6	100.0	42.4	8.3	49.2	30.2
150–299 percent	58.1	100.0	39.5	9.6	50.8	29.4
300 percent or higher	68.2	100.0	38.8	8.1	53.1	28.3
Race and Hispanic origin						
Hispanic	62.2	100.0	42.7	7.1	50.2	26.7
Non-Hispanic white	59.1	100.0	38.5	8.1	53.3	29.8
Non-Hispanic black	25.1	100.0	45.0	14.0	40.9	22.9

[1]Includes babies born to women of other race and origin groups not shown separately.
[2]Limited to women 22-44 years of age at time of interview.
[3]GED Is general equivalency diploma.
NOTES: To compute mean duration for all ever-breastfed babies born 1990-93, babies currently being breastfed at interview were assigned the value 83 weeks, which was the mean duration of breastfeeding for all babies born 1990-93 who were breastfed 12 months or longer. In duration of breastfeeding, 0-2 months equals 0-12 weeks, 3-4 months equals 13-20 weeks, 5 or more months equals 21 weeks or more. Percents may not add to 100 due to rounding.

D1-36 Number of Women 15–44 Years of Age Who Had a Live Birth in 1991–95 and Percent Distribution by Method of Payment for the Most Recent Delivery, According to Selected Characteristics: United States, 1995

Characteristic	Number in thousands	income Total	Own Insurance only	only	Own income and insurance	Medicaid at all	Other government sources at all	All other sources
				Percent distribution				
All women[1]	13,999	100.0	6.8	37.3	21.2	33.6	0.7	0.4
Age at time of birth								
Under 20 years	1,535	100.0	4.0	20.6	5.6	67.5	1.8	0.5
20-24 years	3,402	100.0	5.1	27.9	13.5	51.5	1.4	0.6
25-29 years	4,212	100.0	8.3	40.7	24.3	26.3	0.3	0.0
30-44 years	4,850	100.0	7.5	46.2	28.9	16.5	0.2	0.5
Birth order								
First	5,342	100.0	7.4	38.5	19.9	32.2	1.2	0.7
Second	4,865	100.0	6.0	39.1	26.4	28.2	0.2	0.2
Third or higher	3,792	100.0	7.0	33.3	16.5	42.3	0.7	0.3
Wantedness status at conception								
Intended	9,618	100.0	7.2	41.0	25.4	25.5	0.4	0.4
Mistimed	3,052	100.0	5.3	31.3	12.4	48.9	1.8	0.3
Unwanted	1,308	100.0	6.9	25.1	11.3	55.8	0.2	0.3
Marital status at time of birth								
Never married	3,124	100.0	2.8	20.1	6.5	68.0	1.7	0.9
Married	10,087	100.0	8.1	44.1	27.0	20.1	0.4	0.2
Formerly married	788	100.0	4.9	18.9	5.3	69.2	1.1	0.7
Residence at interview								
Metropolitan, central city	4,388	100.0	7.2	32.7	14.5	44.5	0.4	0.7
Metropolitan, suburban	6,677	100.0	6.9	44.3	23.6	24.2	0.8	0.3
Nonmetropolitan	2,933	100.0	6.1	28.4	26.0	38.5	0.9	0.1
Education at interview[2]								
No high school diploma or GED[3]	1,791	100.0	5.5	20.8	2.7	70.3	0.6	0.1
High school diploma or GED	5,036	100.0	5.6	38.0	21.8	33.4	0.8	0.4
Some college, no bachelor's degree	2,984	100.0	9.1	44.1	27.6	18.5	0.8	–
Bachelor's degree or higher	2,589	100.0	9.0	49.5	35.5	5.4	0.1	0.5
Race and Hispanic origin								
Hispanic	2,134	100.0	7.3	27.6	8.3	56.3	0.5	–
Non-Hispanic white	9,275	100.0	7.5	42.1	26.1	23.0	0.9	0.4
Non-Hispanic black	1,916	100.0	3.0	26.3	7.6	62.0	–	1.1
Non-Hispanic other	674	100.0	6.7	33.5	33.5	25.5	0.9	–

– Quantity zero.
0.0 Quantity more than zero but less than 0.05.
[1] Includes women for whom wantedness status was inapplicable.
[2] Limited to women 22-44 years of age at time of interview.
[3] GED is general equivalency diploma.
NOTES: In classifying method of payment in these 6 mutually exclusive categories, first priority was given to any mention of Medicaid, and second priority was given to any mention of other government sources. Percents may not add to 100 due to rounding.

D1-37 Number of Women 18–44 Years of Age, Percent Who Are Seeking to Adopt a Child, and Percent Who Have Taken Specified Steps Toward Adoption, by Selected Characteristics: United States, 1995

| Characteristic | Number in thousands | Currently seeking to adopt | Steps toward adoption | |
			Applied to an agency	Got a lawyer
			Percent	
All women[1]	54,748	0.9	0.2	0.0
Age at interview				
18-29 years	22,243	0.4	0.0	–
30-34 years	11,065	0.9	0.1	–
35-39 years	11,211	1.6	0.4	0.1
40-44 years	10,230	1.3	0.3	0.2
Marital status				
Never married	17,300	0.6	0.0	–
Currently married	29,600	1.1	0.2	0.1
Formerly married	7,849	1.1	0.2	–
Parity				
0 births	19,998	1.1	0.2	0.1
1 birth	10,502	0.9	0.2	0.1
2 births	13,871	0.5	0.0	–
3 or more births	10,377	1.1	0.2	–
Ever used infertility services				
Yes	9,217	1.8	0.4	0.2
No	42,387	0.8	0.1	0.0
Education at interview[2]				
No high school diploma or GED[3]	5,424	1.9	0.5	–
High school diploma or GED	18,169	0.8	0.2	0.1
Some college, no bachelor's degree	12,399	0.8	0.1	0.1
Bachelor's degree or higher	11,748	1.0	0.0	0.1
Poverty level income at interview[2]				
0-149 percent	10,080	1.0	0.3	–
0-99 percent	5,992	1.2	0.4	–
150-299 percent	14,932	0.7	0.1	–
300 percent or higher	22,736	1.1	0.2	0.1
Race and Hispanic origin				
Hispanic	6,015	1.2	0.4	–
Non-Hispanic white	38,987	0.7	0.1	0.1
Non-Hispanic black	7,357	1.8	0.2	0.0
Non-Hispanic other	2,390	1.8	0.3	0.3

– Quantity zero.

0.0 Quantity more than zero but less than 0.05.

[1]Includes women with missing information on adoption or infertility services.

[2]Limited to women 22-44 years of age at time of interview.

[3]GED is general equivalency diploma.

2. INTERACTION WITH CHILDREN

D2-1 Average Time Spent with Children: Married Respondents

(1=never or rarely, 2=once a month or less, 3=several times a month, 4=about once a week, 5= several times a week, 6=almost every day)

	Leisure Activities Away from Home	At Home Working or Playing Together	Having Private Talks	Helping with Reading or Homework	Watching Television or Videos
Average	3.4	4.1	4.0	4.3	4.8
Age of Respondent					
18-24	3.4	4.7	4.4	5.0	5.2
25-34	3.6	4.4	4.2	4.8	5.1
35-44	3.5	4.1	1.0	4.3	4.7
45-64	3.1	3.6	3.7	3.6	4.4
Highest Year in School					
Less than h.s.	3.2	4.0	3.8	4.1	5.0
High school	3.4	4.0	3.9	4.2	4.8
Some college	3.5	4.2	4.1	4.4	4.8
16 + years	3.6	4.3	4.2	4.6	4.6
Race of Respondent					
Black	3.3	4.0	4.1	4.5	4.9
White	3.5	4.1	4.0	4.3	4.7
Hispanic	3.4	4.1	3.9	4.3	4.9
Other	3.1	3.5	4.0	4.1	4.7
Sex of Respondent					
Male	3.4	3.9	3.5	3.9	4.6
Female	3.5	4.3	4.4	4.7	4.9

D2-2   The Hours Parents Spend with 5–17 Year Old Child in Various Activities

	N	Alone with child	Checking homework	Helping with homework	Talking about school work	Talking about things learned in school
Average	1967	5.7 hrs	3.9 hrs	2.4 hrs	4.1 hrs	3.9 hrs
Age of Respondent						
18-24	(30)	6.5 hrs	4.5 hrs	3.6 hrs	4.4 hrs	4.6 hrs
25-34	(537)	5.5 hrs	4.4 hrs	3.1 hrs	4.2 hrs	4.2 hrs
35-44	(1048)	5.9 hrs	3.8 hrs	2.3 hrs	4.2 hrs	3.9 hrs
45-64	(346)	5.5 hrs	3.5 hrs	1.6 hrs	3.7 hrs	3.3 hrs
65 +	(6)	–	–	–	–	–
Highest Year in School						
Less than h.s.	(234)	6.5 hrs	3.7 hrs	2.1 hrs	3.7 hrs	3.5 hrs
High school	(741)	5.8 hrs	4.0 hrs	2.4 hrs	3.9 hrs	3.9 hrs
Some college	(495)	5.5 hrs	4.0 hrs	2.5 hrs	4.2 hrs	4.0 hrs
16 + years	(492)	5.6 hrs	3.8 hrs	2.5 hrs	4.5 hrs	4.0 hrs
Marital Status						
Married	(1612)	5.5 hrs	3.9 hrs	2.3 hrs	4.1 hrs	3.9 hrs
Widowed	(26)	5.4 hrs	3.1 hrs	2.3 hrs	4.0 hrs	3.7 hrs
Divorced	(165)	7.2 hrs	4.1 hrs	2.4 hrs	4.2 hrs	4.1 hrs
Separated	(65)	6.8 hrs	3.9 hrs	3.0 hrs	4.2 hrs	4.0 hrs
Never married	(98)	7.4 hrs	4.4 hrs	3.4 hrs	4.1 hrs	4.2 hrs
Race of Respondent						
White	(1502)	5.6 hrs	3.9 hrs	2.4 hrs	4.2 hrs	4.0 hrs
Black	(247)	6.2 hrs	4.2 hrs	2.8 hrs	3.9 hrs	3.9 hrs
Hispanic	(178)	6.3 hrs	3.8 hrs	2.4 hrs	4.2 hrs	4.0 hrs
Other	(37)	5.9 hrs	2.8 hrs	2.2 hrs	3.9 hrs	3.7 hrs
Sex of Respondent						
Male	(841)	4.8 hrs	3.5 hrs	1.9 hrs	3.6 hrs	3.5 hrs
Female	(1126)	6.4 hrs	4.3 hrs	2.8 hrs	4.4 hrs	4.2 hrs

D2-3   Frequency That Parents Reported They Spend with Children Age 5–17 Years in Leisure Activities and Family Meals

Over the past 3 months, about how often have you spent time with child in leisure activities, working on something together or just having private talks? Had a meal together with him or her?

	N	Leisure Activities			Meal Together		
		Never/ Once a month	About once a week	About every day	Never/ Once a month	About once a week	About every day
Total	(1284)	38%	40%	22%	44%	34%	22%
Age of Respondent							
35-44	(391)	40%	37%	23%	42%	32%	26%
45-64	(852)	38%	41%	21%	44%	36%	20%
Highest Year in School							
Less than h.s.	(200)	45%	36%	19%	53%	21%	26%
High school	(531)	38%	40%	22%	46%	31%	23%
Some college	(272)	39%	40%	21%	44%	39%	17%
16 + years	(275)	32%	43%	25%	33%	46%	21%
Marital Status							
Married	(996)	38%	41%	21%	46%	35%	19%
Widowed	(43)	40%	42%	18%	33%	40%	27%
Divorced	(167)	38%	37%	25%	32%	35%	33%
Separated	(55)	47%	33%	20%	49%	22%	29%
Race of Respondent							
White	(1025)	36%	42%	22%	41%	37%	22%
Black	(144)	43%	38%	19%	50%	29%	21%
Hispanic	(97)	47%	20%	33%	61%	10%	29%
Sex of Respondent							
Male	(537)	27%	43%	30%	37%	38%	25%
Female	(747)	46%	37%	17%	49%	32%	19%

D2-4   Frequency Parents Talk to 5–17 Year Old Child About Things That Worry or Excite the Child

	N	Talk about things that worry			Talk about things that excite		
		Almost never	Two/three times per month	Several times per week	Almost never	Two/three times per month	Several times per week
Total	(2600)	20%	47%	33%	62%	16%	22%
Age of Respondent							
18-24	(44)	34%	21%	45%	79%	9%	12%
25-34	(726)	21%	25%	54%	65%	16%	19%
35-44	(1371)	18%	21%	61%	63%	16%	21%
45-64	(450)	22%	15%	63%	60%	19%	21%
Highest Year in School							
Less than h.s.	(349)	27%	17%	54%	55%	15%	30%
High school	(987)	19%	22%	59%	58%	19%	23%
Some college	(650)	18%	21%	61%	64%	14%	22%
16 + years	(610)	20%	22%	58%	71%	15%	14%
Marital Status							
Married	(2010)	18%	21%	61%	64%	17%	18%
Widowed	(33)	30%	21%	49%	66%	17%	17%
Divorced	(294)	21%	22%	57%	56%	16%	28%
Separated	(126)	29%	17%	54%	52%	14%	34%
Never married	(137)	26%	19%	55%	59%	14%	27%
Race of Respondent							
White	(1970)	21%	25%	54%	65%	17%	18%
Black	(319)	41%	31%	28%	59%	17%	24%
Hispanic	(262)	36%	20%	44%	61%	17%	22%
Other	(47)	30%	40%	30%	70%	11%	19%
Sex of Respondent							
Male	(1148)	12%	18%	70%	51%	20%	29%
Female	(1452)	26%	23%	51%	71%	18%	16%

D2-5   Frequency Parents Kiss or Hug Their Children

	N	Gave hug or kiss (% yes)	Average number of times
Total	(1988)	91%	11
Age of Respondent			
18-24	(30)	100%	13
25-34	(543)	95%	12
35-44	(1057)	91%	11
45-64	(352)	82%	9
Highest Year in School			
Less than h.s.	(238)	87%	9
High school	(753)	90%	11
Some college	(498)	91%	12
16 + years	(495)	94%	12
Marital Status			
Married	(1628)	91%	11
Widowed	(26)	77%	10
Divorced	(168)	95%	13
Separated	(65)	94%	10
Never married	(100)	90%	8
Race of Respondent			
White	(1520)	92%	12
Black	(249)	83%	8
Hispanic	(165)	91%	11
Other	(36)	81%	10
Sex of Respondent			
Male	(851)	87%	9
Female	(1137)	94%	13

D2-6   Parents' Report of Pleasant Experiences with 5–17 Year Old Children

	N	Enjoyable Time			Easy to Laugh			Loving Child		
		Once a month or less	About once a week	About once a day	Strongly agree	Agree	Disagree	Strongly agree	Agree	Disagree
Total	(1279)	29%	48%	23%	49%	45%	6%	51%	43%	6%
Age of Respondent										
35-44	(385)	25%	50%	25%	44%	48%	8%	45%	48%	7%
45-64	(850)	30%	48%	22%	51%	43%	6%	53%	41%	6%
65 +	(35)	51%	26%	23%	50%	44%	6%	59%	35%	6%
Highest year in School										
Less than h.s.	(197)	43%	38%	19%	52%	42%	6%	48%	48%	4%
High School	(529)	30%	47%	23%	47%	46%	7%	50%	44%	6%
Some College	(275)	25%	48%	27%	52%	44%	4%	54%	38%	8%
16 + years	(269)	19%	57%	24%	47%	48%	5%	51%	42%	7%
Marital Status										
Married	(1031)	29%	49%	22%	50%	45%	5%	51%	43%	6%
Widowed	(50)	25%	55%	20%	56%	42%	2%	68%	30%	2%
Divorced	(185)	24%	44%	32%	40%	50%	10%	43%	47%	10%
Separated	(62)	44%	36%	20%	57%	31%	12%	62%	33%	5%
Race of Respondent										
White	(1084)	26%	51%	23%	49%	46%	5%	51%	43%	6%
Black	(156)	32%	42%	26%	56%	40%	4%	47%	49%	4%
Hispanic	(96)	50%	28%	22%	49%	40%	11%	51%	39%	10%
Sex of Respondent										
Male	(533)	21%	50%	29%	43%	52%	5%	46%	48%	6%
Female	(746)	34%	46%	20%	53%	41%	6%	53%	40%	7%

D2-7 Frequency of Eating Meals Together

(Asked of those with children under 18)
How many nights a week out of seven does your family eat dinner together at home?

Zero	2%
One	1
Two	7
Three	6
Four	11
Five	20
Six	15
Seven	37
Depends/mixed (vol.)	1
No opinion	----
	100%

Mean number: 5.39   Median number: 6

(Asked of those with children under 18)
At your family meals at home, does anyone say grace or give thanks to God aloud before meals?

	1947	1997
Yes	43%	63%
No	57	37
No opinion	0	-----

- - - - Less than 0.5%

D2-8   Frequency of Friends Visiting in Home of 5–17 Year Old Child and How Many of the Friends the Child's Parent Knows

	N	Frequency friends come to home			Child's friends known by parents		
		Once a month	Several times a month	Several times a week	All or most	About half	Few or none
Total	(1987)						
Age of Respondent							
18-24	(30)	43%	17%	40%	63%	14%	3%
25-34	(540)	29%	33%	38%	75%	23%	2%
35-44	(1060)	25%	37%	38%	79%	20%	1%
45-64	(352)	24%	38%	38%	78%	21%	1%
Highest Year in School							
Less than h.s.	(238)	36%	29%	35%	60%	35%	5%
High school	(252)	26%	33%	41%	75%	23%	2%
Some college	(498)	25%	37%	38%	80%	18%	2%
16 + years	(496)	23%	43%	34%	86%	14%	0%
Marital Status							
Married	(1626)	26%	36%	38%	78%	21%	1%
Widowed	(26)	15%	50%	35%	81%	15%	4%
Divorced	(166)	28%	34%	38%	77%	19%	4%
Separated	(65)	26%	32%	42%	76%	20%	4%
Never married	(100)	30%	31%	19%	70%	28%	2%
Race of Respondent							
White	(1518)	37%	30%	33%	68%	30%	2%
Black	(247)	23%	38%	39%	81%	18%	1%
Hispanic	(181)	37%	28%	35%	66%	30%	4%
Other	(36)	44%	30%	26%	78%	20%	0%
Sex of Respondent							
Male	(849)	25%	36%	39%	69%	29%	2%
Female	(1138)	26%	36%	38%	84%	15%	1%

D2-9　Beliefs about Children and Family Responsibilities

	Strongly Agree	Agree	Neither Agree nor Disagree	Disagree	Strongly Disagree
Children ought to let aging parents live with them when the parents can no longer live by themselves.	9.9	38.6	38.4	10.9	2.3
It is all right for mothers to work full-time when their youngest child is under age 5.	4.2	31.3	31.1	24.6	8.8
A man can have a fully satisfying life without having children.	10.6	41.0	30.2	14.0	4.2
Children ought to provide financial help to aging parents when their parents are having financial difficulty.	14.4	53.7	25.6	4.9	1.4
It is all right for children under three years old to be cared for all day in a day care center.	4.1	20.6	24.0	32.9	18.4
Parents ought to help their children with college expenses.	15.9	56.0	22.1	4.4	1.5
Preschool children are likely to suffer if their mother is employed.	12.9	35.1	25.7	21.2	5.1
Parents ought to provide financial help to their adult children when the children are having financial difficulty.	8.3	42.7	37.4	9.5	2.1
A woman can have a fully satisfying life without children.	11.9	37.2	31.5	14.5	4.8

D2-10 Payment of Allowance to Children 5–17 Years Old

Does your child receive an allowance? Does this allowance pay for work regularly done around the house? Is he/she paid for extra jobs around the house?

	N	Paid allowance	Paid for work	Paid for extra work
Total	(1985)	50%	64%	42%
Age of Respondent				
35-44	(543)	49%	73%	45%
45-64	(1053)	48%	60%	45%
65 +	(352)	55%	60%	30%
Highest Year in School				
Less than h.s.	(233)	54%	60%	37%
High school	(253)	45%	71%	42%
Some college	(498)	50%	66%	43%
16 + years	(495)	55%	54%	45%
Marital Status				
Married	(1625)	49%	64%	42%
Widowed	(65)	57%	65%	40%
Divorced	(168)	48%	67%	47%
Separated	(27)	63%	63%	23%
Never married	(100)	62%	55%	35%
Race of Respondent				
White	(1519)	48%	66%	45%
Black	(249)	64%	58%	38%
Hispanic	(177)	50%	56%	29%
Sex of Respondent				
Male	(849)	51%	64%	40%
Female	(1136)	49%	63%	44%

D2-11 Greater Parental Influence

QUESTION: Looking back on the time when you were growing up, which of your parents would you say had the greater influence on your life — your mother or your father?

	Mother	Father	Both equally (vol.)	Neither/ other (vol.)	No opinion	No. of interviews
National	53%	27%	17%	2%	1%	1036
Sex						
Male	49	32	18	1	•	519
Female	57	22	17	3	1	517
Age						
18-29 years	55	30	12	3	0	199
30-49 years	57	27	14	1	1	227
50-64 years	48	30	21	1	0	215
65 & older	50	18	25	6	1	177
Region						
East	57	24	15	3	1	228
Midwest	50	30	17	2	1	251
South	52	26	18	3	1	336
West	54	25	19	2	0	221
Community						
Urban	56	25	14	4	1	344
Suburban	53	26	18	2	1	462
Rural	49	29	20	1	1	230
Race						
White	51	28	18	2	1	835
Non-white	63	18	16	3	0	189
Education						
College	56	26	16	1	1	149
postgraduate	57	28	14	0	1	170
Bachelor s degree	57	25	16	2	•	298
only	49	28	19	4	•	411
Some college						
High school or less						
Politics						
Republican	48	32	19	1	•	328
Democrat	60	22	16	1	1	341
Independent	52	26	16	5	1	367
Ideology						
Liberal	60	23	14	3	•	168
Moderate	54	29	15	2	•	416
Conservative	51	27	20	2	•	409
Income						
$75,000 & over	45	39	15	0	1	123
$50,000-74,999	56	30	12	1	1	284
$20,000-49,999	56	29	14	1	•	268
Under $20,000	52	28	16	3	1	210
	52	20	23	5	0	199

* Less than one percent

D2-11 Greater Parental Influence *(continued)*

QUESTION: Looking back on the time when you were growing up, which of your parents would you say had the greater influence on your life — your mother or your father?

Greater Influence—Trend

	Total	Fathers	Mothers
Mother			
1997	53%	49%	57%
1951	48	45	41
Father			
1997	27	32	22
1951	22	23	21
Both equally (vol.)			
1997	17	18	17
1951	25	27	24
Neither/other (vol.)			
1997	2	1	3
1951	**	**	**
No opinion			
1997	1	•	1
1951	5	5	4

•Less than one percent
** not recorded

D2-12 Parental Performance

(Based on those with children under 18, 379 respondents, + or – 6%) Using an A, B, C, D, and F grading scale like they do in school, what grade would you give to yourself for the job you are doing in bringing up your children?

Parents' Self-grading—Trend

	A	B	C	D	F	No opinion
1997						
Total	31%	58	8	2	•	1
Fathers	23	62	11	2	•	2
Mothers	38	55	6	1	0	0
1990**	31	54	13	1	0	1

· Less than 0.5%

** Total, based on those with children living at home

(Based on those with children under 18) do you spend more time, less time, or about the same amount of time with your children, compared to the amount of time your [mother, father] spent with you when you were growing up?

	Total	Fathers	Mothers
More time	58%	68%	50%
Less time	19	10	25
About the same amount	22	19	25
Doesn't apply/no opinion	1	3	0
	100%	100%	100%

(Based on those with children, 764 respondents, + or – 4%) And who has had the greater influence on your children—you or the child's [mother/father]?

	Total	Fathers	Mothers
Mother	51%	39%	60%
Father	19	28	11
Both equally (vol.)	27	28	26
Neither/other (vol.)	•	1	1
No opinion	3	4	2
	100%	100%	100%

· Less than 0.5%

3. CHILDREN'S PROBLEM BEHAVIORS AND DISAGREEMENT

D3-1   Parents' Perception of Characteristics of 5–17 Year Old Children

Sometimes, for one reason or another, some children are particularly difficult to raise. Would you describe (child) as particularly difficult (easy) to raise: Has long-lasting physical condition, has long-lasting mental or emotional problem, has seen a therapist or doctor for any emotional or behavioral problem?

	N	Difficult to raise	Easy to raise	Has physical handicap	Has emotional problem	Has seen therapist
Total	(3442)	20%	62%	3.9%	7.1%	15%
Age of Respondent						
18-24	(83)	20%	66%	4.8%	3.7%	20%
25-34	(908)	19%	62%	3.6%	7.0%	13%
35-44	(1753)	21%	61%	4.2%	6.9%	16%
45-64	(81)	20%	62%	3.6%	8.4%	14%
65+	(18)	15%	40%	0.0%	0.0%	31%
Highest Year in School						
Less than h.s.	(495)	22%	64%	5.9%	7.4%	11%
High school	(1312)	20%	62%	3.5%	7.2%	14%
Some college	(863)	19%	63%	4.1%	6.1%	18%
16 + years	(762)	20%	58%	3.1%	7.7%	16%
Marital Status						
Married	(2259)	19%	61%	3.9%	6.3%	13%
Widowed	(164)	27%	69%	3.8%	10.9%	25%
Divorced	(416)	23%	59%	3.7%	10.0%	22%
Separated	(47)	15%	68%	1.8%	13.0%	25%
Never married	(46)	20%	64%	5.7%	6.7%	14%
Race of Respondent						
White	(2556)	21%	59%	3.7%	7.8%	16%
Black	(464)	17%	66%	6.5%	5.6%	11%
Hispanic	(362)	20%	72%	2.1%	5.0%	11%
Other	(54)	13%	75%	4.9%	2.3%	7%
Sex of Respondent						
Male	(1616)	17%	61%	3.5%	5.2%	13%
Female	(1826)	23%	62%	4.2%	8.8%	16%

D3-2   Parents' Perception of School Problems of 5–17 Year Old Children

Has child ever dropped out of school? Ever repeated a grade? Been suspended or expelled? Skipped school, refused to go to school last year? Been asked to meet with teacher or principal during past year?

	N	Dropped out	Repeated a grade	Suspended/ Expelled	Skipped school/ Wouldn't go	Meet with teacher or principal
Total	(3442)	2.4%	17.0%	10.0%	4.7%	9.7%
Age of Respondent						
18-24	(83)	0.0%	5.4%	3.8%	4.7%	9.7%
25-34	(908)	2.1%	17.0%	9.0%	4.9%	18.5%
35-44	(1753)	2.7%	17.0%	10.9%	10.7%	15.2%
45-64	(681)	2.4%	16.0%	9.6%	9.4%	13.4%
65+	(18)	0.0%	7.2%	9.2%	0.0%	0.0%
Highest Year in School						
Less than h.s.	(495)	5.7%	30.0%	18.6%	10.8%	18.6%
High school	(1312)	2.4%	18.8%	11.3%	9.0%	16.2%
Some college	(863)	2.6%	16.3%	8.6%	9.4%	16.8%
16 + years	(762)	0.4%	9.8%	3.3%	6.1%	10.8%
Marital Status						
Married	(2594)	1.8%	14.1%	7.8%	7.5%	13.8%
Widowed	(164)	5.5%	28.9%	19.6%	14.1%	25.3%
Divorced	(416)	4.0%	22.0%	13.1%	13.0%	18.9%
Separated	(47)	7.1%	27.8%	26.4%	14.2%	18.2%
Never married	(216)	3.0%	25.7%	19.3%	9.9%	21.8%
Race of Respondent						
White	(2856)	2.3%	14.0%	7.5%	8.5%	13.0%
Black	(464)	2.8%	28.3%	21.7%	9.0%	26.3%
Hispanic	(364)	2.7%	21.5%	12.2%	8.7%	20.0%
Other	(54)	1.6%	8.2%	10.8%	16.2%	8.8%
Sex of Respondent						
Male	(1616)	1.8%	14.3%	8.1%	8.3%	13.2%
Female	(1826)	2.9%	18.8%	11.6%	9.1%	17.5%

D3-3   Parents' Report of 5-17 Year Old Children's Problems with the Police or Premarital Pregnancy

During the last five years has child ever been in trouble with the police? Has child ever been (or gotten someone) pregnant?	N	Trouble with police	Been pregnant/ Gotten someone pregnant
Total	(3442)	5.5%	1.9%
Age of Respondent			
18-24	(83)	4.3%	0.0%
25-34	(908)	4.3%	3.1%
35-44	(1753)	6.3%	2.0%
45-64	(681)	5.2%	1.4%
65+	(18)	13.4%	0.0%
Highest Year in School			
Less than h.s.	(495)	9.1%	4.8%
High school	(1312)	6.3%	1.9%
Some college	(803)	4.6%	1.6%
16 + years	(702)	3.1%	0.1%
Marital Status			
Married	(2594)	4.4%	1.1%
Widowed	(164)	14.1%	3.5%
Divorced	(416)	8.7%	5.7%
Separated	(47)	9.5%	0.0%
Never married	(216)	6.1%	10.1%
Race of Respondent			
White	(2548)	5.3%	1.2%
Black	(462)	5.9%	5.9%
Hispanic	(364)	6.5%	2.2%
Other	(54)	7.2%	1.0%
Sex of Respondent			
Male	(1616)	4.4%	1.0%
Female	(1826)	6.6%	2.7%

D3-4   Child 5–17 Years of Age Allowed to Be Home Alone

Is child allowed to be at home alone in the afternoon after school, between 3-6pm? At night? Overnight if you went on a trip?

		After School			At Night			Overnight		
	N	Yes	Some-times	No	Yes	Some-times	No	Yes	Some-times	No
Total	(1989)	43%	52%	6%	22%	74%	4%	6%	94%	1%
Age of Respondent										
25-34	(542)	23%	73%	5%	8%	89%	3%	2%	98%	0%
35-44	(1058)	47%	47%	6%	25%	72%	3%	5%	94%	1%
45-64	(353)	63%	31%	6%	39%	53%	8%	13%	86%	1%
Highest Year in School										
Less than h.s.	(239)	38%	57%	8%	19%	78%	3%	8%	92%	0%
High school	(753)	43%	53%	4%	22%	73%	5%	5%	94%	2%
Some college	(499)	44%	50%	6%	23%	74%	3%	7%	93%	1%
16 + years	(495)	43%	51%	6%	23%	73%	5%	5%	95%	0%
Marital Status										
Married	(1629)	43%	51%	6%	22%	74%	4%	5%	94%	1%
Widowed	(65)	41%	55%	3%	25%	74%	2%	6%	94%	0%
Divorced	(168)	48%	49%	3%	27%	69%	5%	7%	91%	2%
Separated	(26)	46%	42%	12%	39%	61%	0%	19%	81%	0%
Never married	(100)	29%	66%	5%	11%	84%	5%	4%	95%	1%
Race of Respondent										
White	(1521)	44%	51%	5%	24%	72%	5%	5%	94%	1%
Black	(249)	35%	60%	5%	12%	84%	4%	4%	96%	1%
Hispanic	(36)	64%	30%	6%	38%	62%	0%	19%	78%	3%
Other	(181)	37%	53%	11%	20%	79%	1%	7%	93%	0%
Sex of Respondent										
Male	(852)	44%	51%	6%	23%	72%	5%	7%	93%	1%
Female	(1137)	42%	53%	5%	21%	75%	4%	5%	94%	1%

D3-5   Parents' Restriction of TV Watching of Children Age 5–17

Do you restrict the amount of television that your child watches? Do you restrict the type of program that he/she watches?

	N	Restrict Time Watching			Restrict Type of Program		
		Yes	No	Try	Yes	No	Try
Total	(1973)	42%	49%	9%	74%	19%	7%
Age of Respondent							
25-34	(540)	45%	49%	6%	86%	9%	5%
35-44	(1051)	44%	46%	10%	75%	19%	7%
45-64	(345)	32%	55%	13%	53%	37%	10%
Highest Year in School							
Less than h.s.	(234)	31%	62%	7%	73%	22%	6%
High school	(750)	38%	54%	8%	73%	21%	6%
Some college	(498)	45%	46%	9%	75%	16%	9%
16 + years	(487)	52%	36%	12%	76%	19%	6%
Marital Status							
Married	(1631)	43%	48%	10%	74%	19%	7%
Widowed	(64)	36%	53%	11%	66%	23%	11%
Divorced	(168)	40%	53%	7%	72%	21%	7%
Separated	(26)	46%	46%	8%	59%	37%	4%
Never married	(99)	39%	53%	8%	82%	12%	6%
Race of Respondent							
White	(1507)	40%	50%	10%	74%	19%	7%
Black	(249)	52%	41%	7%	80%	15%	5%
Hispanic	(177)	44%	45%	11%	72%	19%	9%
Sex of Respondent							
Male	(840)	40%	45%	15%	71%	21%	8%
Female	(1133)	44%	45%	11%	77%	18%	6%

D3-6   How Parents Discipline 5-17 Year Old Children When They Do Something Especially Bad

When (child) does somehting especially bad, how often do you talk to, yell at, take away privileges from, or spank him/her for what he/she did wrong?

	N	Talk to			Yell at			Take away privileges			Spank		
		Less than half the time	About half the time	More than half the time	Less than half the time	About half the time	More than half the time	Less than half the time	About half the time	More than half the time	Less than half the time	About half the time	More than half the time
Total	(1988)	3%	6%	91%	44%	24%	32%	44%	24%	72%	79%	10%	11%
Age of Respondent													
18-24	(29)	0%	3%	97%	30%	43%	27%	30%	23%	47%	79%	10%	11%
25-34	(544)	1%	7%	92%	35%	30%	35%	39%	28%	33%	89%	8%	3%
35-44	(1059)	3%	5%	92%	45%	22%	32%	45%	22%	29%	95%	3%	2%
45-64	(353)	4%	8%	88%	53%	16%	31%	50%	22%	16%	97%	2%	1%
Highest Year in School													
Less than h.s.	(237)	4%	10%	86%	41%	27%	32%	43%	31%	26%	90%	7%	3%
High School	(754)	3%	7%	90%	40%	25%	35%	44%	23%	33%	92%	5%	3%
Some college	(499)	2%	3%	95%	40%	26%	34%	42%	26%	32%	95%	3%	2%
16+ years	(496)	3%	4%	92%	53%	17%	30%	49%	19%	32%	96%	3%	1%
Marital Status													
Married	(1629)	3%	5%	92%	46%	23%	31%	46%	23%	31%	94%	4%	2%
Widowed	(26)	0%	19%	81%	38%	33%	29%	40%	40%	20%	96%	4%	0%
Divorced	(168)	2%	5%	93%	36%	24%	40%	31%	25%	44%	93%	5%	2%
Separated	(65)	5%	5%	90%	35%	22%	43%	36%	32%	32%	94%	5%	1%
Never married	(100)	0%	10%	90%	28%	37%	35%	44%	24%	32%	84%	11%	5%
Race of Respondent													
White	(1520)	2%	5%	93%	44%	23%	33%	46%	23%	31%	95%	4%	1%
Black	(248)	2%	8%	92%	41%	25%	34%	36%	24%	40%	84%	9%	7%
Hispanic	(180)	6%	9%	85%	41%	27%	32%	41%	31%	23%	94%	5%	1%
Other	(37)	5%	16%	79%	40%	27%	33%	57%	24%	29%	100%	0%	0%
Sex of Respondent													
Male	(852)	4%	7%	89%	49%	21%	30%	51%	23%	26%	94%	4%	2%
Female	(1136)	2%	5%	93%	39%	25%	36%	40%	24%	36%	93%	5%	2%

D3-7   Parents' Disagreement with 5–17 Year Old Children about Helping Around the House, School, and Getting Along with Family

In the past 3 months, how often have you and child had open disagreements about each of the following: helping around the house, school, and getting along with family members?

	N	Helping around Home			School			Getting along with Family		
		Never/ Rarely	Once a month or less	Once a week or more	Never/ Rarely	Once a month or less	Once a week or more	Never/ Rarely	Once a month or less	Once a week or more
Total	(2595)	47%	35%	18%	78%	15%	7%	55%	25%	20%
Age of Respondent										
25-34	(723)	43%	38%	19%	78%	15%	7%	50%	27%	23%
35-44	(1369)	48%	34%	18%	79%	15%	6%	52%	26%	22%
45-64	(448)	49%	34%	17%	76%	15%	9%	68%	16%	16%
Highest Year in School										
Less than h.s.	(348)	50%	24%	26%	80%	9%	11%	62%	17%	21%
High school	(984)	46%	36%	18%	78%	15%	7%	59%	24%	17%
Some college	(679)	44%	39%	17%	73%	19%	8%	52%	26%	22%
16+ years	(610)	50%	35%	15%	83%	12%	5%	46%	30%	24%
Marital Status										
Married	(2010)	47%	36%	17%	79%	15%	6%	52%	27%	22%
Widowed	(127)	52%	28%	20%	76%	14%	10%	56%	24%	20%
Divorced	(290)	50%	31%	19%	76%	14%	10%	66%	19%	15%
Separated	(34)	35%	50%	15%	73%	21%	6%	64%	12%	24%
Never married	(133)	46%	28%	26%	73%	12%	15%	67%	13%	20%
Race of Respondent										
White	(1966)	46%	37%	17%	77%	13%	10%	50%	28%	22%
Black	(316)	51%	27%	22%	79%	15%	6%	69%	15%	16%
Hispanic	(262)	53%	26%	21%	81%	12%	7%	69%	12%	19%
Sex of Respondent										
Male	(1145)	54%	32%	14%	82%	13%	5%	59%	26%	15%
Female	(1450)	41%	37%	22%	75%	16%	9%	51%	24%	25%

D3-8 Parents' Disagreement with 5–17 Year Old Children about Money and Staying Out Late

In the past 3 months, how often have you and child had open disagreements about each of the following: Money? Staying out late?

	N	Money Never/ Rarely	Money Once a month or less	Money More than once a month	Staying out late Never/ Rarely	Staying out late Once a month or less	Staying out late More than month
Total	(2593)	85%	11%	4%	90%	8%	3%
Age of Respondent							
25-34	(722)	83%	12%	5%	94%	3%	3%
35-44	(1366)	85%	12%	3%	90%	8%	2%
45-64	(449)	88%	8%	4%	88%	9%	3%
Highest Year in School							
Less than h.s.	(345)	84%	9%	7%	85%	10%	5%
High school	(986)	83%	13%	4%	90%	6%	4%
Some college	(652)	84%	12%	3%	92%	7%	1%
16+ years	(606)	90%	6%	3%	89%	10%	2%
Marital Status							
Married	(2004)	87%	10%	3%	90%	7%	3%
Widowed	(128)	73%	20%	7%	86%	9%	5%
Divorced	(292)	82%	13%	5%	89%	7%	4%
Separated	(33)	88%	9%	3%	89%	11%	0%
Never married	(132)	80%	12%	8%	88%	8%	4%
Race of Respondent							
White	(1965)	86%	11%	3%	90%	7%	3%
Black	(317)	81%	11%	8%	93%	5%	3%
Hispanic	(261)	82%	13%	5%	86%	11%	3%
Sex of Respondent							
Male	(1144)	88%	10%	2%	91%	8%	1%
Female	(1449)	83%	12%	5%	89%	7%	4%

D3-9   Parents' Disagreement with 5–17 Year Old Children about Sex, Smoking, Drinking, and Drugs

		Sexual behavior			Smoking, drinking, and drug use		
In the past three months, how often have you and child had open disagreement about each of the following: Sexual behavior? Smoking, drinking, and drug use?							
	N	Never/ Rarely	Once a month or less	More than once a month	Never/ Rarely	Once a month or less	More than once a month
Total	(1077)	97%	2%	1%	97%	2%	1%
Age of Respondent							
25-34	(125)	94%	4%	2%	97%	2%	1%
35-44	(638)	97%	2%	1%	97%	2%	1%
45-64	(305)	99%	1%	0%	97%	3%	0%
Highest Year in School							
Less than h.s.	(159)	96%	2%	2%	97%	3%	0%
High school	(408)	96%	2%	2%	97%	2%	1%
Some college	(275)	98%	1%	1%	97%	3%	0%
16+ years	(233)	99%	1%	0%	97%	2%	0%
Marital Status							
Married	(828)	98%	2%	1%	97%	2%	0%
Widowed	(53)	100%	0%	0%	93%	7%	0%
Divorced	(128)	93%	5%	2%	96%	3%	1%
Never married	(49)	94%	2%	4%	96%	2%	2%
Race of Respondent							
White	(766)	97%	2%	1%	97%	3%	0%
Black	(146)	97%	2%	1%	99%	0%	1%
Hispanic	(129)	97%	0%	3%	96%	4%	1%
Sex of Respondent							
Male	(517)	98%	1%	1%	98%	2%	0%
Female	(560)	97%	2%	1%	97%	2%	1%

D3-10 Parents' Disagreement about Dress and Friends with 5–17 Year Old Children

In the past three months, how often have you and child had open disagreements about each of the following: How he/she dresses, boy/girl friend, or friends?

		Dress			Boy/Girl friend			Friends		
	N	Never/ Rarely	Once a month or less	Once a week or more	Never/ Rarely	Once a month or less	Once a week or more	Never/ Rarely	Once a month or less	Once a week or more
Total	(2600)	73%	18%	9%	92%	5%	3%	91%	7%	2%
Age of Respondent										
25-34	(724)	67%	21%	12%	86%	9%	5%	90%	8%	2%
35-44	(1370)	75%	18%	7%	92%	4%	4%	93%	5%	2%
45-64	(449)	82%	14%	2%	96%	3%	1%	87%	11%	2%
Highest Year in School										
Less than h.s.	(348)	63%	19%	18%	85%	9%	6%	84%	10%	6%
High school	(986)	75%	18%	7%	92%	6%	2%	90%	8%	2%
Some college	(649)	73%	19%	8%	94%	3%	3%	93%	6%	1%
16 + years	(609)	77%	18%	5%	96%	3%	1%	94%	5%	1%
Marital Status										
Married	(2011)	74%	19%	7%	92%	5%	3%	92%	6%	2%
Widowed	(128)	69%	16%	15%	87%	7%	7%	81%	13%	6%
Divorced	(294)	70%	19%	11%	92%	7%	1%	89%	8%	3%
Separated	(33)	88%	9%	3%	—	—	—	68%	29%	2%
Never married	(133)	61%	17%	22%	87%	6%	7%	88%	9%	3%
Race of Respondent										
White	(1967)	74%	18%	8%	94%	4%	2%	92%	6%	2%
Black	(317)	65%	22%	13%	90%	6%	4%	88%	8%	4%
Hispanic	(263)	77%	12%	11%	87%	9%	4%	83%	11%	6%
Sex of Respondent										
Male	(1148)	82%	14%	4%	93%	4%	3%	93%	6%	1%
Female	(1452)	66%	22%	12%	89%	6%	5%	89%	8%	3%

D3-11 How Parents Deal with Disagreements with 5–17 Year Old Children

There are various ways parents deal with serious disagreements with their sons and daughter. How often do you handle disagreements with child by: refusing to talk about it? letting child have way? discussing calmly? arguing heatedly or shouting?

	N	Refuse to Talk			Let Have Own Way			Calm Discussion			Argue and Shout		
		Never/ seldom	Some- times	Often/ always	Never/ seldom	Some- times	Often/ always	Never/ seldom	Some- times	Often/ always	Never/ seldom	Some times	Often/ always
Total	1131	80%	4%	16%	72%	14%	14%	29%	39%	32%	90%	7%	3%
Age of Respondent													
35-44	341	77%	4%	19%	78%	12%	10%	33%	38%	29%	87%	10%	3%
45-64	757	83%	4%	13%	70%	15%	15%	28%	39%	33%	91%	5%	4%
Highest Year in School													
Less than h.s.	159	72%	7%	21%	55%	21%	24%	32%	30%	38%	88%	8%	4%
High School	455	82%	3%	15%	71%	16%	13%	28%	40%	32%	89%	10%	1%
Some college	257	79%	5%	16%	74%	13%	13%	31%	33%	36%	94%	2%	4%
16 + years	256	85%	5%	10%	80%	9%	11%	27%	48%	25%	90%	7%	3%
Marital Status													
Married	679	82%	4%	16%	71%	15%	14%	29%	40%	31%	90%	7%	3%
Divorced	145	69%	7%	24%	73%	13%	14%	32%	40%	28%	87%	10%	3%
Separated	47	82%	3%	15%	75%	14%	11%	23%	36%	41%	95%	5%	0%
Race of Respondent													
White	906	81%	4%	15%	71%	15%	14%	28%	41%	31%	91%	6%	3%
Black	130	74%	3%	23%	74%	13%	13%	38%	26%	36%	85%	9%	6%
Hispanic	86	81%	5%	14%	75%	12%	13%	31%	28%	41%	84%	13%	3%
Sex of Respondent													
Male	465	77%	3%	20%	70%	14%	16%	30%	38%	32%	89%	5%	6%
Female	666	82%	5%	13%	73%	15%	12%	28%	40%	32%	90%	9%	1%

4. CHILDREN OF DIVORCE AND SEPARATION

D4-1 Parental Contact with Child Living with Other Parent

About how often did child talk on telephone or receive a letter from (his/her) (mother/father) during the last 12 months since (he/she) and child stopped living together?		Talk on Phone			See Parent in Person			Stay Overnight
	N	Once a year	Several times a year	About weekly	Once a year	Several times a year	About weekly	Yes
Total	(687)	35%	32%	33%	36%	36%	28%	65%
Age of Respondent								
18-24	(45)	51%	29%	20%	42%	38%	20%	53%
25-34	(279)	40%	31%	29%	38%	34%	29%	64%
35-44	(299)	32%	32%	36%	36%	37%	27%	70%
45-64	(65)	17%	40%	43%	29%	43%	28%	58%
Highest Year in School								
Less than h.s.	(142)	53%	25%	22%	49%	30%	21%	65%
High school	(304)	35%	30%	35%	34%	36%	30%	60%
Some college	(171)	29%	36%	35%	32%	42%	26%	74%
16 + years	(70)	14%	41%	45%	30%	37%	23%	65%
Marital Status								
Married	(199)	37%	37%	26%	43%	43%	14%	89%
Widowed	(99)	31%	28%	41%	32%	31%	37%	63%
Divorced	(248)	27%	33%	40%	30%	38%	32%	65%
Separated	(6)	33%	33%	34%	17%	67%	16%	40%
Never married	(438)	48%	25%	27%	43%	26%	31%	44%
Race of Respondent								
White	(399)	32%	33%	35%	35%	40%	25%	74%
Black	(190)	33%	35%	32%	35%	35%	30%	51%
Hispanic	(89)	51%	20%	29%	47%	24%	29%	52%
Sex of Respondent								
Male	(90)	20%	26%	54%	25%	35%	40%	85%
Female	(598)	37%	33%	20%	38%	36%	26%	62%

D4-2   Help or Interference Divorced Parents Received from Each Other in Raising Children

During the last 12 months, how much help did you get from child's (mother/father) with raising (him/her)? How much did (mother/father) interfere with the way you raised children?

	N	Receive Help None/ A little	Receive Help Some	Receive Help Pretty much/ A great deal	Interference None/ A little	Interference Some	Interference Pretty much/ A great deal
Total	(451)	70%	13%	17%	83%	10%	7%
Age of Respondent							
25-34	(178)	64%	15%	21%	82%	11%	7%
35-44	(205)	66%	17%	17%	83%	10%	7%
45-64	(44)	59%	23%	18%	89%	7%	6%
Highest Year in School							
Less than h.s.	(78)	74%	12%	14%	89%	6%	8%
High school	(198)	65%	16%	19%	82%	9%	9%
Some college	(122)	66%	17%	17%	84%	10%	6%
16 + years	(51)	55%	22%	23%	79%	17%	4%
Race of Respondent							
White	(273)	67%	17%	16%	82%	10%	8%
Black	(126)	61%	17%	22%	87%	6%	7%
Hispanic	(49)	67%	8%	25%	77%	14%	9%
Sex of Respondent							
Male	(65)	58%	15%	27%	86%	9%	5%
Female	(388)	67%	16%	17%	83%	10%	7%

D4-3 Conflict Between Separated/Divorced Parents Over Children 5–17 Years Old Concerning Where Children Live, How They Are Raised, and How Custodial Parent Spends Money on Children

I am going to read you a list of issues that you and your child's (mother/father) may have conflict over. For each one, tell me how much conflict you have.

| | N | *Where Child Living* | | | *How Child is Raised* | | | *How you Spend Money* | | |
		None/ Little	Some	Pretty much/ Great deal	None/ Little	Some	Pretty much Great deal	None/ Little	Some	Pretty much/ Great deal
Total	(185)	36%	24%	40%	51%	25%	24%	40%	30%	30%

| | N | *How Other Parent Spends* | | | *Time Other Parent Spends* | | | *Financial Support Other Partent* | | |
		None/ Little	Some	Pretty much/ Great deal	None/ Little	Some	Pretty much/ Great deal	None/ Little	Some	Pretty much/ Great deal
Total	(212)	34%	25%	41%	31%	31%	38%	19%	22%	59%

D4-4   Problems with Child Arrangements for Divorced or Separated Parents

I'm going to read a list of things that sometimes happen with arrangements for children to spend time with the other parent. How often, if even, did child's (mother/father) NOT show up for a visit, make last minute changes, and YOU make last minute changes?

	N	NOT Show Up			Make Changes			YOU Make Changes		
		Never/ Seldom	Some- times	Very often/ Always	Never/ Seldom	Some- times	Very often/ Always	Never/ Seldom	Some- times	Very often/ Always
Total	(424)	67%	17%	16%	56%	21%	23%	87%	11%	3%
Age of Respondent										
25-34	(728)	64%	21%	15%	58%	20%	22%	83%	15%	2%
35-44	(1374)	70%	16%	14%	55%	21%	24%	91%	7%	2%
45-64	(450)	73%	16%	11%	58%	26%	16%	91%	7%	2%
Highest Year in School										
Less than h.s.	(70)	59%	17%	24%	54%	19%	28%	77%	19%	4%
High school	(193)	66%	20%	14%	58%	20%	22%	89%	8%	3%
Some college	(110)	71%	15%	14%	55%	19%	26%	86%	13%	1%
16 + years	(50)	78%	12%	10%	54%	31%	15%	94%	6%	0%
Marital Status										
Married	(195)	69%	17%	14%	52%	25%	24%	87%	12%	1%
Widowed	(42)	71%	12%	17%	61%	20%	19%	90%	10%	0%
Divorced	(96)	65%	17%	19%	56%	21%	23%	90%	7%	3%
Never married	(88)	63%	22%	15%	61%	14%	25%	81%	14%	5%
Race of Respondent										
White	(258)	71%	16%	13%	50%	24%	26%	87%	10%	3%
Black	(117)	63%	17%	20%	64%	16%	20%	86%	12%	2%
Hispanic	(45)	56%	27%	17%	67%	16%	17%	84%	12%	5%
Sex of Respondent										
Male	(65)	71%	19%	11%	46%	23%	31%	91%	6%	3%
Female	(358)	67%	17%	16%	57%	20%	23%	86%	12%	2%

D4-5 Percent of Separated/Divorced Parents Who Keep Children 5–17 Years Old from Knowing about Conflict Between Them

How much do you try to keep child age 5-17 years old from knowing about your serious disagreements with his/her mother/father?

	N	A little	*Hide Conflict* Some	Pretty much	Great deal
Total	(447)	18%	18%	23%	42%

D4-6 Influence Divorced Parents Have on Major Decisions about Children

How much influence does child's (mother/father) have in making major decisions about such things as education, religion, and health care?

	N	None	A little	Some	Pretty much	A great deal
Total	(666)	59%	12%	13%	7%	10%
Age of Respondent						
18-24	(43)	74%	14%	2%	5%	5%
25-34	(265)	60%	10%	14%	5%	11%
35-44	(292)	56%	13%	12%	8%	10%
45-64	(63)	54%	13%	22%	5%	6%
Highest Year in School						
Less than h.s.	(138)	69%	5%	10%	4%	12%
High school	(295)	59%	16%	11%	6%	9%
Some college	(164)	54%	12%	18%	6%	10%
16 + years	(69)	46%	10%	19%	17%	8%
Race of Respondent						
White	(385)	59%	13%	14%	7%	7%
Black	(185)	58%	10%	11%	8%	12%
Hispanic	(87)	55%	12%	15%	5%	14%
Sex of Respondent						
Male	(95)	44%	15%	20%	7%	14%
Female	(571)	61%	12%	12%	7%	9%

5. PHYSICAL PUNISHMENT AND CHILD ABUSE

D5-1   Attitudes Regarding Spanking

Do you strongly agree, agree, disagree, or strongly disagree that it is sometimes necessary to discipline a child with a good hard spanking?

Spanking — Trend

	Agree strongly	Agree	Disagree	Disagree strongly	No opinion
1994 Mar. 28–30	21%	46%	23%	9%	1%

National Opinion Research Center — General Social Survey

	Agree strongly	Agree	Disagree	Disagree strongly	No opinion
1993 Feb.	23	50	20	7	1
1991 Feb.	26	48	19	6	2
1990 Feb.	28	50	17	4	1
1980 Feb.	31	45	17	5	1
1986 Feb.	28	56	13	3	1

Spanking, by Sex and Age

	Total agree	Total disagree	No opinion
Total	67%	32%	1%
Males	76	23	1
18-30	66	36	1
31-50	78	21	1
51 & over	81	18	1
Females	60	39	1
18-30	61	38	1
31-50	55	44	1
51 & over	65	33	3

Do you personally know any children you suspect have been physically or sexually abused?

Yes	13%
No	87%
No opinion	·
	100%

· Less than 0.5%

Have you reported your concerns to authorities, or talked with the child's parents or guardians, or talked with someone else who might speak with the parents, or were you not able to do anything about it?

Reported to authorities	35%
Spoke with parents	17
Spoke with someone else	13
Did not do anything	18
Did something else to try to stop abuse (vol.)	9
Did more than one thing	7
No opinion	1
	100%

D5-2 Frequency Parents Spank or Hit Children

Sometimes children behave well and sometimes they don't. In the last week, have you had to spank or hit (child) when she/he behaved badly?

	N	Child 5-17 years spanked or hit	Average number of times
Total	(1988)	10%	2
Age of Respondent			
18-24	(30)	37%	2
25-34	(543)	18%	2
35-44	(1058)	7%	1
45-64	(352)	2%	1
Highest Year in School			
Less than h.s.	(237)	14%	2
High school	(753)	10%	2
Some college	(499)	8%	2
16 + years	(495)	8%	1
Marital Status			
Married	(1629)	9%	2
Widowed	(26)	4%	1
Divorced	(168)	10%	1
Separated	(65)	11%	2
Never married	(100)	29%	2
Race of Respondent			
White	(1520)	9%	2
Black	(248)	15%	2
Other	(36)	6%	2
Hispanic	(181)	8%	2
Sex of Respondent			
Male	(852)	7%	2
Female	(1136)	12%	2

D5-3   Attitudes about Dealing with Child Abuse

For each of the following examples, please tell me whether or not you think it should be reported as child abuse or neglect: If a young child under the age of 6 is frequently left at home without a parent or other guardian for several hours; if a child is repeatedly slapped or spanked by parents or guardians; if a child is hit hard enough by a parent or guardian to leave bruises; if parents or adults in the house frequently use illegal drugs, or are frequently drunk from alcohol; if there is no food in the house and the house is filthy. (Follow-up): Do you think that situation justifies removing the children from the family—either temporarily or permanently, or not at all?

Report?

	Yes	No	No opinion
Left home unsupervised	93%	6%	1%
Repeatedly slapped/spanked	69	25	6
Bruised by beatings	84	12	4
Adults excessive drugs/alcohol	92	7	1
No food, house filthy	94	4	2

Remove?

	Temporarily	Permanently	Not at all	No opinion
Left home unsupervised	69%	12%	16%	3%
Repeatedly slapped/spanked	70	17	10	3
Bruised by beatings	65	21	11	3
Adults excessive drugs/alcohol	65	27	4	4
No food, house filthy	72	18	8	2

(SPLIT SAMPLE)

Form A: 545 respondents

Sometimes when children are removed from abusive families, they find permanent foster homes, but sometimes permanent foster homes are not available and the children are kept in state orphanages. If the choice for an abused child—who has been bruised frequently from physical beatings—is either being placed in a state orphanage or being returned to the parents who beat the child, which do you think would be better for the child: going to a state orphanage, or staying with parents?

State orphanage	77%
Stay with parents	13
Unsure	9
No opinion	1
	100%

Form B: 469 respondents

Sometimes when children are removed from abusive families, they find permanent foster homes, but sometimes permanent foster homes are not available and the children are moved from one temporary foster home to another. If the choice for an abused child—who has been bruised frequently from physical beatings—is either being moved from one foster home to another OR being returned to the parents who beat the child, which do you think would be better for the child: moving from foster home to foster home or staying with the parents?

Move from foster home to foster home	71%
Stay with parents	16
Unsure	12
No opinion	1
	100%

D5-4   Rating How Government, Society Deal with Child Abuse

QUESTION: Now on a related subject — how do you rate the way your state government, including social workers and the courts, deal with the problem of child abuse. Do you think the state government does an excellent job, good, fair, or a poor job? How do you rate the way society deals with the problem of child abuse? By society I mean doctors, teachers, friends, and neighbors. Do you think society does an excellent job, good, fair, or a poor job?

	Government response?					Societal response?					No. of interviews
	Excellent	Good	Fair	Poor	No opinion	Excellent	Good	Fair	Poor	No opinion	
National	1%	36%	24%	31%	8%	2%	45%	31%	19%	3%	1014
Sex											
Male	1	36	24	31	8	2	44	30	20	4	517
Female	1	36	25	31	7	2	46	31	18	3	497
Age											
18-29 years	1	40	23	30	6	4	50	27	18	1	185
20-49 years	1	37	26	30	6	2	47	33	18	•	439
50-64 years	1	34	25	33	7	3	42	30	21	4	188
65 & older	1	34	23	31	11	0	41	30	19	10	190
Region											
East	1	34	29	27	9	1	42	29	25	3	252
Midwest	•	40	23	26	11	3	49	30	13	5	244
South	1	36	21	37	5	3	46	28	21	2	308
West	1	34	25	34	6	1	44	36	16	3	210
Community											
Urban	1	34	25	33	7	3	41	31	21	4	403
Suburban	1	38	26	27	8	2	42	34	19	3	335
Rural	2	38	21	33	6	1	54	26	16	3	263
Race											
White	1	37	25	30	7	2	45	32	18	3	875
Non-white	3	34	20	37	6	3	47	25	23	2	126
Education											
College	1	38	21	33	7	3	42	34	20	1	168
Postgraduate	2	38	25	27	8	1	42	37	18	2	324
College graduate	•	36	26	28	10	2	45	33	18	2	294
Some college	1	35	24	34	6	2	48	26	20	4	388
No college											
Politics											
Republican	1	37	24	30	8	2	48	30	16	4	311
Democrat	1	37	28	29	5	2	50	30	17	1	309
Independent	1	35	22	33	9	2	40	31	22	5	394
Ideology											
Liberal	•	34	22	39	5	3	42	29	24	2	140
Moderate	1	39	27	27	6	2	48	31	18	1	422
Conservative	1	35	24	32	8	2	44	31	19	4	416
Income											
$50,000 & over	•	36	24	33	7	2	41	36	20	1	277
$30,000-49,999	2	38	26	29	5	2	49	33	14	2	259
$20,000-29,999	•	36	31	27	6	2	46	30	18	4	177
Under $20,000	1	35	22	33	9	2	46	27	22	3	231

•Less than one percent

D5-5 Number of Substantiated Cases of Child Abuse

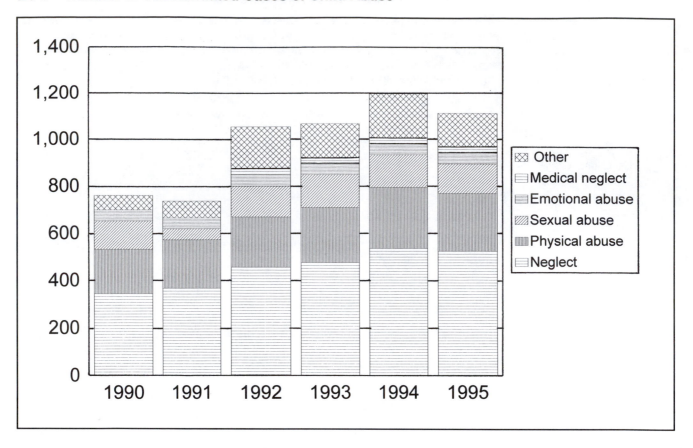

D5-6   Child Abuse and Neglect Cases Substantiated and Indicated—Victim Characteristics: 1990–1995

ITEM	1990 Number	1990 Percent	1993 Number	1993 Percent	1994 Number	1994 Percent	1995 Number	1995 Percent
TYPES OF SUBSTANTIATED MALTREATMENT								
Victims, total [1]	690,658	(X)	966,163	(X)	1,011,595	(X)	1,000,502	(X)
Neglect	338,770	49.1	472,170	48.9	520,550	51.5	523,049	52.3
Physical abuse	186,801	27.0	231,111	23.9	241,338	23.9	244,903	24.5
Sexual abuse	119,506	17.3	137,265	14.2	136,362	13.5	126,095	12.6
Emotional maltreatment	45,621	6.6	47,643	4.9	47,337	4.7	44,648	4.5
Medical Neglect	(NA)	(NA)	23,009	2.4	24,593	2.4	29,454	2.9
Other and unknown	61,477	8.9	145,096	15.0	153,894	15.2	144,733	14.5
SEX OF VICTIM								
Victims, total	794,101	100.0	926,322	100.0	903,195	100.0	834,174	100.0
Male	357,367	45.0	413,277	44.6	420,817	46.6	393,227	47.1
Female	405,409	51.1	470,658	50.8	472,535	52.3	437,407	52.4
Unknown	31,325	3.9	42,387	4.6	9,843	1.1	3,540	0.4
AGE OF VICTIM								
Victims, total	807,965	100.0	926,674	100.0	901,573	100.0	833,115	100.0
1 year and younger	106,507	13.2	121,700	13.1	119,203	13.2	105,375	12.6
2 to 5 years old	192,018	23.8	236,997	25.6	240,925	26.7	222,243	26.7
6 to 9 years old	175,609	21.7	209,292	22.6	210,334	23.3	202,315	24.3
10 to 13 years old	150,507	18.6	177,581	19.2	172,800	19.2	160,107	19.2
14 to 17 years old	116,015	14.4	133,866	14.4	132,566	14.7	125,221	15.0
18 and over	5,464	0.7	6,799	0.7	6,821	0.8	8,029	1.0
Unknown	61,845	7.7	40,439	4.4	18,924	2.1	9,825	1.2
RACE/ETHNIC GROUP OF VICTIM [2]								
Victims, total	793,773	100.0	926,924	100.0	895,831	100.0	822,609	100.0
White	428,506	54.0	497,924	53.7	499,485	55.8	456,163	55.5
Black	198,365	25.0	229,724	24.8	239,798	26.8	222,638	27.1
Asian and Pacific Islander	6,479	0.8	7,775	0.8	7,981	0.9	8,098	1.0
American Indian, Eskimo, and Aleut	10,323	1.3	13,657	1.5	15,098	1.7	14,819	1.8
Other races	11,088	1.4	13,659	1.5	13,678	1.5	15,412	1.9
Hispanic origin	73,590	9.3	85,067	9.2	85,332	9.5	84,754	10.3
Unknown	65,422	8.2	79,118	8.5	34,459	3.8	20,725	2.5

X Not applicable.   [1] More than one type of maltreatment may be substantiated per child. Therefore, totals for this category will add up to more than 100%. Victim totals and maltreatment types are based on subset of states which reported both the number of child victims and maltreatment incidences by type for that year. [2] Some States were unable to report on the number of Hispanic victims, thus it is probable that nationwide the percentage of Hispanic victims is higher.

D5-7   Child Abuse and Neglect Cases Reported and Investigated, by State: 1994 and 1995

STATE	1994				1995			
		Reports		Investigation disposition, number of children substantiated [2]		Reports		Investigation disposition, number of children substantiated [2]
	Population under 18 years old	Number of reports [1]	Number of children subject of a report		Population under 18 years old	Number of reports [1]	Number of children subject of a report	
United States . . .	68,024.000	1,979,797	2,939,170	1,011,595	68,739.952	1,988,514	2,959,237	1,000.502
Alabama	1,080,000	26,515	40,164	21,591	1,080,145	25,704	38,559	18,120
Alaska.	192,000	[3]10,071	10,071	6,774	189,253	9,898	9,898	8,142
Arizona	1,139,000	28,275	48,722	29,531	1,193,270	[3]26,180	43,762	25,154
Arkansas.	640,000	18,429	18,429	7,915	649,521	17,612	28,563	8,169
California.	8,677,000	352,059	449,177	159,031	8,793,616	364,432	458,262	166,418
Colorado	970,000	27,797	44,390	(NA)	981,200	32,382	52,517	7,602
Connecticut	788,000	24,038	37,043	27,618	797,733	24,669	38,701	23,762
Delaware.	175,000	5,275	9,441	2,542	178,826	5,448	9,659	2,300
District of Columbia . . .	119,000	5,612	13,369	5,636	114,652	5,185	12,341	5,916
Florida.	3,262,000	108,943	164,945	77,101	3,371,328	115,108	170,727	77,976
Georgia.	1,893,000	55,578	89,958	63,721	1,923,594	57,118	95,925	57,250
Hawaii.	304,000	[3]5,944	5,944	2,380	309,262	[3]5,601	5,601	2,635
Idaho	339,000	13,592	34,313	9,461	347,924	13,406	35,968	10,743
Illinois.	3,083,000	77,289	140,651	53,056	3,125,894	73,904	132,570	49,217
Indiana	1,473,000	41,725	62,553	25,343	1,487,359	43,429	67,390	22,493
Iowa	729,000	21,210	31,240	9,172	724,511	22,131	32,801	9,967
Kansas	690,000	[3]33,928	33,928	3,644	692,761	[3]30,552	30,552	3,264
Kentucky	970,000	37,911	59,540	25,940	972,708	40,470	63,313	28,630
Louisiana.	1,235,000	28,094	44,901	15,015	1,239,214	27,587	45,326	14,194
Maine	306,000	4,010	8,902	4,769	304,895	4,106	8,291	4,628
Maryland	1,263,000	25,908	41,373	(NA)	1,271,966	26,114	42,352	(NA)
Massachusetts	1,424,000	33,844	56,178	23,964	1,431,854	33,522	56,175	25,375
Michigan	2,525,000	57,394	136,989	21,951	2,519,455	57,914	139,289	21,165
Minnesota	1,241,000	17,967	28,286	10,438	1,245,492	16,991	26,213	10,142
Mississippi	756,000	17,322	27,123	7,982	761,909	16,786	27,224	5,588
Missouri.	1,379,000	52,754	86,007	15,842	1,381,552	52,931	85,927	17,764
Montana	238,000	8,905	13,528	4,194	236,134	8,905	13,528	4,194
Nebraska.	442,000	8,405	17,508	4,514	443,297	7,858	16,109	3,510
Nevada	376,000	13,329	21,286	8,037	398,586	12,716	20,623	7,791
New Hampshire	292,000	6,118	9,770	1,043	294,969	5,639	7,778	1,059
New Jersey	1,931,000	[3]65,954	65,954	9,519	1,963,523	[3]63,684	63,684	9,279
New Mexico	498,000	[3]24,933	24,933	7,356	500,099	[3]28,034	28,034	8,842
New York.	4,511,000	128,111	210,997	54,993	4,536,862	128,896	211,445	57,699
North Carolina	1,756,000	59,135	95,144	30,013	1,799,119	59,968	98,690	30,935
North Dakota	172,000	4,518	7,753	3,617	170,445	4,642	7,673	3,340
Ohio	2,854,000	96,747	156,635	61,806	2,859,848	95,001	156,975	58,416
Oklahoma	880,000	[3]34,846	34,846	10,891	878,039	[3]39,831	39,831	11,700
Oregon	783,000	26,436	42,216	7,946	797,040	26,765	43,407	8,991
Pennsylvania	2,898,000	[3]23,722	23,722	7,038	2,909,302	[3]24,109	24,109	6,891
Rhode Island	240,000	8,862	14,303	3,207	237,611	8,951	14,492	4,437
South Carolina	952,000	21,656	40,461	11,628	944,384	22,756	43,503	11,439
South Dakota	208,000	[3]10,156	10,156	1,923	206,436	[4]8,821	9,063	2,526
Tennessee	1,297,000	[3]34,714	34,714	12,175	1,310,297	[3]36,286	36,286	12,166
Texas	5,301,000	110,742	173,644	55,266	5,400,417	103,029	158,352	46,768
Utah	672,000	17,125	29,112	10,430	674,618	16,114	26,447	8,848
Vermont	146,000	2,579	3,025	1,234	146,760	2,197	2,618	1,122
Virginia	1,603,000	36,431	56,331	10,264	1,612,527	35,992	55,553	10,416
Washington	1,408,000	41,050	57,100	44,197	1,418,404	42,109	58,926	44,893
West Virginia	429,000	12,370	19,754	(NA)	421,868	12,370	19,544	(NA)
Wisconsin	1,347,000	[3]47,561	47,561	18,185	1,353,205	[3]44,661	44,661	17,118
Wyoming	138,000	3,908	5,080	1,702	136,268	(NA)	(NA)	1,508

NA Not available.   [1] Except as noted, reports are on incident/family based basis or based on number of reported incidents regardless of the number of children involved in the incidents.   [2] Type of investigation disposition that determines that there is sufficient evidence under State law to conclude that maltreatment occurred or that the child is at risk of maltreatment.   [3] Child-based report that enumerates each child who is a subject of a report.   [4] South Dakota has both child and incident based reports.

D5-8   Own Experience of Childhood Abuse

QUESTIONS: When you were growing up, do you remember any time when you were punched or kicked or choked by a parent or other adult guardian? Do you remember ever receiving a more serious physical punishment from a parent or adult guardian than being punched, kicked, or choked?

| | Punched, kicked, choked? | | | | Even more serious? | | | | |
	Yes	No	Not sure	No opinion	Yes	No	Not sure	No opinion	No. of interviews
National	12%	88%	•	•	5%	94%	1%	•	1014
Sex									
Male	13	85	1	1	5	94	1	•	517
Female	10	90	•	0	5	95	•	•	497
Age									
18-29 years	15	85	•	0	7	93	0	0	185
20-49 years	13	87	0	•	5	95	0	•	439
50-64 years	8	91	1	0	3	96	1	0	188
65 & older	8	90	1	1	4	94	1	1	190
Region									
East	14	86	0	•	5	95	0	0	252
Midwest	9	90	1	0	1	98	1	0	244
South	9	91	0	0	5	94	0	1	308
West	15	82	1	2	10	90	•	0	210
Community									
Urban	10	89	•	1	5	94	1	•	403
Suburban	13	87	0	0	5	95	•	0	335
Rural	12	87	•	•	6	94	0	•	263
Race									
White	12	88	•	•	5	95	•	•	875
Non-white	9	90	1	0	9	91	•	0	126
Education									
College	8	91	0	1	5	94	•	1	168
postgraduate	8	92	•	•	4	96	•	•	324
College graduate	8	87	•	0	8	92	0	0	294
Some college	13	86	•	•	4	95	1	•	388
No college	13								
Politics									
Republicans	6	94	0	0	3	96	1	0	311
Democrats	11	89	•	•	5	95	•	•	309
Independents	16	82	1	1	7	93	•	•	394
Ideology									
Liberal	21	76	0	3	9	91	0	0	140
Moderate	10	90	•	0	5	94	0	1	422
Conservative	10	90	•	•	3	96	1	•	416
Income									
$50,000 & over	6	94	0	0	2	98	0	•	277
$30,000-49,999	12	88	0	0	5	94	1	0	259
$20,000-29,999	11	89	•	0	7	93	0	0	177
Under $20,000	17	82	1	•	8	91	0	•	231

•Less than one percent

E. Sexual Attitudes and Behaviors and Contraceptive Use

1. SEXUAL EXPERIENCE

Although sexual activity is not necessarily a family characteristic, the biological connection between sexual intercourse and childbearing, the expectation that marriage incorporates sexual intimacy, and attitudes opposing extramarital sex clearly link sexual experience with family life. Because some of the information on sexual activity is derived from fertility studies, that information is only available about women. A majority of people experience first sexual intercourse in mid-to-late adolescence and before marriage (see Figure E1-6). Affection, curiosity, and readiness for sex are the most common reasons given for having voluntary sex the first time, and partners are often going steady at the time of first intercourse (Figure E1-8). Women often state that their first partner was older (Figure E1-6).

Frequency of sexual intercourse ranges from seldom or never to many times per week, but most adults fall within a more narrow range of more than once a month and less than three times per week (Table E1-12). Frequency of intercourse declines with age, and varies by race and marital status.

A majority of adults report having had sexual intercourse in the last year and nearly a third of women have had more than one partner in the last 12 months (Table E1-13). About one in five women have exhibited behaviors that place them at risk of HIV in the last 12 months, usually by having a male partner who has recently had other female partners (Table E1-14). About eight percent of women aged 15-44 have been treated for pelvic inflammatory disease.

2. ATTITUDES TOWARD PREMARITAL SEX AND OTHER SEXUAL ISSUES

Trends in attitudes toward sexual issues have been fairly stable since 1972 (Figure E2-1). The percentage who say premarital sex is wrong has declined and, in the last decade, the percentage saying homosexual relations are wrong has also declined. There is still strong disapproval for extramarital sex and strong approval for sex education in the school. Attitudes toward premarital sex and homosexual relationships vary by age, education, and marital status (Table E2-3). The population is about evenly divided on the issue of cohabitation (Table E2-5).

An increasing percentage of the population believes that homosexuality is an inborn trait, but 40 percent believe that upbringing or environment plays a role (Table E2-6). Fifty-six percent of the population now believe that homosexuals should reveal their homosexuality and 84 percent believe that employers should not discriminate on the basis of sexual orientation (Table E2-7 and Table E2-8), but 47 percent believe that homosexual relations between consenting adults should not be legal (Table E2-8).

A majority of women report that they have received some form of formal sex education (Table E2-9). Instruction on birth control and sexually transmitted infections is somewhat more common than instruction on prevention of HIV or how to say "no" to sex.

3. CONTRACEPTIVE USE AND ABORTION

A majority of women aged 15-44 are currently using some form of birth control (Table E3-1). Surgical sterilization has become the most common method of birth control. Many of those who are not using a method are pregnant, noncontraceptively sterile, or not sexually active (Table E3-1). Only about 5 percent are exposed to the risk of an unwanted pregnancy and are not contraceptive users. However, 40 percent of these women did not use contraceptives at first intercourse (Table E3-4).

The abortion rate has dropped noticeably since the mid-1980s (Table E3-5). In contrast, percentages concerning attitudes toward abortion have been fairly level (Figure E3-8). A substantial majority favor legal abortions if the baby has a serious defect, the mother's health is in danger, or if the pregnancy resulted from rape (Table E3-9). In cases where the mother is single, she wants no more kids, or she is too poor to support another child, attitudes are very divided. Finally, a majority favors legalization of the French abortion pill (Table E3-11).

4. INVOLUNTARY INTERCOURSE AND RAPE

After a steady increase in the 1980s and early 1990s, the rate of rape has declined somewhat in the last few years (Figure E4-1). One fifth of women aged 15-44 have been forced to have sexual intercourse (Table E4-2). Rates are particularly high for women who were formerly married, who lived with a nonbiological parent, or did not complete high school. Nearly 8 percent of women had involuntary sex at first intercourse. Involuntary first intercourse is particularly high when it occurs before age 16 (Table E4-4).

1. SEXUAL EXPERIENCE

E1-1   Average Age at First Sexual Intercourse

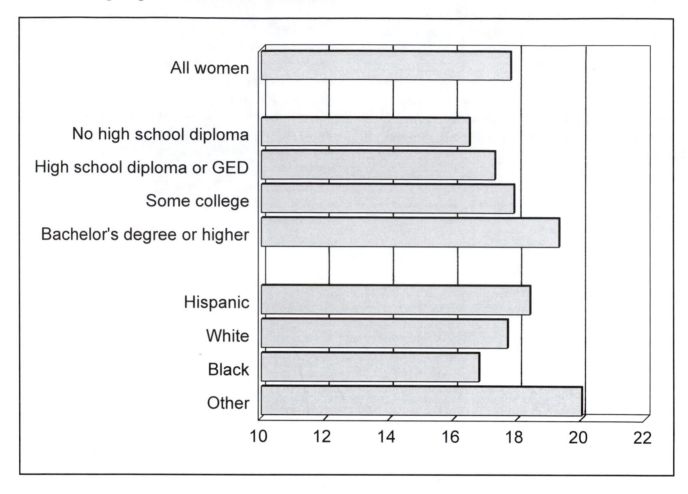

E1-2   Number of Women 15–44 Years of Age and Percent Who Have Ever Had Sexual Intercourse After Menarche for All Women and Never-Married Women, by Age at Interview and by Age and Race and Hispanic Origin for Teenagers: United States, 1995

Age and race and Hispanic origin	All women		Never-married women	
	Number in thousands	Percent	Number in thousands	Percent
All women[1]	60,201	89.3	22,679	71.5
Age at interview				
15 years	1,690	22.1	1,674	21.4
16 years	1,874	38.0	1,874	38.0
17 years	1,889	51.1	1,831	49.6
18 years	1,771	65.4	1,641	62.7
19 years	1,737	75.5	1,542	72.4
15-19 years	8,961	50.4	8,562	48.1
15-17 years	5,452	37.6	5,379	36.8
18-19 years	3,508	70.4	3,183	67.4
20-24 years	9,041	88.6	5,939	82.6
25-29 years	9,693	95.9	3,456	88.6
30-44 years	32,506	98.2	4,722	87.4
Age at interview and race and Hispanic origin				
15-19 years:				
Hispanic	1,150	55.0	1,078	52.0
Non-Hispanic white	5,962	49.5	5,693	47.1
Non-Hispanic black	1,392	59.5	1,351	58.3
15-17 years:				
Hispanic	688	50.0	673	48.8
Non-Hispanic white	3,534	34.9	3,485	33.9
Non-Hispanic black	853	48.2	853	48.2
18-19 years:				
Hispanic	462	62.5	405	57.2
Non-Hispanic white	2,428	70.7	2,208	67.8
Non-Hispanic black	538	77.4	498	75.5

[1]Includes women of other race and origin groups not shown separately.

E1-3   Number of Women 20–44 Years of Age and Cumulative Percent Who Have Ever Had Sexual Intercourse After Menarche and Before Reaching Selected Ages: United States, 1995

Characteristic	Number in thousands	Exact age in years			Mean age at first intercourse[1]
		15	18	20	
All women	51,240	9.2	52.3	75.0	17.8
Age at interview					
20-24 years	9,041	13.6	62.2	80.2	16.6
25-29 years	9,693	10.9	54.9	75.0	17.5
30-34 years	11,065	10.1	53.1	75.8	17.8
35-39 years	11,211	7.6	52.2	75.2	18.0
40-44 years	10,230	4.6	40.6	69.2	18.6
Family background					
Both parents from birth[2]	32,825	6.4	45.6	70.3	18.2
Single parent from birth	1,548	18.4	66.2	84.9	16.6
Both parents, then 1 parent	6,469	11.5	60.6	79.4	17.3
Stepparent[3]	6,655	15.2	70.4	88.1	16.6
Other	3,743	15.6	59.8	81.5	17.1
Education at interview[4]					
No high school diploma or GED[5]	5,424	20.4	73.0	87.1	16.5
High school diploma or GED	18,169	11.2	59.8	83.1	17.3
Some college, no bachelor's degree	12,399	7.0	49.5	73.6	17.9
Bachelor's degree or higher	11,748	2.2	31.7	56.6	19.3
Mother's education					
0-11 years	15,798	11.5	55.3	77.1	17.6
12 years	21,813	9.1	54.0	77.5	17.6
13-15 years	6,866	7.2	47.8	70.1	18.1
16 years or more	6,466	5.1	43.0	65.7	18.3
No mother figure identified	307	31.8	81.5	90.9	15.9
Race and Hispanic origin					
Hispanic	5,553	7.6	42.2	66.7	18.4
Non-Hispanic white	36,560	8.3	52.8	76.0	17.7
Non-Hispanic black	6,818	16.1	66.9	85.6	16.8
Non-Hispanic other	2,309	8.1	28.4	48.1	20.0

[1]Mean ages are based only on women who ever had intercourse after menarche.
[2]Includes women who lived with either both biological or both adoptive parents until they left home.
[3]Parents separated or divorced, then custodial parent remarried.
[4]Limited to women 22-44 years of age at time of interview.
[5]GED is general equivalency diploma.

E1-4 Number of Ever-Married Women 15–44 Years of Age and Percent Distribution by Timing of First Sexual Intercourse After Menarche in Relation to First Marriage, According to Selected Characteristics: United States, 1995

Characteristic	Number in thousands	Total	First intercourse after or same month as marriage	Months from first intercourse to marriage intercourse			
				Less than 12 months	12-35 months	36-59 months	60 months or more
All women	37,521	100.0	17.8	11.5	20.6	17.6	32.5
Age at interview							
15-19 years	399	100.0	17.3	11.6	29.9	36.1	5.1
20-24 years	3,102	100.0	13.6	8.0	25.5	25.9	27.0
25-29 years	6,237	100.0	15.7	7.9	18.3	18.8	39.3
30-34 years	8,846	100.0	13.5	9.6	18.1	18.7	40.2
35-39 years	9,694	100.0	17.7	12.3	21.0	16.3	32.8
40-44 years	9,244	100.0	25.0	16.1	22.2	13.6	23.2
Year of first marriage							
1990-95	8,240	100.0	11.0	3.8	11.6	17.5	56.1
1985-89	7,753	100.0	13.0	6.5	16.8	17.9	45.8
1980-84	7,747	100.0	16.4	10.2	19.1	20.3	33.9
1975-79	7,031	100.0	21.2	14.1	27.7	19.3	17.6
1965-74	6,751	100.0	29.6	25.4	30.4	12.5	2.1
Family background							
Both parents from birth[1]	25,000	100.0	20.3	11.7	20.7	16.8	30.6
Single parent from birth	859	100.0	15.8	11.1	18.1	19.5	35.5
Both parents, then 1 parent	4,227	100.0	13.7	10.5	19.6	17.8	38.4
Stepparent[2]	4,878	100.0	8.9	11.4	21.5	22.0	36.3
Other	2,557	100.0	17.5	11.9	20.8	16.5	33.4
Mother's education							
0-11 years	12,250	100.0	24.6	15.9	20.3	14.4	24.8
12 years	16,497	100.0	14.0	10.0	22.8	19.9	33.3
13-15 years	4,607	100.0	16.5	9.5	19.3	16.6	38.1
16 years or more	3,930	100.0	14.5	6.8	14.7	19.3	44.7
No mother figure identified	238	100.0	9.3	4.8	13.1	15.7	57.1
Poverty level income at interview[3]							
0-149 percent	6,788	100.0	21.7	14.6	21.0	16.1	26.6
0-99 percent	3,832	100.0	21.9	13.7	21.6	16.0	26.9
150-299 percent	11,473	100.0	19.8	12.6	22.4	19.4	25.9
300 percent or higher	18,102	100.0	15.2	9.8	18.7	16.0	40.4
Race and Hispanic origin							
Hispanic	4,116	100.0	37.7	14.9	15.3	11.1	20.9
Non-Hispanic white	28,250	100.0	14.6	11.4	22.2	19.0	32.8
Non-Hispanic black	3,536	100.0	8.1	9.3	17.4	18.1	47.2
Non-Hispanic other	1,619	100.0	44.4	9.8	13.8	8.2	23.8

[1]Includes women who lived with either both biological or both adoptive parents until they left home.
[2]Parents separated or divorced, then custodial parent remarried.
[3]Limited to women 22-44 years of age at time of interview.
NOTE: Percents may not add to 100 due to rounding.

E1-5   Relationship with First Partner

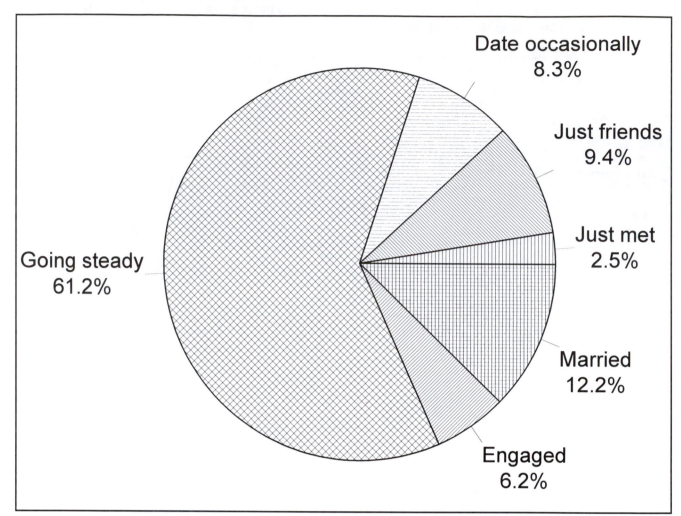

E1-6   Age of First Voluntary Partner

E1-7 Number of Women 15–44 Years of Age Who Have Ever Had Voluntary Sexual Intercourse and Percent Distribution by Age of First Voluntary Partner, According to Age at First Intercourse and Race and Hispanic Origin: United States, 1995

Age at first intercourse and race and Hispanic origin	Number in thousands	Total	Age of first voluntary partner in years					
			under 16	16-17	18-19	20-22	23-24	25 and over
			Percent Distribution					
All women[1]	53,614	100.0	5.8	23.4	26.3	22.3	8.4	13.9
Age at first intercourse								
Under 16 years	12,757	100.0	22.0	43.8	21.2	7.1	2.1	4.0
16 years	8,840	100.0	2.4	41.8	34.5	13.9	3.7	3.7
17 years	8,984	100.0	0.6	27.7	41.6	19.2	5.3	5.6
18 years	7,215	100.0	0.5	7.7	36.7	33.3	9.7	9.1
19 years	48,688	100.0	–	2.0	24.1	45.9	11.4	16.7
20-22 years	7,298	100.0	0.0	0.6	7.2	43.2	19.5	29.5
23-24 years	1,835	100.0	–	0.5	1.8	15.6	29.3	52.8
25 years and over	1,817	100.0	–	0.9	0.5	2.9	11.5	84.2
Race and Hispanic origin and age at first intercourse								
Hispanic	5,887	100.0	4.7	17.9	21.1	25.8	10.3	20.3
Under 16 years	1,305	100.0	17.3	37.3	22.3	14.1	2.9	6.1
16-19 years	2,960	100.0	1.4	18.3	28.4	30.0	9.4	12.6
20 years and over	1,622	100.0	–	1.0	6.7	27.8	18.2	46.2
Non-Hispanic white	38,110	100.0	5.3	24.0	27.2	22.8	8.6	12.2
Under 16 years	8,411	100.0	21.2	45.9	20.8	6.6	2.0	3.5
16-19 years	22,166	100.0	1.1	23.5	37.1	24.7	6.9	6.7
20 years and over	7,534	100.0	–	0.7	5.4	35.3	20.7	38.1
Non-Hispanic black	7,462	100.0	9.7	27.5	28.9	18.2	5.4	10.3
Under 16 years	2,684	100.0	26.0	41.1	21.6	5.7	1.7	4.0
16-19 years	3,946	100.0	0.5	23.8	39.1	24.2	5.2	7.2
20 years and over	832	100.0	0.2	0.3	3.9	31.0	18.7	46.0

- Quantity zero
0.0 Quantity more than zero but less than 0.05.
[1]Includes women of other race and origin groups not shown separately.
NOTE: Percents may not add to 100 due to rounding.

E1-8 Reasons for Having First Sexual Intercourse

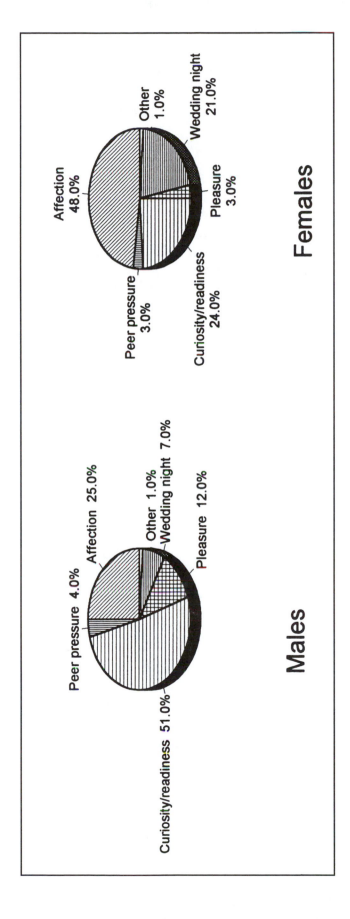

Females

Affection 48.0%

Other 1.0%

Wedding night 21.0%

Pleasure 3.0%

Curiosity/readiness 24.0%

Peer pressure 3.0%

Males

Peer pressure 4.0%

Affection 25.0%

Other 1.0%

Wedding night 7.0%

Pleasure 12.0%

Curiosity/readiness 51.0%

E1-9   Number of Women 15–44 Years of Age Who Have Ever Had Voluntary Sexual Intercourse and Percent Distribution by Type of Relationship with Partner at First Voluntary Intercourse, According to Selected Characteristics: United States, 1995

Characteristic	Number in thousands	Total	Just met	Just friends	Went out once in a while	Going steady	Engaged	Married	Other[1]
					Percent distribution				
All women	53,614	100.0	2.5	9.4	8.3	61.0	6.2	12.2	0.4
Age at interview									
15-19 years	4,506	100.0	2.8	10.5	9.7	72.7	2.8	1.5	0.1
20-24 years	7,956	100.0	3.5	10.2	8.3	69.4	2.9	5.4	0.4
25-29 years	9,269	100.0	2.5	10.0	8.5	63.8	5.1	9.9	0.3
30-34 years	10,766	100.0	1.9	9.3	9.4	61.9	6.5	10.5	0.5
35-39 years	11,047	100.0	2.9	9.4	8.2	56.4	7.5	15.2	0.5
40-44 years	10,071	100.0	1.6	8.1	6.6	50.8	9.4	23.0	0.7
Family background									
Both parents from birth[2]	33,137	100.0	2.3	8.2	8.0	59.3	6.8	15.1	0.4
Single parent from birth	1,843	100.0	2.8	14.0	8.5	62.9	4.9	6.0	0.9
Both parents, then 1 parent	7,072	100.0	2.7	11.1	8.1	63.5	6.2	8.0	0.5
Stepparent[3]	7,504	100.0	3.1	10.0	9.4	67.1	4.3	5.6	0.6
Other	4,058	100.0	2.1	13.6	9.6	58.9	4.8	10.6	0.6
Age at first intercourse									
Under 16 years	12,757	100.0	3.2	15.1	8.6	68.4	2.0	1.9	0.8
16 years	8,840	100.0	2.0	9.5	8.1	71.6	4.3	4.2	0.4
17 years	8,984	100.0	2.2	8.1	7.6	70.5	6.7	4.4	0.5
18 years	7,215	100.0	1.8	7.3	9.3	61.3	7.0	13.0	0.3
19 years	4,868	100.0	3.6	5.4	9.5	52.5	10.3	18.4	0.4
20 years and over	10,950	100.0	2.1	7.0	7.7	39.6	9.7	33.7	0.2
Mother's education									
0-11 years	16,321	100.0	2.1	10.2	9.1	53.0	7.8	17.3	0.5
12 years	22,874	100.0	2.5	9.3	7.4	64.1	6.2	10.2	0.4
13-15 years	7,422	100.0	2.6	8.4	8.6	64.3	5.6	10.2	0.3
16 years or more	6,627	100.0	2.8	8.9	9.4	66.7	2.8	9.0	0.5
No mother figure identified	370	100.0	6.8	14.9	7.9	58.1	4.1	5.5	2.7
Race and Hispanic origin									
Hispanic	5,887	100.0	2.0	8.0	7.1	49.2	7.9	25.2	0.6
Non-Hispanic white	7,462	100.0	2.6	8.3	8.6	62.9	6.4	10.8	0.5
Non-Hispanic black	38,110	100.0	1.9	16.2	8.7	65.8	3.6	3.5	0.3
Non-Hispanic other	2,154	100.0	3.8	9.3	6.2	43.1	5.8	31.5	0.3

[1]Other includes living together, family member, and other relationship types not shown separately.
[2]Includes women who lived with either both biological or both adoptive parents until they left home.
[3]Parents separated or divorced, then custodial parent remarried.
NOTE: Percents may not add to 100 due to rounding.

E1-10 Number of Unmarried Women 15–44 Years of Age and Percent Distribution by Number of Male Sexual Partners in the 12 Months Prior to Interview, According to Selected Characteristics, Based on Responses from Self-Administered Questionnaire: United States, 1995

Characteristic	Number in thousands	Total	Number of partners in last 12 months				
			0	1	2	3	4 or more
			Percent distribution				
All women	30,528	100.0	34.5	47.0	11.2	4.1	3.3
Age at interview							
15-19 years	8,619	100.0	55.8	28.6	8.2	3.7	3.7
20-24 years	6,578	100.0	23.1	52.3	14.9	5.2	4.6
25-29 years	4,604	100.0	20.4	58.0	13.7	4.9	2.9
30-34 years	3,912	100.0	24.0	55.8	12.7	4.6	2.9
35-39 years	3,603	100.0	30.6	52.0	11.5	3.3	2.7
40-44 years	3,212	100.0	37.9	53.4	5.4	2.0	1.2
Marital status							
Never married	22,679	100.0	39.4	43.7	10.0	3.8	3.2
Formerly married	7,849	100.0	20.3	56.7	14.5	4.9	3.7
Age at first intercourse							
Under 16 years	8,213	100.0	10.6	57.6	17.4	7.3	7.1
16 years	4,137	100.0	12.3	64.7	14.9	4.8	3.6
17 years	3,982	100.0	14.0	65.1	13.5	4.2	3.3
18 years	2,880	100.0	18.0	60.7	13.8	5.1	2.4
19 years	1,669	100.0	25.5	58.8	10.0	4.0	1.7
20 years and over	3,246	100.0	37.7	51.0	8.0	2.0	1.3
Education at interview[1]							
No high school diploma or GED[2]	2,617	100.0	19.2	63.6	10.6	3.6	3.1
High school diploma or GED	6,635	100.0	21.1	58.0	12.5	5.1	3.2
Some college, no bachelor's degree	5,236	100.0	28.6	51.8	13.3	3.6	2.7
Bachelors degree or higher	4,586	100.0	33.5	49.9	11.1	3.4	2.2
Poverty level income at interview[1]							
0-149 percent	6,190	100.0	22.3	56.0	14.0	5.2	2.6
0-99 percent	4,038	100.0	21.4	57.5	12.9	5.3	2.9
150-299 percent	6,033	100.0	27.2	53.0	12.1	4.7	3.0
300 percent or higher	6,851	100.0	28.0	56.3	10.4	2.6	2.8
Race and Hispanic origin							
Hispanic	3,524	100.0	41.2	45.7	6.9	2.5	3.6
Non-Hispanic white	19,445	100.0	35.1	46.5	11.1	3.9	3.4
Non-Hispanic black	6,141	100.0	23.7	52.5	14.7	6.0	3.1
Non-Hispanic other	1,418	100.0	56.1	32.6	7.0	2.4	1.9

[1]Limited to women 22-44 years of age at time of interview.
[2]GED is general equivalency diploma.
NOTE: Percents may not add to 100 due to rounding.

E1-11 Number of Women 15–44 Years of Age and Percent Distribution of Male Sexual Partners in Lifetime, According to Selected Characteristics, Based on Responses from Self-Administered Questionnaire: United States, 1995

Characteristic	Number in thousands	Total	Number of partners in lifetime							
			0[1]	1	2	3	4	5	6-9	10 or more
						Percent distribution				
All women	60,201	100.0	10.5	23.5	12.3	9.6	8.4	8.1	12.1	15.5
Age at interview										
15-19 years	8,961	100.0	46.8	19.4	11.0	7.9	3.6	2.9	5.7	3.7
20-24 years	9,041	100.0	11.0	21.6	13.4	11.5	9.0	7.7	11.9	13.9
25-29 years	9,693	100.0	4.3	22.0	13.5	10.1	9.2	10.1	13.8	16.9
30-34 years	11,065	100.0	2.8	23.4	11.8	9.1	11.5	9.7	13.7	18.0
35-39 years	11,211	100.0	1.8	24.3	11.7	9.4	8.5	9.3	14.5	20.5
40-44 years	10,230	100.0	2.4	29.4	12.6	9.7	8.0	8.4	11.7	17.7
Marital status at interview										
Married	29,673	100.0	0.5	34.5	13.8	9.9	8.9	8.0	11.2	13.2
Unmarried	30,528	100.0	20.2	12.8	10.9	9.4	7.9	8.2	12.8	17.7
Never married	22,679	100.0	26.8	14.3	11.3	9.2	7.3	6.9	10.7	13.6
Formerly married	7,849	100.0	0.8	8.6	9.7	9.8	9.8	12.0	19.4	29.8
Age at first intercourse										
Under 16 years	13,944	100.0	(NA)	11.3	11.2	10.2	8.6	10.6	18.5	29.0
16 years	8,750	100.0	(NA)	18.6	12.6	12.9	10.9	9.4	16.5	18.8
17 years	8,764	100.0	(NA)	17.3	14.4	11.4	12.3	12.5	13.1	18.8
18 years	6,941	100.0	(NA)	26.0	14.3	11.0	11.0	9.0	13.1	14.9
19 years	4,759	100.0	(NA)	37.6	14.7	11.6	8.0	7.2	11.0	9.2
20 years and over	10,653	100.0	(NA)	52.2	16.5	8.6	6.3	4.7	5.9	4.6
Education at interview[2]										
No high school diploma or GED[3]	5,424	100.0	1.3	27.7	15.8	10.1	7.6	10.1	11.7	15.8
High school diploma or GED	18,169	100.0	2.5	23.5	13.0	10.8	9.8	9.6	13.7	17.1
Some college, no bachelor's degree	12,399	100.0	4.6	22.3	10.3	9.6	9.1	10.2	14.1	19.9
Bachelor's degree or higher	11,748	100.0	4.7	26.1	11.7	8.6	9.5	7.1	13.5	18.9
Poverty level income at interview[2]										
0-149 percent	10,072	100.0	3.8	21.8	13.7	9.9	9.4	10.1	13.6	17.7
0-99 percent	5,992	100.0	4.1	22.3	13.7	9.7	10.0	10.3	12.4	17.6
150-299 percent	14,932	100.0	3.9	25.7	13.4	9.4	9.2	8.7	12.1	17.6
300 percent or higher	22,736	100.0	3.0	24.4	11.0	10.1	9.3	9.1	14.4	18.7
Race and Hispanic origin										
Hispanic	6,702	100.0	12.1	37.1	15.8	8.9	5.1	5.7	6.9	8.5
Non-Hispanic white	42,522	100.0	10.1	22.4	11.7	9.6	8.6	8.0	13.2	16.4
Non-Hispanic black	8,210	100.0	8.3	14.2	12.1	11.4	11.6	11.6	12.1	18.8
Non-Hispanic other	2,767	100.0	19.8	35.9	14.8	5.7	4.0	4.9	7.2	7.8

(NA) Category not applicable.
[1]Never had intercourse, or never had voluntary intercourse if first intercourse was not voluntary.
[2]Limited to women 22-44 years of age at time of interview.
[3]GED is general equivalency diploma
NOTE: Percents may not add to 100 due to rounding.

E1-12 Frequency of Sexual Intercourse in the Last Month: Married Respondents

	Number of Times
Total (percent)	5.4
Age of Respondent	
18-24	8.6
25-34	8.1
35-44	6.3
45-64	4.5
65 +	2.0
Highest Year in School	
Less than high school	4.9
High school	5.6
Some college	6.0
16 + years	4.9
Race of Respondent	
Black	6.3
White	5.3
Hispanic	6.6
Other	5.9
Sex of Respondent	
Male	5.2
Female	5.7

E1-13 Number of Women 15–44 Years of Age and Percent Reporting the Specified HIV Risk Behaviors in the 12 Months Prior to Interview, by Selected Characteristics: United States, 1995

Characteristic	Number in thousands	Respondent injected drugs without prescription in last year	Partner behavior[1] Had sex with other men since 1980	Partner behavior[1] Injected drugs without prescription since 1980	Partner behavior[1] Had sex with other women around same time as sex with respondent
			Percent		
All women[2]	60,201	1.2	2.0	2.5	14.3
Marital status at interview					
Married	29,672	0.6	1.6	1.2	4.2
Unmarried	30,528	1.8	2.4	4.3	28.4
Never married	22,679	1.7	2.4	4.1	28.7
Formerly married	7,849	2.1	2.5	4.9	27.7
Unmarried women Age at interview:					
15-19 years	8,619	2.0	2.6	6.2	29.8
20-24 years	6,578	1.2	2.0	3.2	30.4
25-44 years	15,331	2.0	2.5	4.2	26.9
Number of male sexual partners in last 12 months (based on Audio CASI):[1]					
None	9,447	1.0	–	1.0	10.4
1 man	12,210	1.7	2.0	2.6	15.2
2 men	4,201	2.3	1.7	5.2	39.9
3 or more men	4,204	3.6	4.2	9.0	57.4
Education at interview:[3]					
No high school diploma or GED[4]	2,617	4.3	3.7	7.2	25.5
High school diploma or GED	6,635	2.1	2.8	3.7	28.3
Some college, no bachelor's degree	5,236	1.0	1.8	3.4	26.3
Bachelor's degree or higher	4,586	1.0	2.1	2.1	28.5
Race and Hispanic origin:					
Hispanic	3,524	1.2	3.0	3.9	28.6
Non-Hispanic white	19,445	1.7	1.9	4.6	25.2
Non-Hispanic black	6,141	2.6	2.0	3.3	35.2
Non-Hispanic other	1,418	1.0	11.8	8.1	38.8

–Zero quantity.

[1]Partner behavior questions were inapplicable if respondent reported zero partners in the last 12 months, based on both interviewer-administered and self-administered (Audio CASI) questions. Audio CASI is audio computer-assisted self-interviewing. The partner behavior questions asked only about partners that the respondent had intercourse with in the 12 months prior to interview.

[2]Includes women with missing information on specific HIV risk behaviors, number of partners in last 12 months, or consistency of condom use.

[3]Limited to women 22-44 years of age at time of interview.

[4]GED is general equivalency diploma.

NOTE: HIV is human immunodeficiency virus, the virus that causes acquired immunodeficiency syndrome (AIDS).

E1-14 Number of Women 15–44 Years of Age and Percent Ever Treated for Pelvic Inflammatory Disease, by Race and Hispanic Origin and Selected Characteristics: United States, 1995

Characteristic	Number of women in thousands[1]				Percent ever treated for pelvic inflammatory disease			
	Total[2]	Hispanic	Non-Hispanic white	Non-Hispanic black	Total[2]	Hispanic	Non-Hispanic white	Non-Hispanic black
All women	60,201	6,702	42,522	8,210	7.6	7.9	7.2	10.6
Age at interview								
15-19 years	8,961	1,150	5,962	1,392	2.7	3.4	2.5	3.0
20-24 years	9,041	1,163	6,062	1,328	6.1	5.6	6.6	6.4
25-29 years	9,693	1,217	6,694	1,346	6.7	6.2	5.6	12.8
30-34 years	11,065	1,233	7,870	1,456	8.5	8.7	7.8	13.8
35-39 years	11,211	1,067	8,242	1,439	11.5	15.3	10.8	15.3
40-44 years	10,230	873	7,691	1,249	8.7	9.5	8.3	12.1
Marital status								
Never married	22,679	2,587	14,271	4,674	4.9	4.1	4.0	8.6
Currently married	29,673	3,178	23,077	2,069	8.2	9.5	7.9	13.2
Formerly married	7,849	938	5,174	1,467	12.8	13.3	13.1	13.3
Parity								
0 births	25,242	2,331	18,512	3,061	6.6	4.8	5.5	7.8
1 birth	10,706	1,202	7,331	1,698	8.1	9.1	8.3	8.7
2 births	13,875	1,361	10,293	1,683	8.9	9.3	8.3	12.2
3 or more births	10,377	1,809	6,385	1,769	10.1	10.2	9.2	15.9
Regular douching								
Yes	16,113	2,228	8,818	4,520	11.7	9.9	12.4	11.9
No	43,890	4,447	33,610	3,646	6.1	7.0	5.9	9.2
Number of male sexual partners in lifetime[3]								
1 man	13,978	2,455	9,454	1,065	4.9	8.3	4.4	5.6
2-3 men	13,405	1,739	9,118	1,964	6.6	10.3	6.0	7.5
4-9 men	17,223	1,201	12,598	2,978	9.2	5.6	8.9	11.9
10 or more men	9,585	588	7,183	1,579	14.3	13.6	13.5	19.3
Age at first sexual intercourse								
Never had intercourse[4]	6,612	820	4,431	748	0.7	2.0	0.3	0.8
Under 15 years	5,906	639	3,630	1,443	11.7	8.1	11.8	14.8
15-17 years	24,588	2,206	18,044	3,780	9.7	9.1	9.2	12.5
18-19 years	12,125	1,415	8,866	1,404	6.8	7.8	6.6	8.2
20 years or older	10,969	1,622	7,550	835	5.5	9.4	5.0	7.8

[1]Includes women with missing information on douching.
[2]Includes women of other race and origin groups not shown separately.
[3]Based on interviewer-administered and self-administered (Audio CASI) questions. Audio CASI is audio computer-assisted self- interviewing.
[4]Never had voluntary intercourse, or never had (voluntary) intercourse since first menstrual period.

E1-15 Number of Unmarried Women 15–44 Years of Age Who Have Had Intercourse in the 12 Months Prior to Interview and Percent Distribution by How Often Their Male Partners Used Condoms for Disease Prevention, According to Selected Characteristics: United States, 1995

Characteristic	Number in thousands	Total	Every time	More than half the time	Half the time	Less than half the time	Not at all
				Percent distribution			
All women[1]	12,708	100.0	31.3	13.9	8.4	13.9	32.5
Age at interview and number of male sexual partners in the 12 months prior to interview[2]							
15-29 years	8,570	100.0	32.2	15.1	9.6	13.8	29.3
30-44 years	4,139	100.0	29.5	11.4	5.9	14.1	39.2
1 partner	8,197	100.0	31.6	9.0	6.1	10.9	42.3
2 or more partners	4,504	100.0	30.9	22.7	12.6	19.4	14.5
15-29 years:							
1 partner	5,315	100.0	32.7	10.1	7.3	10.4	39.5
2 or more partners	3,252	100.0	31.4	23.2	13.4	19.4	12.5
30-44 years:							
1 partner	2,882	100.0	29.6	7.0	3.9	11.8	47.6
2 or more partners	1,251	100.0	29.5	21.4	10.4	19.4	19.4
Race and Hispanic origin of woman and number of male sexual partners in the 12 months prior to interview							
Hispanic	1,077	100.0	30.9	15.4	11.3	13.7	28.7
1 partner	707	100.0	29.8	12.5	9.4	11.5	36.8
2 or more partners	370	100.0	33.1	21.0	14.9	17.8	13.2
Non-Hispanic white	8,202	100.0	27.7	13.0	8.1	14.7	36.5
1 partner	5,341	100.0	28.6	7.7	5.9	10.5	47.4
2 or more partners	2,861	100.0	26.2	23.0	12.1	22.5	16.3
Non-Hispanic black	3,042	100.0	39.2	15.4	9.2	12.8	23.4
1 partner	1,890	100.0	38.4	12.0	6.4	12.3	30.8
2 or more partners	1,153	100.0	40.5	21.0	13.8	13.6	11.2
Education at interview[3]							
No high school diploma or GED[4]	2,128	100.0	26.6	13.9	7.6	10.8	41.1
High school diploma or GED	5,247	100.0	26.2	12.5	7.6	14.5	39.1
Some college, no bachelor's degree	3,779	100.0	29.7	10.6	6.1	13.9	39.7
Bachelor's degree or higher	3,111	100.0	32.4	13.6	7.0	12.0	35.1

[1]Includes women with missing information on number of partners in the 12 months prior to interview.
[2]Number of partners is based on the interviewer-administered question.
[3]Limited to women 22-44 years of age at time of interview.
[4]GED is general equivalency diploma.
NOTES: The frequency of condom use for disease prevention was asked only for a subset of respondents. If she reported ever using condoms for disease prevention in her life AND she had at least 1 sexual partner in the past 12 months, she was asked how often she used condoms in the past 12 months for this purpose. Percents may not add to 100 due to rounding.

2. ATTITUDES TOWARD PREMARITAL SEX AND OTHER SEXUAL ISSUES

E2-1   Trend in Attitudes Toward Sex

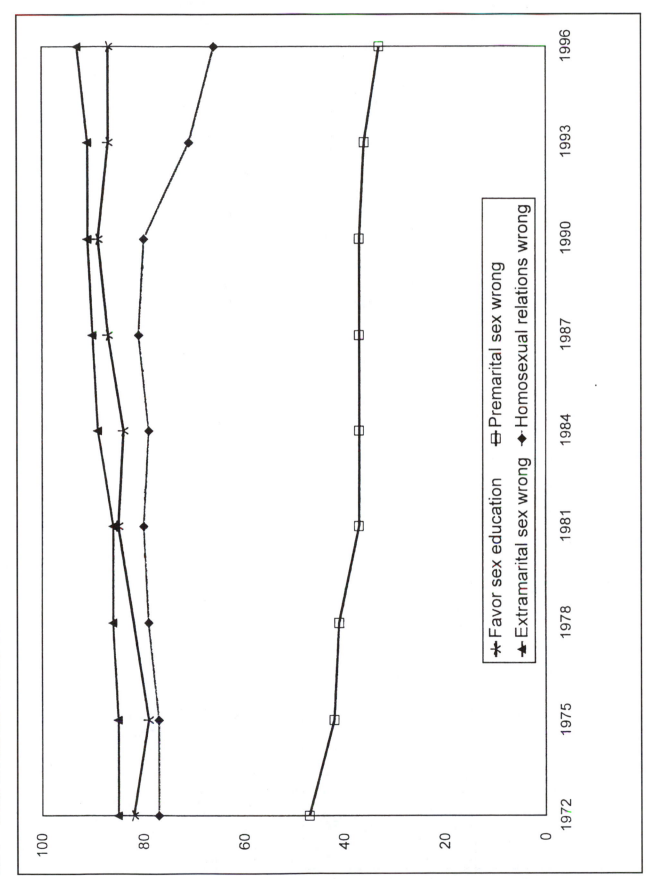

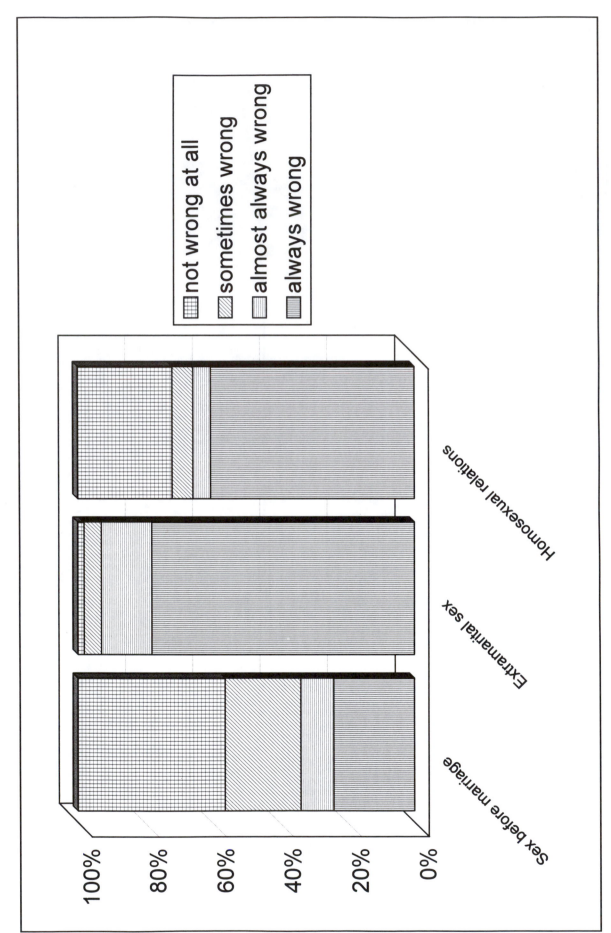

E2-2 Attitudes Toward Sexual Behaviors, 1996

E2-3 Attitudes Toward Sexual Behaviors, 1996

Percent who say behavior is always or almost always wrong:

	premarital sex	extramarital sex	homosexual relations
Total	33.5	92.9	65.6
Age of Respondent			
18-24	22.5	92.0	46.7
25-34	25.1	92.9	58.7
35-44	28.8	92.5	66.6
45-64	35.2	92.9	66.7
65 +	56.5	94.6	85.5
Highest Year in School			
Less than h.s.	41.3	92.5	79.8
High school	34.5	94.7	73.5
Some college	33.4	92.4	63.7
16 + years	27.7	91.9	49.4
Marital Status			
Married	39.0	95.1	71.7
Widowed	51.9	95.7	83.2
Divorced	24.3	91.6	65.0
Separated	28.2	88.6	64.4
Never married	21.5	89.2	46.6
Race of Respondent			
White	32.5	93.7	63.7
Black	39.6	88.4	75.1
Other	31.3	93.1	69.1
Sex of Respondent			
Male	27.3	91.2	67.9
Female	38.3	94.4	63.8

E2-4 Attitudes Toward Sex Education, 1996

Percent who favor sex education in the public schools:

Total	87.4
Age of Respondent	
18-24	95.4
25-34	93.5
35-44	86.4
45-64	86.9
65 +	75.7
Highest Year in School	
Less than h.s.	78.3
High school	87.7
Some college	90.3
16 + years	89.5
Marital Status	
Married	84.1
Widowed	78.4
Divorced	91.3
Separated	86.2
Never married	95.4
Race of Respondent	
White	87.0
Black	89.6
Other	87.2
Sex of Respondent	
Male	86.6
Female	87.9

E2-5   Beliefs About Cohabitation and Sexual Behavior

	Strongly Agree	Agree	Neither Agree nor Disagree	Disagree	Strongly Disagree
It is all right for an unmarried couple to live together even if they have no interest in marriage.	18.4	23.8	26.4	20.9	10.5
It is all right for unmarried 18-year-olds to have sexual relations if they have strong affection for each other.	3.2	17.1	28.2	28.0	23.5
It is all right for an unmarried couple to live together as long as they have plans to marry.	3.4	20.0	37.1	22.8	16.7

E2-6   Homosexuality: Nature or Nurture?

QUESTION: In your view, is homosexuality something a person is born with or is homosexuality due to other factors, such as upbringing or environment?

	Born With	Upbringing/ Environment	Both (vol.)	Neither (vol.)	No opinion	Number of Interviews
National	31%	40	13	3	13	1003
Sex						
Male	26%	46	10	4	14	502
Female	36%	35	16	2	11	501
Age						
18-29 years	21%	52	19	2	6	211
30-49 years	33%	42	12	3	10	443
50-64 years	35%	32	13	1	19	166
65 & older	35%	32	9	3	1	154
Region						
East	39%	35	10	2	14	248
Midwest	29%	40	15	2	14	214
South	27%	46	13	4	10	310
West	31%	36	15	4	14	231
Community						
Urban	30%	42	15	4	9	399
Suburban	35%	36	12	2	15	426
Rural	26%	45	12	4	13	178
Race						
White	32%	39	13	2	14	816
Black	27%	55	9	3	6	101
Education						
College post-graduate	39%	29	18	4	10	155
Bachelor's degree only	35%	34	17	2	12	183
Some college	32%	39	15	3	11	284
High school or less	27%	47	10	2	14	374
Politics						
Republicans	19%	53	12	2	14	288
Democrats	39%	33	15	3	10	370
Independents	33%	37	13	3	14	345
Ideology						
Liberal	38%	34	16	3	9	184
Moderate	40%	32	15	2	11	409
Conservative	19%	53	10	4	14	374
Clinton approval						
Approve	37%	36	14	2	11	589
Disapprove	24%	50	11	3	12	347
Income						
$75,000 & over	37%	26	21	1	15	147
$50,000 & over	36%	35	16	2	11	303
$30,000-49,999	36%	39	10	3	12	266
$20,000-29,999	28%	41	15	3	13	156
Under $20,000	22%	48	15	1	14	201
Religion						
Protestant	29%	44	13	3	11	562
Catholic	36%	36	12	3	13	258
Born-again						
Yes	22%	54	11	4	9	392
No	39%	30	16	1	14	543

	Trend			
	Born with	Upbringing/ Environment	Both (vol.)	Neither/ no opinion
1996	31%	40	13	16
1989	19%	48	12	21
1982	17%	52	13	18
1977	13%	56	14	18

E2-7   Should Homosexuals "Come Out?"

QUESTION: Do you agree or disagree with the following statement: I would prefer that homosexuals stay in the closet, which means that they do not openly reveal their homosexuality.

	Agree (stay in closet)	Disagree (should reveal)	No opinion	No. of interviews
National	37%	56%	7%	1005
Sex				
Male	45	48	7	507
Female	30	63	7	498
Age				
18-29 years	36	62	2	232
30-49 years	33	60	7	424
50-64 years	40	52	8	190
65 & older	46	44	10	148
Region				
East	25	66	9	244
Midwest	37	57	6	263
South	46	46	8	304
West	39	58	3	194
Community				
Urban	33	60	7	441
Suburban	37	58	5	332
Rural	45	46	9	226
Race				
White	38	55	7	886
Non-white	30	65	5	113
Education				
College postgrad.	34	61	5	144
College graduate	31	63	6	304
No college	40	52	8	394
Politics				
Republicans	46	48	6	276
Democrats	29	64	7	310
Independents	37	56	7	419
Ideology				
Liberal	26	70	4	185
Moderate	32	61	7	440
Conservative	49	44	7	354
Clinton approval				
Approve	31	63	6	545
Disapprove	48	45	7	385
Causes of homosexuality				
Inborn	24	71	5	321
Other reasons	45	49	6	477
Not sure	38	49	13	207

E2-8 Attitudes Regarding Homosexual Relationships

Do you think homosexual relations between consenting adults should or should not be legal?

Relations Legal–Trend

	Yes	No	No opinion
1996	44%	47%	9%
1992	48%	44%	8%
1989	47%	36%	17%
1987	33%	55%	12%
1986	33%	54%	13%
1985	44%	47%	9%
1982	45%	39%	16%
1977	43%	43%	14%

As you may know, there has been considerable discussion in the news regarding the rights of homosexual men and women. In general, do you think homosexuals should or should not have equal rights in terms of job opportunities?

Equal Job Opportunities–Trend

	Yes	No	Depends (vol.)/ no opinion
1996	84%	12%	4%
1993	80%	14%	6%
1992	74%	18%	8%
1989	71%	18%	11%
1982	59%	28%	13%
1977	56%	33%	11%

Do you think homosexuals should or should not be hired for each of the following occupations?

Hired in Following Occupations–Trend
(percent saying "yes")

	1977	1982	1985	1987	1989	1992	1996
Salespersons	68%	70%	71%	72%	79%	82%	90%
As a member of the president's cabinet	NA	NA	NA	NA	NA	54%	71%
Doctors	44%	50%	52%	49%	56%	53%	69%
Armed forces	51%	52%	55%	55%	60%	57%	65%
Clergy	36%	38%	41%	42%	44%	43%	60%
High school teachers	NA	NA	NA	NA	47%	47%	60%
Elementary school teachers	27%	32%	36%	33%	42%	41%	55%

E2-9 Number of Women 18–44 Years of Age and Percent Who Had Formal Instruction about the Specified Sex-Education Topics Before They Were 18, by Selected Characteristics: United States, 1995

Characteristic	Received Number in thousands	Birth any formal instruction	Sexually control methods	Topic of formal instruction		
				Safe sex transmitted diseases	How to to prevent HIV[1]	How to say no to sex
All women	54,748	72.8	62.0	62.7	52.0	55.0
Age at interview						
18-19 years	3,508	95.9	86.9	93.2	91.3	89.9
20-24 years	9,041	89.2	80.9	82.1	64.1	80.1
25-29 years	9,692	80.4	71.7	71.1	27.0	62.0
30-34 years	11,065	73.0	62.3	60.8	11.6	49.3
35-39 years	11,211	65.0	53.7	55.5	(NA)	41.5
40-44 years	10,230	51.4	36.2	37.0	(NA)	35.2
Family background						
Both parents from birth[2]	34,610	71.7	60.0	61.2	51.1	53.7
Single parent from birth	1,760	70.5	61.0	60.2	55.7	57.6
Both parents, then 1 parent	6,979	74.6	65.3	64.6	53.5	57.5
Stepparent[3]	7,386	76.3	66.6	67.5	52.4	58.6
Other	4,013	73.9	65.1	64.9	52.4	54.2
Residence at interview						
Metropolitan, central city	16,781	73.5	63.3	63.8	51.0	56.9
Metropolitan, suburban	26,941	73.0	61.4	62.4	50.5	53.8
Nonmetropolitan	11,026	71.0	61.5	62.0	57.0	55.0
Mother's education						
0-11 years	16,454	64.9	54.1	53.9	49.0	49.0
12 years	23,251	74.2	63.0	64.3	51.9	55.9
13-15 years	7,480	79.6	69.0	69.5	56.1	59.6
16 years or more	7,210	79.6	69.0	70.8	51.9	61.2
No mother figure identified	353	74.2	67.0	65.1	61.7	60.1
Poverty level income at interview[4]						
0-149 percent	10,072	65.8	57.0	56.8	39.5	51.0
0-99 percent	5,992	64.2	55.7	54.7	38.2	50.6
150-299 percent	14,932	70.3	59.6	59.4	38.5	51.4
300 percent or higher	22,736	70.9	58.3	59.2	33.2	49.1
Race and Hispanic origin						
Hispanic	6,015	64.8	56.8	55.4	50.2	49.3
Non-Hispanic white	38,987	74.0	62.2	63.6	50.9	55.0
Non-Hispanic black	7,357	76.1	67.1	67.8	59.9	62.5
Non-Hispanic other	2,390	63.1	55.7	51.0	47.4	46.5

[1]NA Category not applicable.
　This question was limited to women 15-29 years of age at interview. HIV is human immunodeficiency virus, the virus that causes acquired immunodeficiency syndrome (AIDS).
[2] Includes women who lived with either both biological or both adoptive parents until they left home.
[3] Parents separated or divorced, then custodial parent remarried.
[4] Limited to women 22-44 years of age at time of interview.
NOTE: Percents do not add to 100 because respondents could report more than 1 type of formal instruction.

3. CONTRACEPTIVE USE AND ABORTION

E3-1   Contraceptive Use by Women, 15–44 Years Old, 1995

CONTRACEPTIVE STATUS AND METHOD	All women [1]	AGE			RACE			MARITAL STATUS		
		15-24 years	25-34 years	35-44 years	Non-Hispanic		His-panic	Never married	Cur-rently married	For-merly married
					White	Black				
All women (1,000)	60,201	18,002	20,758	21,440	42,522	8,210	6,702	22,679	29,673	7,849
PERCENT DISTRIBUTION										
Sterile [2]	29.7	2.6	25.0	57.0	30.2	31.5	28.4	6.9	43.2	45.1
Surgically sterile	27.9	1.8	23.6	54.0	28.5	29.7	26.3	5.7	41.1	42.5
Noncontraceptively sterile [3] .	3.1	0.1	1.2	7.4	3.2	3.7	2.3	0.9	4.1	5.8
Contraceptively sterile [4]	24.8	1.7	22.4	46.6	25.3	26.0	24.0	4.8	37.0	36.7
Nonsurgically sterile [5]	1.7	0.7	1.3	2.8	1.6	1.8	2.0	1.1	2.0	2.2
Pregnant, postpartum	4.6	5.9	6.9	1.3	4.3	4.5	6.3	3.1	6.4	1.9
Seeking pregnancy	4.0	2.1	6.2	3.5	3.7	4.6	4.0	1.5	6.4	2.1
Other nonusers	22.3	44.4	13.3	12.6	21.1	23.1	26.3	46.8	4.7	18.4
Never had intercourse	10.9	30.8	3.4	1.4	10.4	8.9	12.1	28.9	-	0.0
No intercourse in last month [6] .	6.2	7.0	5.3	6.5	5.7	7.2	8.6	11.5	0.5	12.7
Had intercourse in last month [6]	5.2	6.6	4.6	4.7	5.0	7.0	5.6	6.4	4.2	5.7
Nonsurgical contraceptors	39.7	45.0	49.1	26.1	41.2	36.1	35.1	41.8	39.7	32.4
Pill	17.3	23.1	23.7	6.3	18.8	14.8	13.6	20.4	15.6	14.6
IUD	0.5	0.1	0.6	0.8	0.5	0.5	0.9	0.3	0.7	0.4
Diaphragm	1.2	0.2	1.2	2.0	1.5	0.5	0.4	0.5	1.8	0.9
Condom	13.1	13.9	15.0	10.7	13.0	12.5	12.1	13.9	13.3	10.1
Periodic abstinence	1.5	0.5	1.8	2.0	1.6	0.7	1.3	0.6	2.3	0.7
Natural family planning	0.2	-	0.3	0.3	0.3	-	0.1	-	0.4	-
Withdrawal	2.0	1.6	2.3	1.9	2.1	0.9	2.0	1.5	2.3	1.8
Other methods [7]	3.9	5.6	4.2	2.1	3.4	6.2	4.7	4.6	3.3	3.9

- Represents or rounds to zero.   [1] Includes other races, not shown separately.   [2] Total sterile includes male sterile for unknown reasons.   [3] Persons who had sterilizing operation and who gave as one reason that they had medical problems with their female organs.   [4] Includes all other sterilization operations, and sterilization of the husband or current partner.   [5] Persons sterile from illness, accident, or congenital conditions.   [6] Data refer to no intercourse in the 3 months prior to interview.   [7] Includes implants, injectables, morning-after-pill, suppository, Today(TM) sponge and less frequently used methods.

E3-2   Number of Women 15–44 Years of Age and Percent Distribution by Current Contraceptive Status and Method, According to Age at Interview: United States, 1995

Contraceptive status and method	Age in years						
	15-44	15-19	20-24	25-29	30-34	35-39	40-44
	Number in thousands						
All women	60,201	8,961	9,041	9,693	11,065	11,211	10,230
	Percent distribution						
Total	100.0	100.0	100.0	100.0	100.0	100.0	100.0
Using contraception (contraceptors)	64.2	29.8	63.4	69.3	72.7	72.9	71.5
Female sterilization	17.8	0.1	2.5	11.8	21.4	29.8	35.6
Male sterilization	7.0	–	0.7	3.1	7.6	13.6	14.5
Pill	17.3	13.0	33.1	27.0	20.7	8.1	4.2
Implant	0.9	0.8	2.4	1.4	0.5	0.2	0.1
Injectable	1.9	2.9	3.9	2.9	1.3	0.8	0.2
Intrauterine device (IUD)	0.6	–	0.2	0.5	0.6	0.7	0.9
Diaphragm	1.2	0.0	0.4	0.6	1.7	2.2	1.9
Condom	13.1	10.9	16.7	16.8	13.4	12.3	8.8
Female condom	0.0	–	0.1	–	–	–	–
Periodic abstinence	1.5	0.4	0.6	1.2	2.3	2.1	1.8
Natural family planning	0.2	–	0.1	0.2	0.3	0.4	0.2
Withdrawal	2.0	1.2	2.1	2.6	2.1	2.3	1.4
Other methods[1]	1.0	0.3	0.9	1.2	1.3	0.9	1.8
Not using contraception[2]	35.8	70.2	36.6	30.7	27.3	27.1	28.5
Surgically sterile female (noncontraceptive)	3.0	0.1	0.1	0.6	1.7	5.1	9.6
Nonsurgically sterile female	1.3	0.7	0.5	0.7	1.2	2.3	1.9
Pregnant or postpartum	4.6	4.5	7.3	8.4	5.6	2.1	0.4
Seeking pregnancy	4.0	0.9	3.4	6.1	6.2	4.6	2.2
Other nonuse:							
Never had intercourse[3]	10.9	49.8	12.1	4.2	2.7	1.4	1.4
No intercourse in 3 months before interview	6.2	7.1	6.8	5.7	4.9	6.2	6.8
Had intercourse in 3 months before interview	5.2	7.1	6.0	4.7	4.4	4.3	5.1

– Quantity zero.
0.0 Quantity more than zero but less than 0.05.
[1]Includes morning-after pill, foam, cervical cap, Today (TM) sponge, suppository, jelly or cream (without diaphragm), and other methods not shown separately.
[2]Includes other categories not shown separately: "sterile, nonsurgical-male"; "sterile, surgical-male"; "sterile, unknown-male."
[3]Never had voluntary intercourse or never had (voluntary) intercourse since first menstrual period.

NOTES: Percents "using contraception" and "not using contraception" may not add to 100 due to rounding. Due to rounding, percents in specific method categories may not add to total percents using contraception and not using contraception. Also, some methods are not shown separately.

E3-3   Number of Women 15–44 Years of Age Who Have Ever Had Intercourse and Percent Who Have Ever Used the Specified Contraceptive Methods, by Age: United States, 1995

Method	15-44	15-19	20-24	25-29	30-34	35-39	40-44
				Age in years			
				Number in thousands			
All women	53,630	4,496	7,968	9,279	10,772	11,048	10,066
				Percent who ever used			
Any method	98.4	96.9	98.4	98.7	98.3	99.0	98.2
Female sterilization	23.1	0.2	3.0	12.6	23.7	35.4	44.9
Male sterilization	14.6	0.6	2.9	6.1	14.4	24.0	28.0
Pill	82.4	52.1	81.3	86.9	86.8	84.7	85.1
Implant	2.1	2.8	5.0	3.1	1.5	0.9	0.7
Injectable	4.5	9.8	8.1	6.4	3.1	2.3	1.5
Intrauterine device (IUD)	10.0	–	0.8	2.4	7.2	16.5	24.7
Diaphragm	15.2	0.4	2.3	6.6	17.8	25.0	26.5
Condom	82.2	93.5	89.4	86.7	83.0	76.8	72.5
Female condom	1.2	1.1	0.9	1.0	1.4	1.3	1.2
Periodic abstinence	25.5	13.3	15.7	23.7	29.5	31.4	29.9
Natural family planning	4.2	0.4	1.0	2.4	4.9	7.4	5.9
Withdrawal	40.7	42.6	43.7	46.4	41.8	37.0	34.8
Other methods[1]	32.8	11.5	23.1	29.4	38.8	40.2	38.3

– Quantity zero.

[1] Includes morning-after pill, foam, cervical cap, Today (TM) sponge, suppository, jelly or cream (without diaphragm), and other methods not shown separately.

E3-4   Number of Women 15–44 Years of Age Who Have Ever Had Intercourse and Percent Who Used the Specified Contraceptive Method at First Intercourse, According to Race and Hispanic Origin and Year: United States, 1995

Race and Hispanic origin and year	Number in thousands	Used any method	Pill	Condom	Withdrawal	All other methods
			Percent[1]			
All women[2]	53,588	59.0	19.5	29.2	6.8	3.5
Race and Hispanic origin						
Hispanic	5,882	36.2	10.6	19.8	4.1	1.7
Non-Hispanic white	38,090	64.8	21.0	32.0	7.8	4.0
Non-Hispanic black	7,462	60.1	20.5	24.5	2.9	2.2
Year of first intercourse						
1990-95	9,140	75.9	15.5	54.3	4.4	1.6
1985-89	10,063	63.9	19.7	36.4	5.6	2.2
1980-84	10,514	59.4	21.9	25.1	8.0	4.4
Before 1980	23,871	60.2	19.9	18.3	7.6	4.4

[1] For women reporting use of more than one contraceptive method, the method with highest-use effectiveness was coded.
[2] Includes women of other race and origin groups not shown separately.

E3-5   Abortions, Number, Rate, and Ratio, by State: 1980–1992

DIVISION, REGION, AND STATE	NUMBER OF ABORTIONS (1,000)			RATE PER 1,000 WOMEN, 15 TO 44 YEARS OLD			RATIO: ABORTIONS PER 1,000 LIVE BIRTHS		
	1980	1985	1992	1980	1985	1992	1980	1985	1992
United States.......	1,554	1,589	1,529	29.3	28.0	25.9	428	422	379
Northeast..............	396	407	379	34.9	(NA)	32.1	604	(NA)	506
New England	84	85	78	28.9	28.6	25.2	530	504	429
Maine	5	5	4	18.6	18.6	14.7	289	308	282
New Hampshire.......	5	7	4	21.1	29.0	14.6	347	419	269
Vermont............	4	3	3	30.4	26.2	21.2	466	448	393
Massachusetts	46	40	41	33.5	29.3	28.4	609	533	472
Rhode Island	7	8	7	30.7	35.5	30.0	529	572	461
Connecticut	19	22	20	25.6	29.3	26.2	561	550	444
Middle Atlantic	312	322	300	37.0	37.6	34.6	627	607	530
New York..........	188	195	195	45.8	47.4	46.2	780	746	694
New Jersey	56	69	55	32.8	39.6	31.0	591	672	460
Pennsylvania	69	57	50	26.1	21.3	18.6	423	348	302
Midwest..............	318	289	262	23.3	(NA)	18.9	336	(NA)	287
East North Central......	243	221	205	24.9	22.1	20.7	369	356	313
Ohio	67	57	50	26.8	22.4	19.5	397	357	294
Indiana	20	16	16	15.3	12.2	12.0	227	202	185
Illinois	69	65	68	25.9	23.8	25.4	374	372	361
Michigan	65	64	56	29.7	28.7	25.2	457	486	393
Wisconsin	22	18	15	20.1	15.7	13.6	292	246	223
West North Central	75	68	57	19.2	16.7	14.3	260	252	221
Minnesota	20	17	16	20.7	16.6	15.6	288	257	251
Iowa	9	10	7	14.3	15.0	11.4	195	248	185
Missouri...........	22	20	14	19.4	17.3	11.6	273	261	175
North Dakota	3	3	1	21.5	18.5	10.7	235	230	149
South Dakota	1	2	1	9.0	10.6	6.8	103	140	92
Nebraska...........	6	7	6	17.9	18.2	15.7	227	268	246
Kansas	14	10	13	25.6	18.2	22.4	343	264	353
South	457	453	450	25.9	(NA)	22.0	369	(NA)	323
South Atlantic.........	255	257	269	29.4	27.1	25.9	462	429	397
Delaware...........	4	5	6	25.9	30.9	35.2	395	451	502
Maryland	31	30	31	29.2	26.9	26.4	571	480	454
District of Columbia	29	24	21	168.3	145.9	138.4	1,569	1,186	1,104
Virginia	32	34	35	24.2	24.0	22.7	417	412	373
West Virginia	3	5	3	6.9	10.1	7.7	104	185	134
North Carolina.......	32	34	36	22.8	22.6	22.4	377	379	357
South Carolina	14	11	12	18.2	13.7	14.2	274	228	229
Georgia...........	38	38	40	28.4	26.1	24.0	395	397	350
Florida.............	74	77	85	35.5	31.8	30.0	547	465	438
East South Central	65	57	54	19.2	15.8	14.9	271	258	228
Kentucky	13	10	10	15.1	11.0	11.4	215	189	191
Tennessee	26	22	19	23.6	19.1	16.2	352	315	243
Alabama	21	19	17	23.1	20.2	18.2	331	333	277
Mississippi	6	6	8	10.6	9.7	12.4	132	142	176
West South Central	137	139	127	24.5	21.8	19.6	308	290	266
Arkansas...........	6	5	7	12.3	10.1	13.5	173	159	213
Louisiana...........	18	19	14	17.6	17.4	13.4	218	240	195
Oklahoma	11	13	9	16.4	17.1	12.5	221	269	193
Texas	102	101	97	30.0	25.5	23.1	367	320	297
West	383	440	438	36.8	(NA)	34.1	486	(NA)	446
Mountain	68	75	70	25.0	23.6	21.0	302	316	280
Montana	4	4	3	20.1	19.0	18.2	265	288	298
Idaho	3	3	2	12.7	11.1	7.2	141	155	97
Wyoming	1	1	-	9.5	7.9	4.3	107	125	74
Colorado	23	24	20	31.4	28.8	23.6	447	438	362
New Mexico	8	6	6	27.0	17.4	17.7	358	219	228
Arizona	16	22	21	25.0	29.9	24.1	310	373	295
Utah	4	4	4	12.3	11.1	9.3	97	116	104
Nevada	9	10	13	46.6	40.5	44.2	697	641	591
Pacific	315	365	368	41.0	42.8	38.7	561	594	501
Washington	37	31	33	37.5	28.0	27.7	522	458	447
Oregon	18	15	16	28.3	22.3	23.9	396	374	372
California...........	250	304	304	43.7	47.9	42.1	598	640	519
Alaska.............	2	4	2	17.9	27.7	16.5	196	283	222
Hawaii.............	8	11	12	34.4	43.7	46.0	441	611	617

- Represents or rounds to zero.   NA Not available.

E3-6   Abortions, by Selected Characteristics: 1985–1992

CHARACTERISTIC	NUMBER (1,000)			PERCENT DISTRIBUTION			ABORTION RATIO [1]		
	1985	1990 [1]	1992	1985	1990 [1]	1992	1985	1990 [1]	1992
Total abortions	1,589	1,609	1529	100	100	100	297	280	275
Age of woman:									
Less than 15 years old	17	13	13	1	1	1	624	515	511
15 to 19 years old	399	351	295	25	22	19	462	403	370
20 to 24 years old	548	532	526	35	33	34	328	328	333
25 to 29 years old	336	360	341	21	22	22	219	224	228
30 to 34 years old	181	216	213	11	13	14	203	196	192
35 to 39 years old	87	108	110	5	7	7	280	249	239
40 years old and over	21	29	31	1	2	2	409	354	338
Race of woman:									
White	1,076	1,039	944	68	65	62	265	241	229
Black and other	513	570	585	32	35	38	397	396	405
Marital status of woman: [2]									
Married	281	284	257	18	18	17	88	88	84
Unmarried	1,307	1,325	1272	82	82	83	605	527	508
Number of prior live births:									
None	872	780	691	55	49	45	358	316	298
One	349	396	396	22	25	26	219	230	233
Two	240	280	281	15	17	18	288	292	299
Three	85	102	105	5	6	7	281	279	290
Four or more	43	50	57	3	3	4	230	223	244
Number of prior induced abortions:									
None	944	891	810	60	55	53	(NA)	(NA)	(NA)
One	416	443	431	26	28	28	(NA)	(NA)	(NA)
Two or more	228	275	288	14	17	19	(NA)	(NA)	(NA)
Weeks of gestation: [3]									
Less than 9 weeks	779	817	799	49	51	52	(NA)	(NA)	(NA)
9 to 10 weeks	425	418	378	27	26	25	(NA)	(NA)	(NA)
11 to 12 weeks	211	199	182	13	12	12	(NA)	(NA)	(NA)
13 weeks or more	173	175	171	11	11	11	(NA)	(NA)	(NA)

NA Not available.   [1] Number of abortions per 1,000 abortions and live births. Live births are those which occurred from July 1 of year shown through June 30 of the following year (to match time of conception with abortions).   [2] Separated women included with unmarried women.   [3] Data not exactly comparable with prior years because of a change in the method of calculation.

E3-7   Abortions, Number, Rate, and Abortion/Live Birth Ratio, by Race: 1975–1992

YEAR	ALL RACES				WHITE				BLACK AND OTHER			
	Women 15-44 years old (1,000)	Abortions			Women 15-44 years old (1,000)	Abortions			Women 15-44 years old (1,000)	Abortions		
		Num-ber (1,000)	Rate per 1,000 women	Ratio per 1,000 live births [1]		Num-ber (1,000)	Rate per 1,000 women	Ratio per 1,000 live births [1]		Num-ber (1,000)	Rate per 1,000 women	Ratio per 1,000 live births [1]
1975 ..	47,606	1,034	21.7	331	40,857	701	17.2	276	6,749	333	49.3	565
1979 ..	52,016	1,498	28.8	420	44,266	1,062	24.0	373	7,750	435	56.2	625
1980 ..	53,048	1,554	29.3	428	44,942	1,094	24.3	376	8,106	460	56.5	642
1981 ..	53,901	1,577	29.3	430	45,494	1,108	24.3	377	8,407	470	55.9	645
1982 [2] .	54,679	1,574	28.8	428	46,049	1,095	23.8	373	8,630	479	55.5	646
1983 [2] .	55,340	1,575	28.5	436	46,506	1,084	23.3	376	8,834	491	55.5	670
1984 ..	56,061	1,577	28.1	423	47,023	1,087	23.1	366	9,038	491	54.3	646
1985 [2] .	56,754	1,589	28.0	422	47,512	1,076	22.6	360	9,242	513	55.5	659
1986 [2] .	57,483	1,574	27.4	416	48,010	1,045	21.8	350	9,473	529	55.9	661
1987 ..	57,964	1,559	27.1	405	48,288	1,017	21.1	338	9,676	542	56.0	648
1988 [2] .	58,192	1,591	27.3	401	48,325	1,026	21.2	333	9,867	565	57.3	638
1989 [2] .	58,365	1,567	26.8	380	48,104	1,006	20.9	309	10,261	561	54.7	650
1990 [2] .	58,700	1,609	27.4	389	48,224	1,039	21.5	318	10,476	570	54.4	655
1991 ..	59,080	1,557	26.3	379	48,406	982	20.3	303	10,674	574	53.8	661
1992 ..	59,020	1,529	25.9	379	48,161	944	19.6	298	10859	585	53.9	681

[1] Live births are those which occurred from July 1 of year shown through June 30 of the following year (to match time of conception with abortions). Births are classified by race of child 1972-1988, and by race of mother after 1988.   [2] Total numbers of abortions in 1983 and 1986 have been estimated by interpolation; 1989 and 1990 have been estimated using trends in CDC data.

E3-8 Trends in Percent Favoring Legal Abortion for Various Reasons

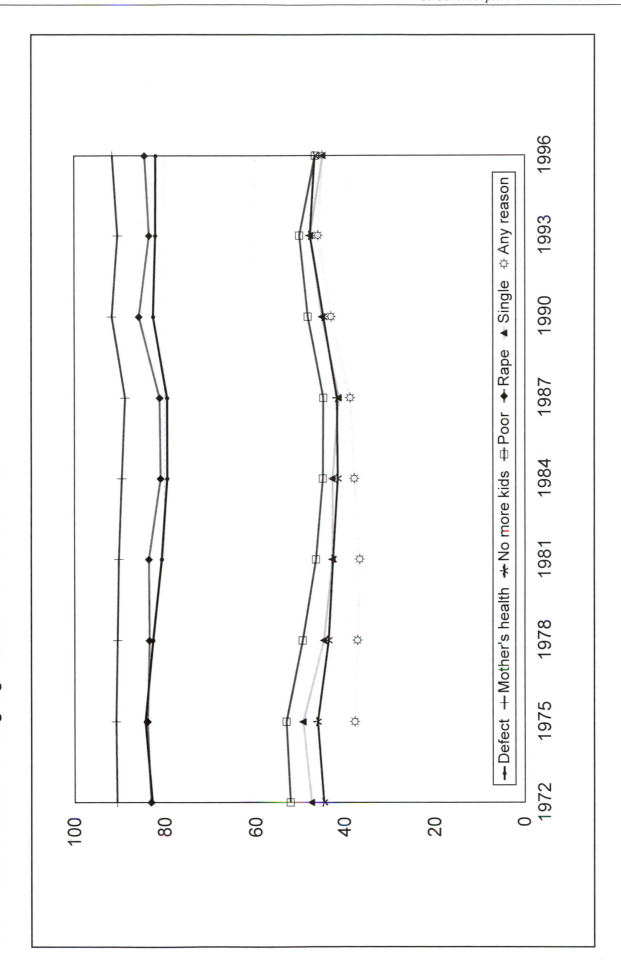

E3-9   Approval of Abortion for Various Reasons (% Approval), 1996

Should it be possible for a pregnant woman to obtain a legal abortion

	for any reason	for serious defect	if woman's health is in danger	if woman doesn't want child	if woman cannot afford child	for rape	if woman does not want to marry the father
Total	45.0	81.8	91.6	46.7	46.6	84.3	44.9
Age of Respondent							
18-24	47.5	81.8	93.0	47.3	49.2	87.0	42.5
25-34	49.5	82.0	93.9	48.9	48.1	87.4	44.0
35-44	44.6	81.6	90.6	46.9	44.2	82.2	44.0
45-64	46.4	81.5	91.1	47.9	49.4	83.9	48.8
65 +	33.7	82.6	89.2	40.1	40.6	81.4	41.5
Highest Year in School							
Less than h.s.	29.7	77.9	89.0	32.4	35.4	77.6	32.2
High school	40.3	83.9	91.8	41.3	40.7	84.0	39.1
Some college	49.2	83.3	93.4	51.0	49.2	88.2	46.8
16 + years	55.7	80.7	91.1	57.7	57.8	85.0	57.3
Marital Status							
Married	41.0	79.6	90.3	44.2	42.4	82.1	43.1
Widowed	35.3	77.0	88.6	36.1	38.6	80.2	39.1
Divorced	46.8	88.8	94.8	50.0	49.1	88.8	48.1
Separated	44.9	80.8	85.7	44.2	47.4	78.2	39.7
Never married	55.8	83.9	94.3	54.4	56.5	88.6	49.5
Race of Respondent							
White	44.6	82.8	92.0	45.8	46.1	85.0	45.5
Black	47.0	77.3	90.5	51.0	50.4	82.3	41.5
Other	45.9	79.2	88.1	49.5	43.9	79.2	44.3
Sex of Respondent							
Male	44.4	81.4	92.2	46.0	46.5	85.9	44.2
Female	45.5	82.1	91.1	47.3	46.7	83.0	45.4

E3-10 Attitudes Toward Legalization of Abortion

Do you think abortions should be legal under any circumstances, legal only under certain circumstances, or illegal in all circumstances?

When Should Abortion Be Legal—Trend

	Always	Under certain circumstances	Never	No opinion
1993 Mar 12-14	32%	51%	13%	4%
1992 Jun	34	48	13	5
1992 Jan	31	53	14	2
1991 Sep	33	49	14	4
1991 May	32	50	17	1
1990 Apr	31	53	12	4
1989 Jul	29	51	17	3
1989 Apr	27	50	18	5
1988	24	57	17	2
1983	23	58	16	3
1981	23	52	21	4
1980	25	53	18	4
1979	22	54	19	5
1977	22	55	19	4
1975	21	54	22	3

Strength of Religious Commitment and Abortion Opinion

	Always	Certain Circumstances	Never	No opinion	(No. of intv.)
Total	32%	51%	13%	4%	(1007)
Importance of religion					
Very	22	55	19	4	(571)
Fairly	41	50	6	3	(329)
Not very	60	33	2	5	(106)
Attended church in last week					
Yes	22	55	20	3	(430)
No	39	49	9	3	(575)

E3-11 Make French Abortion Pill Available Here?

QUESTION: Would you, personally, favor or oppose making this pill available in the United States by prescription?

	Favor	Oppose	No opinion	No. of interviews
National	54%	41%	5%	670
Sex				
Male	61	34	5	333
Female	49	46	5	337
Age				
18-29 years	51	48	1	123
30-49 years	55	40	5	301
50-64 years	56	38	6	146
65 & older	54	36	10	97
Region				
East	59	34	7	169
Midwest	54	44	2	165
South	49	44	7	188
West	57	39	4	148
Community				
Urban	59	38	3	173
Suburban	55	38	7	227
Rural	51	44	5	269
Race				
White	55	40	5	586
Non-white	49	44	7	83
Education				
College graduate	62	34	4	236
Some college	59	37	4	186
No college	46	48	6	246
Politics				
Republicans	38	56	6	178
Democrats	62	32	6	237
Independents	58	38	4	255
1992 vote				
Clinton	69	24	7	233
Bush	38	56	6	190
Perot	65	32	3	102
Did not vote	46	52	2	122
Clinton approval				
Approve	62	33	5	382
Disapprove	44	54	2	219
Income				
$75,000 & over	68	26	6	89
$50,000-74,999	67	28	5	103
$20,000-49,999	51	45	4	290
Under $20,000	48	47	5	162

4. INVOLUNTARY INTERCOURSE AND RAPE

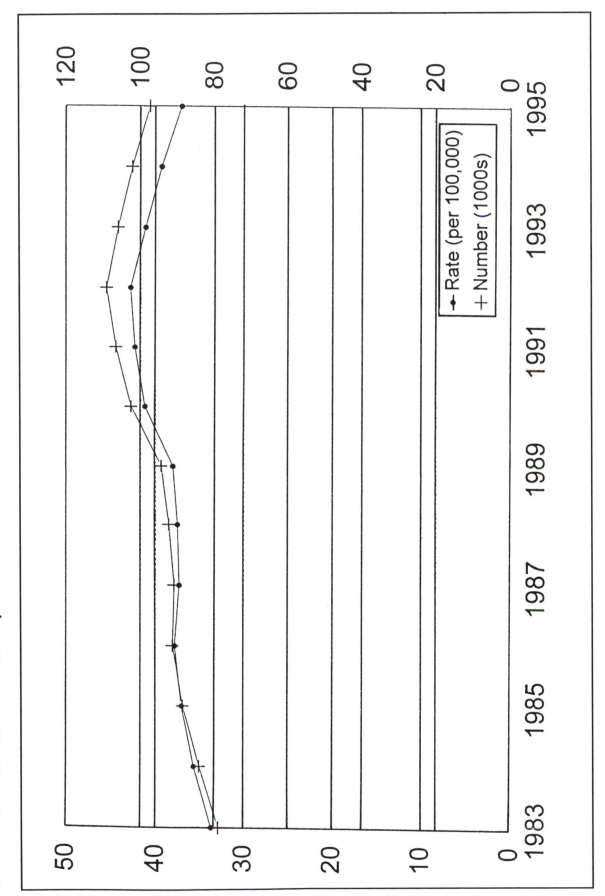

E4-1   Number and Rate of Forcible Rape

E4-2   Number of Women 15–44 Years of Age and Percent Ever Forced to Have Sexual Intercourse, by Age at First Forced Intercourse and Selected Characteristics: United States, 1995

Characteristic	Number in thousands	Ever forced	Age at first forced intercourse[1]			
			Under 15	15-17	18-19	20 and over
			Percent			
All women	60201	20.4	5.8	6.0	2.9	5.3
Age at interview						
15-19 years	8,961	12.5	6.4	5.2	0.6	(NA)
20-24 years	9,041	20.6	7.1	7.5	3.4	2.4
25-29 years	9,693	20.4	6.2	5.5	2.9	5.3
30-34 years	11,065	23.0	6.0	6.3	3.5	6.9
35-39 years	11,211	23.7	5.6	6.8	3.6	7.1
40-44 years	10,230	21.0	3.8	4.5	3.4	8.8
Marital status						
Never married	22,679	17.8	6.1	5.0	2.7	3.7
Currently married	29,673	18.8	4.8	5.6	2.8	5.2
Formerly married	7,849	34.5	9.0	10.3	4.3	10.1
Family background						
Both parents from birth[2]	37,233	17.4	3.8	5.0	3.0	5.3
Single parent from birth	2,093	26.6	11.8	7.1	2.3	4.2
Both parents, then 1 parent	8,003	19.7	5.8	7.2	1.9	4.3
Stepparent[3]	8,378	27.3	10.3	7.3	3.3	5.8
Other	4,493	31.1	11.1	9.0	4.3	6.6
Education at interview[4]						
No high school diploma or GED[5]	5,424	30.4	12.0	10.0	2.7	5.0
High school diploma or GED	18,169	22.1	6.3	6.8	2.9	5.7
Some college, no bachelor's degree	12,399	24.5	5.0	6.2	4.4	8.5
Bachelor's degree or higher	11,748	15.9	2.3	3.1	3.0	7.1
Poverty level income at interview[4]						
0-149 percent	10,072	29.3	9.9	8.2	3.8	6.7
0-99 percent	5,992	29.2	9.7	8.0	4.3	6.7
150-299 percent	14,932	23.2	6.2	6.3	3.7	6.6
300 percent or higher	22,736	18.3	3.4	5.0	2.8	6.7
Race and Hispanic origin						
Hispanic	6,702	18.7	5.3	6.1	2.5	4.1
Non-Hispanic white	42,522	19.8	5.2	5.8	3.0	5.3
Non-Hispanic black	8,210	25.7	8.8	7.3	2.9	6.4
Non-Hispanic other	2,767	19.4	6.9	4.1	3.5	4.5

NA Category not applicable

[1]"Ever forced" means that the woman either responded "yes" to the question asking if she had ever been forced to have intercourse (in the self-administered portion of the interview), or reported her first intercourse as "rape" or "not voluntary" (in the interviewer-administered portion). "Age at first forced intercourse" is based on the self-administered questionnaire unless the only forced intercourse was her first intercourse. For these cases, information is from the interviewer-administered questionnaire.

[2]Includes women who lived with either both biological or both adoptive parents until they left home.

[3]Parents separated or divorced, then custodial parent remarried.

[4]Limited to women 22-44 years of age at time of interview.

[5]GED is general equivalency diploma.

NOTE: Percents may not add to total who were "ever forced" because the total includes respondents with missing information on "age at first forced intercourse."

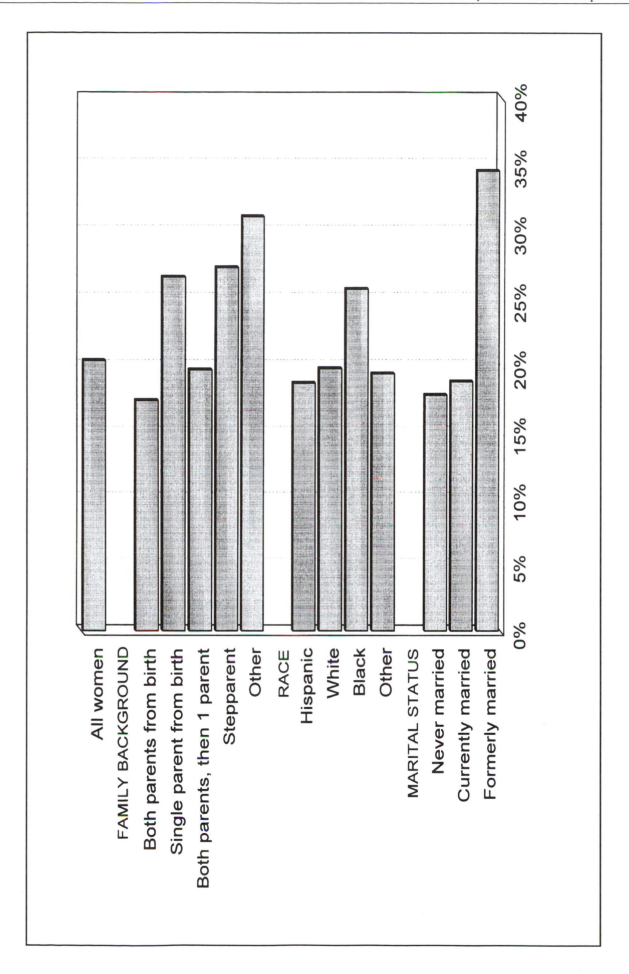

E4-3   Percent of Women Who Were Ever Forced to Have Sexual Intercourse

E4-4   Number of Women 15–44 Years of Age Who Have Ever Had Sexual Intercourse and Percent Whose First Intercourse Was Not Voluntary, by Selected Characteristics: United States, 1995

Characteristic	Number in thousands	Percent whose first intercourse was not voluntary[1]
All women[2]	53,793	7.8
Age at first intercourse		
Under 16 years	13,944	16.1
Under 15 years	7,290	22.1
16 years	8,750	6.5
17 years	8,754	4.9
18 years	6,941	5.1
19 years	4,759	5.0
20 years and over	10,646	3.3
Year of first intercourse		
1990-95	8,978	6.3
1985-89	9,988	6.4
1980-84	10,451	7.1
1975-79	11,005	8.4
1958-74	13,372	9.8
Race and Hispanic origin and age at first intercourse		
Hispanic	5,907	9.4
Under 16 years	1,456	18.1
16-19 years	2,894	7.4
20 years and over	1,558	5.0
Non-Hispanic white	38,212	7.0
Under 16 years	9,219	15.3
16-19 years	21,628	5.0
20 years and over	7,364	2.6
Non-Hispanic black	7,484	9.1
Under 16 years	2,835	15.0
16-19 years	3,852	5.5
20 years and over	796	5.1
Family Background		
Both parents from birth[3]	33,232	6.4
Single parent from birth	1,850	13.0
Both parents, then 1 parent	7,083	7.5
Stepparent[4]	7,529	9.8
Other	4,098	13.2

[1]Includes first intercourse reported as "rape" or "not voluntary."
[2]Includes women of other race and origin groups not shown separately.
[3]Includes women who lived with either both biological or both adoptive parents until they left home.
[4]Parents separated or divorced, then custodial parent remarried.

E4-5 Percent of Women Whose First Intercourse Was Involuntary

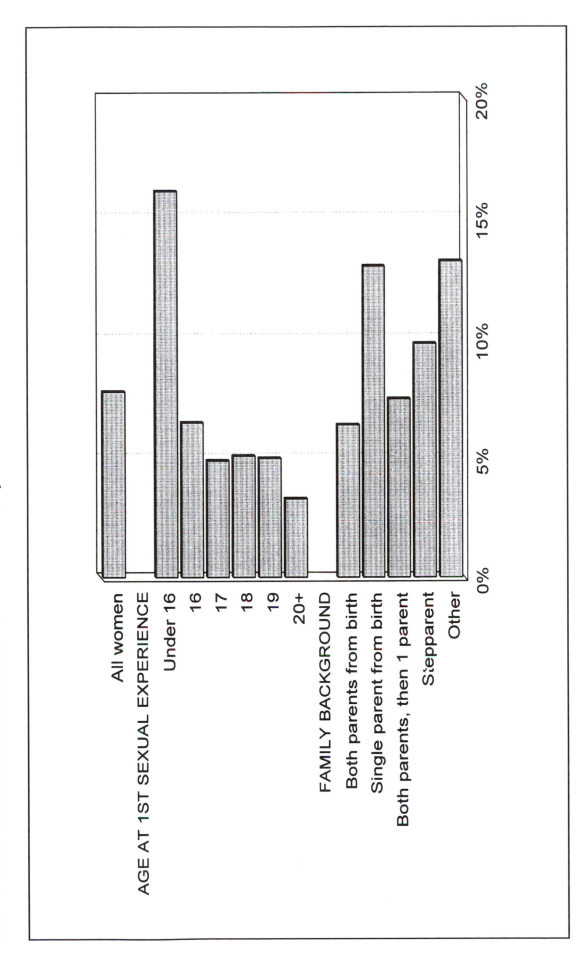

F. Living Arrangements and Kinship Ties

1. LIVING ARRANGEMENTS

The number of households in the United States continued to increase during the 1990s. In 1950 there were 43.6 million households in the country and the number rose to 99.6 million in 1996 (see Table F1-12). Modest population growth, primarily from immigration, has contributed to the expansion in the number of households. In addition, young people are marrying later and many are leaving home and establishing a substantial number of single-person households. Finally, the increased number of divorced individuals maintaining separate households has also added to the total.

In 1996, the most frequently appearing household type was that of a married couple with no children (Figure F1-1). Either the couple had not had any children or else the children had left the nest. Married couples without children in their home accounted for 29 percent of all households. A fourth of all households were occupied by married couples with children and another fourth by individuals living alone. Female-headed households with children constituted 8 percent of all households in the United States.

Given the growth in the number of households occupied by single individuals, it is not surprising that non-family households constitute a greater proportion. In 1960, non-family households accounted for 15 percent of those in this country; in 1996, such households had doubled to 30 percent (Figure F1-2).

Another important trend reported in this chapter is that American families are getting smaller. As can be seen in Table F1-7, the average family in 1970 included 3.58 individuals. Family size declined until 1990 when the average size was 3.17 persons, and since then, it has remained around 3.20 individuals. Related to this, Section D, which focuses on children, contains information about the fertility of American women.

One consequence of changes in household composition is that fewer children live with both parents. Over 80 percent of white children lived with both parents in 1980 and the number had declined to 75 percent in 1995 (Figure F1-15). Seventy-five percent of Hispanic children lived with both parents in 1980 and in 1995 the percent had shrunk to 62 percent. For black children, the percent dropped from 42 to 33 (Figure F1-16).

2. COHABITATION

Cohabitation remains an alternative to marriage for some and a path to marriage for others. Seven percent of American women between the ages of 15 and 44 were cohabiting during 1995 (Table F2-1). Over 40 percent of the women surveyed acknowledged they had cohabited at some time during their lives. Most had done so before their first marriage. Over half of the men and women in a large sample of cohabiting couples included in the NSFH study predicted they "probably" or "definitely" will get married (Table F2-6). It is interesting that only about a third indicate their cohabiting relationship is "very happy." This is considerably lower than the 60-plus percentage of married individuals who evaluate their marital relationship as very happy.

Significantly, more non-cohabiting men under the age of 36 than women in the NSFH study revealed they would like to "live with someone before getting married" (see Table F2-7). On the other hand, 59 percent of the men indicated they would like to get married someday, as compared with only 41 percent of the women.

3. KINSHIP

Kinship ties involve maintaining relationships, spending time together, keeping in touch, and giving support to and receiving it from members of the extended family. It has been thought that modern society, with its emphasis on the nuclear family, has witnessed a decline in kinship ties during this century. Until the NSFH study, national data concerning kinship ties were rather limited. This study provides detailed information about kinship ties in 1994 and 1995.

Adults in the study reported a fairly high level of contact with their brothers and sisters, as 19 percent reported they talk to them on the phone or exchange letters with them more than once a week (Table F3-1). Only 9 percent indicated no contact with their siblings during the past year. The adult men and women in the NSFH study indicated their parents or their adult children were those to whom they most often gave help such as child care, giving rides, helping with housework, or providing emotional support. Not surprising, close family members, parents, or adult children were the most frequent sources of such assistance (Table F3-2).

Parents detailed how they spent, on average, nearly six hours during the past month assisting adult children with child care, shopping, transportation, and emotional encouragement (Table F3-3). A large number of grandparents stated they tended their grandchildren while the parents worked, or so the parents could have some time free from childcare responsibility. Adult children helped their parents with emotional support, shopping, transportation, housework, and yard work. Interestingly, the parents reported they received only four hours of assistance from their adult children, compared with the six hours they gave (Table F3-4). Obviously, parents of adult children feel they give more assistance than they receive.

More than 10 percent of the grandparents in the study indicated they are primarily responsible for raising one or more grandchildren (Table F3-5). On average, grandparents claim a close relationship, 8.7 on a 10-point scale, with their grandchildren.

4. ELDERLY FAMILIES

Most elderly individuals and families in the NSFH study lived by themselves in their own apartments or houses at the time of the study (Table F4-1). As parents got older, more moved in with adult children or into nursing homes. Regardless of where their aged parents lived, adult children had a strong relationship with them (Table F4-2). The adult children averaged an 8.1 relationship with their mothers and a 7.4 average with their fathers, where "10" equals an "absolutely perfect" relationship. Adult children had a fairly high level of contact with their aged mothers (Table F4-3). Over 40 percent visited their mothers at least once a week, and over 60 percent called them on the phone or exchanged a letter with them that often.

A pattern of helping each other persists even as parents age (Tables F4-4 and F4-5). The adult children more often helped with transportation needs, household chores, and yard work of their aged parents. On the other hand, elderly parents gave more emotional support than they received. They also gave considerable childcare help, as noted above under Kinship.

1. LIVING ARRANGEMENTS

F1-1   Distribution of Household Types, 1996

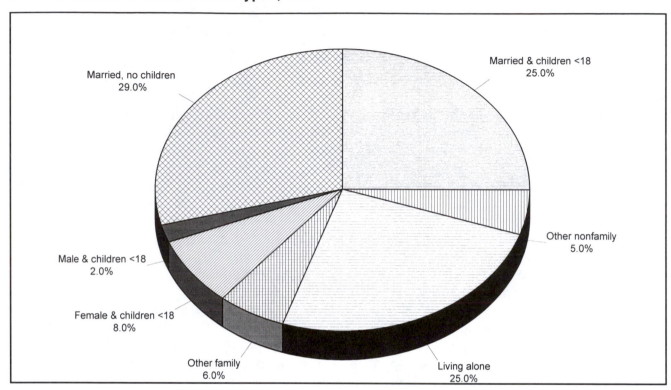

Married & children <18
25.0%

Married, no children
29.0%

Other nonfamily
5.0%

Male & children <18
2.0%

Female & children <18
8.0%

Other family
6.0%

Living alone
25.0%

F1-2   Household Structure

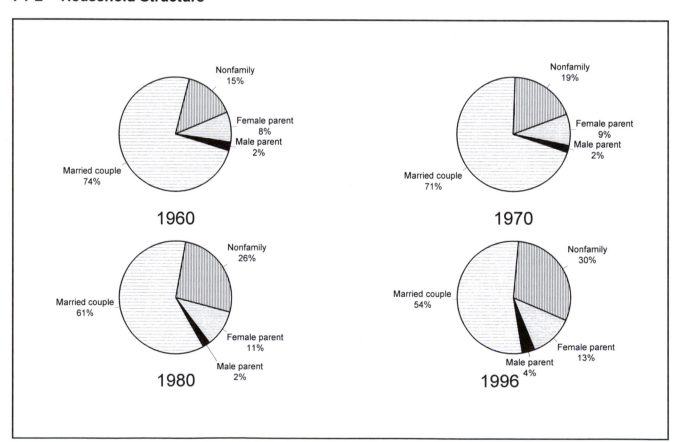

Nonfamily
15%

Female parent
8%

Male parent
2%

Married couple
74%

1960

Nonfamily
19%

Female parent
9%

Male parent
2%

Married couple
71%

1970

Nonfamily
26%

Married couple
61%

Female parent
11%

Male parent
2%

1980

Nonfamily
30%

Married couple
54%

Female parent
13%

Male parent
4%

1996

F1-3   Household Composition: 1970–1993

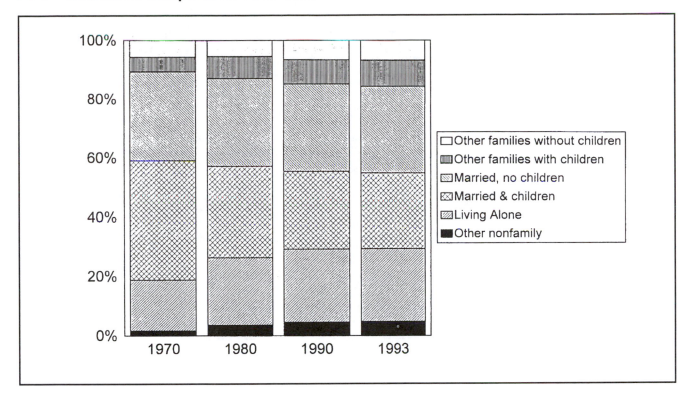

F1-4   Household Composition, by Presence of Own Children under 18: 1993, 1990, 1980, and 1970

(Number in Thousands)	1993		1990		1980		1970	
Type of Household	Number	Percent	Number	Percent	Number	Percent	Number	Percent
All Households	96,391	100.0	93,347	100.0	80,776	100.0	63,401	100.0
Family households	68,144	70.7	66,090	70.8	59,550	73.7	51,456	81.2
No own children under 18	34,887	36.2	33,801	36.2	28,528	35.3	22,725	35.8
With own children under 18	33,257	34.5	32,289	34.6	31,022	38.4	28,732	45.3
Married-couple family	53,171	55.2	52,317	56.0	49,112	60.8	44,728	70.5
No own children under 18	28,464	29.5	27,780	29.8	24,151	29.9	19,196	30.3
With own children under 18	24,707	25.6	24,537	26.3	24,961	30.9	25,532	40.3
Other family, female	3,026	3.1	2,884	3.1	1,733	2.1	1,228	1.9
No own children under 18	1,702	1.8	1,731	1.9	1,117	1.4	887	1.4
With own children under 18	1,324	1.4	1,153	1.2	616	0.8	341	0.5
Nonfamily households	28,247	29.3	27,257	29.2	21,226	26.3	11,945	18.8
Living alone	23,642	24.5	22,999	24.6	18,296	22.7	10,851	17.1
Male householder	12,254	12.7	11,606	12.4	8,807	10.9	4,063	6.4
Living alone	9,436	9.8	9,049	9.7	6,966	8.6	3,532	5.6
Female householder	15,993	16.6	15,651	16.8	12,419	15.4	7,882	12.4
Living alone	14,206	14.7	13,950	14.9	11,330	14.0	7,319	11.5

F1-5   Living Arrangements of Persons 15 Years Old and Over, by Selected Characteristics, 1996

LIVING ARRANGEMENT	Total	15 to 19 years old	20 to 24 years old	25 to 34 years old	35 to 44 years old	45 to 54 years old	55 to 64 years old	65 to 74 years old	75 years old and over
Total [1]	204,625	18,648	17,653	40,919	43,077	31,584	21,084	18,270	13,388
Alone	24,900	80	992	3,736	3,803	3,506	2,941	4,377	5,464
With spouse.	109,335	349	3,598	21,888	28,678	22,423	15,272	11,600	5,526
With other persons	70,390	18,219	13,063	15,295	10,596	5,655	2,871	2,293	2,398
White	171,597	14,769	14,094	33,487	35,794	26,820	18,196	16,306	12,129
Alone.	21,194	67	821	2,991	3,149	2,877	2,434	3,844	5,011
With spouse.	97,338	317	3,221	19,371	25,065	19,795	13,664	10,754	5,152
With other persons	53,065	14,385	10,052	11,125	7,580	4,148	2,098	1,708	1,966
Black	24,214	2,959	2,540	5,354	5,303	3,457	2,125	1,482	997
Alone.	3,055	11	131	536	525	568	431	449	405
With spouse.	7,496	24	240	1,510	2,200	1,619	1,061	585	257
With other persons	13,663	2,924	2,169	3,308	2,578	1,270	633	448	335
Hispanic origin [2]	19,580	2,433	2,606	5,355	4,065	2,171	1,492	983	475
Alone.	1,260	10	69	205	236	191	181	222	146
With spouse.	9,240	92	768	2,862	2,501	1,385	939	543	151
With other persons	9,080	2,331	1,769	2,288	1,328	595	372	218	178

[1] Includes other races and persons not of Hispanic origin, not shown separately.   [2] Persons of Hispanic origin may be of any race.

F1-6   Living Arrangements of Young Adults: 1980–1995

LIVING ARRANGEMENTS AND SEX	PERSONS 18 TO 24 YEARS OLD				PERSONS 25 TO 34 YEARS OLD			
	1980	1985	1990	1995	1980	1985	1990	1995
Total (1,000)	29,122	27,844	25,310	25,158	36,796	40,857	43,240	41,389
Percent distribution:								
Child of householder [1]	48	54	53	53	9	11	12	12
Family householder or spouse . . .	29	24	22	21	72	68	65	63
Nonfamily householder.	10	8	9	9	12	13	13	13
Other	13	14	16	17	7	9	11	13
Male (1,000)	14,278	13,695	12,450	12,545	18,107	20,184	21,462	20,589
Percent distribution:								
Child of householder [1]	54	60	58	58	11	13	15	15
Family householder or spouse . . .	21	16	15	13	66	60	56	53
Nonfamily householder.	11	10	10	10	15	16	16	16
Other	13	14	17	18	8	11	13	15
Female (1,000)	14,844	14,149	12,860	12,613	18,689	20,673	21,779	20,800
Percent distribution:								
Child of householder [1]	43	48	48	47	7	8	8	8
Family householder or spouse . . .	36	32	30	28	78	76	73	72
Nonfamily householder.	8	7	8	9	9	10	10	10
Other	13	13	15	16	6	7	9	10

[1] Includes unmarried college students living in dormitories.

F1-7   Households, Families, Subfamilies, Married Couples, and Unrelated Individuals: 1970–1996

TYPE OF UNIT	1970	1975	1980	1985	1990	1994	1995	1996	PERCENT CHANGE 1970-80	1980-90	1990-96
Households	63,401	71,120	80,776	86,789	93,347	97,107	98,990	99,627	27	16	7
Average size	3.14	2.94	2.76	2.69	2.63	2.67	2.65	2.65	(X)	(X)	(X)
Family households	51,456	55,563	59,550	62,706	66,090	68,490	69,305	69,594	16	11	5
Married couple	44,728	46,951	49,112	50,350	52,317	53,171	53,858	53,567	10	7	2
Male householder \1	1,228	1,485	1,733	2,228	2,884	2,913	3,226	3,513	41	66	22
Female householder \1	5,500	7,127	8,705	10,129	10,890	12,406	12,220	12,514	58	25	15
Nonfamily households	11,945	15,557	21,226	24,082	27,257	28,617	29,686	30,033	78	28	10
Male householder	4,063	5,912	8,807	10,114	11,606	12,462	13,190	13,348	117	32	15
Female householder	7,882	9,645	12,419	13,968	15,651	16,155	16,496	16,685	58	26	7
One person	10,851	13,939	18,296	20,602	22,999	23,611	24,732	24,900	69	26	8
Families	51,586	55,712	59,550	62,706	66,090	68,490	69,305	69,594	15	11	5
Average size	3.58	3.42	3.29	3.23	3.17	3.20	3.19	3.20	(X)	(X)	(X)
Married couple	44,755	46,971	49,112	50,350	52,317	53,171	53,858	53,567	10	7	2
Male householder \1	1,239	1,499	1,733	2,228	2,884	2,913	3,226	3,513	40	66	22
Female householder \1	5,591	7,242	8,705	10,129	10,890	12,406	12,220	12,514	56	25	15
Unrelated subfamilies	130	149	360	526	534	716	674	588	177	48	10
Married couple	27	20	20	46	68	66	64	51	(B)	(B)	(B)
Male reference persons \1	11	14	36	85	45	78	59	45	(B)	(B)	(B)
Female reference persons \	91	115	304	395	421	571	550	493	234	39	17
Related subfamilies	1,150	1,349	1,150	2,228	2,403	2,813	2,878	2,942	0	109	22
Married couple	617	576	582	719	871	1,014	1,015	1,046	-6	50	20
Father-child \1	48	69	54	116	153	164	195	189	(B)	(B)	24
Mother-child \1	484	705	512	1,392	1,378	1,636	1,668	1,706	6	169	24
Married couples	45,373	47,547	49,714	51,114	53,256	54,251	54,937	54,664	10	7	3
With own household	44,728	46,951	49,112	50,350	52,317	53,171	53,858	53,567	10	7	2
Without own househol	645	596	602	764	939	1,080	1,079	1,097	-7	56	17
Percent without	1.4	1.3	1.2	1.5	1.8	2.0	2.0	2.0	(X)	(X)	(X)
Unrelated individuals	14,988	19,100	26,426	30,518	35,384	38,469	39,048	40,077	76	34	13
Nonfamily householders	11,945	15,557	21,226	24,082	27,257	28,617	29,686	30,033	78	28	10
Secondary individuals	3,043	3,543	5,200	6,436	8,127	9,852	9,362	10,044	71	56	24
Male	1,631	2,087	3,006	3,743	4,711	5,892	5,442	5,739	84	57	22
Female	1,412	1,456	2,194	2,693	3,416	3,961	3,920	4,305	55	56	26

- Represents or rounds to zero. B Not shown; base less than 75,000.
X Not applicable. \1 No spouse present.

F1-8   Households—Projections, by Type of Household: 1997–2010

TYPE OF HOUSEHOLD	1997	1998	1999	2000	2005	2010
TOTAL HOUSEHOLDS						
Series 1	99,965	101,043	102,119	103,246	108,819	114,825
Series 2	99,880	100,924	101,966	103,058	108,426	114,200
Series 3	99,680	100,684	101,683	102,734	107,892	113,426
TYPE OF HOUSEHOLD (Series 1)						
Total	99,965	101,043	102,119	103,246	108,819	114,825
Family households	69,761	70,387	71,015	71,669	74,733	77,895
Married couple	54,319	54,707	55,092	55,496	57,371	59,308
Female householder, no spouse present	11,774	11,935	12,101	12,272	13,084	13,927
Male householder, no spouse present......	3,668	3,745	3,822	3,901	4,278	4,660
With children under 18................	32,951	33,001	33,058	33,117	32,699	32,203
Married couple	24,770	24,740	24,713	24,686	23,958	23,126
Female householder, no spouse present ...	6,571	6,624	6,679	6,737	6,944	7,189
Male householder, no spouse present	1,610	1,638	1,666	1,694	1,797	1,888
Without children under 18...............	36,810	37,386	37,957	38,552	42,034	45,692
Married couple	29,549	29,968	30,378	30,810	33,413	36,182
Female householder, no spouse present ...	5,202	5,311	5,422	5,535	6,140	6,738
Male householder, no spouse present	2,058	2,107	2,157	2,208	2,481	2,772
Nonfamily households.................	30,204	30,656	31,104	31,577	34,086	36,931
Female householder, total...............	16,464	16,671	16,875	17,095	18,301	19,702
Living alone [1]	14,480	14,664	14,844	15,035	16,093	17,327
Male householder, total	13,741	13,985	14,228	14,482	15,784	17,229
Living alone [1]	10,587	10,789	10,989	11,195	12,244	13,400

[1] These counts cover individuals 15 years of age or older.

F1-9   Households, 1980–1996, and Persons in Households in 1996, by Type of Household and Presence of Children

TYPE OF HOUSEHOLD AND PRESENCE OF CHILDREN	HOUSEHOLDS					PERSONS IN HOUSEHOLDS, 1996		Persons per house-hold, 1996
	Number (1,000)			Percent distribution		Number (1,000)	Percent distribution	
	1980	1990	1996	1990	1996			
Total households	80,776	93,347	99,627	100	100	264,234	100	2.65
Family households	59,550	66,090	69,594	71	70	226,811	86	3.26
With own children under 18........	31,022	32,289	34,203	35	34	136,001	51	3.98
Without own children under 18......	28,528	33,801	35,391	36	36	90,810	34	2.57
Married couple family..............	49,112	52,317	53,567	56	54	174,985	66	3.27
With own children under 18........	24,961	24,537	24,920	26	25	104,667	40	4.20
Without own children under 18......	24,151	27,780	28,647	30	29	70,318	26	2.44
Male householder, no spouse present...	1,733	2,884	3,513	3	4	11,168	4	3.18
With own children under 18........	616	1,153	1,628	1	2	5,522	2	3.39
Without own children under 18......	1,117	1,731	1,885	2	2	5,646	2	3.00
Female householder, no spouse present.	8,705	10,890	12,514	12	13	40,658	15	3.25
With own children under 18........	5,445	6,599	7,656	7	8	25,812	10	3.37
Without own children under 18......	3,261	4,290	4,859	5	5	14,846	6	3.06
Nonfamily households..............	21,226	27,257	30,033	29	30	37,424	14	1.25
Living alone	18,296	22,999	24,900	25	25	24,900	9	1.00
Male householder..............	8,807	11,606	13,348	12	13	18,072	7	1.35
Living alone	6,966	9,049	10,288	10	10	10,288	4	1.00
Female householder..............	12,419	15,651	16,685	17	17	19,352	7	1.16
Living alone	11,330	13,950	14,612	15	15	14,612	6	1.00

F1-10 Household Characteristics, by Type of Household, 1995

CHARACTERISTIC	NUMBER OF HOUSEHOLDS (1,000)					PERCENT DISTRIBUTION				
		Family households			Non-family house-holds		Family households			Non-family house-holds
	Total	Total [1]	Married couple	Female house-holder [2]		Total	Total [1]	Married couple	Female house-holder [2]	
Total..............	98,990	69,305	53,858	12,220	29,686	100	100	100	100	100
Age of householder:										
15 to 24 years old.......	5,444	3,079	1,632	1,124	2,365	5	4	3	9	8
25 to 29 years old......	8,400	5,575	3,959	1,234	2,825	8	8	7	10	10
30 to 34 years old......	11,052	8,502	6,357	1,731	2,551	11	12	12	14	9
35 to 44 years old......	22,914	18,273	13,919	3,502	4,641	23	26	26	29	16
45 to 54 years old......	17,590	13,746	11,153	2,037	3,845	18	20	21	17	13
55 to 64 years old......	12,224	8,894	7,552	1,056	3,330	12	13	14	9	11
65 to 74 years old......	11,803	7,268	6,169	853	4,535	12	10	11	7	15
75 years old and over	9,562	3,969	3,117	683	5,593	10	6	6	6	19
Region:										
Northeast	19,593	13,482	10,336	2,515	6,111	20	19	19	21	21
Midwest	23,683	16,264	12,836	2,754	7,418	24	23	24	23	25
South	34,766	24,871	19,201	4,590	9,895	35	36	36	38	33
West................	20,948	14,687	11,485	2,363	6,261	21	21	21	19	21
Size of household:										
One person	24,732	(X)	(X)	(X)	24,732	25	(X)	(X)	(X)	83
Two persons	31,834	27,875	21,366	5,065	3,959	32	40	40	41	13
Three persons	16,827	16,212	11,485	3,809	614	17	23	21	31	2
Four persons	15,321	15,056	12,741	1,837	265	15	22	24	15	1
Five persons	6,616	6,530	5,433	904	86	7	9	10	7	(Z)
Six persons	2,279	2,260	1,823	337	19	2	3	3	3	(Z)
Seven persons or more ...	1,382	1,372	1,010	269	10	1	2	2	2	(Z)
Marital status of householder:										
Never married (single)	15,802	4,421	(X)	3,240	11,381	16	6	(X)	27	38
Married, spouse present...	53,858	53,858	53,858	(X)	(X)	54	78	100	(X)	(X)
Married, spouse absent ...	4,708	2,645	(X)	2,160	2,063	5	4	(X)	18	7
Widowed.............	11,450	2,715	(X)	2,283	8,734	12	4	(X)	19	29
Divorced	13,174	5,666	(X)	4,537	7,508	13	8	(X)	37	25
Tenure:										
Owner occupied	64,045	49,970	42,780	5,440	14,075	65	72	79	45	47
Renter occupied	34,946	19,335	11,078	6,781	15,611	35	28	21	55	53

X Not applicable.   Z Less than 0.5 percent.   [1] Includes male householder, no spouse present.   [2] No spouse present.

F1-11 Households, by States: 1980–1996

REGION, DIVISION, AND STATE	NUMBER (1,000)					1996		PERCENT CHANGE		PERSONS PER HOUSEHOLD		
	1980	1990	1993	1994	1995	Total	Householder 65 yrs. and over	1980-90	1990-96	1980	1990	1996
U.S.	80,390	91,946	95,358	95,988	97,386	98,751	21,381	14.4	7.4	2.75	2.63	2.62
Northeast . . .	17,471	18,873	19,080	19,058	19,180	19,298	4,567	8.0	2.3	2.74	2.61	2.64
N.E.	4,362	4,943	4,980	4,982	5,030	5,078	1,158	13.3	2.7	2.74	2.58	2.61
ME	395	465	474	473	477	483	109	17.7	3.8	2.75	2.56	2.54
NH.	323	411	419	423	431	439	85	27.1	6.7	2.75	2.62	2.62
VT.	178	211	218	220	223	227	45	18.1	7.5	2.75	2.57	2.57
MA	2,033	2,247	2,264	2,269	2,297	2,322	536	10.5	3.3	2.72	2.58	2.61
RI	339	378	378	376	376	378	96	11.6	-0.1	2.70	2.55	2.56
CT	1,094	1,230	1,227	1,222	1,225	1,231	287	12.5	-	2.76	2.59	2.65
M.A.	13,109	13,930	14,100	14,077	14,150	14,219	3,409	6.3	2.1	2.74	2.62	2.65
NY. . . .	6,340	6,639	6,702	6,684	6,709	6,737	1,524	4.7	1.5	2.70	2.63	2.65
NJ. . . .	2,549	2,795	2,839	2,841	2,866	2,889	674	9.7	3.4	2.84	2.70	2.75
PA. . . .	4,220	4,496	4,559	4,552	4,575	4,594	1,211	6.6	2.2	2.74	2.57	2.58
Midwest	20,859	22,317	22,878	22,928	23,156	23,390	5,184	7.0	4.8	2.75	2.60	2.59
E.N.C	14,654	15,597	16,008	16,029	16,178	16,339	3,567	6.4	4.8	2.78	2.63	2.61
OH	3,834	4,088	4,187	4,187	4,223	4,260	956	6.6	4.2	2.76	2.59	2.54
IN	1,927	2,065	2,149	2,156	2,182	2,209	472	7.2	6.9	2.77	2.61	2.57
IL	4,045	4,202	4,294	4,295	4,322	4,352	942	3.9	3.6	2.76	2.65	2.65
MI	3,195	3,419	3,494	3,500	3,534	3,576	765	7.0	4.6	2.84	2.66	2.66
WI	1,652	1,822	1,883	1,891	1,917	1,943	432	10.3	6.6	2.77	2.61	2.61
W.N.C	6,205	6,720	6,870	6,899	6,978	7,051	1,617	8.3	4.9	2.68	2.55	2.54
MN	1,445	1,648	1,702	1,716	1,740	1,763	366	14.0	7.0	2.74	2.58	2.58
IA	1,053	1,064	1,084	1,084	1,093	1,103	275	1.1	3.6	2.68	2.52	2.51
MO	1,793	1,961	2,001	2,009	2,031	2,052	478	9.4	4.6	2.67	2.53	2.51
ND. . . .	228	241	242	242	244	247	60	5.8	2.4	2.75	2.55	2.51
SD. . . .	243	259	265	267	270	273	68	6.8	5.4	2.74	2.59	2.56
NE. . . .	571	602	615	616	624	631	147	5.4	4.8	2.66	2.54	2.54
KS. . . .	872	945	962	965	975	982	224	8.3	3.9	2.62	2.53	2.54
South	26,486	31,821	33,363	33,733	34,351	34,949	7,535	20.1	9.8	2.77	2.61	2.58
S.A.	13,160	16,502	17,325	17,525	17,837	18,146	4,102	25.4	10.0	2.73	2.56	2.56
DE. . . .	207	247	262	264	270	276	58	19.5	11.4	2.79	2.61	2.62
MD	1,461	1,749	1,816	1,830	1,853	1,871	356	19.7	7.0	2.82	2.67	2.70
DC. . . .	253	250	243	238	233	231	50	-1.4	-7.3	2.40	2.26	2.24
VA. . . .	1,863	2,292	2,414	2,439	2,476	2,511	469	23.0	9.6	2.77	2.61	2.61
WV	686	689	705	705	709	714	187	0.3	3.7	2.79	2.55	2.50
NC. . . .	2,043	2,517	2,646	2,680	2,738	2,796	589	23.2	11.1	2.78	2.54	2.53
SC. . . .	1,030	1,258	1,328	1,331	1,352	1,376	289	22.1	9.4	2.93	2.68	2.64
GA. . . .	1,872	2,366	2,533	2,587	2,654	2,723	465	26.4	15.1	2.84	2.66	2.65
FL	3,744	5,135	5,379	5,451	5,551	5,648	1,640	37.1	10.0	2.55	2.46	2.45
E.S.C	5,051	5,652	5,886	5,933	6,026	6,122	1,342	11.9	8.3	2.83	2.62	2.56
KY. . . .	1,263	1,380	1,430	1,437	1,457	1,478	322	9.2	7.1	2.82	2.60	2.55
TN. . . .	1,619	1,854	1,941	1,965	2,002	2,041	431	14.5	10.1	2.77	2.56	2.52
AL. . . .	1,342	1,507	1,574	1,582	1,603	1,624	367	12.3	7.8	2.84	2.62	2.56
MS	827	911	941	948	964	979	222	10.2	7.4	2.97	2.75	2.66
W.S.C	8,276	9,667	10,152	10,276	10,488	10,681	2,091	16.8	10.5	2.80	2.69	2.65
AR.	816	891	919	925	938	951	236	9.2	6.7	2.74	2.57	2.51
LA. . . .	1,412	1,499	1,539	1,543	1,559	1,572	324	6.2	4.8	2.91	2.74	2.67
OK. . . .	1,119	1,206	1,235	1,238	1,250	1,265	291	7.8	4.9	2.62	2.53	2.50
TX. . . .	4,929	6,071	6,458	6,570	6,741	6,894	1,240	23.2	13.6	2.82	2.73	2.69
West.	15,574	18,935	20,038	20,269	20,699	21,113	4,096	21.6	11.5	2.71	2.72	2.70
Mountain . .	3,986	5,033	5,444	5,607	5,844	6,022	1,157	26.3	19.6	2.79	2.65	2.61
MT.	284	306	321	326	335	341	75	7.9	11.3	2.70	2.53	2.50
ID	324	361	395	405	419	430	86	11.3	19.1	2.85	2.73	2.68
WY	166	169	176	178	181	184	35	1.9	8.8	2.78	2.63	2.55
CO	1,061	1,282	1,388	1,424	1,466	1,502	246	20.8	17.1	2.65	2.51	2.47
NM	441	543	578	592	607	619	122	22.9	14.1	2.90	2.74	2.64
AZ. . . .	957	1,369	1,466	1,518	1,624	1,687	366	43.0	23.3	2.79	2.62	2.59
UT.	449	537	586	600	621	639	112	19.8	19.0	3.20	3.15	3.06
NV.	304	466	535	562	591	619	115	53.2	32.8	2.59	2.53	2.53
Pacific. . . .	11,587	13,902	14,593	14,662	14,855	15,092	2,939	20.0	8.6	2.68	2.74	2.73
WA	1,541	1,872	2,019	2,049	2,097	2,139	406	21.5	14.2	2.61	2.53	2.53
OR	992	1,103	1,180	1,197	1,223	1,249	273	11.3	13.2	2.60	2.52	2.51
CA.	8,630	10,381	10,812	10,829	10,941	11,101	2,153	20.3	6.9	2.68	2.79	2.79
AK.	131	189	206	207	210	214	20	43.7	13.4	2.93	2.80	2.76
HI	294	356	376	380	384	389	87	21.2	9.0	3.15	3.01	2.97

- Represents or rounds to zero.

F1-12   Family and Nonfamily Households, by Race, Hispanic Origin, and Type: 1980–1996

RACE, HISPANIC ORIGIN, AND TYPE	NUMBER (1,000)					PERCENT DISTRIBUTION				
	1980	1985	1990	1995	1996	1980	1985	1990	1995	1996
TOTAL HOUSEHOLDS										
Total [1]	80,776	86,789	93,347	98,990	99,627	100	100	100	100	100
White	70,766	75,328	80,163	83,737	84,511	88	87	86	85	85
Black	8,586	9,480	10,486	11,655	11,577	11	11	11	12	12
Hispanic [2]	3,684	4,883	5,933	7,735	7,939	5	6	6	8	8
FAMILY HOUSEHOLDS										
White, total	52,243	54,400	56,590	58,437	58,869	100	100	100	100	100
Married couple	44,751	45,643	46,981	47,899	47,873	86	84	83	82	81
Male householder [3]	1,441	1,816	2,303	2,507	2,712	3	3	4	4	5
Female householder [3]	6,052	6,941	7,306	8,031	8,284	12	13	13	14	14
Black, total	6,184	6,778	7,470	8,093	8,055	100	100	100	100	100
Married couple	3,433	3,469	3,750	3,842	3,713	56	51	50	47	46
Male householder [3]	256	344	446	536	573	4	5	6	7	7
Female householder [3]	2,495	2,964	3,275	3,716	3,769	40	44	44	46	47
Asian or Pacific Islander, total [4]	818	(NA)	1,531	1,588	2,125	100	(NA)	100	100	100
Married couple	691	(NA)	1,256	1,290	1,692	84	(NA)	82	81	80
Male householder [3]	39	(NA)	86	98	173	5	(NA)	6	6	8
Female householder [3]	88	(NA)	188	200	260	11	(NA)	12	13	12
Hispanic, total [2]	3,029	3,939	4,840	6,200	6,287	100	100	100	100	100
Married couple	2,282	2,824	3,395	4,235	4,247	75	72	70	68	68
Male householder [3]	138	210	329	479	436	5	5	7	8	7
Female householder [3]	610	905	1,116	1,485	1,604	20	23	23	24	26
NONFAMILY HOUSEHOLDS										
White, total	18,522	20,928	23,573	25,300	25,642	100	100	100	100	100
Male householder	7,499	8,608	9,951	11,093	11,367	40	41	42	44	44
Female householder	11,023	12,320	13,622	14,207	14,275	60	59	58	56	56
Black, total	2,402	2,703	3,015	3,562	3,521	100	100	100	100	100
Male householder	1,146	1,244	1,313	1,653	1,532	48	46	44	46	44
Female householder	1,256	1,459	1,702	1,909	1,989	52	54	56	54	56
Hispanic, total [2]	654	944	1,093	1,535	1,652	100	100	100	100	100
Male householder	365	509	587	790	865	56	54	54	51	52
Female householder	289	435	506	745	787	44	46	46	49	48

NA Not available.   [1] Includes other races not shown separately.   [2] Hispanic persons may be of any race.   [3] No spouse present.   [4] 1980 data as of April and are from 1980 Census of Population. When comparing 1995 estimates of number of households with other years. caution should be used.

F1-13   Family Groups with Children under 18 Years Old, by Race and Hispanic Origin: 1980–1996

RACE AND HISPANIC ORIGIN OF HOUSEHOLDER OR REFERENCE PERSON	NUMBER (1,000)				PERCENT DISTRIBUTION			
	1980	1990	1995	1996	1980	1990	1995	1996
All races, total [1]	32,150	34,670	37,168	37,077	100	100	100	100
Two-parent family groups	25,231	24,921	25,640	25,361	79	72	69	68
One-parent family groups	6,920	9,749	11,528	11,717	22	28	31	32
Maintained by mother	6,230	8,398	9,834	9,855	19	24	26	27
Maintained by father	690	1,351	1,694	1,862	2	4	5	5
White, total	27,294	28,294	29,846	29,947	100	100	100	100
Two-parent family groups	22,628	21,905	22,320	22,178	83	77	75	74
One-parent family groups	4,664	6,389	7,525	7,769	17	23	25	26
Maintained by mother	4,122	5,310	6,239	6,329	15	19	21	21
Maintained by father	542	1,079	1,286	1,440	2	4	4	5
Black, total	4,074	5,087	5,491	5,434	100	100	100	100
Two-parent family groups	1,961	2,006	1,962	1,942	48	39	36	36
One-parent family groups	2,114	3,081	3,529	3,493	52	61	64	64
Maintained by mother	1,984	2,860	3,197	3,171	49	56	58	58
Maintained by father	129	221	332	322	3	4	6	6
Hispanic, total [2]	2,194	3,429	4,527	4,560	100	100	100	100
Two-parent family groups	1,626	2,289	2,879	2,858	74	67	64	63
One-parent family groups	568	1,140	1,647	1,702	26	33	36	37
Maintained by mother	526	1,003	1,404	1,483	24	29	31	33
Maintained by father	42	138	243	219	2	4	5	5

[1] Includes other races. not shown separately.   [2] Hispanic persons may be of any race.

F1-14 Percent Living Alone, by Age, 1994

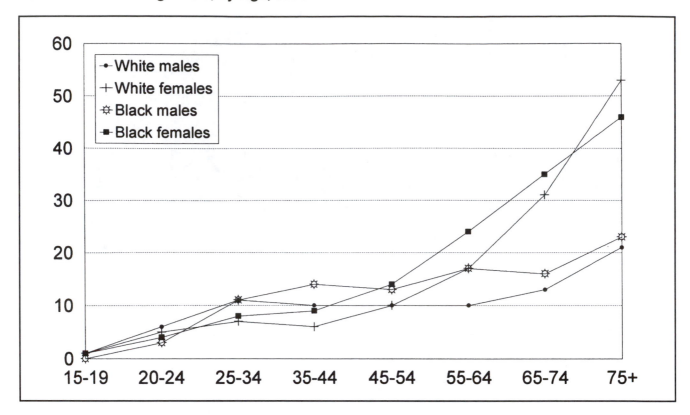

F1-15 Percent of Children under 18 Living with Both Parents: 1980–1990

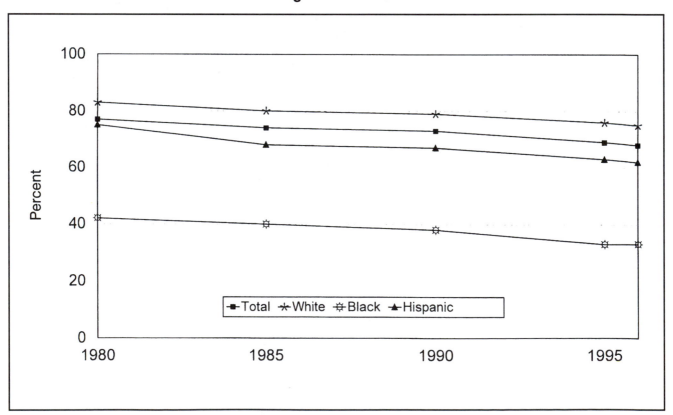

F1-16 Percent of Children Living with Both Parents: 1970–1996

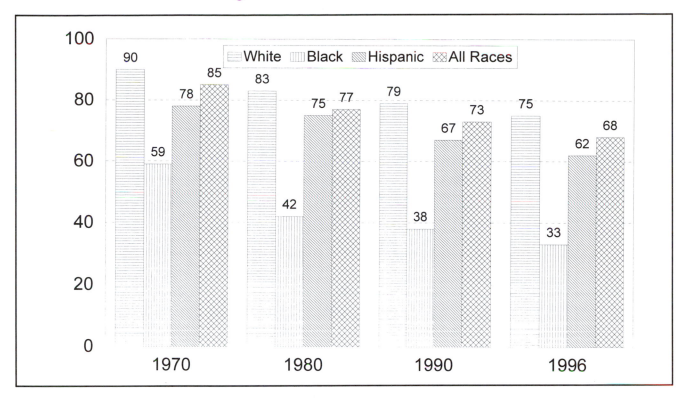

F1-17 Average Size of Households and Families: 1960–1993

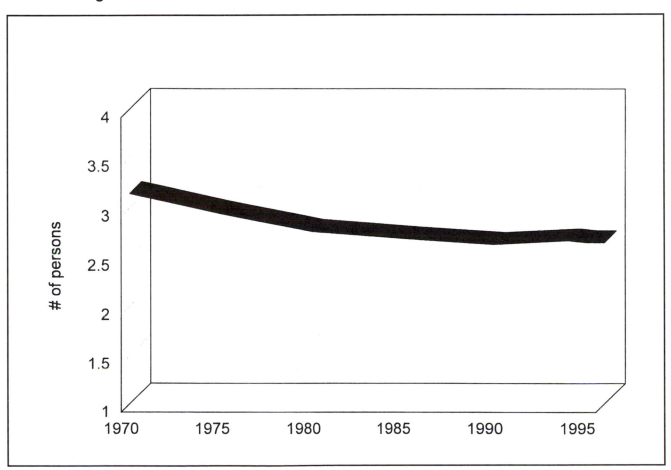

F1-18 Household Size and Population: 1993, 1990, 1980, and 1970

(Number in thousands)

Subject	1993		1990		1980		1970	
	Number	Percent	Number	Percent	Number	Percent	Number	Percent
Total households	93,391	100.0	93,347	100.0	80,776	100.0	63,401	100.0
1 person	23,642	24.5	22,999	24.6	18,296	22.7	10,851	17.1
2 persons	31,175	32.3	30,114	32.3	25,327	31.4	18,333	28.9
3 persons	16,895	17.5	16,128	17.3	14,130	17.5	10,949	17.3
4 persons	14,926	15.5	14,456	15.5	12,666	15.7	9,991	15.8
5 persons	6,357	6.6	6,213	6.7	6,059	7.5	6,548	10.3
6 persons	2,180	2.3	2,143	2.3	2,519	3.1	3,534	5.6
7 or more persons	1,215	1.3	1,295	1.4	1,778	2.2	3,195	5.0
Population in households	253,924	100.0	245,774	100.0	222,540	100.0	199,030	100.0
Under 18 years	67,062	26.4	64,303	26.2	63,492	28.5	69,152	34.7
18 years and over	186,862	73.6	181,471	73.8	159,048	71.5	129,878	65.3
Persons per household	2.63	(X)	2.63	(X)	2.76	(X)	3.14	(X)
Under 18 years	0.70	(X)	0.69	(X)	0.79	(X)	1.09	(X)
18 years and over	1.94	(X)	1.94	(X)	1.97	(X)	2.05	(X)

(X) Not applicable

2. COHABITATION

F2-1   Number of Women 15-44 Years of Age and Percent Who Have Ever Cohabited, Are Currently Cohabiting, Have Ever Married, or Have Ever Married or Cohabited: United States, 1995

Characteristic	Number in thousands	Ever cohabited	Currently cohabiting	Ever married	Ever married or cohabited
			Percent		
All women	60,201	41.1	7.0	62.3	72.5
Age at interview					
15-19 years	8,961	8.9	4.1	4.5	11.4
20-24 years	9,041	38.4	11.2	34.3	54.5
25-29 years	9,693	49.3	9.8	64.3	79.7
30-34 years	11,065	51.4	7.5	79.9	89.2
35-39 years	11,211	50.0	5.2	86.5	92.9
40-44 years	10,230	43.0	4.4	90.4	94.5
Marital status at interview					
Never married	22,679	27.0	11.4	NA	27.0
Currently married	29,673	45.4	NA	100.0	100.0
Formerly married	7,849	65.4	20.7	100.0	100.0
Parity					
0 births	25,242	29.4	7.4	28.3	42.0
1 birth	10,706	52.5	8.2	76.9	98.5
2 births	13,875	47.4	6.4	91.3	97.1
3 or more births	10,377	49.2	6.7	91.2	97.2
Education at interview[1]					
No high school diploma or GED[2]	5,424	60.1	11.6	76.8	91.4
High school diploma or GED	18,169	52.0	8.0	81.9	91.3
Some college, no bachelors degree	12,399	46.3	6.8	72.8	82.9
Bachelor's degree or higher	11,748	37.8	5.1	70.5	79.8
Poverty level income at interview[1]					
0-149 percent	10,072	53.5	7.7	67.4	83.2
0-99 percent	5,992	54.4	7.2	64.0	81.6
150-299 percent	14,932	46.2	7.3	76.8	86.1
300 percent or higher	22,736	46.6	7.3	79.6	87.8
Race and Hispanic origin					
Hispanic	6,702	36.7	8.2	61.4	71.8
Non-Hispanic white	42,522	42.6	7.0	66.4	75.3
Non-Hispanic black	8,210	40.1	6.9	43.1	60.3
Non-Hispanic other	2,767	31.7	4.6	68.5	66.8

NA Category not applicable.
[1]Limited to women 22-44 years of age at time of interview.
[2]GED is general equivalency diploma.

F2-2   Number of Women 15–44 Years of Age and Percent Distribution by Cohabitation Experience Relative to First Marriage, According to Selected Characteristics: United States, 1995

Characteristic	Number in thousands	Total	Ever cohabited			
			Never cohabited	Never married	Before first marriage	After first marriage
			Percent distribution			
All women	60,201	100.0	58.9	10.2	23.6	7.3
Age at interview						
15-19 years	8,961	100.0	91.1	7.0	1.8	0.1
20-24 years	9,041	100.0	61.6	20.2	17.2	0.9
25-29 years	9,693	100.0	50.7	15.4	30.1	3.8
30-34 years	11,065	100.0	48.6	9.3	33.8	8.3
35-39 years	11,211	100.0	50.0	6.4	31.0	12.6
40-44 years	10,230	100.0	57.0	4.1	23.0	15.9
Marital status at interview						
Never married	22,679	100.0	73.0	27.0	(NA)	(NA)
Currently married	29,673	100.0	54.6	(NA)	36.8	8.6
Formerly married	7,849	100.0	34.6	(NA)	41.8	23.7
Parity						
0 births	25,242	100.0	70.6	13.7	13.4	2.3
1 birth	10,706	100.0	47.5	11.6	32.6	8.3
2 births	13,875	100.0	52.6	5.8	31.1	10.6
3 or more births	10,377	100.0	50.8	6.0	29.0	14.2
Education at interview[1]						
No high school diploma or GED[2]	5,424	100.0	39.9	14.6	31.1	14.5
High school diploma or GED	18,169	100.0	48.0	9.4	30.1	12.5
Some college, no bachelor's degree	12,399	100.0	53.7	10.1	28.7	7.5
Bachelor's degree or higher	11,748	100.0	62.2	9.2	25.1	3.5
Poverty level income at interview[1]						
0-149 percent	10,072	100.0	46.5	15.8	27.8	9.9
0-99 percent	5,992	100.0	45.6	17.7	27.0	9.7
150-299 percent	14,932	100.0	53.8	9.2	27.4	9.6
300 percent or higher	22,736	100.0	53.4	8.2	29.8	8.7
Race and Hispanic origin						
Hispanic	6,702	100.0	63.3	10.4	19.2	7.1
Non-Hispanic white	42,522	100.0	57.4	8.9	25.6	8.1
Non-Hispanic black	8,210	100.0	59.9	17.3	17.9	5.0
Non-Hispanic other	2,767	100.0	68.3	8.3	19.8	3.6

NA Category not applicable.
[1] Limited to women 22-44 years of age at time of interview.
[2] GED is general equivalency diploma.

NOTE: Percents may not add to 100 due to rounding.

F2-3   Number of Women 15–44 Years of Age Who Have Ever Cohabited and Percent Distribution by Status of First Cohabitation, According to Selected Characteristics: United States, 1995

Characteristic	Number in thousands	Intact total	Dissolved cohabitation	Intact cohabitation	Dissolved marriage	marriage
All women	24,737	100.0	9.8	32.8	36.5	20.8
Age at interview						
15-19 years	797	100.0	45.3	35.2	17.5	2.0
20-24 years	3,469	100.0	21.6	38.5	29.4	10.0
25-29 years	4,780	100.0	11.7	35.7	39.4	13.2
30-34 years	5,687	100.0	5.6	33.6	37.5	23.3
35-39 years	5,603	100.0	4.4	29.9	39.9	25.8
40-44 years	4,400	100.0	4.4	27.6	36.6	31.3
Marital status at interview						
Never married	6,117	100.0	30.5	69.5	(NA)	(NA)
Currently married	13,485	100.0	(NA)	18.7	67.0	14.3
Formerly married	5,135	100.0	11.0	26.4	(NA)	62.6
Parity						
0 births	7,428	100.0	17.7	43.7	27.3	11.3
1 birth	5,619	100.0	8.6	32.7	37.4	21.4
2 births	6,583	100.0	5.0	25.3	45.8	23.9
3 or more births	5,107	100.0	6.0	27.0	37.1	29.9
Education at interview[1]						
No high school diploma or GED[2]	3,262	100.0	9.6	34.4	27.9	28.1
High school diploma or GED	9,449	100.0	7.3	30.0	39.1	23.6
Some college, no bachelor's degree	5,736	100.0	7.4	32.9	37.5	32.9
Bachelor's degree or higher	4,443	100.0	8.4	35.0	41.9	14.7
Poverty level income at interview[1]						
0-149 percent	5,386	100.0	6.3	41.3	23.8	28.6
0-99 percent	3,257	100.0	5.5	45.6	20.9	28.0
150-299 percent	6,898	100.0	8.4	28.2	38.9	24.5
300 percent or higher	10,605	100.0	8.3	30.4	43.9	17.4
Race and Hispanic origin						
Hispanic	2,460	100.0	13.2	33.2	35.3	18.3
Non-Hispanic white	18,104	100.0	9.5	29.8	39.3	21.4
Non-Hispanic black	3,295	100.0	9.8	49.1	22.8	18.3
Non-Hispanic other	878	100.0	6.8	32.8	35.0	25.3

NA Category not applicable.
[1]Limited to women 22-44 years of age at time of interview.
[2]GED is general equivalency diploma.
NOTE: Percents may not add to 100 due to rounding.

F2-4   Marital and Cohabiting Experience of Women Aged 15–44

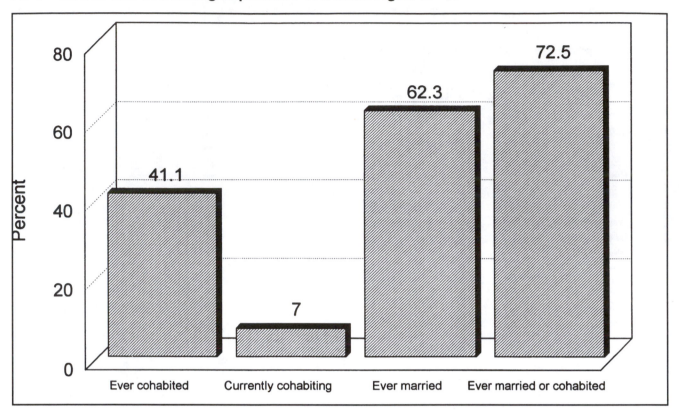

F2-5   Cohabitation Experience Relative to First Marriage, Women Aged 15–44

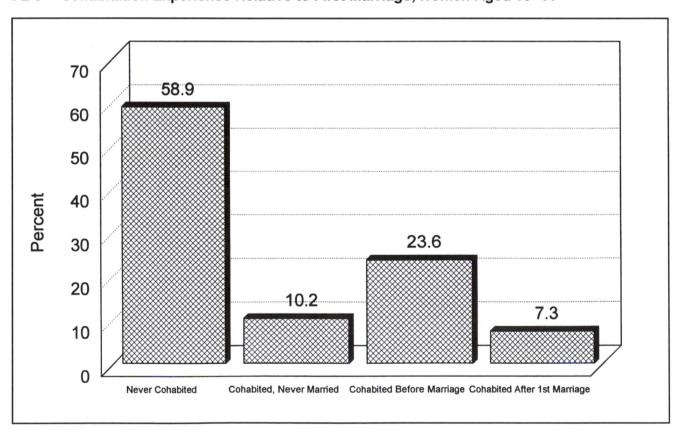

F2-6   Attitudes of Cohabiting Couples, by Sex

	Males	Females	Average
Percent saying their relationship is very happy	39	32	36
Percent saying they probably or definitely will get married	53	52	52
Percent saying they are very happy with:			
Understanding from partner	32	22	27
Love and affection	44	38	41
Time with partner	23	20	22
Demands partner places on you	18	23	20
Sexual relationship	40	33	37
Way partner spends money	25	24	25
Work partner does around the house	42	27	35
Partner as a parent	42	36	40
Percent saying that relationship is fair:			
Household chores	75	51	64
Working for pay	81	76	79
Spending money	80	71	76
Child care	45	48	46

F2-7   Feelings about Marriage, Dating, and Cohabitation: Unmarried Respondents Aged 18–35 Who Are Not Cohabiting, by Sex

	Males	Females	Average
Marriage would limit my independence too much.			
Strongly agree	9	17	14
Agree	22	23	23
Neither agree nor disagree	30	23	26
Disagree	30	26	28
Strongly disagree	9	11	10
I would like to be married now.			
Strongly agree	11	8	9
Agree	18	17	17
Neither agree nor disagree	26	21	23
Disagree	29	27	28
Strongly disagree	16	28	24
I would like to get married someday.			
Strongly agree	24	16	19
Agree	35	25	29
Neither agree nor disagree	18	16	16
Disagree	13	16	15
Strongly disagree	10	27	21
I would like to date more frequently than I do now.			
Strongly agree	16	9	12
Agree	32	24	27
Neither agree nor disagree	21	15	17
Disagree	19	23	22
Strongly disagree	11	29	22
I would like to live with someone before getting married.			
Strongly agree	16	7	10
Agree	27	10	16
Neither agree nor disagree	22	16	18
Disagree	18	22	20
Strongly disagree	18	46	36

3. KINSHIP

F3-1   Reported Contact with Adult Brothers and Sisters

During the past 12 months, how often did you see your brother and sister? Talk on phone or receive letter?

	N	Not at all	About once a year	Several times a year	1-3 times per month	Once a week	More than once a week
Total	(9217)	9%	12%	29%	17%	13%	19%

F3-2   Types of Help Given to and Received from Family Members

Types of Help	Friends / Neighbors	Parents / Children	Brothers / Sisters	Other Relatives
Percent who have given help to:				
Child Care	14	17	10	7
Transportation	27	28	8	8
Work around the house	15	27	6	6
Advice, encouragement, support	42	59	28	18
Percent who have received help from:				
Child Care	8	14	5	4
Transportation	17	17	5	4
Work around the house	11	23	4	5
Advice, encouragement, support	34	49	22	14

F3-3   Assistance Given to Adult Children

Next we are interested in help and support that you may have given to your children age 19 and older. During the last month, have you given help: with shopping/transportation? advice, encouragement, moral, or emotional support? child care while parents work? child care at time other then when working? About how many hours would you say you spent helping your children in the past week?

	N	Shopping/ Transportation	Encouragement/ Emotional support	Child care (working)	Child care (not working)	Number of hours last week
Total	(5011)	17%	74%	24%	32%	5.6
Age of Respondent						
35-44	(707)	24%	77%	28%	43%	6.4
45-64	(2586)	21%	81%	30%	43%	5.7
65 +	(1665)	9%	62%	17%	17%	5.0
Highest Year in School						
Less than h.s.	(1229)	14%	61%	20%	20%	7.7
High school	(2026)	18%	76%	28%	36%	6.1
Some college	(901)	21%	79%	25%	38%	4.5
16 + years	(838)	18%	82%	19%	35%	3.3
Marital Status						
Married	(3497)	18%	76%	26%	35%	5.1
Widowed	(134)	11%	72%	25%	27%	6.6
Divorced	(554)	22%	78%	23%	29%	6.1
Separated	(745)	11%	63%	19%	20%	7.5
Never married	(81)	16%	63%	14%	27%	8.0
Race of Respondent						
White	(4131)	17%	74%	23%	33%	5.1
Black	(526)	16%	72%	26%	28%	7.5
Hispanic	(310)	19%	78%	32%	28%	8.5
Sex of Respondent						
Male	(2207)	20%	69%	20%	27%	3.8
Female	(2804)	15%	78%	27%	35%	6.9

F3-4   Assistance Received from Adult Children

Next we are interested in the help and support that you have received from your children age 19 or older. During the last month, have you received help from your children with: shopping or transportation? housework or yard work? advice, encouragement, moral, or emotional support? In an average week, about how many hours do your children spend helping you?

	N	Shopping/ Transportation	Housework/ Yard work	Encouragement/ Emotional support	Hours of help received in average week
Total	(5011)	28%	29%	50%	3.9
Age of Respondent					
35-44	(707)	33%	33%	45%	4.4
45-64	(2586)	28%	31%	52%	3.6
65 +	(1665)	28%	25%	51%	4.0
Highest Year in School					
Less than h.s.	(1230)	35%	32%	47%	6.0
High school	(2026)	29%	30%	49%	3.7
Some college	(901)	26%	26%	54%	3.1
16 + years	(838)	20%	27%	52%	2.0
Marital Status					
Married	(3497)	25%	27%	47%	3.1
Widowed	(134)	33%	24%	51%	5.4
Divorced	(554)	30%	30%	56%	4.6
Separated	(745)	43%	39%	60%	5.8
Never married	(81)	35%	27%	43%	6.1
Race of Respondent					
White	(4132)	26%	27%	49%	3.3
Black	(525)	39%	36%	51%	6.2
Hispanic	(310)	40%	35%	55%	5.7
Sex of Respondent					
Male	(2207)	20%	24%	38%	2.9
Female	(2804)	35%	33%	59%	4.4

F3-5 Grandparents' Interaction with Grandchildren

The next questions are about grandchildren. How many grandchildren do you have? On a scale of 0 to 10, how would you describe your relationship with your grandchildren? Have you ever had primary responsibility for raising a grandchild?

	N	Number of grandchildren	Closeness to grandchildren (0-not at all close 10=very close)	Primary responsibility (% yes)
Total	(3501)	5.3	8.7	11%
Age of Respondent				
35-44	(239)	1.8	8.4	11%
45-64	(1732)	4.6	8.8	11%
65 +	(1523)	6.8	8.6	12%
Highest Year in School				
Less than h.s.	(1041)	6.9	8.7	18%
High school	(1453)	5.1	8.8	9%
Some college	(545)	4.1	8.6	9%
16 + years	(451)	4.0	8.2	3%
Marital Status				
Married	(2345)	5.0	8.7	9%
Widowed	(90)	5.4	8.0	18%
Divorced	(356)	4.3	8.1	11%
Separated	(670)	6.9	8.8	16%
Never married	(39)	3.0	8.9	26%
Race of Respondent				
White	(2873)	5.1	8.6	9%
Black	(392)	5.7	9.1	23%
Hispanic	(218)	7.0	8.8	14%
Sex of Respondent				
Male	(1507)	4.9	8.3	6%
Female	(1994)	5.6	9.0	15%

4. ELDERLY FAMILIES

F4-1   Residence of Aged Parents

Do/Does your parents/ mother/father live in:	N	House Apartment	Home of child/ relation	Adult care/ old folks home	Nursing home	Some-place close	Total
Total	(5519)	92%	4%	0%	3%	1%	100%
Age of Respondent							
18-24	(312)	93%	6%	0%	0%	1%	100%
25-34	(1766)	97%	2%	0%	0%	0%	99%
35-44	(1907)	95%	3%	0%	1%	0%	99%
45-64	(1425)	86%	6%	1%	6%	0%	99%
65+	(108)	55%	13%	2%	30%	1%	101+
Highest Year in School							
Less than h.s.	(647)	87%	8%	0%	3%	1%	99%
High school	(1985)	92%	4%	0%	2%	1%	99%
Some college	(1548)	93%	4%	1%	2%	0%	100%
16+ years	(1331)	93%	2%	1%	3%	1%	100%
Marital Status							
Married	(3800)	92%	4%	0%	3%	1%	100%
Widowed	(120)	71%	17%	1%	10%	1%	100%
Divorced	(612)	91%	5%	1%	3%	1%	101%
Separated	(168)	93%	4%	0%	2%	1%	100%
Never married	(819)	97%	2%	0%	1%	0%	100%
Race of Respondent							
White	(4466)	93%	3%	1%	3%	0%	100%
Black	(528)	90%	7%	0%	2%	1%	100%
Hispanic	(441)	88%	10%	0%	1%	1%	100%
Other	(83)	86%	10%	0%	4%	0%	100%
Sex of Respondent							
Male	(2706)	92%	4%	0%	3%	1%	100%
Female	(2813)	92%	4%	1%	3%	0%	100%

F4-2　Respondents' Reported Relationships with Aged Parents

Taking all these together, how would you describe your relationship with your mother (father)?	Relationship with Mother (N=6004)	Relationship with Father (N=4331)
Total	8.1[a]	7.4
Age of Respondent		
18-24	8.2	7.1
25-34	8.1	7.2
35-44	8.0	7.4
45-64	8.2	7.7
65+	8.3	8.8
Highest Year in School		
Less than h.s.	8.2	7.0
High school	8.3	7.4
Some college	7.9	7.3
16+ years	7.9	7.6
Marital Status		
Married	8.1	7.5
Widowed	8.0	6.9
Divorced	7.8	7.0
Separated	7.8	7.0
Never married	8.2	7.2
Race of Respondent		
White	8.0	7.4
Black	8.7	7.1
Hispanic	8.2	7.2
Other	8.0	7.6
Sex of Respondent		
Male	8.1	7.4
Female	8.1	7.3

[a] Mean varying between "0" equals "really bad" to "10" equals "absolutely perfect"

F4-3   Frequency Adult Respondents Have Contact with Their Aged Mothers

During the past 12 months, about how often did you see (phone or write) your mother?

		Visit mother			Phone or write mother		
		Never/once a year	Several times a year	Once a week or more	Never/once a year	Several times a year	Once a week or more
Total	(5515)	14%	43%	43%	7%	31%	62%
Age of Respondent							
18-24	(309)	5%	26%	69%	10%	15%	75%
25-34	(1764)	11%	40%	49%	6%	25%	69%
35-44	(1907)	15%	49%	36%	5%	37%	59%
45-64	(1425)	18%	45%	38%	7%	34%	59%
65+	(108)	21%	35%	44%	29%	27%	44%
Highest Year in School							
Less than h.s.	(643)	20%	29%	51%	19%	27%	54%
High school	(1988)	13%	37%	50%	8%	29%	63%
Some college	(1540)	12%	45%	43%	4%	32%	64%
16+ years	(1333)	14%	58%	28%	2%	35%	63%
Marital Status							
Married	(3804)	14%	46%	40%	6%	32%	62%
Widowed	(119)	16%	25%	59%	10%	21%	69%
Divorced	(611)	16%	41%	43%	8%	31%	61%
Separated	(164)	12%	40%	48%	8%	27%	65%
Never married	(815)	13%	38%	49%	7%	25%	68%
Race of Respondent							
White	(4467)	13%	45%	42%	6%	31%	63%
Black	(523)	11%	35%	54%	6%	23%	71%
Hispanic	(436)	25%	36%	39%	12%	34%	54%
Other	(83)	33%	27%	40%	6%	39%	55%
Sex of Respondent							
Male	(2705)	15%	47%	38%	8%	38%	54%
Female	(2310)	13%	40%	47%	6%	24%	70%

F4-4 Percent of Respondents Who Gave Help to Aged Parents during the Past Month

Have you GIVEN help to your parents DURING THE LAST MONTH with the following?

	Shopping, transportation, running errands (N=7323)	Housework, yard, car repairs (N=7323)	Advice, encouragement, moral or emotional support (N=7306)
Average	34%	29%	64%
Age of Respondent			
18-24	49%	54%	68%
25-34	38%	36%	65%
35-44	30%	26%	63%
45-64	33%	23%	66%
65+	33%	19%	65%
Highest Year in School			
Less than h.s.	36%	31%	53%
High school	38%	32%	61%
Some college	34%	31%	68%
16 + years	27%	23%	71%
Marital Status			
Married	30%	24%	63%
Widowed	46%	28%	69%
Divorced	34%	30%	66%
Separated	34%	35%	62%
Never married	49%	50%	69%
Race of Respondent			
White	32%	29%	66%
Black	45%	36%	62%
Hispanic	39%	28%	57%
Other	37%	29%	69%
Sex of Respondent			
Male	32%	32%	59%
Female	36%	26%	70%

F4-5   Percent of Respondents Who Received Help from Aged Parents during the Past Month

DURING THE LAST MONTH, have you RECEIVED help from your parents?

	Shopping, errands, transportation (N=7323)	Advice, encouragement, moral or emotional support (N=7321)	Child care while you worked (N=28613)	Child care other than when working (N=3630)
Average	17%	56%	29%	30%
Age of Respondent				
18-24	45%	75%	48%	53%
25-34	28%	67%	35%	24%
35-44	15%	54%	24%	25%
46-64	6%	46%	17%	10%
65 +	0%	25%	0%	0%
Highest Year in School				
Less than h.s.	16%	47%	25%	24%
High school	18%	53%	30%	32%
Some college	20%	63%	32%	31%
16 + years	13%	56%	25%	30%
Marital Status				
Married	12%	49%	29%	29%
Widowed	9%	55%	42%	21%
Divorced	20%	64%	30%	30%
Separated	25%	70%	31%	37%
Never married	35%	74%	29%	40%
Race of Respondent				
White	16%	55%	29%	31%
Black	23%	63%	36%	35%
Hispanic	17%	64%	22%	19%
Other	19%	55%	39%	26%
Sex of Respondent				
Male	17%	51%	32%	29%
Female	18%	61%	26%	32%

G. Working Women, Wives, and Mothers

1. WORKING WOMEN

In 1996, over 61 million women were in the labor force in the United States (see Table G1-1). Since the end of World War II, the number of working women has drawn closer to the number of men in the labor force, which was, as of 1996, over 61 million, versus 72 million. As a consequence, women currently constitute nearly half, 46 percent, of the labor force in American society. The number of working women has tripled in the last 35 years. Women's participation in the labor force has risen from 38 percent of all civilian women 16 years and older in 1960 to more than 59 percent in 1996. Men's labor force participation in 1996 was 75 percent, so there is considerable room for more women to enter the labor force before they match men's employment patterns. Employment specialists project that in the year 2005, men's labor force participation will remain at or near 75 percent while women's rate is projected to increase slightly, to 62 percent.

Single women continue to have a higher rate of labor force participation than married women, but the gap has narrowed. The traditional norm in American society was for single women to support themselves while married women remained in the home as wife and mother. But times have changed and many more married women have left the home for the workplace. In 1960, 59 percent of all single women worked, compared to 32 percent of married women. Thus, 27 percent more single women than married women were in the labor force. By 1996, the gap had shrunk to only 6 percent, 67 percent of single women compared to 61 percent of married women. Divorced, separated, and widowed women had a lower rate of employment than either single or married women in 1996. Only 48 percent of these women were employed. Obviously, many widows are over 65 years of age and thus may be out of the labor force. In addition, some divorced and separated women have young children, which makes it difficult for them to consistently engage in full-time employment.

Married women between the age of 35 and 44 years had the highest rate of labor force participation in 1996 (Table G1-2). Nearly 76 percent of married women in this age category worked outside the home. As will be discussed below, younger women have more younger children who influence, to a degree, their mothers' labor force participation.

Both husband and wife worked in 1993 among 54 percent of married couples (Table G1-3). In 23 percent of the married couples, only the husband worked and only the wife worked in 5 percent of married couples. Neither the husband nor the wife worked in 17 percent of the couples living in this country. These percentages are similar for both black and Hispanic married couples (Tables G1-4 and G1-5).

Today, the presence of children, at home or in school, makes only a modest difference in whether married mothers work (Table G1-6). In 1996, 53.4 percent of wives/mothers whose husbands were present in the home and who had no children under the age of 18 were employed compared to 70 percent of mothers with children in that age group. Mothers with young children had a rate of labor force participation a few percentage points lower than mothers with older children. For obvious reasons, including maternity leave, fewer women with a child under one year of age worked in 1996. The highest rate, 78 percent, was reported by women with children between the ages of 14 and 17 years.

Information concerning who cares for the children of employed mothers is presented in Section I, Child Care. The division of family roles between working wives and their husbands is discussed in Section B, Quality of Marriage and Family Life.

1. WORKING WOMEN

G1-1   Marital Status of Women in the Civilian Labor Force: 1960–1996

YEAR	FEMALE LABOR FORCE (1,000)				FEMALE PARTICIPATION RATE			
	Total	Single	Married[1]	Other[2]	Total	Single	Married[1]	Other[2]
1960	23,240	5,410	12,893	4,937	37.7	58.6	31.9	41.6
1965	26,200	5,976	14,829	5,396	39.3	54.5	34.9	40.7
1970	31,543	7,265	18,475	5,804	43.3	56.8	40.5	40.3
1975	37,475	9,125	21,484	6,866	46.3	59.8	44.3	40.1
1980	45,487	11,865	24,980	8,643	51.5	64.4	49.9	43.6
1981	46,696	12,124	25,428	9,144	52.1	64.5	50.5	44.6
1982	47,755	12,460	25,971	9,324	52.6	65.1	51.1	44.8
1983	48,503	12,659	26,468	9,376	52.9	65.0	51.8	44.4
1984	49,709	12,867	27,199	9,644	53.6	65.6	52.8	44.7
1985	51,050	13,163	27,894	9,993	54.5	66.6	53.8	45.1
1986	52,413	13,512	28,623	10,277	55.3	67.2	54.9	45.6
1987	53,658	13,885	29,381	10,393	56.0	67.4	55.9	45.7
1988	54,742	14,194	29,921	10,627	56.6	67.7	56.7	46.2
1989	56,030	14,377	30,548	11,104	57.4	68.0	57.8	47.0
1990	56,829	14,612	30,901	11,315	57.5	66.7	58.4	47.2
1991	57,178	14,681	31,112	11,385	57.4	66.2	58.5	46.8
1992	58,141	14,872	31,700	11,570	57.8	66.2	59.3	47.1
1993	58,795	15,031	31,980	11,784	57.9	66.2	59.4	47.2
1994	60,239	15,333	32,888	12,018	58.8	66.7	60.7	47.5
1995	60,944	15,467	33,359	12,118	58.9	66.8	61.0	47.4
1996	61,857	15,842	33,618	12,397	59.3	67.1	61.2	48.1

[1]Husband present.
[2]Widowed, divorced, or separated.

G1-2   Labor Force Participation Rates of Married Women by Age: 1960–1996

Year	Married Women Participation Rate						
	Total	16-19 years	20-24 years	25-34 years	35-44 years	45-64 years	65 and over
Married:							
1960	31.9	27.2	31.7	28.8	37.2	36.0	6.7
1970	40.5	37.8	47.9	38.8	46.8	44.0	7.3
1975	44.3	46.2	57.0	48.4	52.0	43.8	7.0
1980	49.8	49.3	61.4	58.8	61.8	46.9	7.3
1985	53.8	49.6	65.7	65.8	68.1	49.4	6.6
1990	58.4	49.5	66.1	69.6	74.0	56.5	8.5
1995	61.0	51.6	64.7	72.0	75.7	62.7	9.1
1996	61.2	48.6	66.0	71.7	75.8	63.7	9.0

G1-3   Labor Force Status of Married Couples by Age, Age of Children, and Income, 1993

Characteristic	Number	In Labor Force			
		Husband and Wife	Husband Only	Wife Only	Neither
All Married Couples					
Total	53,171	54%	23%	5%	17%
Age:					
15-24	1,463	64	32	2	2
25-34	10,654	70	27	2	1
35-44	13,541	71	26	2	2
45-54	10,550	68	24	5	3
55-64	7,674	43	26	12	19
65 and older	9,306	6	10	9	75
Children:					
Under 18	24,707	65	30	3	2
Under 6 only	6,456	60	37	2	1
Under 6 & 6 to 17	5,486	56	40	2	2
6 to 17 only	12,765	72	23	4	2
Family Income:					
Under $10,000	2,369	19	26	7	49
10,000-24,999	10,544	27	27	8	38
25,000-39,999	11,953	49	25	7	19
40,000-49,999	7,172	63	22	5	10
50,000-74,999	12,163	72	20	3	5
75,000 and over	8,970	72	21	3	5

G1-4   Labor Force Status of Black Married Couples by Age, Age of Children, and Income, 1993

Characteristic	Number	In Labor Force			
		Husband and Wife	Husband Only	Wife Only	Neither
Black Married Couples					
Total	3,748	57%	18%	8%	16%
Age:					
15-24	114	56	38	5	1
25-34	794	75	19	4	2
35-44	997	76	16	4	3
45-54	735	69	18	8	5
55-64	527	35	26	18	21
65 and older	581	4	9	13	74
Children:					
Under 18	1,945	71	20	5	4
Under 6 only	466	67	25	5	4
Under 6 & 6 to 17	450	69	25	3	3
6 to 17 only	1,029	73	16	7	4
Family Income:					
Under $10,000	361	19	19	12	50
10,000-24,999	985	36	24	12	28
25,000-39,999	848	58	20	10	12
40,000-49,999	478	71	19	5	5
50,000-74,999	704	81	10	6	3
75,000 and over	373	87	7	2	4

G1-5   Labor Force Status of Hispanic Married Couples by Age, Age of Children, and Income, 1993

Characteristic	Number	In Labor Force			
		Husband and Wife	Husband Only	Wife Only	Neither
Hispanic Married Couples					
Total	3,674	50%	35%	4%	11%
Age:					
15-24	205	53	40	3	4
25-34	1,058	57	40	2	1
35-44	1,028	60	34	3	3
45-54	669	53	38	5	5
55-64	402	33	36	10	21
65 and older	310	4	11	7	77
Children:					
Under 18	2,355	53	40	3	4
Under 6 only	67	48	47	2	3
Under 6 & 6 to 17	691	48	46	3	3
6 to 17 only	1,047	61	31	4	4
Family Income:					
Under $10,000	365	20	45	7	29
10,000-24,999	1,185	33	46	4	17
25,000-39,999	922	54	35	5	6
40,000-49,999	399	68	26	2	4
50,000-74,999	534	73	20	3	5
75,000 and over	268	75	19	4	3

G1-6   Labor Force Participation Rates for Wives, Husband Present, by Age of Own Youngest Child: 1975–1996

PRESENCE AND AGE OF CHILD	TOTAL			WHITE			BLACK		
	1975	1985	1996 [1]	1975	1985	1996 [1]	1975	1985	1996 [1]
Wives, total	44.4	54.2	61.1	43.6	53.3	60.6	54.1	63.8	67.3
No children under 18	43.8	48.2	53.4	43.6	47.5	53.1	47.6	55.2	54.9
With children under 18	44.9	60.8	70.0	43.6	59.9	69.6	58.4	71.7	79.2
Under 6, total.	36.7	53.4	62.7	34.7	52.1	62.2	54.9	69.6	76.1
Under 3	32.7	50.5	60.5	30.7	49.4	60.2	50.1	66.2	70.7
1 year or under	30.8	49.4	59.3	29.2	48.6	59.1	50.0	63.7	70.2
2 years.	37.1	54.0	64.1	35.1	52.7	64.0	56.4	69.9	72.6
3 to 5 years	42.2	58.4	66.0	40.1	56.6	65.1	61.2	73.8	83.8
3 years.	41.2	55.1	61.9	39.0	52.7	61.2	62.7	72.3	80.0
4 years.	41.2	59.7	69.1	38.7	58.4	67.5	64.9	70.6	82.6
5 years.	44.4	62.1	68.2	43.8	59.9	67.8	56.3	79.1	83.5
6 to 13 years	51.8	68.2	76.0	50.7	67.7	75.8	65.7	73.3	81.6
14 to 17 years	53.5	67.0	78.4	53.4	66.6	78.2	52.3	74.4	82.3

G1-7   Employment Status of Women, by Marital Status and Presence and Age of Children: 1960–1996

| ITEM | TOTAL | | | WITH ANY CHILDREN | | | | | | | | |
| | | | | Total | | | Children 6 to 17 only | | | Children under 6 | | |
	Single	Married[1]	Other[2]	Single	Married[1]	Other[2]	Single	Married[1]	Other[2]	Single	Married[1]	Other[2]
IN LABOR FORCE (mil.)												
1960	5.4	12.3	4.9	(NA)	6.6	1.5	(NA)	4.1	1.0	(NA)	2.5	0.4
1970	7.0	18.4	5.9	(NA)	10.2	1.9	(NA)	6.3	1.3	(NA)	3.9	0.6
1980	11.2	24.9	8.8	0.6	13.7	3.6	0.2	8.4	2.6	0.3	5.2	1.0
1985	12.9	27.7	10.3	1.1	14.9	4.0	0.4	8.5	2.9	0.7	6.4	1.1
1990	14.0	31.0	11.2	1.5	16.5	4.2	0.6	9.3	3.0	0.9	7.2	1.2
1993	14.1	32.2	11.3	1.9	16.9	4.2	0.7	9.7	3.0	1.1	7.3	1.2
1994[3]	14.9	32.9	11.9	2.2	17.6	4.4	0.8	9.9	3.2	1.4	7.7	1.2
1995	15.0	33.6	12.0	2.1	18.0	4.6	0.8	10.2	3.3	1.3	7.8	1.3
1996	15.4	33.4	12.4	2.2	17.8	4.7	0.9	10.2	3.4	1.4	7.6	1.3
PARTICIPATION RATE[4]												
1960	44.1	30.5	40.0	(NA)	27.6	56.0	(NA)	39.0	65.9	(NA)	18.6	40.5
1970	53.0	40.8	39.1	(NA)	39.7	60.7	(NA)	49.2	66.9	(NA)	30.3	52.2
1980	61.5	50.1	44.0	52.0	54.1	69.4	67.6	61.7	74.6	44.1	45.1	60.3
1985	65.2	54.2	45.6	51.6	60.8	71.9	64.1	67.8	77.8	46.5	53.4	59.7
1990	66.4	58.2	46.8	55.2	66.3	74.2	69.7	73.6	79.7	48.7	58.9	63.6
1993	64.5	59.4	45.9	54.4	67.5	72.1	70.2	74.9	78.3	47.4	59.6	60.0
1994[3]	65.1	60.6	47.3	56.9	69.0	73.1	67.5	76.0	78.4	52.2	61.7	62.2
1995	65.5	61.1	47.3	57.5	70.2	75.3	67.0	76.2	79.5	53.0	63.5	66.3
1996	65.2	61.1	48.2	60.5	70.0	77.0	71.8	76.7	80.6	55.1	62.7	69.2
EMPLOYMENT (mil.)												
1960	5.1	11.6	4.6	(NA)	6.2	1.3	(NA)	3.9	0.9	(NA)	2.3	0.4
1970	6.5	17.5	5.6	(NA)	9.6	1.8	(NA)	6.0	1.2	(NA)	3.6	0.6
1980	10.1	23.6	8.2	0.4	12.8	3.3	0.2	8.1	2.4	0.2	4.8	0.9
1985	11.6	26.1	9.4	0.9	13.9	3.5	0.3	8.1	2.6	0.5	5.9	0.9
1990	12.9	29.9	10.5	1.2	15.8	3.8	0.5	8.9	2.7	0.7	6.9	1.1
1993	12.7	30.8	10.5	1.5	16.1	3.9	0.6	9.3	2.8	0.9	6.8	1.1
1994[3]	13.4	31.4	11.0	1.7	16.8	4.0	0.7	9.5	2.9	1.1	7.3	1.0
1995	13.7	32.3	11.3	1.8	17.2	4.2	0.7	9.8	3.1	1.1	7.3	1.2
1996	14.1	32.3	11.7	1.8	17.1	4.4	0.7	9.8	3.2	1.1	7.3	1.2
UNEMPLOYMENT RATE[5]												
1960	6.0	5.4	6.2	(NA)	6.0	8.4	(NA)	4.9	6.8	(NA)	7.8	12.5
1970	7.1	4.8	4.8	(NA)	6.0	7.2	(NA)	4.8	5.9	(NA)	7.9	9.8
1980	10.3	5.3	6.4	23.2	5.9	9.2	15.6	4.4	7.9	29.2	8.3	12.8
1985	10.2	5.7	8.5	23.8	6.6	12.1	15.4	5.5	10.6	28.5	8.0	16.1
1990	8.2	3.5	5.7	18.4	4.2	8.5	14.5	3.8	7.7	20.8	4.8	10.2
1993	9.8	4.4	6.9	19.2	4.8	8.5	13.7	3.8	7.0	22.8	6.2	12.5
1994[3]	10.0	4.5	7.4	19.5	5.0	9.8	13.2	4.5	7.7	23.0	5.6	15.1
1995	8.7	3.9	5.8	16.6	4.3	8.1	11.8	3.6	7.1	19.5	5.3	10.8
1996	8.6	3.4	5.5	18.5	3.5	6.4	15.7	3.2	5.1	20.3	3.9	9.7

NA Not available.   [1] Husband present.   [2] Widowed, divorced, or separated.   [3] Data beginning 1994 not strictly comparable with data for earlier years. See text, section 13, and February 1994 and March 1996 issues of *Employment and Earnings.* [4] Percent of women in each specific category in the labor force.   [5] Unemployed as a percent of civilian labor force in specified group.

G1-8   Median Income of Married-Couple Families, by Work Experience of Husbands and Wives and Presence of Children, 1995

WORK EXPERIENCE OF HUSBAND OR WIFE	NUMBER (1,000)					MEDIAN INCOME (dollars)				
	All married-couple families	No related children	One or more related children under 18 years old			All married-couple families	No related children	One or more related children under 18 years old		
			Total	One child	Two children or more			Total	One child	Two children or more
All married-couple families	53,570	27,537	26,034	9,859	16,175	47,062	44,316	49,969	51,105	49,103
Husband worked.	42,736	18,143	24,593	9,201	15,392	52,839	55,843	51,118	52,710	50,295
Wife worked	32,118	13,698	18,420	7,309	11,111	17,943	8,559	9,384	4,225	5,159
Wife year-round, f.t. worker	17,943	8,559	9,384	4,225	5,159	62,205	65,166	60,373	61,629	59,300
Wife did not work.	10,618	4,445	6,173	1,892	4,281	39,700	41,777	37,518	36,105	38,126
Husband year-round, full-time worker.	34,698	13,735	20,962	7,808	13,154	56,256	60,580	53,764	55,763	52,497
Wife worked	26,672	10,892	15,780	6,243	9,537	59,878	63,759	57,259	59,136	56,274
Wife year-round, f.t. worker	15,359	7,212	8,148	3,656	4,491	64,283	67,418	61,857	63,526	60,872
Wife did not work.	8,025	2,843	5,182	1,565	3,617	43,128	46,704	41,146	40,044	41,671
Husband did not work	10,834	9,393	1,441	658	783	25,732	26,030	23,089	24,056	21,714
Wife worked	2,780	1,971	809	358	451	34,658	36,362	30,523	31,205	30,108
Wife year-round, f.t. worker	1,459	965	493	222	272	40,486	42,908	34,743	36,277	33,950
Wife did not work.	8,054	7,422	632	300	332	23,205	23,851	15,466	17,158	14,065

G1-9   Female Labor Force Participation (Aged 16+)

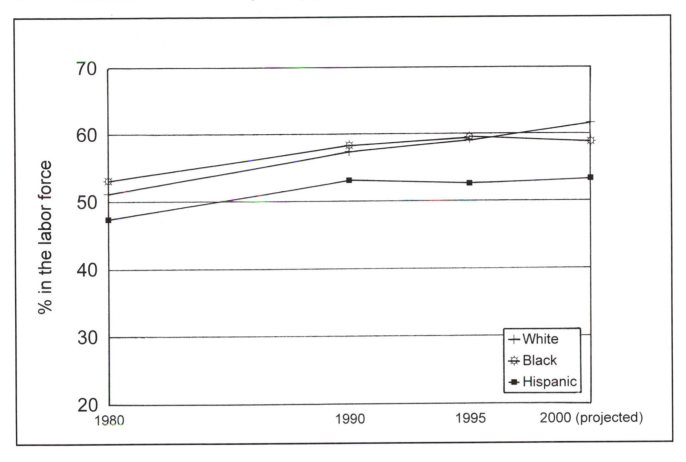

G1-10 Labor Force Participation Rate for Wives, Husband Present, by Age of Youngest Child

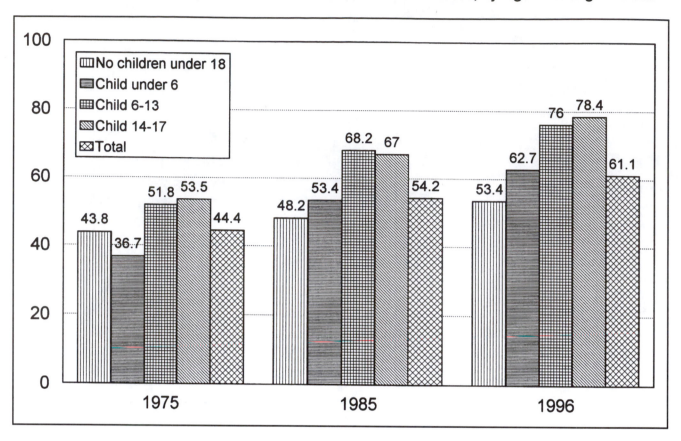

H. Demographic and Economic Context

1. DEMOGRAPHIC STRUCTURE

Several aspects of demographic and economic structure set a context within which families exist. Projections of the population suggest important trends that have implications for families. First, the population is projected to increase over the next 50 years (see Table H1-1). The sex ratio will not change very much as a result of this growth, but the racial mix will. The white population will decline as a percentage of the total while blacks and other races (mostly Asians) will increase. The Hispanic population is projected to grow the most.

As the life span increases and baby boomers reach old age, the elderly population will increase dramatically (Table H1-2). Aging of the population will alter the composition of families, reducing the number of families with children, but increasing the relative number of grandparents.

Mobility rates have remained fairly stable over the last 15 years (Table H1-6). Because mobility rates peak for people in their 20s, it is possible that they will decline as the population ages.

During the 1990s, educational attainment has increased somewhat while employment has remained relatively stable (Table H1-7). Female-headed households have increased slightly, but so has home ownership (Table H1-8). Economic trends are examined in detail in the next sections.

2. INCOME

After adjusting for inflation, household incomes have increased only modestly since 1970 (Figure H2-1). Minority groups were less likely, on average, to benefit from income growth. Moreover, the greatest increases were experienced by dual-income households (Figure H2-2). Overall, income increases with age of the householder up to the mid-40s, and decreases thereafter (Table H2-6). Income is also larger in married-couple households and among those with the greatest educational attainment. In 1995, Alaska reported the highest average household income and West Virginia the lowest (Table H2-9).

Income inequality has been increasing over the last quarter of a century as the income going to the richest fifth of families has increased and the income going to the poorest fifth has declined (Figure H2-12). Low-income families are concentrated among the young, minorities, female-headed households, and those with lower educational attainment (Table H2-14).

In 1995, the median net worth of families was estimated to be about $56,000 (Table H2-15). In contrast, the mean net worth was over $200,000. This difference exists because a small number of families control large amounts of wealth. This wealth comes from a variety of sources including savings and investments, retirement accounts, and life insurance policies (Table H2-20). On the other hand, the average family has about $75,000 of debt, the largest single source of this being home mortgages (Table H2-22).

3. POVERTY AND PUBLIC ASSISTANCE

The percentage of children experiencing poverty increased in the 1970s and early 1980s, and then leveled off (Figure H3-1). One-fifth of America's children now live in poverty (Table H3-3). The percentage is much higher among minority groups. By 1996, the poverty threshold for a family of four was $15,569.

Approximately 14 percent of the population receives welfare (Table H3-13). Aid to Families with Dependent Children, Medicaid, and food stamps are the most common forms of public assistance, and female-headed households are most likely to receive each of these types of assistance.

4. HOME OWNERSHIP AND CONSUMER PATTERNS

Owners live in about two-thirds of the occupied housing in this country (Figure H4-1). Most of these units are financed through conventional mortgages (Table H4-3). In 1996, the median sales price of homes was $140,000, double the value in 1982 (Table H4-5). There is substantial variation in the size and other characteristics of these housing units.

Studies of household expenditures indicate the cost of energy has remained relatively stable, but that food costs have increased since 1990 (Tables H4-16 and H4-17). About a third of households own a dog, and cat ownership is nearly as common (Table H4-19). Most households spend some time in lawn care and gardening (Table H4-20). Most households also give modest amounts of money to charity each year (Figure H4-21).

5. HEALTH INSURANCE

Increased economic inequality and rising costs have made it increasingly difficult for some families to obtain adequate health care. The problem has been compounded by the growing percentage of the population that is not covered by health insurance (Figure H5-1). Younger adults, minority groups, the poor, and the less educated are less likely to be covered by any form of health insurance (Table H5-2).

1. DEMOGRAPHIC STRUCTURE

H1-1   Resident Population—Selected Characteristics, 1790–1996, and Projections, 2000–2050

DATE	SEX		RACE					Hispanic origin[1]
					Other			
	Male	Female	White	Black	Total	American Indian, Eskimo, Aleut	Asian and Pacific Islanders	
1790 (Aug. 2)[2]	(NA)	(NA)	3,172	757	(NA)	(NA)	(NA)	(NA)
1800 (Aug. 4)[2]	(NA)	(NA)	4,306	1,002	(NA)	(NA)	(NA)	(NA)
1850 (June 1)[2]	11,838	11,354	19,553	3,639	(NA)	(NA)	(NA)	(NA)
1860 (June 1)[2]	16,085	15,358	26,923	4,442	79	(NA)	(NA)	(NA)
1870 (June 1)[2]	19,494	19,065	33,589	4,880	89	(NA)	(NA)	(NA)
1880 (June 1)[2]	25,519	24,637	43,403	6,581	172	(NA)	(NA)	(NA)
1890 (June 1)[2]	32,237	30,711	55,101	7,489	358	(NA)	(NA)	(NA)
1900 (June 1)[2]	38,816	37,178	66,809	8,834	351	(NA)	(NA)	(NA)
1910 (Apr. 15)[2]	47,332	44,640	81,732	9,828	413	(NA)	(NA)	(NA)
1920 (Jan. 1)[2]	53,900	51,810	94,821	10,463	427	(NA)	(NA)	(NA)
1930 (Apr. 1)[2]	62,137	60,638	110,287	11,891	597	(NA)	(NA)	(NA)
1940 (Apr. 1)[2]	66,062	65,608	118,215	12,866	589	(NA)	(NA)	(NA)
1950 (Apr. 1)[2]	74,833	75,864	134,942	15,042	713	(NA)	(NA)	(NA)
1950 (Apr. 1)	75,187	76,139	135,150	15,045	1,131	(NA)	(NA)	(NA)
1960 (Apr. 1)	88,331	90,992	158,832	18,872	1,620	(NA)	(NA)	(NA)
1970 (Apr. 1)[3]	98,926	104,309	178,098	22,581	2,557	(NA)	(NA)	(NA)
1980 (Apr. 1)[4]	110,053	116,493	194,713	26,683	5,150	1,420	3,729	14,609
1990 (Apr. 1)[4,5]	121,244	127,474	208,710	30,486	9,523	2,065	7,458	22,354
1990 (July 1)[6]	121,600	127,798	209,173	30,598	9,627	2,073	7,554	22,558
1991 (July 1)[6]	122,984	129,122	210,979	31,107	10,020	2,110	7,911	23,416
1992 (July 1)[6]	124,511	130,500	212,910	31,654	10,448	2,147	8,300	24,349
1993 (July 1)[6]	125,938	131,858	214,760	32,168	10,867	2,184	8,683	25,326
1994 (July 1)[6]	127,261	133,111	216,480	32,647	11,245	2,220	9,025	26,300
1995 (July 1)[6]	128,569	134,321	218,149	33,095	11,646	2,254	9,392	27,277
1996 (July 1)[6]	129,810	135,474	219,749	33,503	12,032	2,288	9,743	28,269
1997 (July 1)[7]	130,712	136,933	221,163	34,075	12,407	2,305	10,102	28,680
1998 (July 1)[7]	131,883	138,119	222,648	34,537	12,817	2,337	10,480	29,566
1999 (July 1)[7]	133,039	139,291	224,103	34,997	13,230	2,369	10,861	30,461
2000 (July 1)[7]	134,181	140,453	225,532	35,454	13,647	2,402	11,245	31,366
2005 (July 1)[7]	139,785	146,196	232,463	37,734	15,784	2,572	13,212	36,057
2010 (July 1)[7]	145,584	152,132	239,588	40,109	18,019	2,754	15,265	41,139
2015 (July 1)[7]	151,750	158,383	247,193	42,586	20,355	2,941	17,413	46,705
2020 (July 1)[7]	158,021	164,721	254,887	45,075	22,780	3,129	19,651	52,652
2025 (July 1)[7]	164,119	170,931	262,227	47,539	25,284	3,319	21,965	58,930
2050 (July 1)[7]	193,234	200,696	294,615	60,592	38,724	4,371	34,352	96,508

NA Not available.

[1]Persons of Hispanic origin may be of any race.

[2]Excludes Alaska and Hawaii.

[3]The revised 1970 resident population count is 203,302,031; which incorporates changes due to errors found after tabulations were completed. The race and sex data shown here reflect the official 1970 census count.

[4]The race data shown have been modified.

[5]The April 1, 1990, census count (248,718,291) includes count question resolution corrections processed through March 1994 and does not include adjustments for census coverage errors.

[6]Estimated.

[7]Middle series projection.

H1-2   Resident Population Characteristics—Percent Distribution and Median Age, 1850–1996, and Projections, 2000–2050

DATE	SEX		RACE			Hispanic origin[1]	Median age (years)
	Male	Female	White	Black	Other		
1850 (June 1)[2]	51.0	49.0	84.3	15.7	(NA)	(NA)	18.9
1900 (June 1)[2]	51.1	48.9	87.9	11.6	0.5	(NA)	22.9
1910 (Apr. 15)[2]	51.5	48.5	88.9	10.7	0.4	(NA)	24.1
1920 (Jan. 1)[2]	51.0	49.0	89.7	9.9	0.4	(NA)	25.3
1930 (Apr. 1)[2]	50.6	49.4	89.8	9.7	0.5	(NA)	26.4
1940 (Apr. 1)[2]	50.2	49.8	89.8	9.8	0.4	(NA)	29.0
1950 (Apr. 1)[2]	49.7	50.3	89.5	10.0	0.5	(NA)	30.2
1950 (Apr. 1)	49.7	50.3	89.3	9.9	0.7	(NA)	30.2
1960 (Apr. 1)	49.3	50.7	88.6	10.5	0.9	(NA)	29.5
1970 (Apr. 1)	48.7	51.3	87.6	11.1	1.3	(NA)	28.0
1980 (Apr. 1)[3]	48.6	51.4	85.9	11.8	2.3	6.4	30.0
1990 (Apr. 1)[3]	48.7	51.3	83.9	12.3	3.8	9.0	32.8
1995 (July 1)	48.9	51.1	83.0	12.6	4.4	10.4	34.3
1996 (July 1)	48.9	51.1	82.8	12.6	4.5	10.7	34.6
2000 (July 1)	48.9	51.1	82.1	12.9	5.0	11.4	35.7
2025 (July 1)	49.0	51.0	78.3	14.2	7.5	17.6	38.0
2050 (July 1)	49.1	50.9	74.8	15.4	9.8	24.5	38.1

NA Not available.

[1] Persons of Hispanic origin may be of any race.

[2] Excludes Alaska and Hawaii.

[3] The Race data shown have been modified.

H1-3   Aging of the Population (Actual and Projected)

H1-4   Expectation of Life at Birth, 1970–1995, and Projections, 1995–2010

[In years. Excludes deaths of nonresidents of the United States]

YEAR	TOTAL			WHITE			BLACK AND OTHER			BLACK		
	Total	Male	Female	Total	Male	Female	Total	Male	Female	Total	Male	Female
1970.............	70.8	67.1	74.7	71.7	68.0	75.6	65.3	61.3	69.4	64.1	60.0	68.3
1975.............	72.6	68.8	76.6	73.4	69.5	77.3	68.0	63.7	72.4	66.8	62.4	71.3
1980.............	73.7	70.0	77.4	74.4	70.7	78.1	69.5	65.3	73.6	68.1	63.8	72.5
1982.............	74.5	70.8	78.1	75.1	71.5	78.7	70.9	66.8	74.9	69.4	65.1	73.6
1983.............	74.6	71.0	78.1	75.2	71.6	78.7	70.9	67.0	74.7	69.4	65.2	73.5
1984.............	74.7	71.1	78.2	75.3	71.8	78.7	71.1	67.2	74.9	69.5	65.3	73.6
1985.............	74.7	71.1	78.2	75.3	71.8	78.7	71.0	67.0	74.8	69.3	65.0	73.4
1986.............	74.7	71.2	78.2	75.4	71.9	78.8	70.9	66.8	74.9	69.1	64.8	73.4
1987.............	74.9	71.4	78.3	75.6	72.1	78.9	71.0	66.9	75.0	69.1	64.7	73.4
1988.............	74.9	71.4	78.3	75.6	72.2	78.9	70.8	66.7	74.8	68.9	64.4	73.2
1989.............	75.1	71.7	78.5	75.9	72.5	79.2	70.9	66.7	74.9	68.8	64.3	73.3
1990.............	75.4	71.8	78.8	76.1	72.7	79.4	71.2	67.0	75.2	69.1	64.5	73.6
1991.............	75.5	72.0	78.9	76.3	72.9	79.6	71.5	67.3	75.5	69.3	64.6	73.8
1992.............	75.8	72.3	79.1	76.5	73.2	79.8	71.8	67.7	75.7	69.6	65.0	73.9
1993.............	75.5	72.2	78.8	76.3	73.1	79.5	71.5	67.3	75.5	69.2	64.6	73.7
1994.............	75.7	72.3	79.0	76.4	73.2	79.6	71.7	67.5	75.8	69.6	64.9	74.1
1995.............	75.8	72.6	78.9	76.5	73.4	79.6	(NA)	(NA)	(NA)	69.8	65.4	74.0
Projections: 1995 ...	(NA)	72.5	79.3	(NA)	73.6	80.1	(NA)	(NA)	(NA)	(NA)	64.8	74.5
2000 ...	(NA)	73.0	79.7	(NA)	74.2	80.5	(NA)	(NA)	(NA)	(NA)	64.6	74.7
2005 ...	(NA)	73.5	80.2	(NA)	74.7	81.0	(NA)	(NA)	(NA)	(NA)	64.5	75.0
2010 ...	(NA)	74.1	80.6	(NA)	75.5	81.6	(NA)	(NA)	(NA)	(NA)	65.1	75.5

H1-5   Selected Life Table Values: 1979–1994

AGE AND SEX	TOTAL [1]			WHITE			BLACK		
	1979-1981	1990	1994	1979-1981	1990	1994	1979-1981	1990	1994
AVERAGE EXPECTATION OF LIFE IN YEARS									
At birth: Male	70.1	71.8	72.4	70.8	72.7	73.3	64.1	64.5	64.9
Female	77.6	78.8	79.0	78.2	79.4	79.6	72.9	73.6	73.9
Age 20: Male	51.9	53.3	53.6	52.5	54.0	54.4	46.4	46.7	47.1
Female	59.0	59.8	59.9	59.4	60.3	60.4	54.9	55.3	55.5
Age 40: Male	33.6	35.1	35.5	34.0	35.6	36.0	29.5	30.1	30.5
Female	39.8	40.6	40.7	40.2	41.0	41.1	36.3	36.8	37.0
Age 50: Male	25.0	26.4	26.9	25.3	26.7	27.2	22.0	22.5	23.1
Female	30.7	31.3	31.5	31.0	31.6	31.7	27.8	28.2	28.5
Age 65: Male	14.2	15.1	15.5	14.3	15.2	15.6	13.3	13.2	13.6
Female	18.4	18.9	19.0	18.6	19.1	19.1	17.1	17.2	17.2
EXPECTED DEATHS PER 1,000 ALIVE AT SPECIFIED AGE									
At birth: Male	13.9	10.3	8.7	12.3	8.6	(NA)	23.0	19.7	(NA)
Female	11.2	8.2	7.1	9.7	6.6	(NA)	19.3	16.3	(NA)
Age 20: Male	1.8	1.6	1.5	1.8	1.4	(NA)	2.2	2.7	(NA)
Female	0.6	0.5	0.4	0.6	0.5	(NA)	0.7	0.7	(NA)
Age 40: Male	3.0	3.1	3.4	2.6	2.7	(NA)	6.9	7.1	(NA)
Female	1.6	1.4	1.4	1.4	1.2	(NA)	3.2	3.1	(NA)
Age 50: Male	7.8	6.2	6.1	7.1	5.6	(NA)	14.9	12.8	(NA)
Female	4.2	3.5	3.4	3.8	3.2	(NA)	7.7	6.6	(NA)
Age 65: Male	28.2	12.9	22.8	27.4	23.0	(NA)	38.5	36.8	(NA)
Female	14.3	13.5	(NA)	13.6	12.8	(NA)	21.6	21.4	(NA)
NUMBER SURVIVING TO SPECIFIED AGE PER 1,000 BORN ALIVE									
Age 20: Male	973	979	980	975	981	(NA)	961	963	(NA)
Female	982	986	987	984	988	(NA)	972	976	(NA)
Age 40: Male	933	938	939	940	946	(NA)	885	880	(NA)
Female	965	971	971	969	975	(NA)	941	944	(NA)
Age 50: Male	890	899	899	901	912	(NA)	801	801	(NA)
Female	941	950	950	947	957	(NA)	896	904	(NA)
Age 65: Male	706	741	748	724	760	(NA)	551	571	(NA)
Female	835	851	855	848	864	(NA)	733	751	(NA)

NA Not available.   [1] Includes other races not shown separately.

H1-6   Mobility Status of the Population, by Selected Characteristics: 1980–1996

MOBILITY PERIOD, AGE, AND REGION	Total (1,000)	PERCENT DISTRIBUTION						
		Non-movers	Movers (different house in United States)					Movers from abroad
			Total	Same county	Different county			
					Total	Same State	Different State	
1980-81.	221,641	83	17	10	6	3	3	1
1985-86.	232,998	82	18	11	7	4	3	1
1990-91.	244,884	83	16	10	6	3	3	1
1991-92.	247,380	83	17	11	6	3	3	1
1992-93.	250,210	83	16	11	6	3	3	1
1993-94.	255,774	83	17	10	6	3	3	1
1995-96, total	260,406	84	16	10	6	3	3	1
1 to 4 years old.	16,160	75	24	17	7	4	3	1
5 to 9 years old.	20,171	82	18	12	6	3	3	1
10 to 14 years old	19,449	85	14	10	5	2	2	(Z)
15 to 19 years old	18,649	85	15	10	5	3	2	1
20 to 24 years old	17,653	66	33	21	11	6	5	1
25 to 29 years old	19,462	67	32	20	12	7	5	1
30 to 44 years old	64,534	83	16	10	6	3	3	1
45 to 64 years old	52,668	92	7	4	3	2	1	(Z)
65 to 74 years old	18,270	96	4	3	2	1	1	(Z)
75 to 84 years old	10,568	96	4	2	2	1	1	(Z)
85 years old and over	2,819	95	5	3	2	2	1	(Z)
Northeast.	50,832	88	11	8	4	2	2	1
Midwest.	61,044	86	14	9	5	3	2	(Z)
South	90,909	83	17	10	7	4	3	1
West.	57,621	79	20	14	6	3	3	1

Z Less than 0.5 percent.

H1-7 Social and Economic Characteristics of the White and Black Populations: 1990–1996

CHARACTERISTIC	NUMBER (1,000)						PERCENT DISTRIBUTION			
	White			Black			White		Black	
	1990	1995	1996	1990	1995	1996	1990	1996	1990	1996
Total persons	206,983	216,751	218,442	30,392	33,531	33,889	100.0	100.0	100.0	100.0
Under 5 years old	15,161	15,915	15,736	2,932	3,342	3,243	7.3	7.2	9.6	9.6
5 to 14 years old	28,405	30,786	31,110	5,546	6,268	6,432	13.7	14.2	18.2	19.0
15 to 44 years old	96,656	97,876	98,146	14,660	16,101	16,154	46.6	44.9	48.2	47.7
45 to 64 years old	40,282	44,189	45,016	4,766	5,264	5,582	19.5	20.6	15.7	16.5
65 years old and over	26,479	27,985	28,436	2,487	2,557	2,478	12.8	13.0	8.2	7.3
EDUCATIONAL ATTAINMENT										
Persons 25 years old and over	134,687	141,113	142,733	16,751	18,457	18,715	100.0	100.0	100.0	100.0
Elementary: 0 to 8 years	14,131	11,101	11,141	2,701	1,800	1,734	10.5	7.8	16.1	9.3
High school: 1 to 3 years	14,080	[1]12,882	[1]13,461	2,969	[1]3,041	[1]3,085	10.5	[1]9.4	17.7	[1]16.5
4 years	52,449	[2]47,986	[2]48,356	6,239	[2]6,686	[2]6,576	38.9	[2]33.9	37.2	[2]35.1
College: 1 to 3 years	24,350	[3]35,321	[3]35,161	2,952	[3]4,486	[3]4,769	18.1	[3]24.6	17.6	[3]25.5
4 years or more	29,677	[4]33,824	[4]34,614	1,890	[4]2,444	[4]2,551	22.0	[4]24.3	11.3	[4]13.6
LABOR FORCE STATUS [5]										
Civilians 16 years old and over	160,625	166,914	168,317	21,477	23,246	23,604	100.0	100.0	100.0	100.0
Civilian labor force	107,447	111,950	113,108	13,740	14,817	15,134	66.9	67.2	64.0	64.1
Employed	102,261	106,490	107,808	12,175	13,279	13,542	63.7	64.1	56.7	57.4
Unemployed	5,186	5,459	5,300	1,565	1,538	1,592	3.2	3.1	7.3	6.7
Unemployment rate [6]	4.8	4.9	4.7	11.4	10.4	10.5	(X)	(X)	(X)	(X)
Not in labor force	53,178	54,965	55,209	7,737	8,429	8,470	33.1	32.8	36.0	35.9
FAMILY TYPE										
Total families	56,590	58,437	58,869	7,470	8,093	8,055	100.0	100.0	100.0	100.0
With own children [7]	26,718	27,951	28,086	4,378	4,682	4,583	47.2	47.7	58.6	56.9
Married couple [7]	46,981	47,899	47,873	3,750	3,842	3,713	83.0	81.3	50.2	46.1
With own children [7]	21,579	22,005	21,835	1,972	1,926	1,901	38.1	37.1	26.4	23.6
Female householder, no spouse present [7]	7,306	8,031	8,284	3,275	3,716	3,769	12.9	14.1	43.8	46.8
With own children [7]	4,199	4,841	4,975	2,232	2,489	2,404	7.4	8.5	29.9	29.8
Male householder, no spouse present [7]	2,303	2,507	2,712	446	536	573	4.1	4.6	6.0	7.1
With own children [7]	939	1,105	1,276	173	267	278	1.7	2.2	2.3	3.4
FAMILY INCOME IN PREVIOUS YEAR IN CONSTANT (1995) DOLLARS										
Total families	56,590	58,437	58,869	7,470	8,093	8,055	100.0	100.0	100.0	100.0
Less than $5,000	1,132	1,286	1,163	627	647	632	2.0	2.0	8.4	7.9
$5,000 to $9,999	2,037	2,572	2,228	934	1,028	926	3.6	3.8	12.5	11.5
$10,000 to $14,999	3,056	3,507	3,425	837	882	881	5.4	5.8	11.2	10.9
$15,000 to $24,999	7,413	8,299	8,204	1,374	1,449	1,478	13.1	13.9	18.4	18.3
$25,000 to $34,999	7,696	8,299	8,372	956	1,117	1,149	13.6	14.2	12.8	14.3
$35,000-$49,999	11,148	10,754	11,095	1,173	1,198	1,279	19.7	18.8	15.7	15.9
$50,000 or more	24,051	23,728	24,385	1,569	1,772	1,710	42.5	41.4	21.0	21.3
Median income (dol.)	44,214	42,043	42,646	24,838	25,398	25,970	(X)	(X)	(X)	(X)
Families below poverty level	4,409	5,312	4,994	2,077	2,212	2,127	7.8	8.5	27.8	26.4
Persons below poverty level	20,785	25,379	24,423	9,302	10,196	9,872	10.0	11.2	30.7	29.3
HOUSING TENURE										
Total occupied units	80,163	83,737	84,511	10,486	11,655	11,577	100.0	100.0	100.0	100.0
Owner-occupied	54,094	57,449	58,282	4,445	4,888	5,085	67.5	69.0	42.4	43.9
Renter-occupied	24,685	24,793	24,798	5,862	6,547	6,290	30.8	29.3	55.9	54.3
No cash rent	1,384	1,494	1,430	178	220	201	1.7	1.7	1.7	1.7

X Not applicable. [1] Represents those who completed ninth to twelfth grade, but have no high school diploma. [2] High school graduate. [3] Some college or associate degree. [4] Bachelor's or advanced degree. [5] Source: U.S. Bureau of Labor Statistics, *Employment and Earnings*, January issues. [6] Total unemployment as percent of civilian labor force. [7] Children under 18 years old.

H1-8   Social and Economic Characteristics of the Hispanic Population, 1995

CHARACTERISTIC	NUMBER (1,000)						PERCENT DISTRIBUTION					
	His-panic, total	Mexi-can	Puer-to Rican	Cuban	Central and South American	Other His-panic	His-panic, total	Mexi-can	Puer-to Rican	Cuban	Central and South American	Other His-panic
Total persons	27,521	17,982	2,730	1,156	3,686	1,967	100.0	100.0	100.0	100.0	100.0	100.0
Under 5 years old	3,318	2,413	272	68	360	205	12.1	13.4	10.0	5.9	9.8	10.4
5 to 14 years old	5,215	3,611	539	131	577	356	18.9	20.1	19.7	11.3	15.7	18.1
15 to 44 years old.	13,894	9,049	1,323	486	2,102	933	50.5	50.3	48.5	42.0	57.0	47.4
45 to 64 years old.	3,666	2,127	466	265	489	320	13.3	11.8	17.1	22.9	13.3	16.3
65 years old and over	1,428	781	130	207	159	154	5.2	4.3	4.8	17.9	4.3	7.8
EDUCATIONAL ATTAINMENT												
Persons 25 years old and over	14,171	8,737	1,437	820	2,082	1,095	100.0	100.0	100.0	100.0	100.0	100.0
High school graduate or higher	7,563	4,067	880	531	1,337	749	53.4	46.5	61.3	64.7	64.2	68.4
Bachelor's degree or higher . .	1,312	572	153	158	272	156	9.3	6.5	10.7	19.3	13.1	14.2
LABOR FORCE STATUS												
Civilians 16 years old and over	18,629	11,609	1,896	1,019	2,686	1,419	100.0	100.0	100.0	100.0	100.0	100.0
Civilian labor force	12,267	7,765	1,098	613	1,885	906	65.8	66.9	57.9	60.2	70.2	63.8
Employed.	11,127	7,016	974	568	1,734	835	59.7	60.4	51.4	55.7	64.6	58.8
Unemployed.	1,140	750	123	45	150	72	6.1	6.5	6.5	4.4	5.6	5.1
Unemployment rate ' . . .	9.3	9.7	11.2	7.4	8.0	7.9	(X)	(X)	(X)	(X)	(X)	(X)
Not in labor force	6,362	3,844	798	406	802	512	34.2	33.1	42.1	39.8	29.9	36.1
FAMILY TYPE												
Total families	6,200	3,847	729	315	817	491	100.0	100.0	100.0	100.0	100.0	100.0
Married couple	4,235	2,745	386	235	541	328	68.3	71.4	52.9	74.6	66.1	66.8
Female householder, no spouse present.	1,485	766	300	67	208	145	24.0	19.9	41.2	21.3	25.4	29.5
Male householder, no spouse present.	479	336	43	13	69	18	7.7	8.7	5.9	4.0	8.5	3.7
FAMILY INCOME IN 1994												
Total families	6,200	3,847	729	315	817	491	100.0	100.0	100.0	100.0	100.0	100.0
Less than $5,000	375	232	54	14	45	30	6.0	6.0	7.4	4.4	5.6	6.0
$5,000 to $9,999	730	446	136	27	73	49	11.8	11.6	18.6	8.5	8.9	9.9
$10,000 to $14,999.	779	517	97	24	92	50	12.6	13.4	13.3	7.5	11.3	10.1
$15,000 to $24,999.	1,301	844	122	68	180	88	21.0	21.9	16.7	21.5	22.0	17.9
$25,000 to $34,999.	923	583	92	46	133	68	14.9	15.2	12.6	14.5	16.3	13.9
$35,000 to $49,999.	924	575	80	38	139	92	14.9	14.9	10.9	12.0	17.1	18.7
$50,000 or more.	1,168	650	149	100	154	115	18.8	16.9	20.4	31.7	18.8	23.4
Median income (dol.)	24,313	23,609	20,929	30,584	26,558	28,658	(X)	(X)	(X)	(X)	(X)	(X)
Families below poverty level .	1,724	1,138	242	43	196	105	27.8	29.6	33.2	13.6	23.9	21.4
Persons below poverty level .	8,416	5,781	981	205	949	500	30.7	32.3	36.0	17.8	25.8	25.5
HOUSING TENURE												
Total occupied units . . .	7,735	4,653	935	451	1,040	656	100.0	100.0	100.0	100.0	100.0	100.0
Owner-occupied	3,278	2,145	268	236	304	325	42.4	46.1	28.7	52.3	29.2	49.6
Renter-occupied	4,457	2,508	667	215	736	331	57.6	53.9	71.3	47.7	70.8	50.4

X Not applicable.

2. INCOME

H2-1   Median Household Income in Constant (1995) Dollars

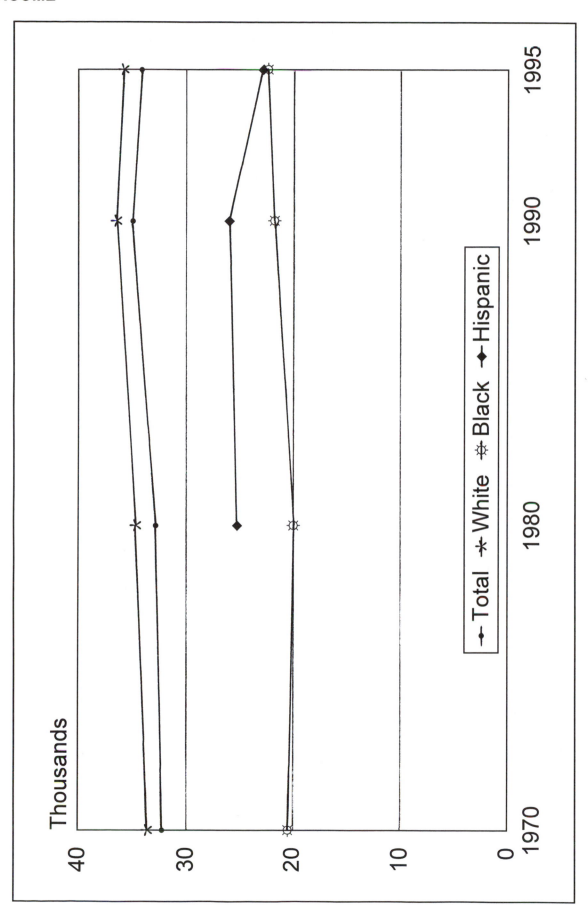

H2-2 Median Family Income in Constant (1993) Dollars

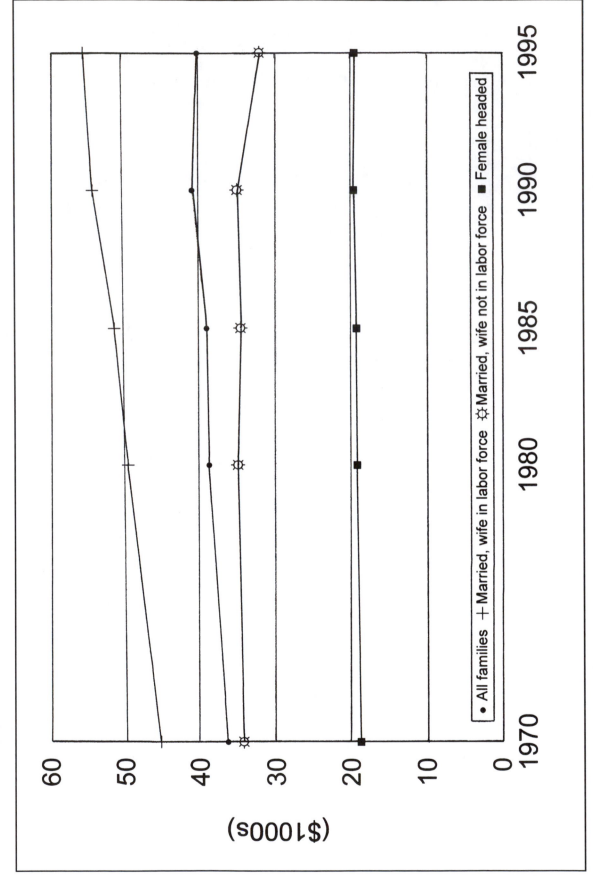

H2-3 Median Family Income, by Race and Hispanic Origin, 1994

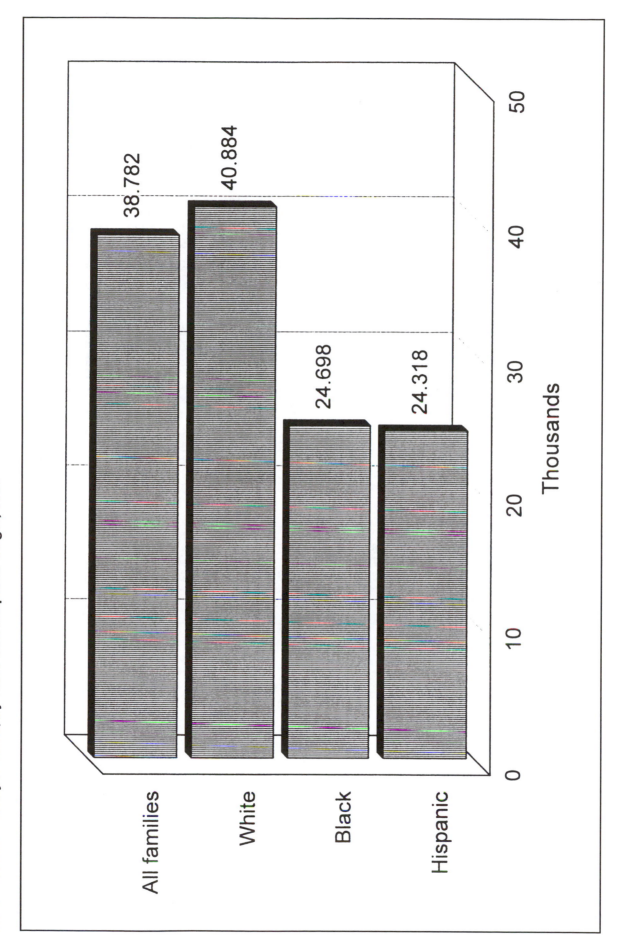

H2-4 Money Income of Households–Percent Distribution, by Income Level, Race, and Hispanic Origin, in Constant (1995) Dollars: 1970–1995

YEAR	Number of families (1,000)	PERCENT DISTRIBUTION							Median income (dollars)
		Under $10,000	$10,000-$14,999	$15,000-$24,999	$25,000-$34,999	$35,000-$49,999	$50,000-$74,999	$75,000 and over	
ALL FAMILIES [1]									
1970	52,227	7.7	6.7	15.4	18.0	24.5	19.0	8.8	36,410
1980	60,309	7.3	6.7	15.2	14.9	21.9	21.3	12.8	38,930
1985	63,558	8.3	6.4	14.7	14.6	19.8	20.8	15.5	39,283
1990	66,322	7.7	6.1	13.7	14.2	19.4	21.0	18.0	41,223
1992	68,216	8.8	6.5	14.4	14.3	18.5	20.6	16.8	39,727
1993	68,506	9.1	6.7	14.6	14.5	17.6	20.0	17.4	38,980
1994	69,313	8.5	6.7	14.6	14.1	17.9	20.0	18.3	39,881
1995	69,597	7.5	6.5	14.4	14.1	18.5	20.4	18.6	40,611
WHITE									
1970	46,535	6.5	6.1	14.6	18.1	25.4	20.0	9.4	37,772
1980	52,710	5.8	5.9	14.5	15.1	22.7	22.4	13.8	40,561
1990	56,803	5.7	5.4	13.2	14.3	19.9	22.2	19.1	43,044
1994	58,444	6.6	6.0	14.2	14.2	18.4	21.0	19.6	42,043
1995	58,872	5.8	5.8	13.9	14.2	18.8	21.4	20.0	42,646
BLACK									
1970	4,928	18.6	12.6	23.0	16.9	16.5	9.8	2.6	23,170
1980	6,317	19.1	13.4	21.2	14.0	15.8	12.3	4.3	23,469
1990	7,471	21.4	11.2	17.5	13.7	15.6	12.8	7.8	24,980
1994	8,093	20.7	10.9	17.9	13.8	14.8	13.4	8.5	25,398
1995	8,055	19.4	10.9	18.3	14.3	15.9	13.3	8.0	25,970
HISPANIC ORIGIN [2]									
1980	3,235	13.2	11.5	21.2	17.1	18.4	13.4	5.3	27,251
1990	4,981	14.6	12.0	19.3	16.0	17.3	13.0	7.8	27,321
1994	6,202	17.2	12.4	20.5	14.9	15.1	12.2	7.6	25,007
1995	6,287	16.2	11.8	22.8	16.2	13.8	12.7	6.6	24,570

[1] Includes other races not shown separately. [2] Persons of Hispanic origin may be of any race.

H2-5   Money Income of Households—Median Income, by Race and Hispanic Origin, in Current and Constant (1995) Dollars: 1970–1995

YEAR	MEDIAN INCOME IN CURRENT DOLLARS					MEDIAN INCOME IN CONSTANT (1995) DOLLARS				
	All families [1]	White	Black	Asian, Pacific Islander	His-panic [2]	All families [1]	White	Black	Asian, Pacific Islander	His-panic [2]
1970	9,867	10,236	6,279	(NA)	(NA)	36,410	37,772	23,170	(NA)	(NA)
1980	21,023	21,904	12,674	(NA)	14,716	38,930	40,561	23,469	(NA)	27,251
1981	22,388	23,517	13,266	(NA)	16,401	37,868	39,778	22,439	(NA)	27,742
1982	23,433	24,603	13,598	(NA)	16,227	37,356	39,221	21,677	(NA)	25,868
1983 [3]	24,580	25,757	14,506	(NA)	16,956	37,610	39,411	22,196	(NA)	25,945
1984 [3]	26,433	27,686	15,431	(NA)	18,832	38,772	40,610	22,634	(NA)	27,623
1985	27,735	29,152	16,786	(NA)	19,027	39,283	41,290	23,775	(NA)	26,949
1986 [4]	29,458	30,809	17,604	(NA)	19,995	40,962	42,840	24,479	(NA)	27,803
1987 [4]	30,970	32,385	18,406	(NA)	20,300	41,548	43,446	24,693	(NA)	27,233
1988	32,191	33,915	19,329	36,560	21,769	41,470	43,691	24,901	47,098	28,044
1989	34,213	35,975	20,209	40,351	23,446	42,049	44,214	24,838	49,593	28,816
1990	35,353	36,915	21,423	42,246	23,431	41,223	43,044	24,980	49,260	27,321
1991 [5]	35,939	37,783	21,548	40,974	23,895	40,214	42,277	24,111	45,848	26,737
1992 [5]	36,573	38,670	21,103	42,255	23,555	39,727	42,005	22,923	45,899	25,586
1993	36,959	39,300	21,542	44,456	23,654	38,980	41,449	22,720	46,886	24,947
1994	38,782	40,884	24,698	46,122	24,318	39,881	42,043	25,398	47,429	25,007
1995	40,611	42,646	25,970	46,356	24,570	40,611	42,646	25,970	46,356	24,570

NA Not available.   [1] Includes other races not shown separately.   [2] Persons of Hispanic origin may be of any race. [3] Beginning 1984, data based on revised Hispanic population controls and not directly comparable with prior years.   [4] Beginning 1987, data based on revised processing procedures and not directly comparable with prior years.   [5] Based on 1990 census population controls.

H2-6   Money Income of Households—Percent Distribution, by Income Level and Selected Characteristics, 1995

CHARACTERISTIC	Number of house-holds (1,000)	PERCENT DISTRIBUTION							Median income (dollars)
		Under $10,000	$10,000-$14,999	$15,000-$24,999	$25,000-$34,999	$35,000-$49,999	$50,000-$74,999	$75,000 and over	
Total [1]	99,627	12,189	8,716	15,848	14,167	16,876	17,038	14,792	34,076
Age of householder:									
15 to 24 years	5,282	1,157	707	1,245	947	699	416	114	20,979
25 to 34 years	19,225	1,937	1,385	3,071	3,299	4,065	3,457	2,007	34,701
35 to 44 years	23,226	1,632	1,275	2,883	3,154	4,504	5,454	4,326	43,465
45 to 54 years	18,008	1,367	807	1,913	2,106	3,184	3,942	4,689	48,058
55 to 64 years	12,401	1,463	863	1,748	1,602	2,099	2,189	2,435	38,077
65 years and over	21,486	4,634	3,679	4,988	3,059	2,326	1,577	1,221	19,096
White	84,511	8,939	7,083	13,192	12,148	14,584	15,093	13,472	35,766
Black	11,577	2,783	1,336	2,178	1,568	1,695	1,299	719	22,393
Hispanic [2]	7,939	1,578	971	1,707	1,222	1,058	918	485	22,860
Northeast	19,695	2,527	1,666	2,700	2,656	3,198	3,580	3,370	36,111
Midwest	23,707	2,429	2,028	3,707	3,415	4,212	4,446	3,471	35,839
South	35,143	4,917	3,288	6,024	5,298	5,922	5,329	4,364	30,942
West	21,082	2,317	1,735	3,418	2,798	3,544	3,683	3,587	35,979
Size of household:									
One person	24,900	7,000	4,030	5,234	3,469	2,776	1,549	844	17,063
Two persons	32,526	2,384	2,562	5,680	5,280	6,103	5,622	4,890	35,700
Three persons	16,724	1,312	943	2,165	2,270	3,147	3,652	3,229	42,244
Four persons	15,118	816	600	1,507	1,778	2,940	3,836	3,640	49,531
Five persons	6,631	448	330	759	829	1,242	1,528	1,497	45,710
Six persons	2,357	139	151	301	319	385	586	475	44,263
Seven or more persons	1,372	90	100	201	222	282	266	209	39,013
Type of Household:									
Family households	69,594	4,841	4,378	9,870	9,824	13,077	14,432	13,173	41,224
Married-couple	53,567	1,736	2,398	6,615	7,292	10,445	12,752	12,326	47,129
Male householder, wife absent	3,513	291	293	669	570	738	576	375	33,534
Female householder, husband absent	12,514	2,812	1,686	2,586	1,962	1,892	1,105	472	21,348
Nonfamily households	30,033	7,349	4,339	5,978	4,343	3,801	2,606	1,618	19,929
Male householder	13,348	2,266	1,495	2,634	2,195	2,117	1,545	1,094	26,023
Female householder	16,685	5,084	2,844	3,345	2,147	1,683	1,062	524	15,892
Educational attainment of householder: [3]									
Total	94,346	11,033	8,010	14,603	13,220	16,178	16,623	14,678	35,235
Less than 9th grade	8,062	2,569	1,452	1,771	966	688	449	166	15,043
9th to 12th grade (no diploma)	9,683	2,363	1,551	2,259	1,285	1,175	731	320	18,298
High school graduate	29,507	3,363	2,682	5,379	4,976	5,572	4,975	2,559	31,376
Some college, no degree	16,951	1,525	1,271	2,516	2,591	3,339	3,374	2,335	37,156
Associate degree	6,719	435	326	914	978	1,376	1,647	1,041	42,118
Bachelor's degree or more	23,424	778	726	1,764	2,424	4,030	5,446	8,256	58,052
Bachelor's degree	14,871	567	549	1,315	1,759	2,730	3,556	4,394	52,857
Master's degree	5,706	152	115	322	458	947	1,386	2,325	64,960
Professional degree	1,641	32	36	86	137	190	264	896	82,010
Doctorate degree	1,206	27	26	39	69	161	240	640	80,005
Tenure:									
Owner occupied	65,143	4,944	4,351	8,751	8,720	11,837	13,627	12,911	41,832
Renter occupied	32,768	6,816	4,139	6,714	5,187	4,821	3,285	1,805	22,563
Occupier paid no cash rent	1,716	429	225	383	258	219	127	74	19,910

[1] Includes other races not shown separately.   [2] Persons of Hispanic origin may be of any race.   [3] 25 years old and over.

H2-7 Money Income of Households—Median Income and Income Level, by Household Type, 1995

| ITEM | All house-holds | FAMILY HOUSEHOLDS | | | | NONFAMILY HOUSEHOLDS | | |
| | | Total | Married couple | Male house-holder, wife absent | Female house-holder, husband absent | Total [1] | Single-person household | |
							Male house-holder	Female house-holder
MEDIAN INCOME (dollars)								
All households	34,076	41,224	47,129	33,534	21,348	19,929	26,023	15,892
White	35,766	43,265	47,608	35,129	24,431	20,585	26,898	16,325
Black	22,393	26,838	41,362	27,071	15,589	15,007	19,172	11,872
Hispanic [2]	22,860	25,491	30,195	25,053	14,755	13,780	17,339	10,196
NUMBER (1,000)								
All households	99,627	69,594	53,567	3,513	12,514	30,033	13,348	16,685
Under $5,000	3,651	1,708	566	95	1,046	1,943	787	1,156
$5,000 to $9,999	8,538	3,133	1,170	196	1,766	5,406	1,479	3,928
$10,000 to $14,999	8,716	4,378	2,398	293	1,686	4,339	1,495	2,844
$15,000 to $19,999	8,294	4,923	3,187	321	1,415	3,370	1,357	2,014
$20,000 to $24,999	7,554	4,947	3,428	348	1,171	2,608	1,277	1,331
$25,000 to $34,999	14,167	9,824	7,292	570	1,962	4,343	2,195	2,147
$35,000 to $49,999	16,876	13,077	10,445	738	1,892	3,801	2,117	1,683
$50,000 to $74,999	17,038	14,432	12,752	576	1,105	2,606	1,545	1,062
$75,000 to $99,999	7,678	6,803	6,293	221	289	874	577	297
$100,000 and over	7,114	6,370	6,033	154	183	744	517	227

[1] Includes other nonfamily households not shown separately.   [2] Persons of Hispanic origin may be of any race.

H2-8   Money Income of Households—Percent Distribution, by Income Quintile and Top Five Percent, 1995

CHARACTERISTIC	Number (1,000)	PERCENT DISTRIBUTION						
		Total	Lowest fifth	Second fifth	Third fifth	Fourth fifth	Highest fifth	Top 5 percent
Total	99,627	100.0	20.0	20.0	20.0	20.0	20.0	5.0
Age of householder:								
15 to 24 years old	5,282	100.0	33.6	29.0	21.8	11.8	3.8	0.3
25 to 34 years old	19,225	100.0	16.7	20.3	24.4	23.4	15.2	2.7
35 to 44 years old	23,226	100.0	11.8	16.1	20.3	26.2	25.6	5.9
45 to 54 years old	18,008	100.0	11.7	13.3	18.3	22.9	33.8	9.4
55 to 64 years old	12,401	100.0	18.2	17.3	19.3	20.0	25.2	7.3
65 years old and over	21,486	100.0	36.5	28.9	17.0	9.9	7.6	2.2
White	84,511	100.0	18.0	19.8	20.2	20.8	21.3	5.4
Black	11,577	100.0	34.3	22.7	19.0	14.2	9.8	1.4
Hispanic origin [1]	7,939	100.0	30.9	26.2	19.7	14.3	9.0	1.6
Northeast	19,695	100.0	20.5	17.1	19.5	20.4	22.5	6.4
Midwest	23,707	100.0	17.8	19.6	20.3	22.0	20.3	4.5
South	35,143	100.0	22.2	21.7	20.9	18.3	16.9	4.3
West	21,082	100.0	18.2	20.4	18.7	20.2	22.4	5.5
Family households	69,594	100.0	12.5	17.8	20.8	23.5	25.4	6.4
Married-couple families	53,567	100.0	7.2	15.6	20.5	26.2	30.5	7.9
Male householder	3,513	100.0	15.4	23.9	24.0	20.9	15.8	2.8
Female householder	12,514	100.0	34.6	25.2	21.5	12.7	6.1	0.9
Nonfamily households	30,033	100.0	37.3	25.2	18.1	11.8	7.6	1.8
Male householder	13,348	100.0	26.9	25.3	21.3	15.2	11.3	2.8
Living alone	10,288	100.0	31.4	27.3	20.8	12.9	7.6	2.2
Female householder	16,685	100.0	45.7	25.1	15.5	9.1	4.6	0.9
Living alone	14,612	100.0	50.4	25.8	14.1	7.0	2.7	0.5
Worked	71,070	100.0	10.2	17.6	22.0	24.5	25.7	6.4
Worked at full-time jobs	61,729	100.0	7.6	16.8	22.5	25.7	27.4	6.7
Worked at part-time jobs	9,341	100.0	27.6	23.4	18.5	16.4	14.2	4.2
Did not work	28,557	100.0	44.3	25.9	15.0	8.9	5.9	1.6

[1] Persons of Hispanic origin may be of any race.

H2-9 Money Income of Households—Median Income, by State, in Constant (1995) Dollars: 1985–1995

STATE	1985	1988 [1]	1989	1990	1991	1992 [2]	1993 [3]	1994	1995
United States....	33,452	35,073	35,526	34,914	33,709	33,278	32,949	33,178	34,076
Alabama............	25,966	25,698	26,159	27,235	27,242	28,034	26,453	27,967	25,991
Alaska	49,264	42,645	44,253	45,823	45,443	45,407	45,278	46,653	47,954
Arizona............	33,818	34,055	35,091	34,076	34,393	31,890	32,178	32,180	30,863
Arkansas	24,717	25,987	26,342	26,569	26,222	25,942	24,299	26,290	25,814
California	38,215	39,017	40,569	38,817	37,668	37,913	35,936	36,332	37,009
Colorado...........	39,916	33,770	32,945	35,836	35,246	35,286	36,373	38,905	40,706
Connecticut.........	44,035	46,651	52,014	45,324	47,168	44,363	41,676	42,262	40,243
Delaware	32,548	39,298	39,413	35,918	36,461	38,755	38,036	36,890	34,928
District of Columbia	29,851	34,449	32,879	31,940	33,440	32,856	28,797	30,969	30,748
Florida	30,229	32,729	32,059	31,115	30,493	29,708	30,111	30,124	29,745
Georgia	29,813	34,224	33,850	32,137	30,449	31,281	33,394	32,359	34,099
Hawaii	41,019	42,543	43,059	45,383	41,676	45,745	44,994	43,453	42,851
Idaho..............	29,405	30,209	30,301	29,506	29,222	30,093	32,705	32,430	32,676
Illinois	35,225	38,034	38,469	37,945	35,676	34,272	34,653	36,075	38,071
Indiana............	32,116	33,872	31,829	31,399	30,311	30,991	31,086	28,647	33,385
Iowa	29,640	31,311	32,281	31,819	31,949	31,222	30,230	34,016	35,519
Kansas............	32,276	32,935	33,014	34,884	32,779	32,963	31,398	29,125	30,341
Kentucky	24,589	25,645	28,616	28,894	26,591	25,510	25,709	27,349	29,810
Louisiana	29,997	26,405	28,097	26,125	28,308	27,633	27,751	26,404	27,949
Maine..............	29,062	34,012	34,685	32,024	31,183	32,171	28,938	31,175	33,858
Maryland	42,683	47,088	44,265	45,308	41,347	40,412	42,123	40,309	41,041
Massachusetts........	39,951	42,787	44,351	42,265	39,962	39,495	39,090	41,648	38,574
Michigan...........	34,335	37,967	37,823	34,907	35,937	35,050	34,448	36,284	36,426
Minnesota..........	33,789	37,471	37,098	36,689	32,985	33,653	35,523	34,597	37,933
Mississippi	23,247	23,402	24,479	23,528	21,791	22,344	23,404	26,120	26,538
Missouri	31,073	30,200	32,566	31,870	31,248	29,721	30,250	31,046	34,825
Montana...........	28,661	28,639	29,118	27,256	27,780	28,813	27,917	28,414	27,757
Nebraska	30,875	32,411	32,347	32,045	33,064	32,639	32,703	32,695	32,929
Nevada	32,964	36,049	36,060	37,340	36,855	34,660	37,772	36,888	36,084
New Hampshire.......	37,396	44,606	46,128	47,580	40,318	42,837	40,040	36,244	39,171
New Jersey.........	43,879	46,747	48,080	45,165	44,813	42,364	42,714	43,478	43,924
New Mexico	28,926	24,858	27,779	29,196	29,697	28,090	28,221	27,667	25,991
New York	33,481	37,250	38,710	36,836	35,576	33,729	33,430	32,803	33,028
North Carolina.......	30,382	31,453	32,454	30,700	30,047	30,166	30,396	30,967	31,979
North Dakota........	30,034	31,037	31,007	29,459	28,972	29,284	29,655	29,079	29,089
Ohio	35,655	35,736	35,668	34,996	33,333	34,112	32,995	32,758	34,941
Oklahoma..........	30,034	30,489	29,088	28,432	28,491	27,465	27,696	27,756	26,311
Oregon............	31,010	35,746	35,063	34,142	33,781	34,681	34,950	32,347	36,374
Pennsylvania........	32,402	34,450	35,261	33,821	33,979	32,459	32,690	32,975	34,524
Rhode Island........	34,878	38,444	37,023	37,276	34,504	33,057	35,341	32,833	35,359
South Carolina.......	28,378	32,893	29,249	33,506	30,730	29,956	27,477	30,692	29,071
South Dakota	25,696	28,720	29,630	28,650	27,570	28,524	29,253	30,576	29,578
Tennessee	25,180	26,868	27,790	26,343	27,362	26,415	26,474	29,451	29,015
Texas..............	33,629	32,159	31,815	32,915	31,032	30,364	30,298	31,627	32,039
Utah	35,746	33,898	37,752	35,146	31,348	37,205	37,742	36,728	36,480
Vermont	36,825	37,344	38,463	36,261	32,623	35,580	32,763	36,817	33,824
Virginia............	40,266	42,059	41,932	40,896	40,435	41,492	38,425	38,714	36,222
Washington.........	33,993	41,645	39,281	37,444	38,010	36,824	37,604	34,483	35,568
West Virginia........	22,638	24,932	26,642	25,812	25,900	22,019	23,647	24,232	24,880
Wisconsin..........	32,925	38,100	35,793	35,810	34,836	36,181	33,503	36,391	40,955
Wyoming	31,275	34,034	36,282	34,351	32,505	32,814	31,052	34,079	31,529

[1] Beginning 1988, data based on revised processing procedures and not directly comparable with prior years. [2] Implementation of 1990 census population controls. [3] Data collection method changed from paper and pencil to computer assisted interviewing. In addition, the March 1994 income supplement was revised to allow for the coding of different income amounts on selected questionnaire items.

H2-10 Money Income of Families—Percent Distribution, by Income Level, Race, and Hispanic Origin, in Constant (1995) Dollars: 1970–1995

YEAR	Number of families (1,000)	PERCENT DISTRIBUTION							Median income (dollars)
		Under $10,000	$10,000-$14,999	$15,000-$24,999	$25,000-$34,999	$35,000-$49,999	$50,000-$74,999	$75,000 and over	
ALL FAMILIES [1]									
1970	52,227	7.7	6.7	15.4	18.0	24.5	19.0	8.8	36,410
1980	60,309	7.3	6.7	15.2	14.9	21.9	21.3	12.8	38,930
1985	63,558	8.3	6.4	14.7	14.6	19.8	20.8	15.5	39,283
1990	66,322	7.7	6.1	13.7	14.2	19.4	21.0	18.0	41,223
1992	68,216	8.8	6.5	14.4	14.3	18.5	20.6	16.8	39,727
1993	68,506	9.1	6.7	14.6	14.5	17.6	20.0	17.4	38,980
1994	69,313	8.5	6.7	14.6	14.1	17.9	20.0	18.3	39,881
1995	69,597	7.5	6.5	14.4	14.1	18.5	20.4	18.6	40,611
WHITE									
1970	46,535	6.5	6.1	14.6	18.1	25.4	20.0	9.4	37,772
1980	52,710	5.8	5.9	14.5	15.1	22.7	22.4	13.8	40,561
1990	56,803	5.7	5.4	13.2	14.3	19.9	22.2	19.1	43,044
1994	58,444	6.6	6.0	14.2	14.2	18.4	21.0	19.6	42,043
1995	58,872	5.8	5.8	13.9	14.2	18.8	21.4	20.0	42,646
BLACK									
1970	4,928	18.6	12.6	23.0	16.9	16.5	9.8	2.6	23,170
1980	6,317	19.1	13.4	21.2	14.0	15.8	12.3	4.3	23,469
1990	7,471	21.4	11.2	17.5	13.7	15.6	12.8	7.8	24,980
1994	8,093	20.7	10.9	17.9	13.8	14.8	13.4	8.5	25,398
1995	8,055	19.4	10.9	18.3	14.3	15.9	13.3	8.0	25,970
HISPANIC ORIGIN [2]									
1980	3,235	13.2	11.5	21.2	17.1	18.4	13.4	5.3	27,251
1990	4,981	14.6	12.0	19.3	16.0	17.3	13.0	7.8	27,321
1994	6,202	17.2	12.4	20.5	14.9	15.1	12.2	7.6	25,007
1995	6,287	16.2	11.8	22.8	16.2	13.8	12.7	6.6	24,570

[1] Includes other races not shown separately.   [2] Persons of Hispanic origin may be of any race.

H2-11 Money Income of Families—Median Income, by Race and Hispanic Origin, in Current and Constant (1995) Dollars: 1970–1995

YEAR	MEDIAN INCOME IN CURRENT DOLLARS					MEDIAN INCOME IN CONSTANT (1995) DOLLARS				
	All families [1]	White	Black	Asian, Pacific Islander	His-panic [2]	All families [1]	White	Black	Asian, Pacific Islander	His-panic [2]
1970	9,867	10,236	6,279	(NA)	(NA)	36,410	37,772	23,170	(NA)	(NA)
1980	21,023	21,904	12,674	(NA)	14,716	38,930	40,561	23,469	(NA)	27,251
1981	22,388	23,517	13,266	(NA)	16,401	37,868	39,778	22,439	(NA)	27,742
1982	23,433	24,603	13,598	(NA)	16,227	37,356	39,221	21,677	(NA)	25,868
1983	24,580	25,757	14,506	(NA)	16,956	37,610	39,411	22,196	(NA)	25,945
1984 [3]	26,433	27,686	15,431	(NA)	18,832	38,772	40,610	22,634	(NA)	27,623
1985	27,735	29,152	16,786	(NA)	19,027	39,283	41,290	23,775	(NA)	26,949
1986	29,458	30,809	17,604	(NA)	19,995	40,962	42,840	24,479	(NA)	27,803
1987 [4]	30,970	32,385	18,406	(NA)	20,300	41,548	43,446	24,693	(NA)	27,233
1988	32,191	33,915	19,329	36,560	21,769	41,470	43,691	24,901	47,098	28,044
1989	34,213	35,975	20,209	40,351	23,446	42,049	44,214	24,838	49,593	28,816
1990	35,353	36,915	21,423	42,246	23,431	41,223	43,044	24,980	49,260	27,321
1991 [5]	35,939	37,783	21,548	40,974	23,895	40,214	42,277	24,111	45,848	26,737
1992 [5]	36,573	38,670	21,103	42,255	23,555	39,727	42,005	22,923	45,899	25,586
1993	36,959	39,300	21,542	44,456	23,654	38,980	41,449	22,720	46,886	24,947
1994	38,782	40,884	24,698	46,122	24,318	39,881	42,043	25,398	47,429	25,007
1995	40,611	42,646	25,970	46,356	24,570	40,611	42,646	25,970	46,356	24,570

NA Not available.   [1] Includes other races not shown separately.   [2] Persons of Hispanic origin may be of any race. [3] Beginning 1984, data based on revised Hispanic population controls and not directly comparable with prior years.   [4] Beginning 1987, data based on revised processing procedures and not directly comparable with prior years.   [5] Based on 1990 census population controls.

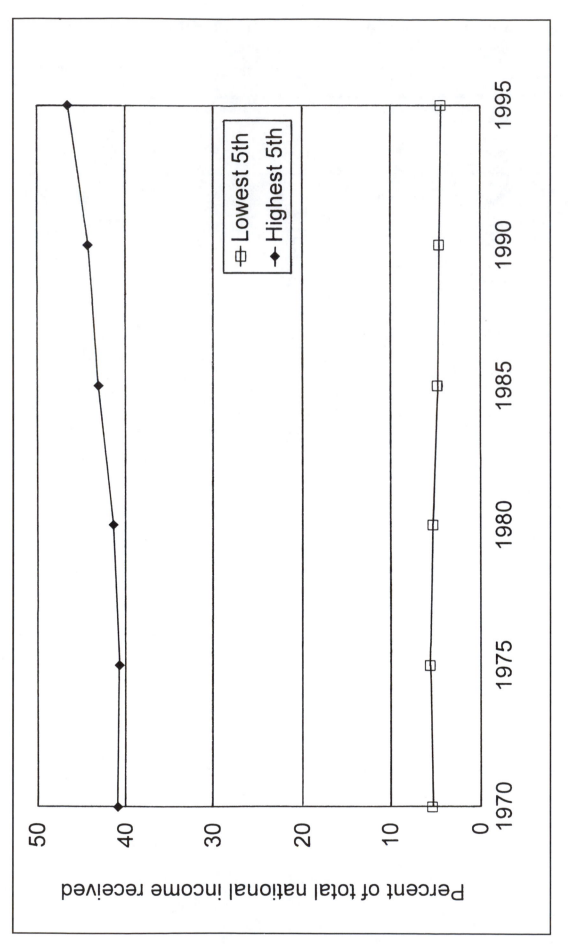

H2-12 Shares of Income Received by the Poorest and Richest Fifths of Families

H2-13 Share of Aggregate Income Received by Each Fifth and Top Five Percent of Families, by Race and Hispanic Origin of Householder: 1970–1995

YEAR	Number (1,000)	Upper limit of each fifth				Top 5 per-cent	Low-est 5th	Sec-ond 5th	Third 5th	Fourth 5th	High-est 5th	Top 5 per-cent
		Lowest	Second	Third	Fourth							
1970	52,227	18,819	30,701	41,694	57,311	89,484	5.4	12.2	17.6	23.8	40.9	15.6
1975	56,245	18,947	31,199	43,388	60,073	94,098	5.6	11.9	17.7	24.2	40.7	14.9
1980	60,309	19,258	32,424	45,924	64,441	101,847	5.3	11.6	17.6	24.4	41.1	14.6
1981	61,019	18,631	31,715	45,260	63,937	101,474	5.3	11.4	17.5	24.6	41.2	14.4
1982	61,393	18,172	31,121	44,556	63,928	104,118	5.0	11.3	17.2	24.4	42.2	15.3
1983 [1]	62,015	18,109	31,017	45,100	64,490	106,134	4.9	11.2	17.2	24.5	42.4	15.3
1984	62,706	18,445	32,085	46,474	66,832	109,423	4.8	11.1	17.1	24.5	42.5	15.4
1985	63,558	18,816	32,415	46,955	68,309	111,843	4.8	11.0	16.9	24.3	43.1	16.1
1986	64,491	19,467	33,511	48,835	70,318	115,969	4.7	10.9	16.9	24.1	43.4	16.5
1987 [2]	65,204	19,584	33,783	49,370	71,545	116,646	4.6	10.7	16.8	24.0	43.8	17.2
1988	65,837	19,455	33,729	49,598	72,021	118,520	4.6	10.7	16.7	24.0	44.0	17.2
1989	66,090	19,668	34,413	50,145	73,189	121,629	4.6	10.6	16.5	23.7	44.6	17.9
1990	66,322	19,643	33,866	49,020	71,699	119,352	4.6	10.8	16.6	23.8	44.3	17.4
1991	67,173	19,022	32,574	48,115	70,483	115,054	4.5	10.7	16.6	24.1	44.2	17.1
1992 [3]	68,216	18,154	32,233	47,795	69,574	115,155	4.3	10.5	16.5	24.0	44.7	17.6
1993	68,506	17,898	31,640	47,492	70,446	119,370	4.1	9.9	15.7	23.3	47.0	20.3
1994	69,313	18,448	32,187	48,332	71,982	123,445	4.2	10.0	15.7	23.3	46.9	20.1
1995	69,597	19,070	32,985	48,985	72,260	123,656	4.4	10.1	15.8	23.2	46.5	20.0
White	58,872	20,916	35,046	51,000	75,000	127,196	4.8	10.4	16.0	23.0	45.8	19.5
Black	8,055	10,200	20,000	32,296	51,016	84,744	3.3	8.7	15.2	24.1	48.7	20.0
Hispanic origin [4]	6,287	11,479	19,677	30,022	48,492	82,380	4.1	9.5	15.1	23.2	48.1	19.9

[1] Beginning 1983, data based on revised Hispanic population controls and not directly comparable with prior years. [2] Beginning 1987, data based on revised processing procedures and not directly comparable with prior years. [3] Based on 1990 census population controls. [4] Persons of Hispanic origin may be of any race.

H2-14 Money Income of Families—Percent Distribution, by Income Quintile and Top Five Percent: 1995

CHARACTERISTIC	Number (1,000)	PERCENT DISTRIBUTION						
		Total	Lowest fifth	Second fifth	Third fifth	Fourth fifth	Highest fifth	Top 5 percent
All families.................	69,597	100.0	20.0	20.0	20.0	20.0	20.0	5.0
Age of householder:								
15 to 24 years old.............	3,019	100.0	50.4	26.2	15.1	6.5	1.9	0.2
25 to 34 years old.............	13,727	100.0	24.3	21.3	22.8	19.3	12.2	2.1
35 to 44 years old.............	18,504	100.0	15.8	16.8	20.4	24.7	22.3	5.3
45 to 54 years old.............	13,908	100.0	10.9	13.5	18.8	24.1	32.6	8.6
55 to 64 years old.............	9,134	100.0	16.5	17.8	19.7	20.0	26.0	7.1
65 years old and over...........	11,306	100.0	27.5	31.6	19.0	11.6	10.2	3.1
White.....................	58,872	100.0	17.3	19.8	20.4	21.0	21.5	5.4
Black.....................	8,055	100.0	38.0	22.7	17.4	13.2	8.7	1.4
Hispanic origin [1]................	6,287	100.0	38.8	25.2	16.1	12.5	7.3	1.3
Type of family:								
Married-couple families...........	53,570	100.0	12.7	18.5	21.0	23.2	24.5	6.3
Male householder, wife absent......	3,513	100.0	28.5	26.3	20.5	14.6	10.0	1.6
Female householder, husband absent .	12,514	100.0	48.8	24.5	15.5	7.7	3.4	0.5
Presence of related children under 18 years old:								
No related children..............	32,878	100.0	17.2	21.4	20.6	19.6	21.3	5.5
One or more related children.......	36,719	100.0	22.5	18.8	19.5	20.4	18.8	4.6
One child..................	15,046	100.0	22.8	19.5	18.9	19.5	19.3	4.3
Two children or more...........	21,674	100.0	22.3	18.3	19.9	20.9	18.6	4.8
Education attainment of householder: [2]								
Total.....................	66,578	100.0	18.6	19.7	20.2	20.6	20.8	5.2
Less than 9th grade..............	5,063	100.0	46.1	28.6	14.5	7.7	3.0	0.5
9th to 12th grade (no diploma)........	6,477	100.0	39.9	27.1	17.6	10.5	5.0	0.9
High school graduate (includes equivalency)........................	21,468	100.0	19.5	24.3	23.7	20.6	11.9	1.8
Some college, no degree...........	12,166	100.0	15.6	19.4	23.0	23.4	18.5	3.6
Associate degree	4,786	100.0	11.0	16.1	23.1	28.4	21.4	3.8
Bachelor's degree or more..........	16,618	100.0	5.2	9.4	15.6	24.3	45.5	14.3
Bachelor's degree	10,421	100.0	6.1	11.3	17.4	26.0	39.2	10.2
Master's degree................	4,091	100.0	4.2	6.5	13.4	24.0	51.9	15.7
Professional degree.............	1,193	100.0	3.6	6.8	9.7	13.6	66.3	36.4
Doctorate degree...............	913	100.0	2.2	5.1	11.8	19.7	61.2	26.7

[1] Persons of Hispanic origin may be of any race.   [2] 25 years old and over.

H2-15 Family Net Worth—Mean and Median Net Worth in Constant (1995) Dollars, by Selected Family Characteristics: 1989–1995

FAMILY CHARACTERISTIC	1989			1992			1995		
	Percent of families	Net worth		Percent of families	Net worth		Percent of families	Net worth	
		Mean	Median		Mean	Median		Mean	Median
All families	100.0	216.7	56.5	100.0	200.5	52.8	100.0	205.9	56.4
Age of family head:									
Under 35 years old.	27.2	66.3	9.2	25.8	50.3	10.1	24.8	47.2	11.4
35 to 44 years old	23.4	171.3	69.2	22.8	144.3	46.0	23.2	144.5	48.5
45 to 54 years old	14.4	338.9	114.0	16.2	287.8	83.4	17.8	277.8	90.5
55 to 64 years old	13.9	334.4	110.5	13.2	358.6	122.5	12.5	356.2	110.8
65 to 74 years old	12.0	336.8	88.4	12.6	308.3	105.8	11.9	331.6	104.1
75 years old and over.	9.0	250.8	83.2	9.4	231.0	92.8	9.8	276.0	95.0
Family income in constant (1995) dollars:[1]									
Less than $10,000	15.4	26.1	1.6	15.5	30.9	3.3	16.0	45.6	4.8
$10,000 to $24,999	24.3	77.9	25.6	27.8	71.2	28.2	26.5	74.6	30.0
$25,000 to $49,999	30.3	121.8	56.0	29.5	124.4	54.8	31.1	119.3	54.9
$50,000 to $99,999	22.3	229.5	128.1	20.0	240.8	121.2	20.2	256.0	121.1
$100,000 and more	7.7	1,372.9	474.7	7.1	1,283.6	506.1	6.1	1,465.2	485.9
Education of householder:									
No high school diploma.	24.3	92.1	28.5	20.4	75.8	21.6	19.0	87.2	26.3
High school diploma.	32.1	134.4	43.4	29.9	120.6	41.4	31.6	138.2	50.0
Some college	15.1	213.8	56.4	17.7	185.4	62.6	19.0	186.6	43.2
College degree	28.5	416.9	132.1	31.9	363.3	103.1	30.5	361.8	104.1
Tenure:									
Owner occupied	63.8	311.7	119.9	63.9	289.6	106.1	64.7	295.4	102.3
Renter occupied or other. . . .	36.2	49.4	2.4	36.1	42.7	3.6	35.3	42.2	4.5

[1]Income for year preceding the survey.

H2-16 Money Income of Families—Work Experience, by Income Level, 1995

CHARACTERISTIC	Number of families (1,000)	INCOME LEVEL (1,000)							Median income (dollars)
		Under $10,000	$10,000 to $14,999	$15,000 to $24,999	$25,000 to $34,999	$35,000 to $49,999	$50,000 to $74,999	$75,000 and over	
All families..............	69,597	5,216	4,507	10,040	9,828	12,841	14,204	12,961	40,611
Number of earners:									
No earners.................	10,180	2,634	1,660	2,621	1,491	947	513	312	17,713
1 earner....................	19,894	2,104	2,112	4,338	3,621	3,443	2,370	1,906	28,423
2 earners or more...........	39,524	479	735	3,081	4,716	8,451	11,321	10,743	54,008
2 earners	31,041	444	661	2,750	4,094	7,068	8,637	7,387	50,989
3 earners	6,249	28	65	297	522	1,107	2,001	2,229	63,924
4 earners or more	2,234	6	8	34	100	276	683	1,126	75,386
Work experience of householder:									
Total	69,597	5,216	4,507	10,040	9,828	12,841	14,204	12,961	40,611
Worked......................	52,701	2,165	2,326	6,109	7,088	10,543	12,586	11,884	46,983
Worked at full-time jobs	46,285	1,267	1,772	5,032	6,154	9,446	11,606	11,009	49,031
50 weeks or more	39,506	497	1,121	3,913	5,171	8,204	10,419	10,181	51,409
27 to 49 weeks..............	4,576	277	390	728	716	897	907	660	37,639
26 weeks or less.............	2,203	493	261	391	267	345	280	167	24,011
Worked at part-time............	6,416	898	554	1,077	934	1,097	980	875	31,832
50 weeks or more	3,036	256	278	533	404	577	533	456	36,008
27 to 49 weeks..............	1,487	181	103	233	262	257	213	238	32,891
26 weeks or less.............	1,893	462	174	311	269	263	234	180	24,986

H2-17 Median Income of Families, by Type of Family, in Current and Constant (1995) Dollars: 1970–1995

YEAR	CURRENT DOLLARS						CONSTANT (1995) DOLLARS					
	Total	Married-couple families			Male householder, no wife present	Female householder, no husband present	Total	Married-couple families			Male householder, no wife present	Female householder, no husband present
		Total	Wife in paid labor force	Wife not in paid labor force				Total	Wife in paid labor force	Wife not in paid labor force		
1970.......	9,867	10,516	12,276	9,304	9,012	5,093	36,410	38,805	45,299	34,332	33,255	18,794
1980.......	21,023	23,141	26,879	18,972	17,519	10,408	38,930	42,852	49,774	35,132	32,441	19,273
1985.......	27,735	31,100	36,431	24,556	22,622	13,660	39,283	44,049	51,599	34,780	32,041	19,347
1986.......	29,458	32,805	38,346	25,803	24,962	13,647	40,962	45,616	53,321	35,879	34,710	18,976
1987 [1].....	30,970	34,879	40,751	26,640	25,208	14,683	41,548	46,792	54,669	35,739	33,818	19,698
1988.......	32,191	36,389	42,709	27,220	26,827	15,346	41,470	46,878	55,020	35,066	34,560	19,769
1989.......	34,213	38,547	45,266	28,747	27,847	16,442	42,049	47,375	55,633	35,331	34,225	20,208
1990.......	35,353	39,895	46,777	30,265	29,046	16,932	41,223	46,519	54,543	35,290	33,868	19,743
1991.......	35,939	40,995	48,169	30,075	28,351	16,692	40,214	45,871	53,898	33,652	31,723	18,677
1992 [2].....	36,573	41,890	49,775	30,174	27,576	17,025	39,727	45,503	54,068	32,776	29,954	18,493
1993.......	36,959	43,005	51,204	30,218	26,467	17,443	38,980	45,356	54,003	31,870	27,914	18,397
1994.......	38,782	44,959	53,309	31,176	27,751	18,236	39,881	46,233	54,820	32,060	28,537	18,753
1995.......	40,611	47,062	55,823	32,375	30,358	19,691	40,611	47,062	55,823	32,375	30,358	19,691

[1] Beginning 1987, data based on revised processing procedures and not directly comparable with prior years.   [2] Based on 1990 census population controls.

H2-18 Median Income of Persons with Income in Constant (1995) Dollars, by Sex, Race, and Hispanic Origin: 1980–1995

ITEM	FEMALE					MALE				
	1980	1990	1993 [1]	1994 [2]	1995	1980	1990	1993 [1]	1994 [2]	1995
NUMBER WITH INCOME (1,000)										
All races.........	80,826	92,245	94,417	95,147	96,007	78,661	88,220	90,194	91,254	92,066
White...............	70,573	78,566	79,484	80,045	80,608	69,420	76,480	77,650	78,220	79,022
Black...............	8,596	10,687	11,267	11,450	11,607	7,387	8,820	8,947	9,199	9,339
Hispanic [3]	3,617	5,903	7,053	7,298	7,478	3,996	6,767	8,208	8,375	8,577
White, not Hispanic origin .	67,084	72,939	73,128	73,665	73,506	65,564	69,987	70,179	70,919	70,754
MEDIAN INCOME (dol.)										
All races.........	9,111	11,742	11,650	11,791	12,130	23,203	23,652	22,256	22,336	22,562
White...............	9,161	12,030	11,882	11,960	12,316	24,680	24,685	23,183	23,311	23,895
Black...............	8,481	9,711	10,028	10,843	10,961	14,831	15,004	15,403	15,407	16,006
Hispanic [3]	8,157	8,783	8,543	8,857	8,928	17,886	15,706	14,437	14,911	14,840
White, not Hispanic origin .	9,222	12,338	12,233	12,284	12,807	25,334	25,604	24,438	24,806	25,481

[1] Data collection method changed and questionaire was revised to allow for coding of different income amounts. [2] Introduction of new 1990 census sample design. [3] Persons of Hispanic origin may be of any race.

H2-19 Flow of Funds Accounts—Assets of Households: 1980–1996

TYPE OF INSTRUMENT	TOTAL (bil. dol.)							PERCENT DISTRIBUTION		
	1980	1985	1990	1993	1994	1995	1996	1980	1990	1996
Total financial assets	6,296	9,709	14,207	17,733	18,275	20,711	22,768	100.0	100.0	100.0
Deposits...................	1,490	2,460	3,239	3,152	3,144	3,348	3,531	23.7	22.8	15.5
Foreign deposits.............	-	8	13	16	17	19	23	-	0.1	0.1
Checkable deposits and currency ..	224	318	383	562	547	503	450	3.6	2.7	2.0
Time and savings deposits	1,203	1,941	2,478	2,236	2,228	2,378	2,520	19.1	17.4	11.1
Money market fund shares	62	193	365	338	352	448	538	1.0	2.6	2.4
Credit market instruments	423	799	1,494	1,691	1,981	1,932	1,961	6.7	10.5	8.6
Open-market paper...........	38	35	63	46	35	35	47	0.6	0.4	0.2
U.S. Government securities	165	267	514	594	938	881	875	2.6	3.6	3.8
Treasury issues.............	160	239	390	477	669	646	586	2.5	2.7	2.6
Savings bonds...........	73	80	126	172	180	185	187	1.2	0.9	0.8
Other Treasury	88	159	264	305	489	461	399	1.4	1.9	1.8
Agency issues	5	28	124	117	269	235	289	0.1	0.9	1.3
Municipal securities..........	104	346	574	557	505	454	432	1.7	4.0	1.9
Corporate and foreign bonds......	31	75	195	312	311	362	390	0.5	1.4	1.7
Mortgages................	84	76	147	183	193	200	217	1.3	1.0	1.0
Corporate equities [1]	903	1,110	1,753	3,250	3,100	4,167	4,780	14.3	12.3	21.0
Mutual fund shares.............	46	198	467	977	1,027	1,227	1,491	0.7	3.3	6.5
Security credit	16	35	62	102	109	128	158	0.3	0.4	0.7
Life insurance reserves..........	216	257	381	471	505	550	585	3.4	2.7	2.6
Pension fund reserves [2]	960	2,062	3,406	4,639	4,847	5,568	6,319	15.2	24.0	27.8
Investment in bank personal trusts ...	265	384	552	691	699	767	834	4.2	3.9	3.7
Equity in noncorporate business	1,903	2,273	2,629	2,496	2,587	2,700	2,734	30.2	18.5	12.0
Miscellaneous assets	74	133	224	264	275	325	376	1.2	1.6	1.7

- Represents zero.   [1] Only those directly held and those in closed-end funds. Other equities are included in mutual funds, life insurance and pension reserves, and bank personal trusts.

H2-20 Financial Assets Held by Families, by Type of Asset: 1992 and 1995

AGE OF FAMILY HEAD AND FAMILY INCOME	Any financial asset [1]	Transac-tion accounts [2]	Certifi-cates of deposit	Savings bonds	Stocks [3]	Mutual funds [4]	Retirement accounts [5]	Life insur-ance (cash value)	Other man-aged [6]
PERCENT OF FAMILIES OWNING ASSET									
1992, total	90.3	87.0	16.7	22.3	16.9	10.4	37.9	34.8	4.0
1995, total	90.8	87.1	14.1	22.9	15.3	12.0	43.0	31.4	3.8
Under 35 years old	87.0	80.8	7.1	21.1	11.1	8.8	39.2	22.3	1.6
35 to 44 years old	92.0	87.4	8.2	31.0	14.5	10.5	51.5	28.9	3.4
45 to 54 years old	92.4	88.9	12.5	25.1	17.5	16.0	54.3	37.5	2.9
55 to 64 years old	90.5	88.2	16.2	19.6	14.9	15.2	47.2	37.5	7.1
65 to 74 years old	92.0	91.1	23.9	17.0	18.0	13.7	35.0	37.0	5.6
75 years old and over	93.8	93.0	34.1	15.3	21.3	10.4	16.5	35.1	5.7
Less than $10,000.	68.1	61.1	7.2	5.9	2.5	1.8	5.9	15.8	(B)
$10,000 to $24,999	87.6	82.3	16.0	11.8	9.2	4.9	24.2	25.2	3.2
$25,000 to $49,999	97.8	94.7	13.7	27.4	14.3	12.4	52.6	33.1	4.2
$50,000 to $99,999	99.5	98.6	15.6	39.9	26.0	20.9	69.8	42.5	5.3
$100,000 and more	100.0	100.0	21.1	36.3	45.2	38.0	84.6	54.1	8.0
MEDIAN VALUE [7]									
1992, total	12.0	2.5	11.2	0.7	8.7	17.4	15.2	3.3	21.7
1995, total	13.0	2.1	10.0	1.0	8.0	19.0	15.6	5.0	30.0
Under 35 years old	5.3	1.2	6.0	0.5	3.7	5.0	5.2	3.4	3.8
35 to 44 years old	11.6	2.0	6.0	1.0	4.0	10.0	12.0	5.0	10.8
45 to 54 years old	24.8	2.7	12.0	1.0	10.0	17.5	25.0	6.5	43.0
55 to 64 years old	32.3	3.0	14.0	1.1	17.0	55.0	32.8	6.0	42.0
65 to 74 years old	19.1	3.0	17.0	1.5	15.0	50.0	28.5	5.0	26.0
75 years old and over	20.9	5.0	11.0	4.0	25.0	50.0	17.5	5.0	100.0
Less than $10,000.	1.2	0.7	7.0	0.4	2.0	25.0	3.5	1.5	(B)
$10,000 to $24,999	5.4	1.4	10.0	0.8	5.7	8.0	6.0	3.0	19.7
$25,000 to $49,999	12.1	2.0	10.0	0.7	6.9	12.5	10.0	5.0	25.0
$50,000 to $99,999	40.7	4.5	13.0	1.2	5.7	15.0	23.0	7.0	35.0
$100,000 and more	214.5	15.8	15.6	1.5	30.0	48.0	85.0	12.0	62.5

B Base figure too small.   [1] Includes other types of financial assets, not shown separately.   [2] Checking, savings, and money market accounts.   [3] Covers only those stocks that are directly held by families outside mutual funds, IRA's, Keogh or pension accounts.   [4] Excludes money market mutual funds, individual retirement accounts (IRA's), Keogh accounts, and any type of pension plan invested in mutual funds.   [5] Covers IRA's, Keogh accounts, and employer-provided pension plans from which withdrawals can be made, such as 401(k) plans.   [6] Includes trusts, annuities, managed investment accounts, and other such assets.   [7] Median value of financial asset for families holding such assets.

H2-21 Flow of Funds Accounts—Liabilities of Households: 1980–1996

TYPE OF INSTRUMENT	TOTAL (bil. dol.)							PERCENT DISTRIBUTION		
	1980	1985	1990	1993	1994	1995	1996	1980	1990	1996
Total liabilities	1,443	2,350	3,765	4,471	4,850	5,245	5,665	100.0	100.0	100.0
Credit market instruments	1,391	2,260	3,640	4,288	4,660	5,041	5,436	96.4	96.7	96.0
Home mortgages	905	1,410	2,491	2,980	3,178	3,376	3,654	62.7	66.2	64.5
Consumer credit.	355	595	811	864	990	1,132	1,226	24.6	21.5	21.6
Municipal securities.	17	81	86	115	129	135	139	1.2	2.3	2.5
Bank loans, n.e.c. [1]	28	32	12	18	29	42	37	1.9	0.3	0.7
Other loans	55	79	101	127	135	145	144	3.8	2.7	2.5
Commercial mortgages	31	63	139	185	199	212	235	2.2	3.7	4.1
Security credit	25	51	39	76	75	79	93	1.7	1.0	1.6
Trade payables	14	24	69	90	97	107	116	1.0	1.8	2.1
Unpaid life insurance premiums [2]	13	15	16	17	18	18	19	0.9	0.4	0.3

[1] Not elsewhere classified.   [2] Includes deferred premiums.

H2-22 Financial Debt Held by Families, by Type of Debt, 1992 and 1995

AGE OF FAMILY HEAD AND FAMILY INCOME	Any debt	Mortgage, home equity	Installment	Other lines of credit	Credit card	Investment real estate	Other debt [1]
PERCENT OF FAMILIES HOLDING DEBTS							
1992, total	73.6	39.1	46.1	2.4	43.8	7.8	8.8
1995, total	75.2	41.1	46.5	1.9	47.8	6.3	9.0
Under 35 years old	83.8	32.9	62.2	2.6	55.4	2.6	7.8
35 to 44 years old	87.2	54.1	60.7	2.2	55.8	6.5	11.1
45 to 54 years old	86.5	61.9	54.0	2.3	57.3	10.4	14.1
55 to 64 years old	75.2	45.8	36.0	1.4	43.4	12.5	7.5
65 to 74 years old	54.5	24.8	16.7	1.3	31.3	5.0	5.5
75 years old and over	30.1	7.1	9.6	(B)	18.3	1.5	3.6
Less than $10,000.	48.5	8.9	25.9	(B)	25.4	1.6	6.6
$10,000 to $24,999	67.3	24.8	41.3	1.4	41.9	2.5	8.7
$25,000 to $49,999	83.9	47.3	54.3	2.0	56.7	5.8	8.5
$50,000 to $99,999	89.9	68.7	60.7	3.2	62.8	9.5	10.0
$100,000 and more	86.4	73.6	37.0	4.0	37.0	27.9	15.8
MEDIAN DEBT [2]							
1992, total	19.5	47.4	5.0	2.2	1.1	26.0	2.7
1995, total	22.5	51.0	6.1	3.5	1.5	28.0	2.0
Under 35 years old	15.2	63.0	7.0	1.4	1.4	22.8	1.5
35 to 44 years old	37.6	60.0	5.6	2.0	1.8	30.0	1.7
45 to 54 years old	41.0	48.0	7.0	5.7	2.0	28.1	2.5
55 to 64 years old	25.8	36.0	5.9	3.5	1.3	26.0	4.0
65 to 74 years old	7.7	19.0	4.9	3.8	0.8	36.0	2.0
75 years old and over	2.0	15.9	3.9	(B)	0.4	8.0	3.0
Less than $10,000.	2.6	14.0	2.9	(B)	0.6	15.0	2.0
$10,000 to $24,999	9.2	26.0	3.9	3.0	1.2	18.3	1.2
$25,000 to $49,999	23.4	46.0	6.6	3.0	1.4	25.0	1.5
$50,000 to $99,999	65.0	68.0	9.0	2.2	2.2	34.0	2.5
$100,000 and more	112.2	103.4	8.5	19.5	3.0	36.8	7.0

B Base figure too small.   [1] Includes loans on insurance policies, loans against pension accounts, and other unclassified loans.   [2] Median amount of financial debt for families holding such debts.

H2-23 Percent Distribution of Amount of Debt Held by Families, 1992 and 1995

TYPE OF DEBT	1992	1995	PURPOSE OF DEBT	1992	1995	TYPE OF LENDING INSTITUTION	1992	1995
Total..........	100.0	100.0	Total..........	100.0	100.0	Total............	100.0	100.0
Home mortgage and home equity lines of credit	64.2	68.2	Home purchase.....	59.9	65.2	Commercial bank	33.2	35.1
			Home improvement ..	2.3	1.9	Savings and loan	16.6	11.3
			Investment, excluding real estate	1.6	0.9	Credit union	4.0	4.2
Installment loans.....	10.3	11.2				Finance or loan company.	13.5	21.0
Credit card balances..	2.8	3.7	Vehicles..........	6.2	7.1	Brokerage	3.3	1.9
Other lines of credit...	0.7	0.4	Goods and services..	5.0	5.2	Real estate lender.....	14.2	12.9
Investment real estate mortgages	19.8	14.4	Investment real estate.	20.5	15.3	Individual lender	4.5	4.4
			Education.........	2.5	2.5	Other nonfinancial.....	1.5	0.7
Other debt.........	2.2	2.2	Other loans	2.2	2.0	Government.........	1.9	1.7
						Credit and store cards ..	3.0	3.7
						Other loans	4.4	3.1

H2-24 State and Local Government Retirement Systems—Beneficiaries and Finances: 1980–1994

YEAR AND LEVEL OF GOVERNMENT	Number of beneficiaries (1,000)	RECEIPTS					BENEFITS AND WITHDRAWALS			Cash and security holdings
		Total	Employee contributions	Government contributions		Earnings on investments	Total	Benefits	Withdrawals	
				State	Local					
1980: All systems........	(NA)	37.3	6.5	7.6	10.0	13.3	14.0	12.2	1.8	185
State-administered ...	(NA)	28.6	5.3	7.4	5.6	10.3	10.3	8.8	1.4	145
Locally administered..	(NA)	8.7	1.2	0.2	4.3	3.0	3.8	3.4	0.4	41
1990: All systems........	4,026	111.3	13.9	14.0	18.6	64.9	38.4	36.0	2.4	721
State-administered ...	3,232	89.2	11.6	14.0	11.5	52.0	29.6	27.6	2.0	575
Locally administered..	794	22.2	2.2	(Z)	7.0	12.9	8.8	8.4	0.4	145
1993: All systems........	4,562	135.4	16.5	15.2	20.4	83.3	51.6	49.1	2.5	929
State-administered ...	3,643	109.4	13.8	15.2	12.9	67.6	40.0	37.9	2.1	750
Locally administered..	919	26.0	2.7	(Z)	7.5	15.8	11.6	11.2	0.4	180
1994: All systems........	4,889	138.7	17.3	15.5	21.2	84.6	56.4	53.4	3.0	1,025
State-administered ...	3,979	113.2	14.7	15.5	13.6	69.4	43.8	41.2	2.6	826
Locally administered..	910	25.5	2.6	(Z)	7.7	15.2	12.6	12.2	0.5	199

NA Not available.   Z Less than $50 million.

H2-25 Private Pension Plans—Summary, by Type of Plan: 1980–1993

["Pension plan" is defined by the Employee Retirement Income Security Act (ERISA) as "any plan, fund, or program which was heretofore or is hereafter established or maintained by an employer or an employee organization, or by both, to the extent that such plan (a) provides retirement income to employees, or (b) results in a deferral of income by employees for periods extending to the termination of covered employment or beyond, regardless of the method of calculating the contributions made to the plan, the method of calculating the benefits under the plan, or the method of distributing benefits from the plan." A defined benefit plan provides a definite benefit formula for calculating benefit amounts - such as a flat amount per year of service or a percentage of salary times years of service. A defined contribution plan is a pension plan in which the contributions are made to an individual account for each employee. The retirement benefit is dependent upon the account balance at retirement. The balance depends upon amounts contributed, investment experience, and, in the case of profit sharing plans, amounts which may be allocated to the account due to forfeitures by terminating employees. Employee Stock Ownership Plans (ESOP) and 401(k) plans (see table 594) are included among defined contribution plans. Data are based on Form 5500 series reports filed with the Internal Revenue Service]

ITEM	Unit	TOTAL				DEFINED CONTRIBUTION PLAN				DEFINED BENEFIT PLAN			
		1980	1985	1990	1993	1980	1985	1990	1993	1980	1985	1990	1993
Number of plans [1]	1,000...	488.9	632.1	712.3	702.1	340.8	462.0	599.2	618.5	148.1	170.2	113.1	83.6
Total participants [2][3]	Million..	57.9	74.7	76.9	83.9	19.9	35.0	38.1	43.6	38.0	39.7	38.8	40.3
Active participants [2][4]	Million..	49.0	62.3	61.8	64.7	18.9	33.2	35.5	39.6	30.1	29.0	26.3	25.1
Contributions [5]	Bil. dol..	66.2	95.1	98.8	153.6	23.5	53.1	75.8	101.5	42.6	42.0	23.0	52.1
Benefits [6]	Bil. dol..	35.3	101.9	129.4	156.3	13.1	47.4	63.0	77.2	22.1	54.5	66.4	79.1

[1] Excludes all plans covering only one participant. [2] Includes double counting of workers in more than one plan. [3] Total participants include active participants, vested separated workers, and retirees. [4] Any workers currently in employment covered by a plan and who are earning or retaining credited service under a plan. Includes any nonvested former employees who have not yet incurred breaks in service. [5] Includes both employer and employee contributions. [6] Benefits paid directly from trust and premium payments made from plan to insurance carriers. Excludes benefits paid directly by insurance carriers.

H2-26 Pension Plan Coverage of Workers, by Selected Characteristics, 1995

SEX AND AGE	NUMBER WITH COVERAGE (1,000)				PERCENT OF TOTAL WORKERS			
	Total [1]	White	Black	Hispanic [2]	Total [1]	White	Black	Hispanic [2]
Total	57,837	49,435	6,260	3,191	41.2	41.4	41.2	25.1
Male	32,310	28,050	3,059	1,831	43.3	43.6	42.2	24.5
Under 65 years old	31,633	27,458	2,997	1,807	44.0	44.5	42.3	24.5
15 to 24 years old	1,633	1,368	179	138	13.3	13.1	13.8	8.7
25 to 44 years old	18,217	15,661	1,845	1,189	47.3	47.8	46.1	26.7
45 to 64 years old	11,784	10,430	973	480	55.9	56.4	54.5	36.5
65 years old and over	677	592	62	25	23.7	22.7	35.3	21.0
Female	25,527	21,385	3,202	1,360	38.9	38.9	40.3	26.0
Under 65 years old	25,057	20,967	3,157	1,344	39.4	39.5	40.5	26.1
15 to 24 years old	1,092	903	145	95	9.6	9.6	10.4	8.5
25 to 44 years old	14,672	12,099	2,004	869	43.7	43.8	45.1	29.6
45 to 64 years old	9,293	7,965	1,009	380	49.8	49.8	51.7	34.7
65 years old and over	470	418	44	16	22.3	22.0	27.0	24.5

[1] Includes other races, not shown separately. [2] Hispanic persons may be of any race.

H2-27 Social Security-Covered Employment, Earnings, and Contribution Rates: 1980–1995

ITEM	Unit	1980	1985	1988	1989	1990	1991	1992	1993	1994	1995
Workers with insured status [1]	Million	137.4	148.3	155.4	158.3	161.3	164.0	165.9	167.4	168.8	170.6
Male	Million	75.4	79.6	82.6	83.8	85.2	86.4	87.2	87.8	88.3	89.1
Female	Million	62.0	68.6	72.8	74.5	76.1	77.5	78.7	79.6	80.5	81.5
Under 25 years old	Million	25.5	22.4	21.3	21.3	21.4	21.3	20.8	20.1	19.3	19.0
25 to 34 years old	Million	34.9	39.4	41.0	41.3	41.5	41.6	41.3	40.8	40.2	39.8
35 to 44 years old	Million	22.4	28.6	32.3	33.5	34.9	36.4	37.2	38.0	38.9	39.8
45 to 54 years old	Million	18.6	19.0	20.5	21.4	22.1	22.8	24.1	25.5	26.8	28.1
55 to 59 years old	Million	9.2	9.1	8.8	8.7	8.7	8.7	8.8	9.0	9.2	9.5
60 to 64 years old	Million	7.9	8.7	8.7	8.7	8.7	8.8	8.7	8.5	8.4	8.4
65 to 69 years old	Million	6.7	7.3	7.7	7.9	8.1	8.2	8.1	8.2	8.2	8.1
70 years old and over	Million	12.1	13.9	15.0	15.4	15.8	16.3	16.8	17.3	17.7	18.0
Workers reported with—											
Taxable earnings [2]	Million	113	120	130	132	134	133	134	136	139	143
Maximum earnings [2]	Million	10	8	8	8	8	8	8	8	8	8
Earnings in covered employment [2]	Bil. dol.	1,329	1,942	2,432	2,573	2,704	2,761	2,916	3,033	3,171	3,369
Reported taxable [2]	Bil. dol.	1,178	1,725	2,092	2,238	2,358	2,422	2,533	2,644	2,784	2,924
Percent of total	Percent	88.6	88.8	86.0	87.0	87.2	87.7	86.9	87.2	87.8	86.8
Annual maximum taxable earnings [3]	Dollars	25,900	39,600	45,000	48,000	51,300	53,400	55,500	57,600	60,600	61,200
Contribution rates for OASDHI: [4]											
Each employer and employee	Percent	6.13	7.05	7.51	7.51	7.65	7.65	7.65	7.65	7.65	7.65
Self-employed [5]	Percent	8.10	14.10	15.02	15.02	15.30	15.30	15.30	15.30	15.30	15.30
SMI, monthly premium [6]	Dollars	9.60	15.50	24.80	31.90	28.60	29.90	31.80	36.60	41.10	46.10

[1] Fully insured for retirement and/or survivor benefits as of beginning of year. [2] Includes self-employment. [3] The maximum taxable earnings for HI was $125,000 in 1991; $130,200 in 1992, and 135,000 in 1993. Beginning 1994 upper limit on earnings subject to HI taxes was repealed. [4] As of January 1, 1996, and 1997, each employee and employer pays 7.65 percent and the self-employed pay 15.3 percent. [5] Self-employed pays 11.8 percent in 1985 and 13.02 percent in 1988 and 1989. The additional amount is supplied from general revenues. Beginning 1990, self-employed pays 15.3 percent, and half of the tax is deductible for income tax purposes and for computing self-employment income subject to social security tax. [6] 1980, as of July 1; beginning 1985, as of January 1. As of January 1, 1996, the monthly premium is $42.50; as of January 1, 1997, $43.80.

H2-28 Social Security Trust Funds: 1980–1995

TYPE OF TRUST FUND	1980	1985	1989	1990	1991	1992	1993	1994	1995
Old-age and survivors insurance (OASI):									
Net contribution income [1]	103.5	180.2	252.6	272.4	278.4	286.8	296.2	298.3	310.1
Interest received [2]	1.8	1.9	12.0	16.4	20.8	24.3	27.0	29.9	32.8
Benefit payments [3]	105.1	167.2	208.0	223.0	240.5	[4]254.9	[4]267.8	279.1	291.6
Assets, end of year	22.8	[5]35.8	155.1	214.2	267.8	319.2	369.3	413.5	458.5
Disability insurance (DI):									
Net contribution income [1]	13.3	17.4	24.1	28.7	29.3	30.4	31.5	51.7	54.7
Interest received [2]	0.5	0.9	0.7	0.9	1.1	1.1	0.8	1.2	2.2
Benefit payments [3]	15.5	18.8	22.9	24.8	27.7	[4]31.1	[4]34.6	37.7	40.9
Assets, end of year	3.6	[6]6.3	7.9	11.1	12.9	12.3	9.0	22.9	37.6
Hospital insurance (HI):									
Net contribution income [1][7]	23.9	47.7	68.5	71.1	78.4	82.4	84.9	97.9	103.3
Interest received [2]	1.1	3.4	7.3	8.5	9.5	10.5	12.5	10.7	10.8
Benefit payments	25.1	47.5	60.0	66.2	71.5	83.9	93.5	103.3	116.4
Assets, end of year	13.7	[8]20.5	85.6	98.9	115.2	124.0	127.8	132.8	130.3
Supplementary medical insurance (SMI):									
Net premium income	3.0	5.6	10.8	11.3	11.9	14.1	14.2	17.4	19.7
Transfers from general revenue	7.5	18.3	30.9	33.0	37.6	41.4	41.5	36.2	39.0
Interest received	0.4	1.2	1.1	1.6	1.7	1.8	2.0	2.0	1.6
Benefit payments	10.6	22.9	38.4	42.5	47.3	49.3	55.8	58.6	65.0
Assets, end of year	4.5	10.9	12.2	15.5	17.8	24.2	24.1	19.4	13.1

[1] Includes deposits by States and deductions for refund of estimated employee-tax overpayment. Beginning in 1985, includes government contributions on deemed wage credits for military service in 1957 and later. Includes tax credits on net earnings from self-employment in 1985-89. Includes taxation of benefits beginning in 1985 for OASI and DI and in 1994 for HI. [2] In 1985-90, includes interest on advance tax transfers. Beginning 1985, includes interest on reimbursement for unnegotiated checks. Data for 1985 reflect interest on interfund borrowing. [3] Includes payments for vocational rehabilitation services furnished to disabled persons receiving benefits because of their disabilities. Beginning in 1985, amounts reflect deductions for unnegotiated benefit checks. [4] Data adjusted to reflect 12 months of benefit payments. [5] Includes $13.2 billion borrowed from the DI and HI Trust Funds. [6] Excludes $2.5 billion lent to the OASI Trust Fund. [7] Includes premiums from aged ineligibles enrolled in HI. [8] Excludes $10.6 billion lent to the OASI Trust Fund.

H2-29 Private Expenditures for Social Welfare, by Type: 1980–1994

TYPE	1980	1985	1989	1990	1991	1992	1993	1994
Total expenditures	251,507	464,643	671,722	723,154	766,892	833,552	877,604	924,994
Percent of gross domestic product	9.0	11.1	12.4	12.6	13.0	13.3	13.4	13.3
Health	142,500	253,900	369,800	413,100	441,000	477,000	505,100	528,600
Income maintenance	53,564	118,871	167,260	164,772	170,754	187,461	192,340	204,736
Private pension plan payments [1][2]	37,605	98,570	141,286	138,114	143,314	158,857	163,158	174,452
Short-term sickness and disability [2]	8,630	10,570	13,616	13,680	13,844	14,684	15,132	15,901
Long-term disability [2]	1,282	1,937	2,892	2,926	3,172	3,143	2,900	2,895
Life insurance and death	5,075	7,489	9,063	9,278	9,472	10,184	10,693	11,229
Supplemental unemployment	972	305	403	774	952	593	457	259
Education	32,667	52,873	75,350	80,699	86,140	93,069	99,265	105,361
Welfare and other services	22,776	38,999	59,312	64,583	68,998	76,022	80,899	86,297

[1] Covers benefits paid for solely by employers and all benefits of employment-related pension plans to which employee contributions are made. Excludes individual savings plans such as IRA's and Keogh plans. Pension plan benefits include monthly benefits and lump-sum distributions to retired and disabled employees and their dependents and to survivors of deceased employees. Also includes preretirement lump-sum distributions. [2] Covers wage and salary workers in private industry.

H2-30 Public Income-Maintenance Programs—Cash Benefit Payments: 1980–1995

PROGRAM	1980	1985	1987	1988	1989	1990	1991	1992	1993	1994	1995
Total [1]	228.1	335.2	372.0	393.8	421.9	455.8	503.3	541.9	547.2	(NA)	(NA)
Percent of personal income [2]	10.1	9.9	9.8	9.7	9.6	9.8	10.4	10.5	10.2	(NA)	(NA)
OASDI [3]	120.3	186.1	204.7	216.4	229.6	245.6	265.6	284.3	296.3	311.6	327.9
Public employee retirement [4]	40.6	63.0	72.1	78.0	83.8	90.4	97.3	103.7	112.6	(NA)	(NA)
Railroad retirement	4.9	6.3	6.5	6.7	6.9	7.2	7.5	7.3	7.9	8.0	8.1
Veterans' pensions, compensation	11.4	14.1	14.3	14.7	15.3	15.8	16.3	16.5	16.9	18.7	18.0
Unemployment benefits [5]	18.9	14.4	14.4	13.2	16.4	20.0	31.3	37.3	21.5	21.6	22.0
Temporary disability benefits	1.4	1.8	2.5	2.8	2.9	3.2	3.9	4.0	3.3	(NA)	(NA)
Workers' compensation [6]	9.7	22.3	27.1	30.3	33.8	37.6	41.7	44.1	43.4	(NA)	(NA)
Public assistance	12.1	15.3	16.5	17.0	17.4	19.3	20.1	22.4	21.0	23.3	22.8
Supplemental Security Income	7.9	11.1	13.6	14.7	14.9	15.2	18.5	22.3	24.7	26.1	27.9

NA Not available.   [1] Includes lump sum death benefits, not shown separately. Lump sum death benefits for State and local government employee retirement systems are not available beginning 1987.   [2] For base data, see table 703.   [3] Old-age, survivors, and disability insurance under Federal Social Security Act; see text, section 12.   [4] Excludes refunds of contributions to employees who leave service.   [5] Beginning 1985, covers State unemployment insurance, Ex-Servicemen's Compensation Act and railroad unemployment insurance only.   [6] Includes black lung benefits.

H2-31 Number of Families Receiving Specified Sources of Income, by Characteristics of Householder and Family Income, 1995

SOURCE OF INCOME	Total families [1]	Under 65 years old	65 years old and over	White	Black	His-panic origin [2]	Under $15,000	$15,000 to $24,999	$25,000 to $34,999
Total	69,597	58,292	11,306	58,872	8,055	6,287	9,723	10,040	9,828
Earnings	59,055	54,301	4,753	50,186	6,555	5,406	5,358	7,367	8,279
Wages and salary	57,324	52,965	4,359	48,589	6,480	5,276	4,991	7,050	7,937
Social Security, railroad retirement	16,356	5,862	10,494	14,370	1,592	915	2,716	3,885	3,116
Supplemental Security Income (SSI)	2,421	1,921	500	1,592	669	360	1,026	591	323
Public assistance	3,616	3,530	86	2,153	1,262	767	2,493	594	251
Veterans payments	1,735	1,054	681	1,507	172	55	163	247	278
Unemployment compensation	5,022	4,807	215	4,336	514	503	521	732	850
Workers compensation	1,571	1,458	114	1,337	165	137	122	210	265
Retirement income	10,001	4,208	5,792	9,106	697	339	473	1,786	2,019
Private pensions	6,328	2,259	4,069	5,810	410	211	337	1,314	1,425
Military retirement	956	673	283	851	79	29	8	83	131
Federal employee pensions	1,182	445	737	1,030	125	27	47	150	226
State or local employee pensions	1,911	785	1,126	1,746	127	57	70	260	361
Other income	10,322	9,895	427	8,496	1,393	776	1,761	1,509	1,472
Alimony	248	237	11	210	33	12	38	31	46
Child support	4,421	4,378	43	3,645	664	307	1,054	801	774
Education assistance	4,784	4,648	137	3,895	642	371	603	596	591

[1] Includes other items not shown separately.   [2] Persons of Hispanic origin may be of any race.

H2-32 Ratios of Debt Payments to Family Income: 1989–1995

AGE OF FAMILY HEAD AND FAMILY INCOME (constant (1995) dollars)	RATIO OF DEBT PAYMENTS TO FAMILY INCOME						PERCENT OF DEBTORS WITH—					
	Aggregate			Median			Ratios above 40 percent			Any payment 60 days or more past due		
	1989	1992	1995	1989	1992	1995	1989	1992	1995	1989	1992	1995
All families	15.6	15.8	15.4	16.0	15.7	16.7	10.9	11.6	11.1	7.0	6.0	6.9
Under 35 years old	18.4	16.9	17.7	16.5	15.5	16.9	13.1	10.6	11.1	10.8	8.2	8.8
35 to 44 years old	18.8	18.4	17.6	18.4	18.5	18.2	9.2	12.2	9.8	5.9	7.0	7.4
45 to 54 years old	16.2	17.5	17.0	16.8	16.2	17.0	11.7	11.6	11.0	4.6	5.4	7.8
55 to 64 years old	14.6	14.4	14.9	13.5	15.2	15.2	10.0	15.6	15.3	7.5	4.6	2.5
65 to 74 years old	6.8	10.3	9.4	12.3	10.1	13.3	8.5	8.6	9.9	3.3	1.1	5.0
75 years old and over	2.6	4.6	3.8	8.8	3.1	3.8	11.2	9.6	9.5	1.1	2.1	4.2
Less than $10,000	16.2	17.1	21.1	19.3	13.2	15.1	25.6	28.9	26.9	21.4	11.1	8.0
$10,000 to $24,999	12.7	16.5	16.1	17.2	14.7	17.8	13.9	16.0	16.9	11.8	9.2	11.4
$25,000 to $49,999	16.7	17.0	17.2	16.0	16.0	16.9	10.6	9.7	8.5	4.2	6.2	7.8
$50,000 to $99,999	17.4	16.0	16.7	16.1	16.9	16.8	5.7	4.7	4.3	4.0	2.1	2.4
$100,000 and more	14.0	14.2	11.9	13.9	14.6	11.4	6.7	4.5	4.1	2.2	0.5	1.4

H2-33 Selected Financial Institutions—Number and Assets, by Asset Size, 1996

ASSET SIZE	NUMBER OF INSTITUTIONS			ASSETS (bil. dol.)		
	F.D.I.C.-insured		Credit unions [1]	F.D.I.C.-insured		Credit unions [1]
	Commercial banks	Savings institutions		Commercial banks [2]	Savings institutions	
Total	9,528	1,924	11,392	4,578.3	1,028.2	326.9
Less than $5.0 million	52	7	5,520	0.2	(Z)	10.0
$5.0 million to $9.9 million	188	31	1,774	1.5	0.3	12.6
$10.0 million to $24.9 million	1,340	120	1,848	24.2	2.2	29.8
$25.0 million to $49.9 million	2,207	268	966	81.0	10.3	34.0
$50.0 million to $99.9 million	2,416	418	619	173.0	31.0	43.0
$100.0 million to $499.9 million . . .	2,650	789	591	523.4	180.8	119.7
$500.0 million to $999.9 million . . .	277	130	51	190.1	89.3	33.5
$1.0 billion to $2.9 billion	207	98	21	342.6	156.8	31.0
$3.0 billion or more	191	63	2	3,242.2	557.5	13.2
	PERCENT DISTRIBUTION					
Total	100.0	100.0	100.0	100.0	100.0	100.0
Less than $5.0 million	0.5	0.4	48.5	(Z)	(Z)	3.1
$5.0 million to $9.9 million	2.0	1.6	15.6	(Z)	(Z)	3.9
$10.0 million to $24.9 million	14.1	6.2	16.2	0.5	0.2	9.1
$25.0 million to $49.9 million	23.2	13.9	8.5	1.8	1.0	10.4
$50.0 million to $99.9 million	25.4	21.7	5.4	3.8	3.0	13.2
$100.0 million to $499.9 million . . .	27.8	41.0	5.2	11.4	17.6	36.6
$500.0 million to $999.9 million . . .	2.9	6.8	0.4	4.2	8.7	10.2
$1.0 billion to $2.9 billion	2.2	5.1	0.2	7.5	15.3	9.5
$3.0 billion or more	2.0	3.3	(Z)	70.8	54.2	4.0

Z Less than $50 million or 0.05 percent. [1] Source: National Credit Union Administration, *National Credit Union Administration Yearend Statistics 1996*. Excludes nonfederally insured State chartered credit unions and federally insured corporate credit unions. [2] Includes foreign branches of U.S. banks.

H2-34 Banking Offices, by Type of Bank: 1980–1996

[As of **December 31**. Includes Puerto Rico and outlying areas. Covers all FDIC-insured commercial banks and savings institutions. Data for 1980 include automatic teller machines which were reported by many banks as branches]

ITEM	1980	1985	1990	1991	1992	1993	1994	1995	1996
All banking offices	(NA)	85,083	84,672	84,098	82,002	81,745	82,673	81,893	82,476
Number of banks	(NA)	18,043	15,162	14,488	13,856	13,322	12,602	11,970	11,452
Number of branches	(NA)	67,040	69,510	69,610	68,146	68,423	70,071	69,923	71,024
Commercial banks	53,172	57,710	62,753	63,896	63,401	63,828	65,594	66,454	67,316
Number of banks.............	14,434	14,417	12,347	11,927	11,466	10,960	10,450	9,941	9,528
Number of branches	38,738	43,293	50,406	51,969	51,935	52,868	55,144	56,513	57,788
Savings institutions	(NA)	27,373	21,919	20,202	18,601	17,917	17,079	15,439	15,160
Number of banks.............	(NA)	3,626	2,815	2,561	2,390	2,362	2,152	2,029	1,924
Number of branches	(NA)	23,747	19,104	17,641	16,211	15,555	14,927	13,410	13,236

NA Not available.

H2-35 Nonfinancial Assets Held by Families, by Type of Asset, 1995

AGE OF FAMILY HEAD AND FAMILY INCOME	Any nonfinancial asset	Vehicles	Primary residence	Investment real estate	Business	Other nonfinancial
PERCENT OF FAMILIES OWNING ASSET						
1995, total	91.1	84.2	64.7	17.5	11.0	9.0
Age of family head:						
Under 35 years old.	87.6	83.9	37.9	7.2	9.3	7.6
35 to 44 years old	90.9	85.1	64.6	14.4	13.9	10.2
45 to 54 years old	93.7	88.2	75.4	23.9	14.8	10.7
55 to 64 years old	94.0	88.7	82.1	26.9	11.7	9.8
65 to 74 years old	92.5	82.0	79.0	26.5	7.9	8.9
75 years old and over.	90.2	72.8	73.0	16.6	3.8	5.4
Family income:						
Less than $10,000	69.8	57.7	37.6	6.9	4.8	3.8
$10,000 to $24,999	89.4	82.7	55.4	11.5	6.2	6.2
$25,000 to $49,999	96.6	92.2	68.4	16.5	9.8	9.6
$50,000 to $99,999	99.1	93.3	84.4	24.9	17.5	11.5
$100,000 and more	99.4	90.2	91.1	52.3	32.1	22.6
Current work status of householder:						
Professional, managerial	96.7	90.8	71.1	24.6	11.8	14.5
Technical, sales, clerical	92.9	88.0	63.4	10.5	6.4	10.6
Precision production	97.2	93.4	66.9	16.2	7.3	9.0
Machine operators and laborers . .	93.8	91.9	61.2	14.0	5.1	6.5
Service occupations	86.9	83.8	50.5	8.6	3.5	2.0
Self-employed	96.1	85.7	73.9	32.1	58.0	16.1
Retired.	88.3	76.6	70.3	18.6	2.9	5.6
Other not working	67.9	60.6	34.8	8.0	3.7	5.9
Tenure:						
Owner occupied	100.0	90.8	100.0	22.3	13.4	10.3
Renter occupied or other.	74.8	72.2	0.0	8.7	6.4	6.5
MEDIAN VALUE [1]						
1995, total	83.0	10.0	90.0	50.0	41.0	10.0
Age of family head:						
Under 35 years old.	21.5	9.0	80.0	33.5	20.0	5.0
35 to 44 years old	95.6	10.7	95.0	45.0	35.0	9.0
45 to 54 years old	111.7	12.4	100.0	55.0	60.0	12.0
55 to 64 years old	107.0	11.9	85.0	82.5	75.0	10.0
65 to 74 years old	93.5	8.0	80.0	55.0	100.0	16.0
75 years old and over.	79.0	5.3	80.0	20.0	30.0	15.0
Family income:						
Less than $10,000	13.1	3.6	40.0	16.2	50.6	2.5
$10,000 to $24,999	44.5	6.1	65.0	30.0	30.0	8.0
$25,000 to $49,999	81.5	11.1	80.0	40.0	26.3	6.0
$50,000 to $99,999	145.2	16.2	120.0	57.3	30.0	14.0
$100,000 and more	319.3	22.8	200.0	130.0	300.0	20.0
Current work status of householder:						
Professional, managerial	133.5	12.4	130.0	57.3	15.0	10.0
Technical, sales, clerical	83.1	10.4	90.0	40.0	17.5	10.0
Precision production	72.9	12.2	78.0	37.5	30.0	5.0
Machine operators and laborers . .	57.9	10.8	68.0	36.0	24.0	8.0
Service occupations	35.8	7.2	69.0	17.5	80.2	10.0
Self-employed	175.6	12.0	120.0	100.0	71.0	8.0
Retired.	78.0	7.3	76.0	45.0	90.0	10.0
Other not working	17.4	6.2	80.0	59.0	12.0	7.0
Tenure:						
Owner occupied	115.4	11.9	90.0	53.0	50.0	10.0
Renter occupied or other.	7.5	6.4	(B)	35.0	26.0	5.0

[1] Median value of financial asset for families holding such assets.

3. POVERTY AND PUBLIC ASSISTANCE

H3-1   Percent of Children below Poverty Level

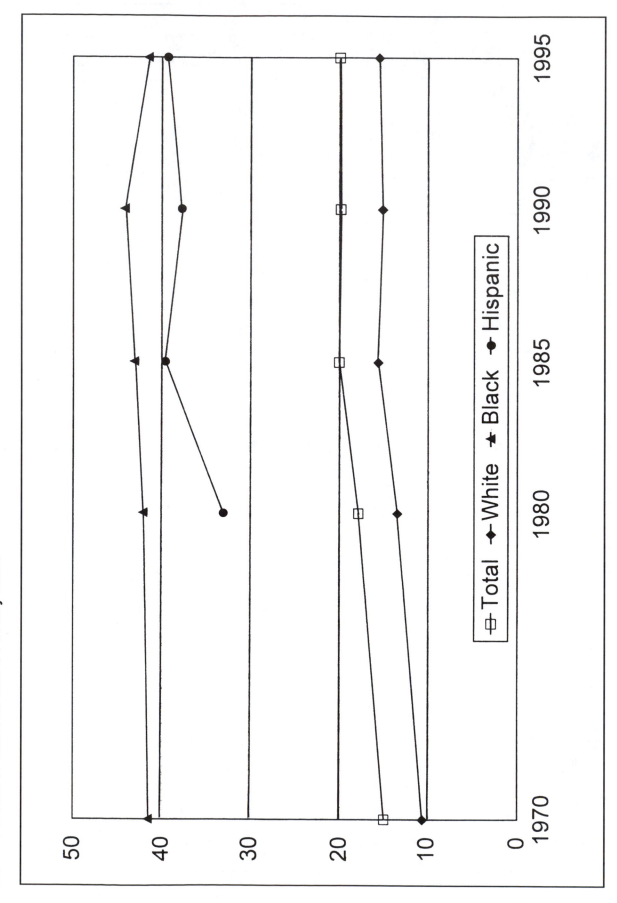

H3-2   Persons below Poverty Level and below 125 Percent of Poverty Level: 1960–1995

YEAR	NUMBER BELOW POVERTY LEVEL (1,000)				PERCENT BELOW POVERTY LEVEL				BELOW 125 PERCENT OF POVERTY LEVEL		AVERAGE INCOME CUTOFFS FOR NONFARM FAMILY OF FOUR [3]	
	All races [1]	White	Black	His-panic [2]	All races [1]	White	Black	His-panic [2]	Number (1,000)	Per-cent of total popula-tion	At poverty level	At 125 percent of poverty level
1960	39,851	28,309	(NA)	(NA)	22.2	17.8	(NA)	(NA)	54,560	30.4	3,022	3,778
1970	25,420	17,484	7,548	(NA)	12.6	9.9	33.5	(NA)	35,624	17.6	3,968	4,960
1975	25,877	17,770	7,545	2,991	12.3	9.7	31.3	23.0	37,182	17.6	5,500	6,875
1976	24,975	16,713	7,595	2,783	11.8	9.1	31.1	26.9	35,509	16.7	5,815	7,269
1977	24,720	16,416	7,726	2,700	11.6	8.9	31.3	24.7	35,659	16.7	6,191	7,739
1978	24,497	16,259	7,625	2,607	11.4	8.7	30.6	22.4	34,155	15.8	6,662	8,328
1979 [4]	26,072	17,214	8,050	2,921	11.7	9.0	31.0	21.6	36,616	16.4	7,412	9,265
1980	29,272	19,699	8,579	3,491	13.0	10.2	32.5	21.8	40,658	18.1	8,414	10,518
1981	31,822	21,553	9,173	3,713	14.0	11.1	34.2	25.7	43,748	19.3	9,287	11,609
1982	34,398	23,517	9,697	4,301	15.0	12.0	35.6	26.5	46,520	20.3	9,862	12,328
1983 [5]	35,303	23,984	9,882	4,633	15.2	12.1	35.7	29.9	47,150	20.3	10,178	12,723
1984	33,700	22,955	9,490	4,806	14.4	11.5	33.8	28.0	45,288	19.4	10,609	13,261
1985	33,064	22,860	8,926	5,236	14.0	11.4	31.3	28.4	44,166	18.7	10,989	13,736
1986	32,370	22,183	8,983	5,117	13.6	11.0	31.1	29.0	43,486	18.2	11,203	14,004
1987 [6]	32,221	21,195	9,520	5,422	13.4	10.4	32.4	27.3	43,032	17.9	11,611	14,514
1988	31,745	20,715	9,356	5,357	13.0	10.1	31.3	28.0	42,551	17.5	12,092	15,115
1989	31,528	20,785	9,302	5,430	12.8	10.0	30.7	26.7	42,653	17.3	12,674	15,843
1990	33,585	22,326	9,837	6,006	13.5	10.7	31.9	26.2	44,837	18.0	13,359	16,699
1991	35,708	23,747	10,242	6,339	14.2	11.3	32.7	28.1	47,527	18.9	13,924	17,405
1992 [7]	38,014	25,259	10,827	7,592	14.8	11.9	33.4	29.6	50,592	19.7	14,335	17,919
1993	39,265	26,226	10,877	8,126	15.1	12.2	33.1	30.6	51,801	20.0	14,763	(NA)
1994	38,059	25,379	10,196	8,416	14.5	11.7	30.6	30.7	50,401	19.3	15,141	18,926
1995	36,425	24,423	9,872	8,574	13.8	11.2	29.3	30.3	48,761	18.5	15,569	19,461

NA Not available.   [1] Includes other races not shown separately.   [2] Persons of Hispanic origin may be of any race.
[3] Beginning 1981, income cutoffs for nonfarm families are applied to all families, both farm and nonfarm.   [4] Population controls based on 1980 census; see text, sections 1 and 14.   [5] Beginning 1983, data based on revised Hispanic population controls and not directly comparable with prior years.   [6] Beginning 1987, data based on revised processing procedures and not directly comparable with prior years.   [7] Beginning 1992, based on 1990 population controls.

H3-3   Children below Poverty Level, by Race and Hispanic Origin: 1970–1995

YEAR	NUMBER BELOW POVERTY LEVEL (1,000)				PERCENT BELOW POVERTY LEVEL			
	All races [1]	White	Black	Hispanic [2]	All races [1]	White	Black	Hispanic [2]
1970	10,235	6,138	3,922	(NA)	14.9	10.5	41.5	(NA)
1980	11,114	6,817	3,906	1,718	17.9	13.4	42.1	33.0
1981	12,068	7,429	4,170	1,874	19.5	14.7	44.9	35.4
1982	13,139	8,282	4,388	2,117	21.3	16.5	47.3	38.9
1983 [3]	13,427	8,534	4,273	2,251	21.8	17.0	46.2	37.7
1984	12,929	8,086	4,320	2,317	21.0	16.1	46.2	38.7
1985	12,483	7,838	4,057	2,512	20.1	15.6	43.1	39.6
1986	12,257	7,714	4,037	2,413	19.8	15.3	42.7	37.1
1987 [4]	12,275	7,398	4,234	2,606	19.7	14.7	44.4	38.9
1988	11,935	7,095	4,148	2,576	19.0	14.0	42.8	37.3
1989	12,001	7,164	4,257	2,496	19.0	14.1	43.2	35.5
1990	12,715	7,696	4,412	2,750	19.9	15.1	44.2	37.7
1991	13,658	8,316	4,637	2,977	21.1	16.1	45.6	39.8
1992 [5]	14,521	8,752	5,015	3,440	21.6	16.5	46.3	39.0
1993	14,961	9,123	5,030	3,666	22.0	17.0	45.9	39.9
1994	14,610	8,826	4,787	3,956	21.2	16.3	43.3	41.1
1995	13,999	8,474	4,644	3,938	20.0	15.5	41.5	39.3

NA Not available.   [1] Includes other races not shown separately.   [2] Persons of Hispanic origin may be of any race.
[3] Beginning 1983, data based on revised Hispanic population controls and not directly comparable with prior years.   [4] Beginning 1987, data based on revised processing procedures and not directly comparable with prior years.   [5] Beginning 1992, based on 1990 population controls.

H3-4   Weighted Average Poverty Thresholds: 1980–1995

SIZE OF UNIT	1980 [1]	1988	1989	1990	1991	1992	1993	1994	1995
One person (unrelated individual) . . .	$4,190	$6,022	$6,310	$6,652	$6,932	$7,143	$7,363	$7,547	$7,763
Under 65 years	4,290	6,155	6,451	6,800	7,086	7,299	$7,518	7,710	7,929
65 years and over	3,949	5,674	5,947	6,268	6,532	6,729	6,930	7,108	7,309
Two persons	5,363	7,704	8,076	8,509	8,865	9,137	9,414	9,661	9,933
Householder under 65 years	5,537	7,958	8,343	8,794	9,165	9,443	9,728	9,976	10,259
Householder 65 years and over . . .	4,983	7,157	7,501	7,905	8,241	8,487	8,740	8,967	9,219
Three persons	6,565	9,435	9,885	10,419	10,860	11,186	11,522	11,821	12,158
Four persons	8,414	12,092	12,674	13,359	13,924	14,335	14,763	15,141	15,569
Five persons	9,966	14,304	14,990	15,792	16,456	16,952	17,449	17,900	18,408
Six persons	11,269	16,146	16,921	17,839	18,587	19,137	19,718	20,235	20,804
Seven persons	12,761	18,232	19,162	20,241	21,058	21,594	22,383	22,923	23,552
Eight persons	14,199	20,253	21,328	22,582	23,605	24,053	24,838	25,427	26,237
Nine or more persons	16,896	24,129	25,480	26,848	27,942	28,745	29,529	30,300	31,280

[1] Poverty levels for nonfarm families.

H3-5 Persons below Poverty Level, by Selected Characteristics, 1995

AGE AND REGION	NUMBER BELOW POVERTY LEVEL (1,000)				PERCENT BELOW POVERTY LEVEL			
	All races [1]	White	Black	Hispanic [2]	All races [1]	White	Black	Hispanic [2]
Total	36,425	24,423	9,872	8,574	13.8	11.2	29.3	30.3
Under 18 years old	14,665	8,981	4,761	4,080	20.8	16.2	41.9	40.0
18 to 24 years old	4,553	3,156	1,117	1,097	18.3	15.9	30.5	30.6
25 to 34 years old	5,196	3,601	1,304	1,325	12.7	10.8	24.4	24.7
35 to 44 years old	4,064	2,812	995	942	9.4	7.9	18.8	23.2
45 to 54 years old	2,470	1,683	630	429	7.8	6.3	18.2	19.7
55 to 59 years old	1,163	840	246	186	10.3	8.7	21.4	23.0
60 to 64 years old	996	777	191	174	10.2	9.2	19.5	25.4
65 years old and over . . .	3,318	2,572	629	342	10.5	9.0	25.4	23.5
65 to 74 years old	1,573	1,196	301	213	8.6	7.3	20.3	21.7
75 years old and over .	1,745	1,375	328	129	13.0	11.3	32.9	27.1
Northeast	6,445	4,289	1,878	1,586	12.5	9.9	30.8	36.5
Midwest	6,785	4,665	1,873	403	11.0	8.6	30.7	21.3
South	14,458	8,712	5,283	2,831	15.7	12.2	28.5	30.4
West	8,736	6,757	837	3,755	14.9	13.8	28.0	29.4

[1] Includes other races not shown separately.   [2] Persons of Hispanic origin may be of any race.

H3-6 Persons 65 Years Old and Over below Poverty Level: 1970–1995

CHARACTERISTIC	NUMBER BELOW POVERTY LEVEL (1,000)					PERCENT BELOW POVERTY LEVEL				
	1970	1979 [1]	1990 [2]	1994	1995	1970	1979 [1]	1990 [2]	1994	1995
Total [3]	4,793	3,682	3,658	3,663	3,318	24.6	15.2	12.2	11.7	10.5
White	4,011	2,911	2,707	2,846	2,572	22.6	13.3	10.1	10.2	9.0
Black	683	740	860	700	629	48.0	36.2	33.8	27.4	25.4
Hispanic [4]	(NA)	154	245	323	342	(NA)	26.8	22.5	22.6	23.5
In families	2,013	1,380	1,172	1,254	1,058	14.8	8.4	5.8	6.0	5.0
Unrelated individuals	2,779	2,299	2,479	2,409	2,260	47.2	29.4	24.7	23.1	21.4

NA Not available.   [1] Population controls based on 1980 census; see text, section 14.   [2] Beginning 1987, data based on revised processing procedures and not directly comparable with prior years.   [3] Beginning 1979, includes members of unrelated subfamilies not shown separately. For earlier years, unrelated subfamily members are included in the "In families" category.   [4] Persons of Hispanic origin may be of any race.

H3-7   Persons below Poverty Level, by State: 1980–1995

STATE	NUMBER BELOW POVERTY LEVEL (1,000)					PERCENT BELOW POVERTY LEVEL				
	1980	1990 [1]	1993	1994	1995	1980	1990 [1]	1993	1994	1995
United States	29,272	33,585	39,265	38,059	36,425	13.0	13.5	15.1	14.5	13.8
Alabama.	810	779	725	704	882	21.2	19.2	17.4	16.4	20.1
Alaska.	36	57	52	61	45	9.6	11.4	9.1	10.2	7.1
Arizona.	354	484	615	673	700	12.8	13.7	15.4	15.9	16.1
Arkansas	484	472	484	369	376	21.5	19.6	20.0	15.3	14.9
California	2,619	4,128	5,803	5,658	5,342	11.0	13.9	18.2	17.9	16.7
Colorado.	247	461	354	335	335	8.6	13.7	9.9	9.0	8.8
Connecticut.	255	196	277	344	318	8.3	6.0	8.5	10.8	9.7
Delaware	68	48	73	57	74	11.8	6.9	10.2	8.3	10.3
District of Columbia	131	120	158	129	122	20.9	21.1	26.4	21.2	22.2
Florida	1,692	1,896	2,507	2,128	2,321	16.7	14.4	17.8	14.9	16.2
Georgia	727	1,001	919	1,012	878	13.9	15.8	13.5	14.0	12.1
Hawaii	81	121	91	97	122	8.5	11.0	8.0	8.7	10.3
Idaho.	138	157	150	137	167	14.7	14.9	13.1	12.0	14.5
Illinois	1,386	1,606	1,600	1,464	1,459	12.3	13.7	13.6	12.4	12.4
Indiana.	645	714	704	816	545	11.8	13.0	12.2	13.7	9.6
Iowa	311	289	290	302	352	10.8	10.4	10.3	10.7	12.2
Kansas.	215	259	327	375	273	9.4	10.3	13.1	14.9	10.8
Kentucky	701	628	763	710	572	19.3	17.3	20.4	18.5	14.7
Louisiana	868	952	1,119	1,117	849	20.3	23.6	26.4	25.7	19.7
Maine.	158	162	196	113	138	14.6	13.1	15.4	9.4	11.2
Maryland	389	468	479	541	520	9.5	9.9	9.7	10.7	10.1
Massachusetts.	542	626	641	585	665	9.5	10.7	10.7	9.7	11.0
Michigan.	1,194	1,315	1,475	1,347	1,174	12.9	14.3	15.4	14.1	12.2
Minnesota.	342	524	506	523	427	8.7	12.0	11.6	11.7	9.2
Mississippi	591	684	639	515	630	24.3	25.7	24.7	19.9	23.5
Missouri	625	700	832	797	484	13.0	13.4	16.1	15.6	9.4
Montana.	102	134	127	97	133	13.2	16.3	14.9	11.5	15.3
Nebraska	199	167	169	146	159	13.0	10.3	10.3	8.8	9.6
Nevada	70	119	141	168	173	8.3	9.8	9.8	11.1	11.1
New Hampshire	63	68	112	87	60	7.0	6.3	9.9	7.7	5.3
New Jersey.	659	711	866	730	617	9.0	9.2	10.9	9.2	7.8
New Mexico	268	319	282	356	457	20.6	20.9	17.4	21.1	25.3
New York	2,391	2,571	2,981	3,097	3,020	13.8	14.3	16.4	17.0	16.5
North Carolina.	877	829	966	980	877	15.0	13.0	14.4	14.2	12.6
North Dakota.	99	87	70	65	76	15.5	13.7	11.2	10.4	12.0
Ohio	1,046	1,256	1,461	1,571	1,285	9.8	11.5	13.0	14.1	11.5
Oklahoma.	406	481	662	540	548	13.9	15.6	19.9	16.7	17.1
Oregon.	309	267	363	373	360	11.5	9.2	11.8	11.8	11.2
Pennsylvania.	1,142	1,328	1,598	1,496	1,464	9.8	11.0	13.2	12.5	12.2
Rhode Island.	97	71	108	99	102	10.7	7.5	11.2	10.3	10.6
South Carolina.	534	548	678	501	744	16.8	16.2	18.7	13.8	19.9
South Dakota	127	93	102	107	103	18.8	13.3	14.2	14.5	14.5
Tennessee	884	833	998	779	846	19.6	16.9	19.6	14.6	15.5
Texas.	2,247	2,684	3,177	3,603	3,270	15.7	15.9	17.4	19.1	17.4
Utah	148	143	203	154	168	10.0	8.2	10.7	8.0	8.4
Vermont	62	61	59	45	61	12.0	10.9	10.0	7.6	10.3
Virginia.	647	705	627	710	648	12.4	11.1	9.7	10.7	10.2
Washington.	538	434	634	614	677	12.7	8.9	12.1	11.7	12.5
West Virginia.	297	328	400	336	300	15.2	18.1	22.2	18.6	16.7
Wisconsin.	403	448	636	453	449	8.5	9.3	12.6	9.0	8.5
Wyoming	49	51	64	45	59	10.4	11.0	13.3	9.3	12.2

[1] Beginning 1990, data based on revised processing procedures and not directly comparable with prior years.

H3-8 Families below Poverty Level and below 125 Percent of Poverty Level: 1960–1995

YEAR	NUMBER BELOW POVERTY LEVEL (1,000)				PERCENT BELOW POVERTY LEVEL				BELOW 125 PERCENT OF POVERTY LEVEL	
	All races [1]	White	Black	His-panic [2]	All races [1]	White	Black	His-panic [2]	Number (1,000)	Percent
1960	8,243	6,115	(NA)	(NA)	18.1	14.9	(NA)	(NA)	11,525	25.4
1970	5,260	3,708	1,481	(NA)	10.1	8.0	29.5	(NA)	7,516	14.4
1971	5,303	3,751	1,484	(NA)	10.0	7.9	28.8	(NA)	(NA)	(NA)
1972	5,075	3,441	1,529	477	9.3	7.1	29.0	20.6	7,347	13.5
1973	4,828	3,219	1,527	468	8.8	6.6	28.1	19.8	7,044	12.8
1974	4,922	3,352	1,479	526	8.8	6.8	26.9	21.2	7,195	12.9
1975	5,450	3,838	1,513	627	9.7	7.7	27.1	25.1	7,974	14.2
1976	5,311	3,560	1,617	598	9.4	7.1	27.9	23.1	7,647	13.5
1977	5,311	3,540	1,637	591	9.3	7.0	28.2	21.4	7,713	13.5
1978	5,280	3,523	1,622	559	9.1	6.9	27.5	20.4	7,417	12.8
1979 [3]	5,461	3,581	1,722	614	9.2	6.9	27.8	20.3	7,784	13.1
1980	6,217	4,195	1,826	751	10.3	8.0	28.9	23.2	8,764	14.5
1981	6,851	4,670	1,972	792	11.2	8.8	30.8	24.0	9,568	15.7
1982	7,512	5,118	2,158	916	12.2	9.6	33.0	27.2	10,279	16.7
1983 [4]	7,647	5,220	2,161	981	12.3	9.7	32.3	25.9	10,358	16.7
1984	7,277	4,925	2,094	991	11.6	9.1	30.9	25.2	9,901	15.8
1985	7,223	4,983	1,983	1,074	11.4	9.1	28.7	25.5	9,753	15.3
1986	7,023	4,811	1,987	1,085	10.9	8.6	28.0	24.7	9,476	14.7
1987 [5]	7,005	4,567	2,117	1,168	10.7	8.1	29.4	25.5	9,338	14.3
1988	6,874	4,471	2,089	1,141	10.4	7.9	28.2	23.7	9,284	14.1
1989	6,784	4,409	2,077	1,133	10.3	7.8	27.8	23.4	9,267	14.0
1990	7,098	4,622	2,193	1,244	10.7	8.1	29.3	25.0	9,564	14.4
1991	7,712	5,022	2,343	1,372	11.5	8.8	30.4	26.5	10,244	15.3
1992 [6]	8,144	5,255	2,484	1,529	11.9	9.1	31.1	26.7	10,959	16.1
1993	8,393	5,452	2,499	1,625	12.3	9.4	31.3	27.3	11,203	16.4
1994	8,053	5,312	2,212	1,724	11.6	9.1	27.3	27.8	10,771	15.5
1995	7,532	4,994	2,127	1,695	10.8	8.5	26.4	27.0	10,223	14.7

NA Not available.   [1] Includes other races not shown separately.   [2] Persons of Hispanic origin may be of any race.
[3] Population controls based on 1980 census; see text, section 14.   [4] Beginning 1983, data based on revised Hispanic population controls and not directly comparable with prior years.   [5] Beginning 1987, data based on revised processing procedures and not directly comparable with prior years.   [6] Beginning 1992, based on 1990 population controls.

H3-9   Families below Poverty Level, by Selected Characteristics, 1995

CHARACTERISTIC	NUMBER BELOW POVERTY LEVEL (1,000)				PERCENT BELOW POVERTY LEVEL			
	All races [1]	White	Black	His-panic [2]	All races [1]	White	Black	His-panic [2]
Total	7,532	4,994	2,127	1,695	10.8	8.5	26.4	27.0
Age of householder:								
15 to 24 years old.	993	653	294	255	33.6	28.4	55.6	44.9
25 to 34 years old.	2,286	1,457	719	571	16.7	13.0	36.9	30.9
35 to 44 years old.	1,959	1,301	536	473	10.6	8.4	23.5	26.5
45 to 54 years old.	947	606	271	183	6.8	5.1	18.3	19.2
55 to 64 years old.	706	521	152	114	7.7	6.6	16.8	19.1
65 years old and over	618	443	151	92	5.5	4.4	17.0	17.8
Education of householder: [3]								
No high school diploma	2,776	1,867	752	967	24.1	20.3	39.5	35.7
High school diploma, no college	2,113	1,371	641	297	9.8	7.5	24.3	20.6
Some college, less than Bachelor's degree	1,222	780	383	144	7.2	5.4	18.9	13.8
Bachelor's degree or more	403	309	53	27	2.4	2.1	5.6	5.3
Work experience of householder:								
Total [4]	6,909	4,548	1,976	1,604	11.9	9.3	27.6	27.8
Worked during year.	3,768	2,658	934	901	7.5	6.2	16.9	19.4
Year-round, full-time.	1,392	1,003	322	406	3.6	3.0	8.1	12.2
Not year-round, full-time	2,375	1,656	612	495	20.5	17.3	39.4	38.0
Did not work	3,141	1,890	1,042	703	39.2	31.6	63.9	62.0

[1] Includes other races not shown separately.   [2] Hispanic persons may be of any race.   [3] Householder 25 years old and over.   [4] Persons 16 years old and over.

H3-10 Persons below Poverty Level, by Definition of Income, 1995

Defi-nition num-ber	DEFINITION	NUMBER BELOW POVERTY LEVEL (1,000)				PERCENT BELOW POVERTY LEVEL			
		All races [1]	White	Black	His-panic [2]	All races [1]	White	Black	His-panic [2]
	All persons	263,733	218,028	33,740	28,344	(X)	(X)	(X)	(X)
	INCOME BEFORE TAXES								
1	Money income excluding capital gains [3]	36,425	24,423	9,872	8,574	13.8	11.2	29.3	30.3
2	Definition 1 less government money transfers .	57,643	42,285	12,563	10,380	21.9	19.4	37.2	36.6
3	Definition 2 plus capital gains.	57,515	42,149	12,567	10,385	21.8	19.3	37.2	36.6
4	Definition 3 plus health insurance supplements to wage or salary income [4] . . .	55,558	40,743	12,117	9,960	21.1	18.7	35.9	35.1
	INCOME AFTER TAXES								
5	Definition 4 less Social Security payroll taxes .	57,930	42,605	12,555	10,453	22.0	19.5	37.2	36.9
6	Definition 5 less Federal income taxes (excluding EITC) [5]	58,388	42,936	12,643	10,540	22.1	19.7	37.5	37.2
7	Definition 6 plus EITC [5]	55,061	40,449	11,980	9,764	20.9	18.6	35.5	34.4
8	Definition 7 less State income taxes	55,505	40,788	12,059	9,807	21.0	18.7	35.7	34.6
9	Definition 8 plus nonmeans-tested government cash transfers [6]	37,176	24,685	10,262	8,564	14.1	11.3	30.4	30.2
10	Definition 9 plus value of Medicare	36,193	23,998	9,979	8,423	13.7	11.0	29.6	29.7
11	Definition 10 plus value of regular-price school lunches.	36,177	23,992	9,970	8,423	13.7	11.0	29.5	29.7
12	Definition 11 plus means-tested government cash transfers [7]	33,062	22,160	8,945	7,818	12.5	10.2	26.5	27.6
13	Definition 12 plus value of Medicaid	30,871	20,725	8,324	7,198	11.7	9.5	24.7	25.4
14	Definition 13 plus means-tested government noncash transfers [8]	27,190	18,492	7,048	6,307	10.3	8.5	20.9	22.3
15	Definition 14 plus net imputed return on equity in own home [9]	24,823	16,647	6,600	6,009	9.4	7.6	19.6	21.2

X Not applicable.   [1] Includes other races not shown separately.   [2] Persons of Hispanic origin may be of any race.   [3] Official definition based on income before taxes and includes government cash transfers.   [4] Employer contributions to the health insurance plans of employees.   [5] Earned Income Tax Credit.   [6] Includes Social Security and Railroad Retirement, veterans payments, unemployment and workers' compensation, Black Lung payments, Pell Grants, and other government educational assistance.   [7] Includes AFDC and other public assistance or welfare payments, Supplemental Security Income, and veterans payments. Households must meet certain eligibility requirements in order to qualify for these benefits.   [8] Includes Medicaid, food stamps, subsidies from free or reduced-price school lunches, and rent subsidies.   [9] Estimated amount of income a household would receive if it chose to shift amount held as home equity into an interest bearing account.

H3-11 Percent of Population Receiving Forms of Government Assistance, 1992

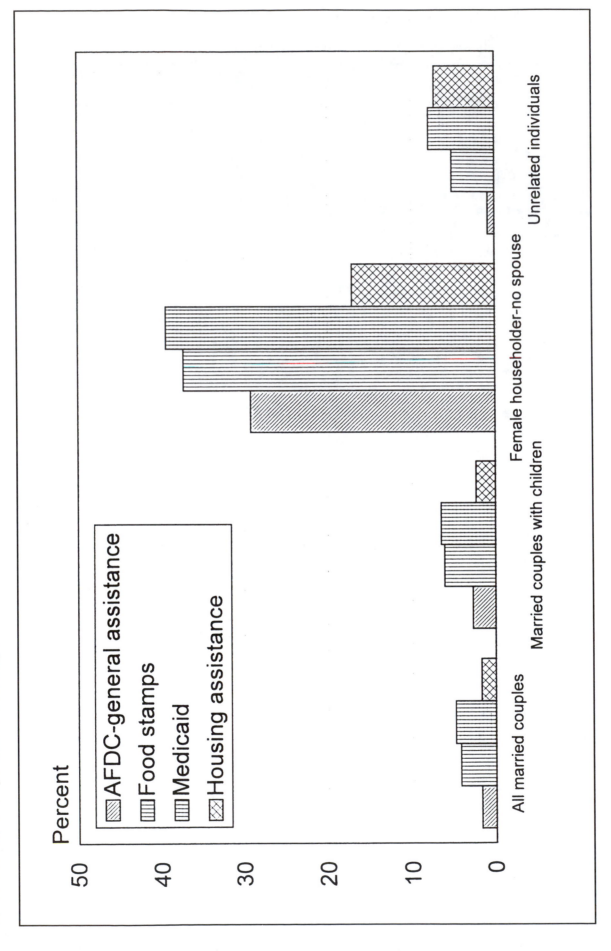

H3-12 Households Receiving Means-Tested Noncash Benefits: 1980–1995

[In thousands, **except percent**. Households as of **March** of following year. Covers civilian noninstitutional population, including persons in the Armed Forces living off post or with their families on post. A means-tested benefit program requires that the household's income and/or assets fall below specified guidelines in order to qualify for benefits. The means-tested noncash benefits covered are food stamps, free or reduced-price school lunches, public or subsidized housing, and Medicaid. There are general trends toward underestimation of noncash beneficiaries. Households are classified according to poverty status of family or nonfamily householder; for explanation of poverty level, see text, section 14. Data for 1980-90 based on 1980 census population controls; beginning 1994, based on 1990 census population controls. Based on Current Population Survey; see text, section 1,

TYPE OF BENEFIT RECEIVED	1980	1985	1990	1994	1995			
					Total	Below poverty level		Above poverty level
						Number	Percent distribution	
Total households	82,368	88,458	94,312	98,990	99,627	12,926	100	86,701
Receiving at least one noncash benefit . .	14,266	14,466	16,098	21,267	21,148	8,298	64	12,850
Not receiving cash public assistance . .	7,860	7,860	8,819	13,269	13,335	3,874	30	9,461
Receiving cash public assistance [1] . . .	6,407	6,607	7,279	7,998	7,813	4,425	34	3,388
Total households receiving—								
Food stamps.	6,769	6,779	7,163	8,925	8,388	5,399	42	2,989
School lunch.	5,532	5,752	6,252	8,534	8,607	3,749	29	4,858
Public housing.	2,777	3,799	4,339	4,946	4,846	2,546	20	2,300
Medicaid	8,287	8,178	10,321	14,119	14,111	6,309	49	7,802

[1] Households receiving money from Aid to Families with Dependent Children program, Supplemental Security Income program or other public assistance programs.

H3-13 Persons Participating in Selected Means-Tested Government Assistance Programs, by Selected Characteristics: 1991 and 1992

[Average monthly participation. Covers noninstitutionalized population. Persons are considered participants in Aid to Families with Dependent Children (AFDC), General Assistance, and the Food Stamp Program if they are the primary recipient or if they are covered under another persons's allotment. Persons receiving Supplemental Security Income (SSI) payments are considered to be participants in an assistance program as are persons covered by Medicaid or living in public or subsidized rental housing. Based on the Survey of Income and Program Participation; for details on sample survey,

YEAR AND SELECTED CHARACTERISTIC	NUMBER OF PARTICIPANTS (1,000)					PERCENT OF POPULATION PARTICIPATING				
	Major means-tested assistance programs [1]	AFDC or General Assistance	Food stamps	Medicaid	Housing assistance	Major means-tested assistance programs [1]	AFDC or General Assistance	Food stamps	Medicaid	Housing assistance
1991	31,695	11,869	19,383	(NA)	(NA)	12.7	4.7	7.8	(NA)	(NA)
1992, total	33,954	11,862	20,700	23,924	10,878	13.4	4.7	8.2	9.4	4.3
Under 18 years old	15,222	7,292	10,780	11,918	4,344	22.5	10.8	15.9	17.6	6.4
18 to 64 years old	14,751	4,492	8,716	9,376	4,789	9.5	2.9	5.6	6.0	3.1
65 years old and over	3,982	78	1,204	2,630	1,745	13.0	0.3	3.9	8.6	5.7
White	21,690	6,379	12,583	14,921	6,178	10.3	3.0	6.0	7.1	2.9
Black	10,507	4,723	7,072	7,683	4,094	33.0	14.8	22.2	24.2	12.9
Hispanic origin [2]	6,410	2,439	4,222	4,635	1,687	26.9	10.2	17.7	19.4	7.1
Poverty status: [3]										
Below the poverty level	20,031	9,288	15,926	15,320	6,050	56.5	26.2	44.9	43.2	17.1
At or above the poverty level	13,923	2,574	4,774	8,604	4,828	6.4	1.2	2.2	3.9	2.2
Family status:										
In married-couple families	12,895	3,012	7,313	8,298	2,964	7.5	1.7	4.2	4.8	1.7
With related children under 18 years old	10,870	2,929	6,654	7,033	2,473	10.0	2.7	6.1	6.5	2.3
In families with female householder, no spouse present	15,068	8,287	10,968	12,012	5,146	40.7	22.4	29.7	32.5	13.9
With related children under 18 years old	13,630	8,116	10,377	10,958	4,765	49.0	29.2	37.3	39.4	17.1
Unrelated individuals	4,891	272	1,853	2,844	2,597	13.5	0.8	5.1	7.9	7.2

NA Not available.   [1] Covers AFDC, General Assistance, SSI, food stamps, Medicaid, and housing assistance.   [2] Persons of Hispanic origin may be of any race.   [3] For explanation of poverty level, see text, section 14.

H3-14 Aid to Families with Dependent Children (AFDC) and Supplemental Security Income (SSI)—Recipients and Payments, by State and Other Areas: 1990–1995

DIVISION AND STATE OR OTHER AREA	AFDC Recipients [1] (1,000)		AFDC Payments for year (mil. dol.)		AFDC Average monthly payment per family		SSI Recipients (1,000)			SSI Payments for year (mil. dol.)		
	1990	1994	1990	1994	1990	1994	1990	1994	1995	1990	1994	1995
Total	12,159	13,974	19,078	22,867	S392	S378	[2]4,817	[2]6,296	[2]6,514	16,133	25,291	27,037
U.S.	11,958	13,790	18,995	22,777	396	382	4,817	6,295	6,513	16,133	25,289	27,035
New England	577	639	1,250	1,497	535	527	209	274	287	652	1,061	1,166
ME.	62	61	104	107	422	393	24	30	31	56	87	96
NH.	21	29	35	62	431	451	[3]7	[3]10	[3]11	[3]19	[3]33	[3]39
VT.	25	27	51	65	527	549	10	13	13	31	46	50
MA.	282	288	647	730	556	553	119	157	164	397	643	700
RI	52	63	104	136	499	499	17	23	24	53	89	100
CT	135	171	309	397	571	553	[3]32	[3]43	[3]45	[3]96	[3]162	[3]181
Middle Atlantic	1,903	2,208	3,623	4,444	472	468	711	957	997	2,533	4,164	4,477
NY	1,031	1,273	2,337	2,993	556	543	415	564	589	1,557	2,542	2,724
NJ	323	324	459	524	352	358	105	140	144	340	562	594
PA	549	611	827	927	382	367	191	252	265	635	1,060	1,159
East North Central .	2,397	2,383	3,611	3,659	379	356	622	898	925	2,021	3,740	3,934
OH.	657	634	896	940	328	318	156	236	248	483	972	1,044
IN	164	203	174	229	263	263	[3]60	[3]86	[3]89	[3]174	[3]324	[3]348
IL.	656	713	868	932	342	322	[3]177	[3]260	[3]267	[3]593	[3]1,107	[3]1,160
MI	684	619	1,232	1,136	464	430	143	207	210	483	870	896
WI	236	214	441	423	464	462	86	110	112	288	467	487
West North Central .	647	690	955	1,072	366	356	216	288	299	584	1,022	1,107
MN.	177	169	355	379	512	513	[3]40	[3]60	[3]62	[3]110	[3]215	[3]235
IA	96	105	154	169	371	356	33	41	42	86	139	148
MO	218	260	237	287	274	260	[3]85	[3]110	[3]114	[3]237	[3]400	[3]431
ND	16	15	24	26	359	381	[3]7	[3]9	[3]9	[3]18	[3]27	[3]29
SD	19	18	22	25	272	307	10	13	14	26	44	47
NE.	44	42	60	62	336	330	[3]16	[3]21	[3]21	[3]42	[3]70	[3]76
KS.	77	82	103	124	332	347	25	36	38	65	127	141
South Atlantic	1,654	2,116	1,844	2,587	272	269	847	1,100	1,151	2,370	3,867	4,218
DE.	22	26	30	40	292	293	8	10	11	22	36	40
MD.	198	227	304	313	370	324	60	[4]79	[4]82	185	[4]308	[4]332
DC.	54	75	87	127	380	389	16	20	20	54	79	83
VA.	158	190	181	253	265	282	[3]95	[3]125	[3]130	[3]257	[3]431	[3]471
WV.	109	109	112	126	249	260	[5]47	[5]64	[5]68	[5]146	[5]255	[5]276
NC.	255	322	257	356	237	227	[3]149	[3]182	[3]191	[3]403	[3]592	[3]639
SC.	118	133	97	115	203	186	[3]90	[3]108	[4]111	[3]234	[3]360	[4]384
GA.	320	390	333	430	265	254	159	194	199	415	646	692
FL	420	645	443	826	263	282	222	[4]317	[4]338	653	[4]1,160	[4]1,300
East South Central .	742	747	510	589	168	167	501	632	651	1,371	2,218	2,387
KY	204	195	185	199	224	210	[3]115	[3]156	[3]165	[3]337	[3]578	[3]635
TN	230	281	176	216	186	164	140	175	180	384	602	648
AL	132	124	63	92	115	155	[3]133	[3]162	[3]165	[3]351	[3]558	[3]600
MS.	176	147	86	82	120	123	114	140	141	300	480	504
West South Central.	1,154	1,248	811	937	180	176	564	735	755	1,478	2,521	2,700
AR.	73	66	57	58	190	188	76	94	94	187	310	326
LA.	279	260	188	169	167	165	133	179	182	378	679	717
OK.	129	127	135	166	279	296	[3]60	[3]72	[3]74	[3]158	[3]246	[3]266
TX.	673	794	431	544	165	159	[5]295	[5]390	[5]404	[5]755	[5]1,286	[5]1,391
Mountain	454	579	523	796	297	323	162	239	252	476	882	966
MT	29	34	40	49	344	344	10	13	14	29	48	53
ID	17	24	20	30	266	285	[3]10	[3]16	[3]17	[3]29	[3]57	[3]63
WY.	16	15	20	21	313	310	[3]3	[3]6	[3]6	[3]9	[3]19	[3]21
CO.	109	115	138	158	320	321	[3]38	[3]55	[3]57	[3]110	[3]203	[3]217
NM.	67	105	66	144	273	352	[3]32	[3]43	[3]45	[3]90	[3]152	[3]166
AZ.	144	198	146	268	268	311	[3]45	[3]69	[3]73	[3]139	[3]259	[3]288
UT.	47	48	65	77	347	364	13	20	20	38	75	80
NV.	25	41	28	48	278	275	11	19	21	33	69	79
Pacific.	2,427	3,179	5,866	7,197	606	548	984	1,172	1,196	4,646	5,811	6,081
WA.	237	289	447	612	452	494	62	88	92	208	368	398
OR.	99	107	150	197	374	395	[3]32	[3]45	[3]47	[3]95	[3]168	[3]183
CA.	2,023	2,682	5,107	6,113	637	556	873	1,014	1,032	4,278	5,174	5,391
AK.	24	37	62	113	651	740	[3]5	[3]6	[3]7	[3]14	[3]24	[3]27
HI	44	65	100	163	581	652	14	18	19	51	76	82
PR	193	173	74	74	103	106	(X)	(X)	(X)	(X)	(X)	(X)
GU	4	7	6	12	418	509	(X)	(X)	(X)	(X)	(X)	(X)
VI	3	4	3	3	279	220	(X)	(X)	(X)	(X)	(X)	(X)
N. Mariana	(X)	(X)	(X)	(X)	(X)	(X)	[5]1	[5]1	[5]1	[5]2	[5]2	[5]2

X Not applicable. [1] See footnote 3, table 602. [2] Includes data for those recipients whose residence was "unknown." [3] Data for persons with Federal SSI payments only; State has State-administered supplementation. [4] Data for Federal SSI payments and federally-administered State supplementation only; State also has State-administered supplementation. [5] Data for persons with Federal SSI payments only; State supplementary payments not made.

H3-15 Mothers Who Receive AFDC and/or Food Stamp Benefits—Socioeconomic Characteristics, 1993

CHARACTERISTIC	AFDC MOTHERS		FOOD STAMP MOTHERS		CHARACTERISTIC	AFDC MOTHERS		FOOD STAMP MOTHERS	
	Number (1,000)	Per-cent distri-bution	Number (1,000)	Per-cent distri-bution		Number (1,000)	Per-cent distri-bution	Number (1,000)	Per-cent distri-bution
Total..........	3,754	100	5,303	100	Married, husband absent [2]	648	17	906	17
Age:					Widowed or divorced..	851	23	1,244	23
15 to 19 years old....	191	5	204	4	Never married	1,783	48	2,065	39
20 to 24 years old....	866	23	1,162	22					
25 to 29 years old....	865	23	1,150	22	Educational attainment:				
30 to 34 years old....	921	25	1,335	25	Not a high school graduate	1,633	44	2,169	41
35 to 39 years old....	604	16	922	17	High school, 4 years ..	1,422	38	2,141	40
40 to 44 years old....	307	8	530	10	College: 1 or more years	698	19	992	19
Race:					Labor force status:				
White	2,074	55	3,176	60	Worked all or some weeks	474	13	1,159	22
Black	1,471	39	1,903	36	No job last month	3,280	87	4,144	78
Hispanic origin:									
Hispanic [1]	784	21	1,060	20	Monthly family income: [3]				
Not Hispanic	2,970	79	4,242	80	Less than $500	1,351	36	1,635	31
					$500 to $999	1,360	36	1,797	34
Marital status:					$1,000 to $1,499	479	13	924	17
Married, husband present	472	13	1,087	20	$1,500 and over	552	15	861	16

[1] Persons of Hispanic origin may be of any race. [2] Includes separated women. [3] Excludes those who did not report income.

H3-16 Federal Food Programs: 1980–1996

[For fiscal years ending in year shown; see text, section 9. Program data include Puerto Rico, Virgin Islands, Guam, American Samoa, Northern Marianas, and the former Trust Territory when a Federal food program was operated in these areas. Participation data are average monthly figures except as noted. Participants are not reported for the nutrition program for the elderly and the commodity distribution programs. Cost data are direct Federal benefits to recipients; they exclude Federal administrative payments and applicable State and local contributions. Federal costs for commodities and cash-in-lieu of commodities are shown separately from direct cash benefits for those programs receiving both]

PROGRAM	Unit	1980	1985	1990	1992	1993	1994	1995	1996
Food Stamp:									
Participants	Million	21.1	19.9	20.1	25.4	27.0	27.5	26.6	25.5
Federal cost	Mil. dol.	8,721	10,744	14,187	20,906	22,006	22,749	22,765	22,456
Monthly average coupon value per recipient	Dollars	34.47	44.99	58.92	68.57	67.96	69.01	71.27	73.28
Nutrition assistance program for Puerto Rico: [1]									
Federal cost	Mil. dol.	(X)	825	937	1,002	1,040	1,079	1,131	1,143
National school lunch program (NSLP): [2]									
Free lunches served	Million	1,671	1,657	1,662	1,891	1,981	2,049	2,090	2,122
Reduced-price lunches served	Million	308	255	273	285	287	298	309	326
Children participating [3]	Million	26.6	23.6	24.1	24.6	24.9	25.3	25.7	25.9
Federal cost	Mil. dol.	2,279	2,578	3,214	3,856	4,081	4,291	4,467	4,649
School breakfast (SB):									
Children participating [3]	Million	3.6	3.4	4.1	4.9	5.4	5.8	6.3	6.6
Federal cost	Mil. dol.	288	379	596	787	869	959	1,048	1,115
Special supplemental food program (WIC): [4]									
Participants	Million	1.9	3.1	4.5	5.4	5.9	6.5	6.9	7.2
Federal cost	Mil. dol.	584	1,193	1,637	1,959	2,115	2,325	2,516	2,693
Commodity supplemental food program: [5]									
Participants	Million	0.1	0.2	0.3	0.3	0.4	0.4	0.4	0.4
Federal cost	Mil. dol.	19	42	71	87	94	87	79	80
Child and adult care (CC): [6]									
Participants [7]	Million	0.7	1.0	1.5	1.8	2.0	2.2	2.4	2.4
Federal cost	Mil. dol.	207	390	720	966	1,082	1,196	1,296	1,356
Summer feeding (SF): [8]									
Children participating [9]	Million	1.9	1.5	1.7	1.9	2.1	2.2	2.1	2.2
Federal cost	Mil. dol.	104	103	145	182	195	205	212	225
Nutrition program for the elderly:									
Meals served	Million	166	225	246	245	244	247	251	246
Federal cost	Mil. dol.	75	134	142	151	153	153	151	143
Federal cost of commodities donated to— [10]									
Child nutrition (NSLP, CC, SF, and SB)	Mil. dol.	930	840	646	740	706	764	733	720

X Not applicable.   [1] Puerto Rico was included in the food stamp program until June 30, 1982.   [2] See headnote, table 608. [3] Nine month (September through May) average daily meals (lunches or breakfasts) served divided by the ratio of average daily attendance to enrollment.   [4] WIC serves women, infants, and children.   [5] Program provides commodities to women, infants, children, and the elderly.   [6] Program provides year-round subsidies to feed preschool children in child care centers and family day care homes. Certain care centers serving disabled or elderly adults also receive meal subsidies.   [7] Quarterly average daily attendance at participating institutions.   [8] Program provides free meals to children in poor areas during summer months. [9] Peak month (July) average daily attendance at participating institutions.   [10] Includes the Federal cost of commodity entitlements. cash-in-lieu of commodities, and bonus foods.

H3-17 Federal Food Stamp and National School Lunch Programs, by State: 1990–1996

[Cost data for years ending Sept. 30. Data on food stamp households and persons are average monthly number participating in year ending Sept. 30. Data on pupils participating in National School Lunch Program are for month in which the highest number of children participated nationwide. For National School Lunch Program, covers public and private elementary and secondary schools and residential child care institutions. Food Stamp costs are for benefits only and exclude administrative expenditures. National School Lunch Program costs include Federal cash reimbursements at rates set by law for each meal served but do not include the value of USDA donated commodities utilized in this program]

REGION, DIVISION, AND STATE	FOOD STAMP PROGRAM								NATIONAL SCHOOL LUNCH PROGRAM					
	Households participating (1,000)		Persons (1,000)			Cost (mil. dol.)			Persons (1,000)			Cost (mil. dol.)		
	1995	1996	1990	1995	1996	1990	1995	1996	1990	1995	1996	1990	1995	1996
Total [1]	10,879	10,553	20,067	26.619	25,534	14.187	22,765	22,456	24,589	26,242	26,438	3,214	4,467	4,649
U.S.	10,867	10,537	20.036	26.579	25,485	14.153	22,714	22,387	24,019	25,690	25,929	3,098	4,343	4,529
Northeast	2,206	2,122	3,589	4,886	4,690	2,462	4,347	4,294	4,033	4,259	4,317	489	711	744
N.E.	430	412	707	979	927	426	769	747	991	1,018	1,035	95	145	154
ME.	60	61	94	132	131	63	112	113	108	105	104	11	16	16
NH.	25	23	31	58	53	20	44	42	91	90	92	6	10	10
VT.	27	26	38	59	56	22	46	44	47	50	52	4	7	7
MA.	178	163	347	410	374	207	315	295	454	476	487	44	67	72
RI.	40	39	64	93	91	42	82	78	60	62	60	7	12	13
CT.	100	100	133	226	223	72	169	175	231	235	240	23	34	36
M.A.	1,776	1,710	2,882	3,907	3,763	2,036	3,578	3,547	3,042	3,241	3,281	393	566	590
NY.	1,027	984	1,548	2,183	2,099	1,086	2,065	2,054	1,546	1,704	1,713	232	332	344
NJ.	233	233	382	551	541	289	506	511	507	534	549	60	91	97
PA.	516	493	952	1,173	1,124	661	1,006	983	990	1,002	1,019	102	143	150
Midwest	2,311	2,181	4,806	5,516	5,147	3,566	4,644	4,398	5,806	6,113	6,140	619	821	843
E.N.C.	1,713	1,598	3,616	4,067	3,758	2,765	3,482	3,270	3,687	3,876	3,891	421	556	573
OH.	506	459	1,089	1,155	1,045	861	1,017	935	919	1,010	1,006	109	138	139
IN.	183	155	311	470	390	226	382	330	635	605	604	54	70	72
IL.	488	470	1,013	1,151	1,105	835	1,056	1,034	932	985	997	131	175	183
MI.	418	409	917	971	935	663	806	773	733	770	772	82	113	117
WI.	119	105	286	320	283	180	220	198	468	506	512	45	60	62
W.N.C	598	583	1,190	1,449	1,388	801	1,162	1,128	2,119	2,237	2,249	197	266	270
MN.	131	128	263	308	295	165	240	221	489	535	542	42	58	59
IA.	75	74	170	184	177	109	141	141	392	397	395	31	40	41
MO.	237	233	431	576	554	312	488	480	547	581	583	58	79	80
ND.	17	16	39	41	40	25	32	32	94	90	89	8	9	10
SD.	19	18	50	50	49	35	40	41	102	109	108	12	14	15
NE.	43	42	95	105	102	59	77	78	191	209	212	18	24	24
KS.	75	72	142	184	172	96	144	135	302	316	319	29	40	41
South	4,240	4,142	8,040	10,695	10,268	5,928	9,201	9,096	9,890	10,487	10,561	1,334	1,836	1,909
S.A.	1,905	1,902	2,993	4,593	4,516	2,223	4,008	4,056	4,454	4,784	4,810	558	816	849
DE.	21	21	33	57	58	25	47	47	59	68	68	6	9	10
MD.	169	165	255	399	375	203	365	362	347	372	378	40	60	62
DC.	43	42	62	94	93	43	93	95	47	50	50	10	14	14
VA.	235	235	346	546	538	247	450	451	586	623	634	60	87	89
WV.	123	121	262	309	300	192	253	252	198	241	206	29	33	33
NC.	258	265	419	614	631	282	495	551	749	769	777	91	123	127
SC.	140	140	299	364	358	240	297	299	451	463	463	60	82	83
GA.	329	323	536	816	793	382	700	703	908	997	1,021	106	159	167
FL.	588	590	781	1,395	1,371	609	1,307	1,296	1,110	1,200	1,213	158	249	263
E.S.C.	863	843	1,938	2,187	2,083	1,386	1.791	1,771	2,085	2,124	2,120	281	349	359
KY.	187	186	458	520	478	334	413	414	498	519	517	61	79	82
TN.	281	274	527	662	638	372	554	542	590	617	623	68	90	93
AL.	209	204	454	525	509	328	441	440	570	568	563	77	93	95
MS.	185	179	499	480	457	352	383	376	428	419	417	76	87	89
W.S.C	1,472	1,397	3,109	3,915	3,670	2,319	3,402	3,269	3,351	3,580	3,631	495	671	700
AR.	107	109	235	272	274	155	212	224	292	318	320	41	53	55
LA.	267	256	727	711	670	549	629	597	694	689	683	104	126	128
OK.	153	147	267	375	354	186	315	308	362	379	376	46	64	66
TX.	946	885	1,880	2,558	2,372	1,429	2,246	2,140	2,003	2,194	2,252	304	429	452
West	2,110	2,092	3,601	5,482	5,381	2,197	4,522	4,599	4,289	4,830	4,911	657	975	1,033
Mountain	529	507	988	1,373	1,297	726	1,152	1,108	1,362	1,558	1,549	170	248	261
MT.	28	29	57	71	71	41	57	58	84	88	87	10	13	13
ID.	30	30	59	80	80	40	59	61	131	142	142	14	19	20
WY.	13	13	28	34	33	21	28	28	57	58	58	5	7	7
CO.	103	101	221	252	244	156	217	210	282	309	315	31	43	45
NM.	87	87	157	239	235	117	196	199	179	191	194	30	40	42
AZ.	178	159	317	480	427	239	414	372	331	422	404	47	77	82
UT.	44	42	99	119	110	71	90	87	233	251	251	24	33	33
NV.	46	46	50	99	98	41	91	91	67	97	98	8	16	18
Pacific	1,581	1,585	2,613	4,109	4.084	1,471	3,371	3,492	2,927	3.272	3,363	487	727	772
WA.	204	206	340	476	476	229	417	426	361	434	441	43	69	73
OR.	132	135	216	289	288	168	254	259	234	257	254	26	39	40
CA.	1,176	1,169	1,955	3,175	3,143	968	2,473	2,556	2,147	2,392	2,471	396	587	624
AK.	15	16	25	45	46	25	50	54	39	48	48	8	13	13
HI.	55	59	77	125	130	81	177	196	145	142	147	14	20	22

[1] Includes Puerto Rico (for NSLP), other outlying areas and Dept. of Defense overseas.

4. HOME OWNERSHIP AND CONSUMER PATTERNS

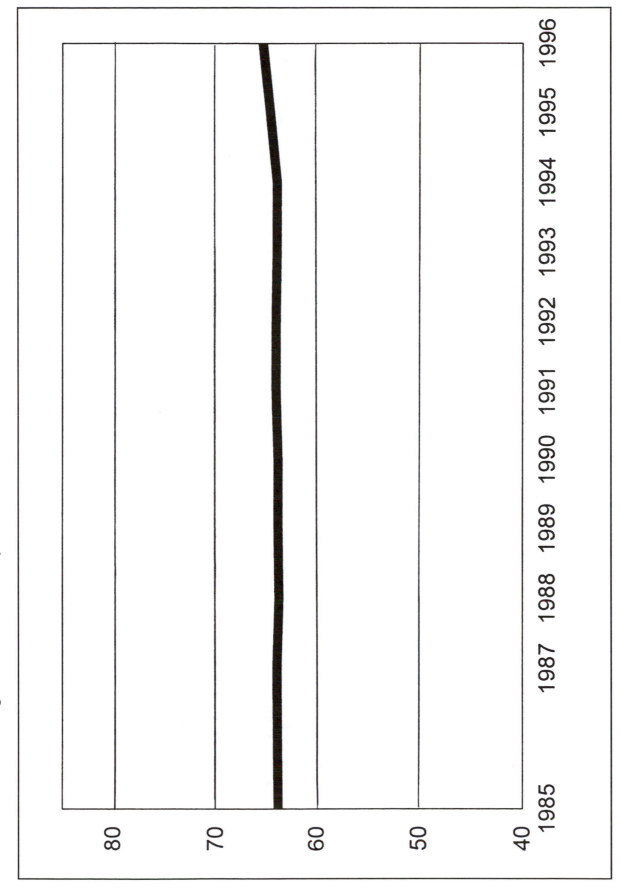

H4-1 Percent of Housing That Is Owner Occupied

H4-2   New Privately Owned Housing Units Started, by State: 1993–1996

REGION, DIVISION, AND STATE	1993	1994	1995	1996, est. Total units	1996, est. Single-family units	REGION, DIVISION, AND STATE	1993	1994	1995	1996, est. Total units	1996, est. Single-family units
U.S...	1,199.0	1,457.0	1,354.0	1,451.0	1,147.0	VA...	46.9	47.4	45.2	48.7	37.6
Northeast.	125.0	138.0	118.0	127.0	107.0	WV..	4.4	5.3	4.8	4.6	4.1
N.E....	38.9	42.6	38.2	40.2	37.3	NC..	60.8	66.9	64.4	67.6	54.9
ME..	4.4	4.9	4.2	4.6	4.4	SC..	23.4	25.6	26.1	30.3	23.3
NH..	4.2	4.6	4.3	4.5	3.7	GA..	57.3	69.4	77.2	79.8	65.8
VT...	2.5	2.5	2.0	2.1	1.9	FL...	115.1	131.0	123.4	122.8	91.2
MA..	16.7	18.3	16.3	16.6	15.6	E.S.C.	87.2	93.9	88.6	95.9	75.5
RI...	2.5	2.6	2.5	2.6	2.4	KY..	20.7	21.5	18.9	20.2	16.8
CT..	8.5	9.7	9.1	9.8	9.3	TN..	33.6	35.5	36.4	40.3	31.0
M.A...	86.1	95.4	79.8	86.6	69.6	AL...	21.9	23.7	21.2	21.9	17.7
NY..	24.9	29.1	23.4	28.6	17.9	MS..	11.1	13.2	12.2	13.6	10.0
NJ...	22.5	25.5	25.3	25.8	23.3	W.S.C.	130.1	162.8	151.0	165.3	130.3
PA...	38.7	40.7	31.1	32.2	28.5	AR..	13.0	15.1	12.2	13.2	10.2
Midwest..	297.9	329.0	290.0	318.0	255.0	LA...	14.3	16.4	14.4	16.5	14.1
E.N.C..	205.2	225.6	203.9	222.7	181.5	OK..	12.9	12.7	11.8	13.4	10.9
OH..	48.8	50.4	43.6	49.0	39.7	TX...	89.9	118.6	112.5	122.2	95.1
IN...	35.7	38.1	36.8	40.3	35.1	West	301.8	351.0	331.0	358.0	273.0
IL...	45.9	53.7	48.8	49.9	40.8	Moun-					
MI...	41.6	49.2	47.6	53.7	45.2	tain...	140.7	176.4	171.8	185.8	139.0
WI...	33.1	34.1	27.1	29.7	20.7	MT..	3.7	3.9	3.1	2.8	1.8
W.N.C..	92.7	103.4	86.1	94.9	73.2	ID...	13.1	13.3	9.5	9.4	8.2
MN..	26.6	27.6	25.0	24.7	21.6	WY..	2.1	2.8	1.9	2.5	2.0
IA...	12.2	13.3	9.4	11.0	7.7	CO..	32.4	41.6	39.7	41.7	32.0
MO..	24.9	30.9	25.6	28.6	24.0	NM..	7.8	9.3	9.7	9.2	7.3
ND..	3.3	3.8	3.2	2.0	1.6	AZ...	38.7	52.9	53.5	57.7	45.3
SD..	4.3	4.7	3.9	4.3	2.8	UT..	19.3	21.6	20.7	21.6	15.7
NE..	8.8	8.5	8.0	9.7	5.9	NV..	23.6	31.1	33.8	41.0	26.8
KS..	12.5	14.6	11.0	14.6	9.7	Pacific .	161.1	174.6	159.2	172.1	133.6
South....	562.8	639.0	615.0	648.0	512.0	WA..	41.1	43.7	37.9	43.4	31.7
S.A....	345.5	382.3	375.4	386.4	306.6	OR..	21.6	24.6	25.0	26.9	18.5
DE..	5.8	5.7	5.3	4.9	4.7	CA..	90.3	97.6	86.9	95.3	78.9
MD..	31.3	30.8	28.9	27.7	24.9	AK..	2.1	2.2	2.5	2.7	1.8
DC..	0.3	0.2	0.1	0.0	0.0	HI...	6.0	6.6	6.9	3.9	2.6

H4-3 Characteristics of New Privately Owned One-Family Houses Completed: 1970–1995

[Percent distribution, except as indicated. Data beginning 1980 show percent distribution of characteristics for all houses completed (includes new houses completed, houses built for sale completed, contractor-built and owner-built houses completed, and houses completed for rent). Data for 1970 cover contractor-built, owner-built, and houses for rent for rent for year construction started and houses sold for year of sale. Percents exclude houses for which characteristics specified were not reported]

CHARACTERISTIC	1970	1980	1990	1995	1996	CHARACTERISTIC	1970	1980	1990	1995	1996
Total houses (1,000)....	793	957	966	1,066	1,129	Bedrooms...........	100	100	100	100	100
						2 or less...........	13	17	15	13	13
Financing...........	100	100	100	100	100	3.................	63	63	57	57	56
Mortgage..........	84	82	82	88	87	4 or more..........	24	20	29	30	31
FHA-insured......	30	16	14	8	9	Bathrooms..........	100	100	100	100	100
VA-guaranteed.....	7	8	4	5	5	1 1/2 or less........	52	27	13	11	9
Conventional......	47	55	62	74	74	2.................	32	48	42	41	41
Rural Housing Serv-						2 1/2 or more.......	16	25	45	48	49
ice [1]..........	([2])	3	2	1	1	Heating fuel........	100	100	100	100	100
Cash or equivalent....	16	18	18	12	11	Electricity..........	28	50	33	28	26
						Gas..............	62	41	59	67	69
Floor area..........	100	100	100	100	100	Oil...............	8	3	5	3	3
Under 1,200 sq. ft....	36	21	11	10	9	Other.............	1	5	3	1	1
1,200 to 1,599 sq. ft...	28	29	22	22	21	Heating system.......	100	100	100	100	100
1,600 to 1,999 sq. ft...	16	22	22	23	23	Warm air furnace.....	71	57	65	67	70
2,000 to 2,399 sq. ft...	21	13	17	17	18	Electric heat pump....	(NA)	24	23	25	23
2,400 sq. ft. and over..	([3])	15	29	28	30	Other.............	29	19	12	9	7
Average (sq. ft.)......	1,500	1,740	2,080	2,095	2,120	Central air-conditioning .	100	100	100	100	100
Median (sq. ft.)......	1,385	1,595	1,905	1,920	1,950	With	34	63	76	80	81
						Without	66	37	24	20	19
Number of stories.....	100	100	100	100	100	Fireplaces..........	100	100	100	100	100
1.................	74	60	46	49	49	No fireplace	65	43	34	37	38
2 or more..........	17	31	49	48	47	1 or more..........	35	56	66	63	62
Split level..........	10	8	4	3	3	Parking facilities	100	100	100	100	100
Foundation..........	100	100	100	100	100	Garage	58	69	82	84	86
Full or partial basement.	37	36	38	39	37	Carport	17	7	2	2	1
Slab	36	45	40	42	44	No garage or carport ..	25	24	16	14	13
Crawl space	27	19	21	19	19						

NA Not available. [1] Prior to 1996, Farmers Home Administration. [2] Included with "Conventional" financing. [3] Included with floor area of 2,000 to 2,399 square feet.

H4-4   New Privately Owned One-Family Houses Sold, by Region and Type of Financing, 1980–1996, and by Sales-Price Group, 1996

[In thousands. Based on a national probability sample of monthly interviews with builders or owners of 1-family houses for which building permits have been issued or, for nonpermit areas, on which construction has started. For details, see source. For composition of regions.

YEAR AND SALES-PRICE GROUP	Total sales	REGION				FINANCING TYPE			
		North-east	Midwest	South	West	Conven-tional	FHA and VA	Rural Housing Service[1]	Cash
1980	545	50	81	267	145	302	196	14	32
1985	688	112	82	323	170	403	208	11	64
1986	750	136	96	322	196	411	268	12	59
1987	671	117	97	271	186	408	190	8	64
1988	676	101	97	276	202	437	171	6	62
1989	650	86	102	260	202	416	162	14	58
1990	534	71	89	225	149	337	138	10	50
1991	509	57	93	215	144	329	128	9	43
1992	610	65	116	259	170	428	134	7	41
1993	666	60	123	295	188	476	147	6	37
1994	670	61	123	295	191	490	130	9	41
1995	667	55	125	300	187	490	129	9	39
1996	757	74	137	337	209	570	140	9	38
Under $70,000	26	(B)	(B)	21	(B)	11	11	3	(B)
$70,000 to $79,999	33	(B)	4	24	4	15	16	(B)	(B)
$80,000 to $99,999	104	5	21	63	16	56	42	(B)	4
$100,000 to $119,999	101	5	20	45	30	65	29	(B)	6
$120,000 to $149,999	159	11	32	69	47	121	27	(B)	10
$150,000 to $199,999	160	18	29	61	51	137	14	(B)	8
$200,000 to $249,999	79	14	14	27	23	74	(B)	(B)	4
$250,000 to $299,999	40	5	6	13	15	38	(B)	(B)	(B)
$300,000 and over	56	13	8	14	21	54	(B)	(B)	3

B Withheld because estimate did not meet publication standards on the basis of sample size.   [1] Formerly, the Farmers Home Administration.

H4-5   Median Sales Price of New Privately Owned One-Family Houses Sold, by Region: 1980–1996

YEAR	U.S.	North-east	Midwest	South	West	YEAR	U.S.	North-east	Midwest	South	West
1980	64,600	69,500	63,400	59,600	72,300	1989	120,000	159,600	108,800	96,400	139,000
1982	69,300	78,200	68,900	66,100	75,000	1990	122,900	159,000	107,900	99,000	147,500
1983	75,300	82,200	79,500	70,900	80,100	1991	120,000	155,900	110,000	100,000	141,100
1984	79,900	88,600	85,400	72,000	87,300	1992	121,500	169,000	115,600	105,500	130,400
1985	84,300	103,300	80,300	75,000	92,600	1993	126,500	162,600	125,000	115,000	135,000
1986	92,000	125,000	88,300	80,200	95,700	1994	130,000	169,000	132,900	116,900	140,400
1987	104,500	140,000	95,000	88,000	111,000	1995	133,900	180,000	134,000	124,500	141,400
1988	112,500	149,000	101,600	92,000	126,500	1996	140,000	186,000	138,000	126,200	153,900

H4-6 New Mobile Homes Placed for Residential Use and Average Sales Price, by Region: 1980–1996

YEAR	UNITS PLACED (1,000)					AVERAGE SALES PRICE (dol.)				
	Total	North-east	Mid-west	South	West	U.S.	North-east	Mid-west	South	West
1980	233.7	12.3	32.3	140.3	48.7	19,800	18,500	18,600	18,200	25,400
1985	283.4	20.2	38.6	187.6	36.9	21,800	22,700	21,500	20,400	28,700
1986	256.1	21.2	37.2	162.3	35.4	22,400	24,400	21,800	20,700	29,900
1987	239.2	23.6	40.0	145.5	30.1	23,700	25,600	23,700	21,900	31,000
1988	224.3	22.7	39.1	130.7	31.8	25,100	27,000	24,600	22,700	33,900
1989	202.8	20.2	39.1	112.8	30.6	27,200	30,200	26,700	24,100	37,800
1990	195.4	18.8	37.7	108.4	30.6	27,800	30,000	27,000	24,500	39,300
1991	174.3	14.3	35.4	97.6	27.0	27,700	30,400	27,600	24,500	38,600
1992	212.0	15.0	42.2	124.4	30.4	28,400	30,900	28,800	25,400	39,000
1993	242.5	15.4	44.5	146.7	35.9	30,500	32,000	31,400	27,700	40,500
1994	286.1	16.2	53.0	174.4	42.5	33,500	33,900	34,600	30,500	44,600
1995	310.7	14.6	56.0	198.3	41.8	36,300	36,600	36,600	34,000	46,800
1996	319.7	15.4	56.6	205.1	42.6	38,400	40,200	39,600	36,100	47,700

H4-7 Total Housing Inventory for the United States: 1970–1996

ITEM	1970	1975	1980	1985	1990	1991	1992	1993	1994	1995	1996
All housing units . . .	69,778	78,821	87,739	97,333	106,283	107,276	108,316	109,611	110,952	112,655	114,139
Vacant	6,137	6,896	8,101	9,446	12,059	12,023	11,926	11,894	12,257	12,669	13,155
Year-round vacant	4,391	5,202	5,996	7,400	9,128	9,137	8,932	8,937	9,229	9,570	9,945
For rent	1,299	1,647	1,575	2,221	2,662	2,780	2,769	2,809	2,858	2,946	3,008
For sale only	427	591	734	1,006	1,064	1,070	970	894	953	1,022	1,082
Rented or sold	427	536	623	664	660	602	628	625	772	810	834
Held off market	2,238	2,429	3,064	3,510	4,742	4,686	4,564	4,609	4,646	4,793	5,022
Occasional use	615	649	814	977	1,485	1,494	1,443	1,508	1,612	1,667	1,709
Usual residence elsewhere	429	470	568	659	1,068	1,084	1,011	994	815	801	852
Other	1,195	1,309	1,683	1,875	2,189	2,107	2,111	2,108	2,219	2,325	2,461
Seasonal [1]	1,746	1,694	2,106	2,046	2,931	2,886	2,994	2,957	3,028	3,099	3,209
Total occupied	63,640	71,925	79,638	87,887	94,224	95,253	96,391	97,717	98,695	99,985	100,984
Owner	40,834	46,463	52,223	56,152	60,248	61,010	61,823	62,533	63,136	64,739	66,041
Renter	22,806	25,462	27,415	31,736	33,976	34,242	34,568	35,184	35,558	35,246	34,943
Percent distribution:											
All housing units	100.0	100.0	100.0	100.0	100.0	100.0	100.0	100.0	100.0	100.0	100.0
Vacant	8.8	8.7	9.2	9.7	11.3	11.2	11.0	10.9	11.0	11.2	11.5
Total occupied	91.2	91.3	90.8	90.3	88.7	88.8	89.0	89.1	89.0	88.8	88.5
Owner	58.5	58.9	59.5	57.7	56.7	56.9	57.1	57.0	56.9	57.5	57.9
Renter	32.7	32.3	31.2	32.6	32.0	31.9	31.9	32.1	32.0	31.3	30.6

[1] Beginning 1990 includes vacant seasonal mobile homes. For years shown, seasonal vacant housing units were underreported prior to 1990.

H4-8   Housing Units—Current Trends for Selected Characteristics: 1991–1995

CHARACTERISTIC	NUMBER OF UNITS (1,000)			PERCENT DISTRIBUTION		
	1991	1993	1995	1991	1993	1995
UNITS IN STRUCTURE						
All housing units....................	104,592	106,611	109,457	100.0	100.0	100.0
1 detached	62,646	64,283	66,169	59.9	60.3	60.5
1 attached..........................	6,156	6,079	6,213	5.9	5.7	5.7
3 or 4..............................	10,890	10,732	10,700	10.4	10.1	9.8
5 or more	17,918	18,444	18,727	17.1	17.3	17.1
5 to 9	5,368	5,521	5,594	5.1	5.2	5.1
10 to 49...........................	8,477	8,851	8,993	8.1	8.3	8.2
50 or more.........................	4,073	4,072	4,140	3.9	3.8	3.8
Mobile home or trailer	6,983	7,072	7,647	6.7	6.6	7.0
PLUMBING FACILITIES						
All housing units....................	104,592	106,611	109,457	100.0	100.0	100.0
Complete plumbing facilities	101,197	104,302	106,942	96.8	97.8	97.7
Lacking complete plumbing facilities..........	3,394	2,309	2,515	3.2	2.2	2.3
VEHICLES KEPT AT HOME						
Occupied housing units	93,147	94,724	97,693	100.0	100.0	100.0
None	10,148	9,793	9,583	10.9	10.3	9.8
1.................................	31,280	31,662	32,731	33.6	33.4	33.5
2.................................	35,290	36,673	38,173	37.9	38.7	39.1
3 or more	16,428	16,596	17,206	17.6	17.5	17.6
TELEPHONE AVAILABLE						
Occupied housing units...............	93,147	94,724	97,693	100.0	100.0	100.0
With telephone........................	87,291	88,442	91,544	93.7	93.4	93.7
No telephone.........................	5,856	6,282	6,149	6.3	6.6	6.3

H4-9   Housing Units—Characteristics, by Tenure and Region, 1995

| CHARACTERISTIC | Total housing units | Sea-sonal | YEAR-ROUND UNITS | | | | | | | Vacant |
| | | | Occupied | | | | | | | |
			Total	Owner	Renter	North-east	Mid-west	South	West	
Total units	109,457	3,054	97,693	63,544	34,150	19,200	23,662	34,236	20,596	8,710
Percent distribution	100.0	2.8	89.3	58.1	31.2	17.5	21.6	31.3	18.8	8.0
Units in structure:										
Single family detached	66,169	1,804	60,826	52,257	8,569	9,818	16,175	22,406	12,427	3,539
Single family attached	6,213	41	5,545	2,936	2,609	1,571	1,053	1,867	1,055	627
2 to 4 units	10,700	124	9,299	1,734	7,565	3,126	2,168	2,083	1,922	1,277
5 to 9 units	5,594	102	4,803	520	4,283	970	1,023	1,592	1,218	690
10 to 19 units	5,092	93	4,342	368	3,974	791	880	1,575	1,096	657
20 to 49 units	3,901	74	3,244	342	2,903	896	559	856	933	583
50 or more units	4,140	55	3,470	550	2,920	1,470	668	641	691	615
Mobile home or trailer	7,647	761	6,164	4,837	1,328	557	1,136	3,216	1,254	722
Stories in structure: [1]										
One story	3,065	35	2,678	279	2,399	158	374	1,204	942	352
2 stories	10,828	149	9,318	1,055	8,263	1,065	1,321	3,594	3,338	1,361
3 stories	8,268	152	7,056	1,179	5,877	2,363	2,451	1,249	992	1,060
4 to 6 stories	4,652	79	3,904	591	3,312	2,287	793	395	429	670
7 or more stories	2,627	32	2,213	415	1,799	1,382	359	312	160	381
Foundation: [2]										
Full or partial basement	32,423	367	30,635	27,080	3,554	9,859	13,077	4,894	2,803	1,420
Crawlspace	18,891	762	16,727	13,155	3,572	573	2,413	9,007	4,735	1,402
Concrete slab	19,255	358	17,722	13,988	3,734	855	1,556	9,610	5,702	1,175
Other	1,813	358	1,287	970	317	101	181	762	243	168
Year structure built:										
1939 and earlier	22,116	544	19,308	11,068	8,239	7,162	6,228	3,574	2,345	2,263
1940 to 1949	8,400	228	7,487	4,671	2,817	1,680	1,750	2,500	1,558	685
1950 to 1959	13,569	371	12,398	8,798	3,600	2,546	3,245	3,936	2,670	800
1960 to 1969	15,806	472	14,267	9,349	4,918	2,415	3,266	5,286	3,300	1,068
1970 to 1979	23,717	784	21,033	13,347	7,685	2,716	4,872	8,358	5,086	1,899
1980 or later	25,849	654	23,201	16,311	6,890	2,679	4,301	10,582	5,639	1,994
Median year	1967	1968	1967	1968	1965	1953	1962	1972	1971	1966
Main heating equipment:										
Warm-air furnace	57,840	838	53,165	38,301	14,863	6,881	17,711	17,212	11,361	3,837
Electric heat pump	10,614	311	9,406	7,027	2,379	433	692	7,003	1,278	897
Steam or hot water system	14,895	87	13,669	7,323	6,345	9,503	2,587	834	745	1,139
Floor, wall, or pipeless furnace	5,674	128	4,963	2,148	2,815	234	389	1,534	2,806	583
Built-in electric units	8,344	422	7,035	2,870	4,166	1,303	1,342	2,286	2,104	887
Room heaters with flue	2,083	178	1,620	869	752	187	245	864	324	285
Room heaters without flue	1,886	49	1,642	964	678	43	31	1,500	69	194
Stoves	2,877	339	2,320	1,735	585	360	379	962	619	218
Fireplaces	1,066	141	850	661	187	37	81	385	347	75
None	1,795	359	1,044	463	581	38	31	457	518	393
Portable electric heaters	950	78	809	413	395	19	18	576	195	63
Other	1,432	124	1,171	768	403	162	156	623	231	137
Kitchen equipment:										
Lacking complete facilities	3,629	391	1,075	461	614	241	281	302	252	2,163
With complete facilities	105,827	2,662	96,618	63,083	33,536	18,959	23,382	33,934	20,344	6,546
Kitchen sink	108,395	2,903	97,034	63,231	33,803	19,033	23,484	34,065	20,452	8,458
Refrigerator	106,872	2,739	97,433	63,469	33,964	19,133	23,597	34,180	20,523	6,701
Burners and oven	107,394	2,795	97,207	63,443	33,764	19,093	23,528	34,113	20,473	7,392
Burners only	151	21	105	31	74	28	17	40	20	25
Oven only	119	4	99	32	68	14	44	19	22	16
Dishwasher	56,635	818	52,508	40,236	12,272	9,084	11,160	19,210	13,054	3,309
Washing machine	79,403	1,129	75,745	60,034	15,711	13,526	18,804	28,015	15,399	2,530
Clothes dryer	74,165	1,062	70,756	57,184	13,571	12,150	18,341	25,694	14,571	2,347
Disposal in kitchen sink	46,353	717	42,451	28,793	13,659	4,159	10,301	14,086	13,906	3,185
Air conditioning: Central	50,824	780	46,577	34,161	12,415	3,856	11,694	23,772	7,255	3,467
Percent of total units	46.4	25.5	47.7	53.8	36.4	20.1	49.4	69.4	35.2	39.8
One or more room units	29,141	530	27,181	16,126	11,054	8,732	7,107	8,361	2,982	1,431
Source of water:										
Public system or private company	94,108	1,767	84,818	52,643	32,175	16,307	19,749	29,445	19,318	7,523
Percent of total units	86.0	57.9	86.8	82.8	94.2	84.9	83.5	86.0	93.8	86.4
Well serving 1 to 5 units	14,265	955	12,270	10,463	1,807	2,783	3,778	4,498	1,211	1,041
Other	1,083	332	606	438	167	110	136	293	67	146
Means of sewage disposal:										
Public sewer	83,308	1,222	75,282	44,527	30,755	14,859	18,618	24,111	17,694	6,804
Percent of total units	76.1	40.0	77.1	70.1	90.1	77.4	78.7	70.4	85.9	78.1
Septic tank, cesspool, chemical toilet	25,635	1,521	22,296	18,937	3,359	4,335	5,029	10,041	2,891	1,819
Other	513	311	116	80	36	6	15	83	11	87

[1] Limited to multiunit structures.   [2] Limited to single-family units.

H4-10 Homeownership Rates, by Age of Householder: 1985–1996

AGE OF HOUSEHOLDER	1985	1987	1988	1989	1990	1991	1992	1993 [1]	1994	1995	1996
United States	63.9	64.0	63.8	63.9	63.9	64.1	64.1	64.0	64.0	64.7	65.4
Less than 35 years old	39.9	39.5	39.3	39.1	38.5	37.8	37.6	37.3	37.3	38.6	39.1
Less than 25 years old	17.2	16.0	15.8	16.6	15.7	15.3	14.9	14.8	14.9	15.9	18.0
25 to 29 years old	37.7	36.4	35.9	35.3	35.2	33.8	33.6	33.6	34.1	34.4	34.7
30 to 34 years old	54.0	53.5	53.2	53.2	51.8	51.2	50.5	50.8	50.6	53.1	53.0
35 to 44 years old	68.1	67.2	66.9	66.6	66.3	65.8	65.1	65.1	64.5	65.2	65.5
35 to 39 years old	65.4	64.1	63.6	63.4	63.0	62.2	61.4	61.8	61.2	62.1	62.1
40 to 44 years old	71.4	70.8	70.7	70.2	69.8	69.5	69.1	68.6	68.2	68.6	69.0
45 to 54 years old	75.9	76.1	75.6	75.5	75.2	74.8	75.1	75.3	75.2	75.2	75.6
45 to 49 years old	74.3	74.6	74.4	74.1	73.9	73.7	74.2	73.7	73.8	73.7	74.4
50 to 54 years old	77.5	77.8	77.1	77.2	76.8	76.1	76.2	77.2	76.8	77.0	77.2
55 to 64 years old	79.5	80.2	79.5	79.6	79.3	80.0	80.2	79.9	79.3	79.5	80.0
55 to 59 years old	79.2	80.0	79.3	79.1	78.8	79.5	79.3	78.9	78.4	78.8	79.4
60 to 64 years old	79.9	80.4	79.8	80.1	79.8	80.5	81.2	80.9	80.1	80.3	80.7
65 years and over	74.8	75.5	75.6	75.8	76.3	77.2	77.1	77.3	77.4	78.1	78.9
65 to 69 years old	79.5	79.5	80.0	80.0	80.0	81.4	80.8	80.7	80.6	81.0	82.4
70 to 74 years old	76.8	77.7	77.7	77.8	78.4	78.8	79.0	79.9	80.1	80.9	81.4
75 years old and over	69.8	70.8	70.8	71.2	72.3	73.1	73.3	73.4	73.5	74.6	75.3

[1] Based on 1990 census controls.

H4-11 Homeownership Rates, by State: 1985–1996

STATE	1985	1990	1993 [1]	1994	1995	1996	STATE	1985	1990	1993 [1]	1994	1995	1996
United States .	63.9	63.9	64.0	64.0	64.7	65.4	Missouri	69.2	64.0	66.4	68.4	69.4	70.2
Alabama	70.4	68.4	70.2	68.5	70.1	71.0	Montana	66.5	69.1	69.7	68.8	68.7	68.6
Alaska	61.2	58.4	55.4	58.8	60.9	62.9	Nebraska	68.5	67.3	67.7	68.0	67.1	66.8
Arizona	64.7	64.5	69.1	67.7	62.9	62.0	Nevada	57.0	55.8	55.8	55.8	58.6	61.1
Arkansas	66.6	67.8	70.5	68.1	67.2	66.6	New Hampshire . . .	65.5	65.0	65.4	65.1	66.0	65.0
California	54.2	53.8	56.0	55.5	55.4	55.0	New Jersey	62.3	65.0	64.5	64.1	64.9	64.6
Colorado	63.6	59.0	61.8	62.9	64.6	64.5	New Mexico	68.2	68.6	69.1	66.8	67.0	67.1
Connecticut	69.0	67.9	64.5	63.8	68.2	69.0	New York	50.3	53.3	52.8	52.5	52.7	52.7
Delaware	70.3	67.7	74.1	70.5	71.7	71.5	North Carolina	68.0	69.0	68.8	68.7	70.1	70.4
Dist of Columbia . . .	37.4	36.4	35.7	37.8	39.2	40.4	North Dakota	69.9	67.2	62.7	63.3	67.3	68.2
Florida	67.2	65.1	65.5	65.7	66.6	67.1	Ohio	67.9	68.7	68.5	67.4	67.9	69.2
Georgia	62.7	64.3	66.5	63.4	66.6	69.3	Oklahoma	70.5	70.3	70.3	68.5	69.8	68.4
Hawaii	51.0	55.5	52.8	52.3	50.2	50.6	Oregon	61.5	64.4	63.8	63.9	63.2	63.1
Idaho	71.0	69.4	72.1	70.7	72.0	71.4	Pennsylvania	71.6	73.8	72.0	71.8	71.5	71.7
Illinois	60.6	63.0	61.8	64.2	66.4	68.2	Rhode Island	61.4	58.5	57.6	56.5	57.9	56.6
Indiana	67.6	67.0	68.7	68.4	71.0	74.2	South Carolina	72.0	71.4	71.1	72.0	71.3	72.9
Iowa	69.9	70.7	68.2	70.1	71.4	72.8	South Dakota	67.6	66.2	65.6	66.4	67.5	67.8
Kansas	68.3	69.0	68.9	69.0	67.5	67.5	Tennessee	67.6	68.3	64.1	65.2	67.0	68.8
Kentucky	68.5	65.8	68.8	70.6	71.2	73.2	Texas	60.5	59.7	58.7	59.7	61.4	61.8
Louisiana	70.2	67.8	65.4	65.8	65.3	64.9	Utah	71.5	70.1	68.9	69.3	71.5	72.7
Maine	73.7	74.2	71.9	72.6	76.7	76.5	Vermont	69.5	72.6	68.5	69.4	70.4	70.3
Maryland	65.6	64.9	65.5	64.1	65.8	66.9	Virginia	68.5	69.8	68.5	69.3	68.1	68.5
Massachusetts	60.5	58.6	60.7	60.6	60.2	61.7	Washington	66.8	61.8	63.1	62.4	61.6	63.1
Michigan	70.7	72.3	72.3	72.0	72.2	73.3	West Virginia	75.9	72.0	73.3	73.7	73.1	74.3
Minnesota	70.0	68.0	65.8	68.9	73.3	75.4	Wisconsin	63.8	68.3	65.7	64.2	67.5	68.2
Mississippi	69.6	69.4	69.7	69.2	71.1	73.0	Wyoming	73.2	68.9	67.1	65.8	69.0	68.0

[1] Based on 1990 population controls.

H4-12 Occupied Housing Units—Costs and Value, by Region, 1995

[As of fall. Specified owner-occupied units are limited to one-unit structures on less than 10 acres and no business on property. Specified renter-occupied units exclude one-unit structures on 10 acres or more. See headnote table 1203 for an explanation of housing costs. Based on the American Housing Survey;

CATEGORY	NUMBER (1,000)					PERCENT DISTRIBUTION				
	Total units	North-east	Mid-west	South	West	Total units	North-east	Mid-west	South	West
OWNER OCCUPIED UNITS										
Total	63,544	11,861	16,567	22,959	12,157	100.0	100.0	100.0	100.0	100.0
Monthly housing costs:										
Less than $300	17,027	1,694	4,633	8,008	2,692	26.8	14.3	27.9	34.9	22.1
$300 to $399	6,360	1,341	1,838	2,144	1,036	10.0	11.3	11.1	9.4	8.5
$400 to $499	5,268	1,143	1,594	1,801	730	8.3	9.6	9.6	7.8	6.0
$500 to $599	4,921	914	1,452	1,811	744	7.7	7.7	8.8	7.9	6.1
$600 to $699	4,356	838	1,267	1,572	679	6.9	7.1	7.6	6.8	5.6
$700 to $799	4,142	751	1,180	1,459	753	6.5	6.3	7.1	6.4	6.2
$800 to $999	6,684	1,373	1,717	2,337	1,257	10.5	11.6	10.4	10.2	10.3
$1,000 to $1,249	5,477	1,253	1,293	1,650	1,280	8.6	10.6	7.8	7.2	10.5
$1,250 to $1,499	3,518	939	685	848	1,047	5.5	7.9	4.1	3.7	8.6
$1,500 or more	5,791	1,616	908	1,328	1,939	9.1	13.6	5.5	5.8	15.9
Median (dol.) [1]	563	700	515	474	726	(X)	(X)	(X)	(X)	(X)
RENTER OCCUPIED UNITS										
Total	34,150	7,338	7,096	11,277	8,439	100.0	100.0	100.0	100.0	100.0
Less than $300	4,815	1,003	1,318	1,766	729	14.1	13.7	18.6	15.7	8.6
$300 to $399	4,285	669	1,265	1,722	629	12.5	9.1	17.8	15.3	7.5
$400 to $499	5,645	956	1,455	2,029	1,206	16.5	13.0	20.5	18.0	14.3
$500 to $599	5,076	1,106	1,070	1,609	1,292	14.9	15.1	15.1	14.3	15.3
$600 to $699	4,188	1,024	730	1,199	1,235	12.3	14.0	10.3	10.6	14.6
$700 to $799	2,910	726	372	846	966	8.5	9.9	5.2	7.5	11.4
$800 to $999	2,856	788	292	694	1,081	8.4	10.7	4.1	6.2	12.8
$1,000 to $1,249	1,244	380	97	239	528	3.6	5.2	1.4	2.1	6.3
$1,250 to $1,499	420	122	25	88	185	1.2	1.7	0.4	0.8	2.2
$1,500 or more	365	114	30	68	152	1.1	1.6	0.4	0.6	1.8
No cash rent	2,344	451	442	1,017	435	6.9	6.1	6.2	9.0	5.2
Median (dol.)	523	574	451	479	612	(X)	(X)	(X)	(X)	(X)

X Not applicable.

H4-13 Occupied Housing Units—Financial Summary, by Selected Characteristics of the Householder, 1995

CHARACTERISTIC	Total occu-pied units	TENURE		BLACK		HISPANIC ORIGIN [1]		ELDERLY [2]		HOUSEHOLDS BELOW POVERTY LEVEL	
		Owner	Renter	Owner	Renter	Owner	Renter	Owner	Renter	Owner	Renter
Total units [3]	97,693	63,544	34,150	5,137	6,637	3,245	4,512	16,299	4,542	6,034	8,661
Monthly housing costs:											
Less than $300	21,844	17,027	4,815	1,721	1,423	883	549	8,833	1,364	3,015	2,682
$300-$399.............	10,644	6,360	4,285	555	1,004	287	529	2,560	558	710	1,305
$400-$499.............	10,913	5,268	5,645	444	1,182	249	762	1,479	583	510	1,345
$500-$599.............	9,997	4,921	5,076	430	928	227	797	947	485	389	904
$600-$699.............	8,544	4,356	4,188	381	698	219	652	585	389	258	621
$700-$799.............	7,052	4,142	2,910	323	409	209	388	455	240	227	420
$800-$999.............	9,540	6,684	2,856	496	417	296	369	582	245	282	309
$1,000 or more	16,815	14,786	2,029	786	167	877	201	855	196	644	166
Median amount (dol.)	543	563	523	465	459	590	535	282	418	300	391
Monthly housing costs as percent of income:											
Less than 5 percent	3,036	2,845	191	174	16	104	19	669	14	17	15
5 to 9 percent	10,508	9,570	938	677	121	455	88	2,749	67	88	55
10 to 14 percent..........	14,002	11,260	2,741	827	446	444	216	3,222	129	223	116
15 to 19 percent..........	14,673	10,637	4,035	755	727	470	424	2,382	192	296	194
20 to 24 percent..........	12,318	8,174	4,144	668	796	397	482	1,724	381	348	297
25 to 29 percent..........	9,519	5,523	3,996	405	758	293	517	1,196	556	319	578
30 to 34 percent..........	6,514	3,586	2,928	298	540	205	410	866	485	338	472
35 to 39 percent..........	4,703	2,402	2,301	227	421	164	370	662	325	262	418
40 percent or more........	18,234	8,377	9,857	964	2,219	649	1,639	2,515	1,826	3,007	4,999
Median amount (percent)....	22	19	29	20	31	21	34	18	38	52	62
Median monthly costs (dol.):											
Electricity	63	69	48	71	52	64	44	59	40	62	46
Piped gas..............	38	42	29	46	35	29	25	41	26	38	30
Fuel oil................	59	61	52	57	54	60	43	61	54	53	52

[1] Persons of Hispanic origin may be of any race.   [2] Householders 65 years old and over.   [3] Includes units with mortgage payment not reported and no cash rent not shown separately.

H4-14 Owner-Occupied Housing Units—Mortgage Characteristics, by Region, 1995

CHARACTERISTIC	NUMBER (1,000)					PERCENT DISTRIBUTION				
	Total units	North-east	Mid-west	South	West	Total units	North-east	Mid-west	South	West
ALL OWNERS										
Total units	63,544	11,861	16,567	22,959	12,157	100.0	100.0	100.0	100.0	100.0
Mortgages currently on property:										
None, owned free and clear. . . .	24,518	4,607	6,479	9,666	3,765	38.6	38.8	39.1	42.1	31.0
Mortgaged	39,026	7,254	10,088	13,292	8,392	61.4	61.2	60.9	57.9	69.0
One mortgage or land contract.	34,730	6,326	8,913	12,183	7,307	54.7	53.3	53.8	53.1	60.1
Two mortgages	4,244	914	1,167	1,102	1,062	6.7	7.7	7.0	4.8	8.7
Three mortgages or more . . .	52	14	7	7	23	0.1	0.1	0.0	0.0	0.2
OWNERS WITH MORTGAGES										
Total units	39,026	7,254	10,088	13,292	8,392	100.0	100.0	100.0	100.0	100.0
Type of primary mortgage:										
FHA	5,172	514	1,182	2,252	1,225	13.3	7.1	11.7	16.9	14.6
VA	2,356	170	467	1,086	632	6.0	2.3	4.6	8.2	7.5
Farmers Home Administration [1] .	381	47	114	158	62	1.0	0.6	1.1	1.2	0.7
Other types.	27,906	5,732	7,793	8,583	5,798	71.5	79.0	77.3	64.6	69.1
Don't know	1,336	265	202	585	284	3.4	3.7	2.0	4.4	3.4
Not reported	1,875	527	330	628	390	4.8	7.3	3.3	4.7	4.6
Payment plan of primary mortgage:										
Fixed payment, self amortizing. .	30,002	5,392	7,925	10,519	6,166	76.9	74.3	78.6	79.1	73.5
Adjustable rate mortgage	4,473	900	1,116	1,233	1,224	11.5	12.4	11.1	9.3	14.6
Graduated payment mortgage . .	370	67	79	114	109	0.9	0.9	0.8	0.9	1.3
Balloon	586	53	244	178	112	1.5	0.7	2.4	1.3	1.3
Other.	567	102	144	200	121	1.5	1.4	1.4	1.5	1.4
Combination	336	71	93	103	69	0.9	1.0	0.9	0.8	0.8
Not reported	2,691	669	486	946	590	6.9	9.2	4.8	7.1	7.0
Home equity loan:										
With a home equity loan	8,474	1,771	2,271	2,384	2,048	21.7	24.4	22.5	17.9	24.4
No home equity loan	27,696	4,906	7,243	9,776	5,770	71.0	67.6	71.8	73.5	68.8
Not reported	2,857	576	574	1,132	574	7.3	7.9	5.7	8.5	6.8

[1] Due to a reorganization, now the Rural Housing Service handles these mortgage functions.

H4-15 Heating Equipment and Fuels for Occupied Units: 1991–1995

TYPE OF EQUIPMENT OR FUEL	NUMBER (1,000)			PERCENT DISTRIBUTION		
	1991	1993	1995	1991	1993	1995
Occupied units, total	93,147	94,724	97,692	100.0	100.0	100.0
Heating equipment:						
Warm air furnace.	49,423	51,248	53,165	53.1	54.1	54.4
Heat pumps	7,638	8,422	9,406	8.2	8.9	9.6
Steam or hot water	13,929	13,657	13,669	15.0	14.4	14.0
Floor, wall, or pipeless furnace.	4,291	4,746	4,963	4.6	5.0	5.1
Built-in electric units.	6,755	6,722	7,035	7.3	7.1	7.2
Room heaters with flue.	2,549	1,766	1,620	2.7	1.9	1.7
Room heaters without flue	2,111	1,597	1,642	2.3	1.7	1.7
Fireplaces, stoves, portable heaters or other . .	5,590	5,654	5,150	6.0	6.0	5.3
None.	861	911	1,044	0.9	1.0	1.1
House main heating fuel:						
Utility gas.	47,018	47,669	49,203	50.5	50.3	50.4
Fuel oil, kerosene, etc	12,462	12,189	12,029	13.4	12.9	12.3
Electricity.	23,714	25,107	26,771	25.5	26.5	27.4
Bottled, tank, or LP gas	3,882	3,922	4,251	4.2	4.1	4.4
Coal or coke.	319	297	210	0.3	0.3	0.2
Wood and other fuel	4,890	4,630	4,186	5.2	4.9	4.3
None.	862	910	1,043	0.9	1.0	1.1
Cooking fuel:						
Electricity.	54,232	55,887	57,621	58.2	59.0	59.0
Gas [1]	38,119	37,996	39,218	40.9	40.1	40.1
Other fuel	424	479	566	0.5	0.5	0.6
None.	372	362	287	0.4	0.4	0.3

[1] Includes utility, bottled, tank, and LP gas.

H4-16 Average Prices of Selected Fuels and Electricity: 1980–1996

[In dollars per unit, except electricity, in cents per kWh. Represents price to end-users, except as noted]

ITEM	Unit [1]	1980	1985	1989	1990	1991	1992	1993	1994	1995	1996
Crude oil, composite [2] . . .	Barrel	28.07	26.75	14.67	17.97	22.22	19.06	18.43	16.41	15.59	17.23
Motor gasoline: [3]											
Unleaded regular	Gallon	1.25	1.20	0.95	1.02	1.16	1.14	1.13	1.11	1.11	1.15
Unleaded premium . . .	Gallon	(NA)	1.34	1.11	1.20	1.35	1.32	1.32	1.30	1.31	1.34
No. 2 heating oil.	Gallon	0.79	0.85	0.54	0.59	0.73	0.67	0.63	0.60	0.57	0.56
No. 2 diesel fuel.	Gallon	0.82	0.79	0.50	0.59	0.73	0.65	0.62	0.60	0.55	0.56
Residual fuel oil	Gallon	0.61	0.61	0.33	0.41	0.47	0.36	0.35	0.34	0.35	(NA)
Natural gas, residential . .	1,000 cu/ft. .	3.68	6.12	5.47	5.64	5.80	5.82	5.89	6.16	6.41	6.06
Electricity, residential. . . .	kWh	5.4	7.8	7.5	7.6	7.9	8.1	8.2	8.3	8.4	8.4

NA Not available. [1] See headnote. [2] Refiner acquisition cost. [3] Average, all service.

H4-17 Weekly Food Costs: 1990 and 1996

[In dollars. Assumes that food for all meals and snacks is purchased at the store and prepared at home. See source for details on estimation procedures]

FAMILY TYPE	DECEMBER 1990				JANUARY 1996			
	Thrifty plan	Low-cost plan	Moderate-cost plan	Liberal plan	Thrifty plan	Low-cost plan	Moderate-cost plan	Liberal plan
FAMILIES								
Family of 2:								
20-50 years.............	48.10	60.60	74.70	92.70	54.70	69.10	85.20	106.30
51 years and over	45.60	58.30	71.80	85.80	51.50	66.40	82.20	98.60
Family of 4:								
Couple, 20-50 years and children—								
1-2 and 3-5 years...........	70.10	87.30	106.60	131.00	79.50	99.60	121.80	150.00
6-8 and 9-11 years	80.10	102.60	128.30	154.40	91.30	117.10	146.20	176.30
INDIVIDUALS [1]								
Child:								
1-2 years	12.70	15.40	18.00	21.80	14.30	17.60	20.60	25.00
3-5 years	13.70	16.80	20.70	24.90	15.50	19.20	23.70	28.40
6-8 years	16.60	22.20	27.90	32.50	19.00	25.40	31.70	36.90
9-11 years	19.80	25.30	32.50	37.60	22.60	28.90	37.00	42.80
Male:								
12-14 years.................	20.60	28.60	35.70	42.00	23.40	32.60	40.50	47.60
15-19 years.................	21.40	29.60	36.80	42.60	24.20	33.60	41.80	48.40
20-50 years.................	22.90	29.30	36.60	44.30	26.10	33.40	41.80	50.70
51 years and over	20.90	27.90	34.30	41.10	23.60	31.90	39.30	47.20
Female:								
12-19 years.................	20.80	24.80	30.10	36.30	23.50	28.20	34.20	41.30
20-50 years.................	20.80	25.80	31.30	40.00	23.60	29.40	35.70	45.90
51 years and over	20.60	25.10	31.00	36.90	23.20	28.50	35.40	42.40

[1] The costs given are for individuals in 4-person families. For individuals in other size families, the following adjustments are suggested: 1-person, add 20 percent; 2-person, add 10 percent; 3-person, add 5 percent; 5- or 6-person, subtract 5 percent; 7- (or more) person, subtract 10 percent.

H4-18 Profile of Consumer Expenditures for Sound Recordings: 1990–1996

[In percent, except total value. Based on monthly telephone surveys of the population 10 years old and over]

ITEM	1990	1995	1996	ITEM	1990	1995	1996
Total value (mil. dol.)	7,541.1	12,320.3	12,533.8	Music club	8.9	14.3	14.3
				Mail order............	2.5	4.0	2.9
PERCENT DISTRIBUTION [1]							
Age: 10 to 14 years........	7.6	8.0	7.9	Music type: [2]			
15 to 19 years.........	18.3	17.1	17.2	Rock................	36.1	33.5	32.6
20 to 24 years.........	16.5	15.3	15.0	Country	9.6	16.7	14.7
25 to 29 years.........	14.6	12.3	12.5	R&B	11.6	11.3	12.1
30 to 34 years.........	13.2	12.1	11.4	Pop.................	13.7	10.1	9.3
35 to 39 years.........	10.2	10.8	11.1	Rap.................	8.5	6.7	8.9
40 to 44 years.........	7.8	7.5	9.1	Classical	3.1	2.9	3.4
45 years and over	11.1	16.1	15.1	Jazz	4.8	3.0	3.3
Sex: Male	54.4	53.0	50.9	Gospel...............	2.5	3.1	4.3
Female	45.6	47.0	49.1	Soundtracks	0.8	0.9	0.8
Sales outlet:				New age	1.1	0.7	0.7
Record store...........	69.8	52.0	49.9	Children's.............	0.5	0.5	0.7
Other store...........	18.5	28.2	31.5	Other................	5.6	7.0	5.2

[1] Percent distributions exclude nonresponses and responses of don't know. [2] As classified by respondent.

H4-19 Household Pet Ownership, 1996

(Based on a sample survey of 80,000 households in 1996; for details, see source)

ITEM	Unit	Dog	Cat	Bird	Horse
Households owning companion pets [1]	Million	31.2	27.0	4.6	1.5
Percent of all households	Percent	31.6	27.3	4.6	1.5
Average number owned	Number	1.7	2.2	2.7	2.7
Total companion pet population [1]	Million	52.9	59.1	12.6	4.0
Households obtaining veterinary care [2]	Percent	88.7	72.9	15.8	66.3
Average visits per household per year	Number	2.6	1.9	0.2	2.3
Average annual costs per household	Dollars	186.80	112.24	10.95	226.26
Total expenditures	Mil. dol.	5,828	3,030	50	339
PERCENT DISTRIBUTION OF HOUSEHOLDS OWNING PETS					
Annual household income: Under $12,500	Percent	12.7	13.9	17.3	9.5
$12,500 to $24,999	Percent	19.1	19.7	20.9	20.3
$25,000 to $39,999	Percent	21.6	21.5	22.0	21.8
$40,000 to $59,999	Percent	21.5	21.2	17.5	23.1
$60,000 and over	Percent	25.2	23.7	22.3	25.4
FAMILY SIZE: [1]					
One person	Percent	13.2	16.8	12.7	12.1
Two persons	Percent	31.0	32.6	27.9	29.1
Three persons	Percent	21.4	20.6	20.4	22.0
Four or more persons	Percent	34.5	29.9	38.9	36.7

[1] As of December. [2] During 1996

H4-20 Household Participation in Lawn and Garden Activities: 1991–1995

[For calendar year. Based on national household sample survey conducted by the Gallup Organization. Subject to sampling variability;

ACTIVITY	PERCENT HOUSEHOLDS ENGAGED IN—					RETAIL SALES (mil. dol.)				
	1991	1992	1993	1994	1995	1991	1992	1993	1994	1995
Total	78	75	71	74	72	22,134	22,824	22,410	25,897	22,242
Lawn care.	62	54	54	56	53	6,890	7,460	6,446	8,417	7,621
Indoor houseplants	42	34	31	37	30	852	926	689	999	864
Flower gardening	41	39	39	44	38	2,302	2,167	2,396	3,147	2,107
Insect control.	35	27	24	28	24	1,260	1,593	1,080	1,127	1,049
Shrub care	32	27	28	30	25	1,030	1,437	1,274	1,133	774
Vegetable gardening	31	31	26	31	28	1,652	1,440	1,063	1,476	1,359
Tree care	27	20	21	22	17	1,443	1,664	2,011	1,408	1,002
Landscaping	26	22	24	26	20	4,828	4,444	5,006	5,797	5,524
Flower bulbs	26	23	22	28	21	520	503	453	635	377
Fruit trees	15	13	13	14	11	371	350	759	389	241
Container gardening	13	9	11	12	12	330	239	441	359	377
Raising transplants [1]	12	8	10	11	8	141	169	201	182	187
Herb gardening	9	7	8	10	8	161	135	175	112	140
Growing berries	7	6	6	6	5	90	62	126	85	55
Ornamental gardening.	7	5	6	5	5	264	235	290	264	144
Water gardening	(NA)	(NA)	(NA)	5	5	(NA)	(NA)	(NA)	367	421

NA Not available.   [1] Starting plants in advance of planting in ground.

H4-21 **Percent of Households Contributing to Charity, by Dollar Amount, 1995**

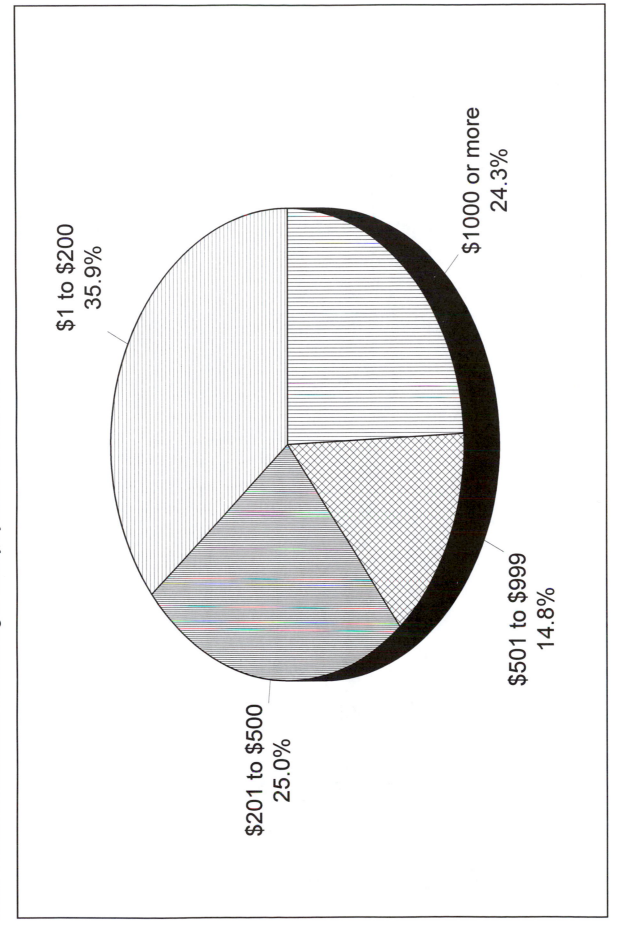

$1 to $200
35.9%

$1000 or more
24.3%

$501 to $999
14.8%

$201 to $500
25.0%

5. HEALTH INSURANCE

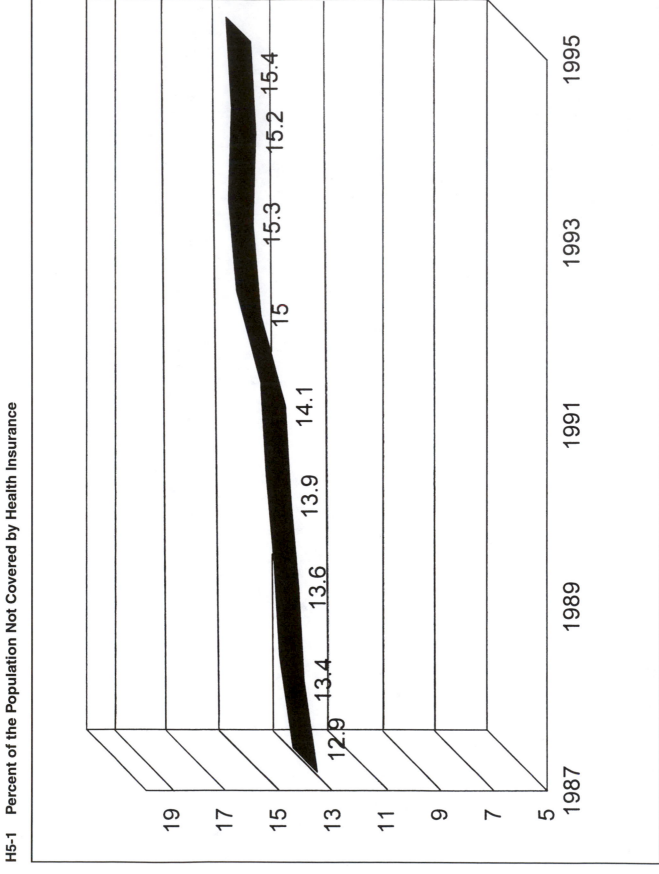

H5-1   Percent of the Population Not Covered by Health Insurance

H5-2   Health Insurance Coverage Status, by Selected Characteristics: 1987–1995

[Persons as of following year for coverage in the year shown. Government health insurance includes Medicare, Medicaid, and military plans. Based on Current Population Survey;

CHARACTERISTIC	NUMBER (mil.)							PERCENT			
	Total persons	Covered by private or Government health insurance					Not covered by health insur- ance	Covered by private or Government health insurance			Not covered by health insur- ance
		Total [1]	Private		Government			Total [1]	Private	Med- icaid	
			Total	Group health [2]	Medi- care	Med- icaid					
1987	241.2	210.2	182.2	149.7	30.5	20.2	31.0	87.1	75.5	8.4	12.9
1988	243.7	211.0	182.0	150.9	30.9	20.7	32.7	86.6	74.7	8.5	13.4
1989	246.2	212.8	183.6	151.6	31.5	21.2	33.4	86.4	74.6	8.6	13.6
1990	248.9	214.2	182.1	150.2	32.3	24.3	34.7	86.1	73.2	9.7	13.9
1991	251.4	216.0	181.4	150.1	32.9	26.9	35.4	85.9	72.1	10.7	14.1
1992 [3]	256.8	218.2	181.5	148.8	33.2	29.4	38.6	85.0	70.7	11.5	15.0
1993 [3]	259.8	220.0	182.4	148.3	33.1	31.7	39.7	84.7	70.2	12.2	15.3
1994 [3]	262.1	222.4	184.3	159.6	33.9	31.6	39.7	84.8	70.3	12.1	15.2
1995, total [3][4] . .	264.3	223.7	185.9	161.5	34.7	31.9	40.6	84.6	70.3	12.1	15.4
Age: Under 18 years.	71.1	61.4	47.0	43.8	0.3	16.5	9.8	86.2	66.1	23.2	13.8
18 to 24 years . . .	24.8	17.8	15.0	12.5	0.1	3.0	7.0	71.8	60.2	12.1	28.2
25 to 34 years . . .	40.9	31.6	27.9	26.0	0.4	3.5	9.4	77.1	68.3	8.5	22.9
35 to 44 years . . .	43.1	35.9	32.8	30.6	0.8	2.9	7.1	83.4	76.2	6.6	16.6
45 to 54 years . . .	31.6	27.4	25.3	23.3	0.9	1.8	4.2	86.7	80.0	5.6	13.3
55 to 64 years . . .	21.1	18.3	16.1	14.1	1.7	1.4	2.8	86.7	76.5	6.7	13.3
65 years and over.	31.7	31.4	21.8	11.1	30.5	2.8	0.3	99.1	68.7	8.9	0.9
Sex: Male	129.1	107.5	91.3	80.7	14.9	13.4	21.6	83.2	70.7	10.4	16.8
Female	135.2	116.2	94.6	80.7	19.8	18.5	18.9	86.0	70.0	13.7	14.0
Race: White	218.4	187.3	161.3	139.2	30.6	20.5	31.1	85.8	73.8	9.4	14.2
Black	33.9	26.8	17.1	15.7	3.3	9.2	7.1	79.0	50.5	27.1	21.0
Hispanic origin [5]	28.4	19.0	12.2	11.3	1.7	6.5	9.5	66.7	42.9	22.8	33.3

[1] Includes other Government insurance, not shown separately. Persons with coverage counted only once in total, even though they may have been covered by more that one type of policy.   [2] Related to employment of self or other family members.
[3] Beginning 1992, data based on 1990 census adjusted population controls.   [4] Includes other races not shown separately.
[5] Persons of Hispanic origin may be of any race.

H5-3   Persons with and without Health Insurance Coverage, by State, 1995

[Based on the Current Population Survey and subject to sampling error;

STATE	Persons covered (1,000)	PERSONS NOT COVERED Number (1,000)	PERSONS NOT COVERED Per-cent of total	STATE	Persons covered (1,000)	PERSONS NOT COVERED Number (1,000)	PERSONS NOT COVERED Per-cent of total
United States	223,733	40,582	15.4	Missouri.................	4,416	756	14.6
Alabama	3,804	595	13.5	Montana	762	111	12.7
Alaska..................	552	79	12.5	Nebraska................	1,504	149	9.0
Arizona	3,461	885	20.4	Nevada	1,271	292	18.7
Arkansas	2,079	454	17.9	New Hampshire.	1,027	114	10.0
California..............	25,517	6,601	20.6	New Jersey	6,782	1,121	14.2
Colorado	3,248	564	14.8	New Mexico	1,344	463	25.6
Connecticut	2,998	289	8.8	New York...............	15,522	2,779	15.2
Delaware	602	112	15.7	North Carolina.	5,951	996	14.3
District of Columbia	459	96	17.3	North Dakota	585	53	8.3
Florida.................	11,724	2,628	18.3	Ohio	9,894	1,336	11.9
Georgia.................	5,966	1,301	17.9	Oklahoma	2,591	615	19.2
Hawaii..................	1,082	106	8.9	Oregon	2,817	403	12.5
Idaho...................	993	161	14.0	Pennsylvania	10,849	1,195	9.9
Illinois................	10,504	1,294	11.0	Rhode Island	839	124	12.9
Indiana	4,972	716	12.6	South Carolina	3,205	546	14.6
Iowa....................	2,569	327	11.3	South Dakota	649	67	9.4
Kansas	2,223	316	12.4	Tennessee	4,669	814	14.8
Kentucky	3,327	567	14.6	Texas	14,190	4,615	24.5
Louisiana...............	3,428	885	20.5	Utah	1,767	235	11.7
Maine	1,060	166	13.5	Vermont.................	519	79	13.2
Maryland	4,350	783	15.3	Virginia	5,521	862	13.5
Massachusetts	5,400	671	11.1	Washington	4,759	676	12.4
Michigan	8,706	938	9.7	West Virginia	1,523	276	15.3
Minnesota	4,260	370	8.0	Wisconsin	4,930	391	7.3
Mississippi	2,159	531	19.7	Wyoming	406	77	15.9

H5-4 Number of Currently Married Women 15–44 Years of Age, and Percent Reporting the Specified Sources of Coverage for Health Insurance, by Selected Characteristics, 1995

Characteristic	Number in thousands	Not covered	Woman's employer	Husband's employer	Medicaid	CHAMPUS/ CHAMPVA[2]	Self-paid
				Percent			
All women	29,673	9.1	38.3	46.7	8.5	3.0	5.5
Age at interview							
15-24 years	2,805	15.5	27.6	31.2	25.9	6.6	2.9
25-29 years	5,089	10.1	40.0	41.7	11.7	3.5	4.5
30-34 years	7,153	10.0	39.0	45.0	8.0	1.9	6.0
35-39 years	7,608	7.7	38.0	51.2	5.2	2.2	6.1
40-44 years	7,018	6.6	41.1	53.1	3.6	3.2	6.2
Work status at interview							
Full time	14,714	6.7	57.9	41.6	3.1	2.3	4.2
Part time	5,428	11.6	20.7	58.8	6.5	2.6	7.1
Not working	9,531	11.5	18.2	47.5	18.1	4.3	6.6
Residence at interview							
Metropolitan, central city	7,102	11.4	39.9	39.6	11.0	3.8	4.5
Metropolitan, suburb	15,880	7.8	39.2	49.8	6.2	3.0	5.3
Nonmetropolitan	6,691	10.0	34.6	46.6	11.5	2.2	7.2
Education at interview[3]							
No high school diploma or GED[4]	2,807	13.3	21.5	30.8	25.6	2.0	2.7
High school diploma or GED	11,534	9.4	36.8	48.2	9.0	2.7	5.5
Some college, no bachelor's degree	7,163	8.1	41.7	47.8	4.2	4.1	5.6
Bachelor's degree or higher	7,162	2.6	46.8	52.3	1.8	2.0	6.8
Poverty level income at interview[3]							
0-149 percent	3,882	24.0	17.0	24.4	38.6	1.5	3.3
0-99 percent	1,954	27.2	11.6	15.6	50.5	1.5	2.0
150-299 percent	8,899	12.2	33.5	47.0	5.3	4.9	5.1
300 percent or higher	15,885	3.0	47.6	63.3	1.3	2.0	6.4
Race and Hispanic origin							
Hispanic	3,178	21.0	31.5	28.3	21.1	2.5	3.2
Non-Hispanic white	23,077	7.5	38.9	49.9	6.4	2.7	6.0
Non-Hispanic black	2,069	9.3	42.3	41.1	13.2	5.0	2.7
Non-Hispanic other	1,349	8.6	38.8	42.5	9.1	6.0	6.5

[1]Includes other sources of health insurance coverage not shown separately.

[2]CHAMPUS is the civilian health and medical program of the uniformed services; CHAMPVA is the Veterans Administration civilian health and medical program.

[3]Limited to women 22-44 years of age at time of interview.

[4]GED is general equivalency diploma.

*NOTE:*Percents do not add to 100 because respondents could report more than one source of coverage.

H5-5   Number of Unmarried Women 15–44 Years of Age and Percent Reporting the Specified Sources of Coverage for Health Insurance, by Selected Characteristics, 1995

Characteristic	Number in thousands	Not covered	Woman's employer	Parents	Medicaid	CHAMPUS/ CHAMPVA[1]	Self- paid	Other source[2]
					Percent			
All women	30,528	14.1	33.9	25.1	22.8	1.9	3.6	4.4
Age at interview								
16-19 years	8,619	11.0	2.9	67.0	18.2	2.0	0.9	1.7
20-24 years	6,578	18.6	26.4	27.2	21.9	3.0	4.9	3.8
25-29 years	4,604	21.1	53.6	1.6	27.5	1.2	3.7	5.7
30-34 years	3,912	14.1	51.3	0.1	29.7	1.5	4.5	6.0
35-39 years	3,603	15.9	52.1	0.1	25.6	0.9	4.1	8.3
40-44 years	3,212	13.8	62.4	0.1	18.8	1.8	6.0	4.8
Marital status								
Never married	22,679	13.6	29.0	33.8	20.5	1.9	3.5	2.3
Formerly married	7,849	15.6	47.8	29.4	1.9	3.7	10.3	10.3
Work status at interview								
Full time	13,091	13.9	66.0	6.1	10.7	1.6	4.2	3.6
Part time	6,218	18.1	12.3	44.5	18.7	2.5	3.7	5.2
Not working	11,219	12.1	8.4	36.4	39.4	1.9	2.7	4.8
Residence at interview								
Metropolitan, central city	11,448	14.2	33.3	19.1	29.7	1.9	4.0	3.5
Metropolitan, suburb	13,423	12.9	37.6	28.5	16.2	1.9	3.6	5.2
Nonmetropolitan	5,657	16.6	26.1	29.2	24.5	1.8	2.8	4.2
Education at interview[3]								
No high school diploma or GED[4]	2,617	19.7	17.0	0.1	61.7	1.0	1.4	3.3
High school diploma or GED	6,635	16.2	47.9	0.5	32.0	1.6	3.4	6.4
Some college, no bachelor's degree	5,236	15.1	53.0	8.8	17.0	2.1	5.0	6.7
Bachelor's degree or higher	4,586	8.5	71.8	5.4	4.9	0.9	8.6	4.2
Poverty level income at interview[3]								
0-149 percent	6,190	15.7	19.0	4.0	57.6	1.3	2.3	7.4
0-99 percent	4,038	15.3	9.6	4.5	69.3	0.8	1.4	6.2
150-299 percent	6,033	17.1	58.4	2.9	15.5	1.8	6.1	5.1
300 percent or higher	6,851	11.3	72.9	4.7	5.2	1.4	6.0	4.2
Race and Hispanic origin								
Hispanic	3,524	20.7	28.1	17.2	33.5	0.8	1.0	2.7
Non-Hispanic white	19,445	13.2	36.1	29.7	14.7	1.8	4.5	2.5
Non-Hispanic black	6,141	12.7	31.3	14.0	42.7	2.5	2.1	5.1
Non-Hispanic other	1,418	16.4	28.3	29.9	21.4	2.3	3.2	7.0

[1]CHAMPUS is the civilian health and medical program of the uniformed services; CHAMPVA is the Veterans Administration civilian health and medical program.

[2]Other sources include school, partner's insurance, former husband's insurance, and other sources not shown separately.

[3]Limited to women 22-44 years of age at time of interview.

[4]GED is general equivalency diploma.

NOTE: Percents do not add to 100 because respondents could report more than one source of coverage.

I. Child Care

1. SOURCES OF CHILD CARE

As discussed in Section G, Working Women, Wives, and Mothers, the number of women with children entering the workplace has risen steadily for the past 50 years until today approximately 60 percent of women with children under the age of 6 are working outside the home. Over 70 percent of mothers, both single and married, with children between the ages of 6 and 17 are also employed. The children of these working women are cared for by a variety of organizations and individuals (see Figure I1-1). Organized day care centers, including those sponsored by employers, provide care for 30 percent of the children. These organizations include day care centers that tend 18 percent of the children, and nurseries or preschools that handle the other 12 percent (Table I1-2) Non-relatives care for 21 percent of working mothers' children. These generally are women in the neighborhood who watch from one to five children in their homes to earn money while remaining at home. A substantial number (17 percent) of the children of working mothers are watched over by their grandparents. The fathers of the children care for 16 percent. Finally, mothers themselves take care of 6 percent of the children while they are at work; their employers allow them to bring their child or children to their workplace with them.

The percent of the children of married women who are cared for by their fathers rose a little in 1991 compared with 1988, but then fell back to the earlier level in 1993 (Figure I1-3). Care by relatives has steadily declined from 1988 to 1993, while the number of children in organized facilities has increased.

Women who work during the day used organized day care facilities more frequently than women who work in the afternoon, evening, and night (Figure I1-4). On the other hand, those who work during the non-day hours use relatives, both the fathers and other relatives, more often. Poor mothers leave their children with relatives more often than other mothers (Figure I1-5). Unmarried mothers use relatives, including grandparents, more frequently than do married women (Table I1-9).

The majority of working mothers took maternity leave when they gave birth (Table I1-7). Less than one percent did not take maternity leave because their employer did not offer it. Clearly, most working women have the option, and some opt to continue working with minimal time off taken for the birth of their child. The percent of mothers taking maternity leave has steadily increased since 1980, probably because more employers offer the opportunity to do so.

Over 10 percent of women between the ages of 18 and 44 have cared for a child to whom they did not give birth (Table I1-12). Children of relatives and stepchildren constitute the majority of children cared for by someone other than their birth mother. Foster children and adopted children are cared for less often in this way.

2. FATHERS' PARTICIPATION IN CHILD CARE

In 1993, one-fourth of fathers with preschool-aged children provided care for them while their mothers were working (Figure I2-1 and Table I2-2). This is a modest increase from the percent of fathers doing so in 1988. Twice as many unemployed fathers (58 percent), compared with those who are working (23 percent), care for one or more of their children (Table

I2-2). Not surprising, more poor fathers than well-to-do fathers care for their children while their wives work (Figure I.2-5). Finally, more Hispanic fathers care for their children while their wives work, fol-lowed by white fathers. Black fathers have the lowest rate of caring for their children when their wives are in the workplace (Table I2-6).

1. SOURCES OF CHILD CARE

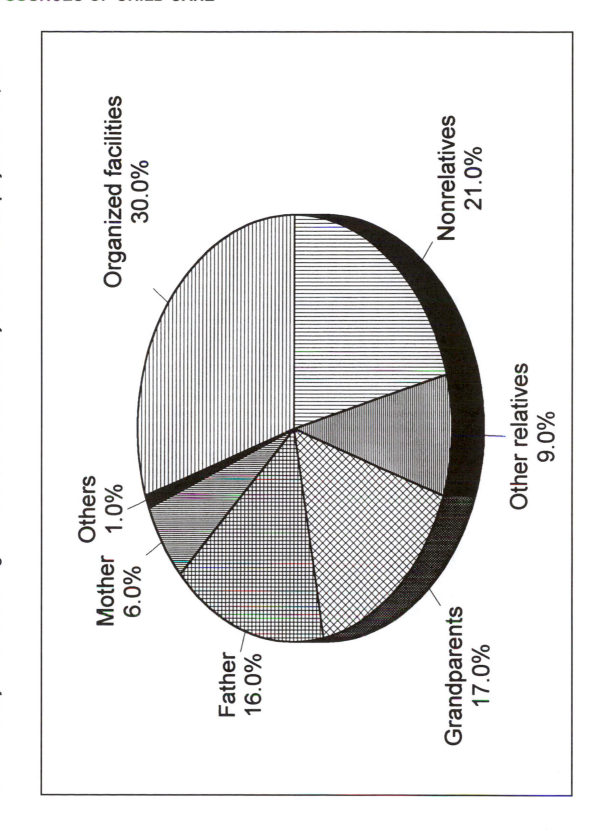

I1-1   Primary Child Care Arrangements for Preschoolers Used by Families with Employed Mothers, 1993

Organized facilities
30.0%

Nonrelatives
21.0%

Other relatives
9.0%

Grandparents
17.0%

Father
16.0%

Mother
6.0%

Others
1.0%

I1-2   Primary Child Care Arrangements of Preschoolers by Mother's Employment Status: Fall 1993

			Employment Status[1]							
	All Preschoolers		Employment Schedule				Shift Work Status			
			Full Time		Part Time		Day Shift		Non-day Shift	
Type of Arrangement	Number	Percent	Number	Percent	Number	Percent	Number	Percent	Number	Percent
All Preschoolers	9,937	100.0	6,426	100.0	3,512	100.0	6,083	100.0	3,855	100.0
Care in child's home	3,054	30.7	1,656	25.8	1,398	39.8	1,465	24.1	1,589	41.2
By father	1,585	15.9	719	11.2	866	24.7	657	10.8	928	24.1
By grandparent	649	6.5	384	6.0	264	7.5	361	5.9	287	7.4
By other relative	328	3.3	227	3.5	101	2.9	166	2.7	162	4.2
By nonrelative	492	5.0	325	5.1	167	4.8	281	4.6	211	5.5
Care in provider's home	3,184	32.0	2,239	34.9	945	26.9	2,095	34.4	1,089	28.3
By grandparent	996	10.0	684	10.6	312	8.9	593	9.7	403	10.5
By other relative	543	5.5	384	6.0	159	4.5	360	5.9	183	4.8
By nonrelative	1,645	16.6	1,171	18.2	474	13.5	1,143	18.8	503	13.0
Organized child care facilities	2,972	29.9	2,166	33.7	806	22.9	2,146	35.3	826	21.4
Day/group care center	1,823	18.3	1,398	21.8	425	12.1	1,369	22.5	453	11.8
Nursery/preschool	1,149	11.6	768	11.9	381	10.9	776	12.8	373	9.7
Mother cares for child at work[2]	616	6.2	280	4.4	336	9.6	296	4.9	321	8.3
Other[3]	111	1.2	84	1.3	26	0.8	81	1.3	30	0.8

[1]Calculations based on mother's principal job only.
[2]Includes women working at home or away from home.
[3]Includes preschoolers in kindergarten and school-based activities.

I1-3   **Changes in Selected Child Care Arrangements: 1988–1993**

(Percent of preschoolers of working mothers in selected arrangements)

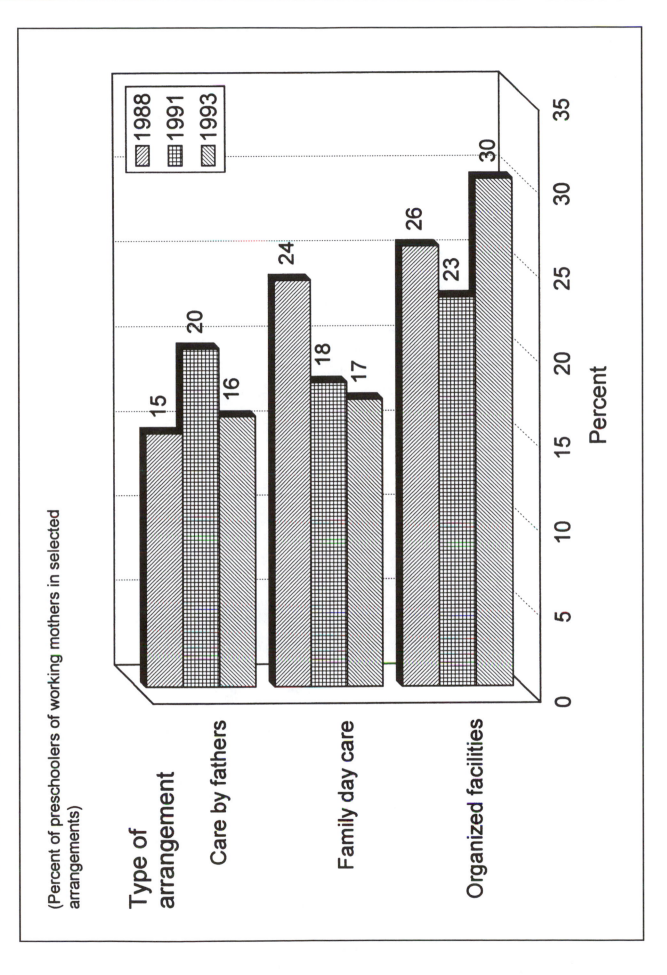

I1-4   Child Care Arrangements for Preschoolers, by Employment Status of Mother, 1993

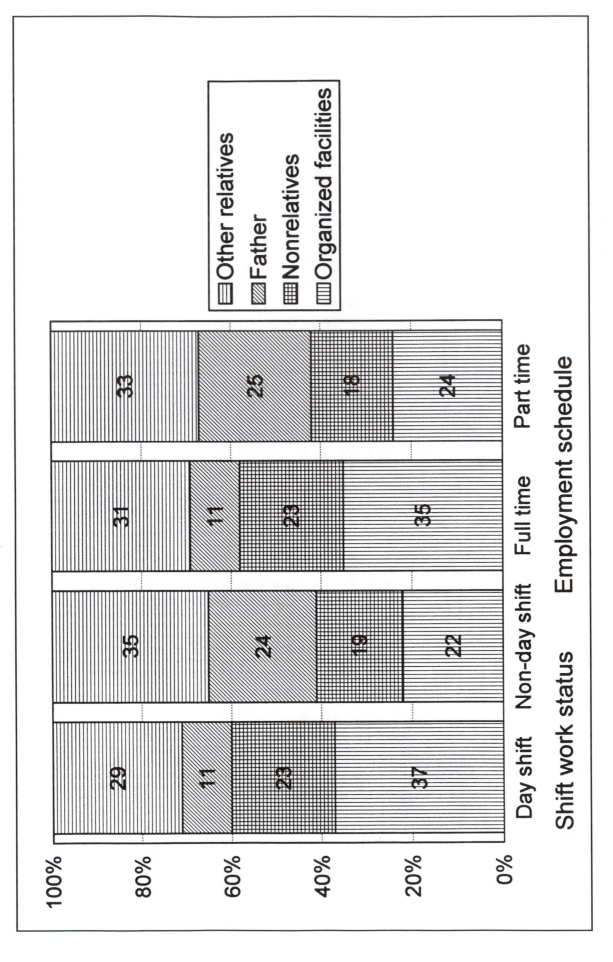

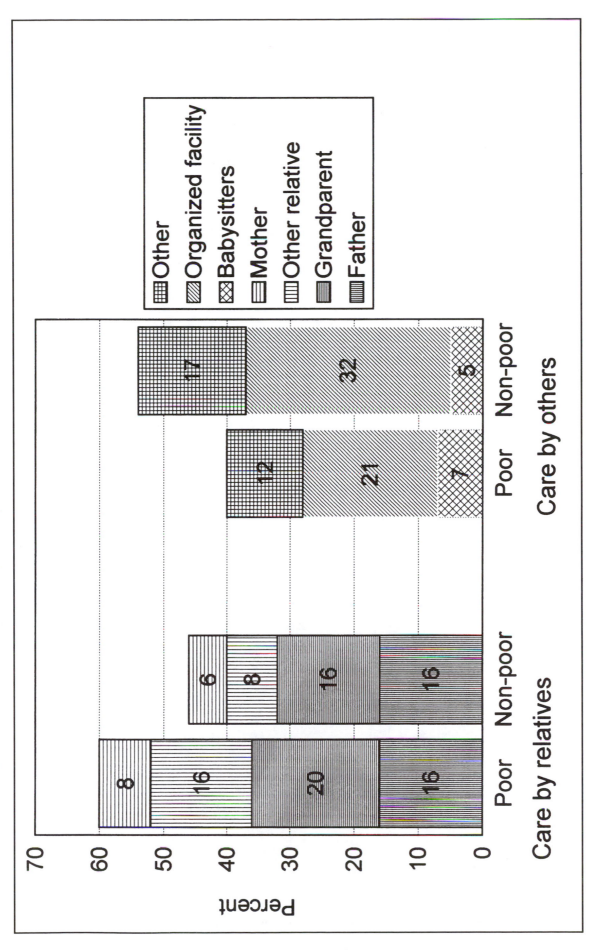

I1-5 **Child Care Arrangements for Preschoolers, by Poverty Status, 1993**

Legend: Other, Organized facility, Babysitters, Mother, Other relative, Grandparent, Father

Care by others: Poor — 12, 21, 7; Non-poor — 17, 32, 5

Care by relatives: Poor — 8, 16, 20, 16; Non-poor — 6, 8, 16, 16

I1-6   Primary Child Care Arrangements Used for Preschoolers by Families with Employed Mothers: Fall 1993

| Characteristic | Number of children | Care in child's home by | | | | Care in another home by | | | Organized facilities | | | |
		Father	Grand-parent	Other relative	Non-relative	Grand-parent	Other relative	Non-relative	Day-care center	Nursery/pre-school	Mother cares for child[1]	Other[2]
All Preschoolers	9,937	1,585	649	328	492	996	543	1,645	1,823	1,149	616	111
Race and Hispanic Origin:												
White, not Hispanic	7,295	1,252	389	141	370	699	299	1,294	1,461	807	529	54
Black, not Hispanic	1,161	101	123	82	17	106	135	164	188	191	33	22
Hispanic origin	1,078	161	86	85	76	158	88	136	110	119	34	26
Other	403	71	50	21	30	33	21	51	64	31	21	9
Age of Child:												
Less than 1 year	1,631	285	123	45	98	183	108	364	284	29	113	–
1 year	2,122	392	186	88	84	229	136	449	408	56	92	3
2 years	1,969	304	117	55	139	247	113	327	392	140	132	3
3 years	2,161	300	128	76	87	172	111	322	424	386	152	3
4 years	2,055	304	95	65	85	166	74	184	314	539	127	102
Marital Status:												
Married, husband present	7,841	1,514	378	183	394	750	360	1,282	1,429	924	543	84
Widowed, separated, divorced	1,012	14	113	70	60	101	90	176	192	137	48	12
Never married	1,084	57	158	75	39	144	94	188	201	88	25	14
Age of Mother:												
15 to 24 years	1,566	225	184	69	61	226	118	279	256	77	60	10
25 to 34 years	5,984	1,040	340	150	263	615	334	982	1,113	713	363	71
35 years and over	2,387	320	124	108	168	155	91	385	454	359	192	30
Educational Attainment:												
Less than high school	1,051	180	109	98	50	90	85	155	116	96	64	8
High school, 4 years	3,549	611	258	115	118	447	253	564	600	346	201	38
College, 1 to 3 years	2,772	447	155	69	123	267	139	437	542	347	210	35
College, 4 or more years	2,566	347	127	46	203	192	66	489	564	360	141	30
Enrollment in School:												
Enrolled in school	742	89	69	27	24	58	30	124	166	101	48	8
Not enrolled in school	9,196	1,496	579	301	468	938	513	1,522	1,657	1,048	569	104
Monthly Family Income[3]:												
Less than $1,200	1,070	170	70	52	61	143	100	161	143	73	83	13
$1,200 to $2,999	3,268	648	177	116	96	370	235	490	516	324	262	35
$3,000 to $4,499	2,578	454	189	70	114	266	86	488	476	275	136	26
$4,500 and over	2,981	313	204	90	219	210	123	498	685	475	127	38
Poverty Level[3]:												
Below poverty	1,068	173	88	65	70	126	104	131	128	83	87	13
Above poverty	8,829	1,412	552	263	419	862	439	1,506	1,692	1,064	521	98
Program Participation:												
All recipients[4]	1,537	198	141	91	62	193	157	229	247	111	98	11
Non-recipient	8,401	1,387	507	237	431	803	386	1,416	1,576	1,038	519	101
AFDC recipient	443	20	44	32	24	43	49	62	81	48	32	2
Non-recipient	9,495	1,565	605	296	468	953	494	1,577	1,742	1,101	584	109
WIC recipient	1,019	139	89	70	28	118	126	178	139	58	67	6
Non-recipient	8,919	1,446	559	258	465	878	417	1,467	1,683	1,091	549	105
Food Stamps recipient	873	93	81	48	38	113	107	93	155	82	52	11
Non-recipient	9,064	1,492	568	280	454	883	436	1,552	1,668	1,067	564	101
Region:												
Northeast	1,748	440	112	78	89	185	93	189	290	152	104	16
Midwest	2,773	453	200	78	92	272	120	609	479	237	211	21
South	3,319	348	203	93	184	337	237	506	695	531	134	50
West	2,097	344	133	80	126	202	93	341	359	229	166	23
Metropolitan Residence:												
Metropolitan	7,746	1,246	507	256	433	761	391	1,234	1,402	960	467	88
In central cities	2,844	495	218	108	147	296	143	471	465	316	150	34
Suburbs	4,902	751	290	148	286	465	247	763	937	644	317	55
Nonmetropolitan	2,191	339	141	72	59	235	152	412	420	189	149	23

– Rounds to or represents zero.

[1] Includes mothers working at home or away from home.

[2] Includes preschoolers in kindergarten and school-based activities.

[3] Omits preschoolers whose families did not report income.

[4] Family receiving either AFDC, Food Stamps, or WIC, or any combination of the three programs. Also includes a small number of preschoolers (18,000) whose families are on General Assistance.

[5] Family not receiving either General Assistance, AFDC, Food Stamps, or WIC.

I1-7   Women Who Took Maternity Leave for Most Recent Birth, 1995

Characteristic of the mother	Number in thousands	Total	Not employed	Took maternity leave	Did not take leave		
					Not needed	Not offered	Other reasons
				Percent distribution			
All women	34,958	100.0	48.0	37.3	2.3	0.9	11.6
Age at time of birth							
15-19 years	3,436	100.0	71.9	14.8	0.7	0.1	12.5
20-24 years	10,094	100.0	52.8	29.8	1.3	1.3	14.9
25-29 years	11,629	100.0	44.8	41.1	2.7	0.8	10.5
30-44 years	9,799	100.0	38.3	48.3	3.5	0.8	9.1
Year of child's birth							
1991-95	13,999	100.0	43.2	43.5	2.2	0.9	10.3
1981-90	16,344	100.0	47.4	37.2	2.7	0.8	11.8
1980 and before	5,616	100.0	61.5	22.0	1.6	0.9	14.0
Marital status at time of birth							
Never married	6,379	100.0	58.4	26.8	0.8	1.0	13.0
Married	26,439	100.0	44.9	40.3	2.8	0.8	11.1
Formerly married	2,140	100.0	54.3	31.1	0.8	1.3	12.5
Birth order							
First	10,901	100.0	35.8	46.9	1.8	1.1	14.4
Second	13,965	100.0	47.7	38.1	2.6	1.0	10.7
Third or higher	10,092	100.0	61.5	25.8	2.5	0.4	9.7
Education at interview[2]							
No high school diploma or GED[3]	4,961	100.0	69.6	16.5	0.7	0.4	12.8
High school diploma or GED	14,295	100.0	48.8	36.2	1.6	1.0	12.4
Some college, no bachelor's deg.	7,967	100.0	40.1	44.4	2.6	1.1	11.8
Bachelor's degree or higher	5,929	100.0	32.8	52.8	5.6	0.9	7.9
Race and Hispanic origin							
Hispanic	4,372	100.0	57.8	28.9	1.1	0.8	11.4
Non-Hispanic white	24,009	100.0	44.7	39.6	3.0	0.9	12.0
Non-Hispanic black	5,149	100.0	53.5	34.5	0.4	1.1	10.6
Non-Hispanic other	1,428	100.0	53.7	34.8	1.5	0.6	9.4

[2] Limited to women 22-44 years of age at time of interview.
[3] GED is general equivalency diploma.
NOTE: Percents may not add to 100 due to rounding.

I1-8   Child Care Arrangements Used by Working Women, 1995

Characteristic	Number in thousands	Other parent or stepparent	Grandparent or other relative	Non-relative	Day care center or preschool	Brother or sister	Child cares for self	School (regular hours)	Other arrangement[1]
					Percent				
All women	7,493	16.5	22.4	13.3	14.8	13.6	5.9	14.2	9.1
Marital status									
Never married	653	8.7	39.6	14.3	16.8	6.8	3.3	13.2	4.5
Currently married	5,189	20.7	17.2	12.8	13.2	14.2	6.0	15.1	10.5
Formerly married	1,651	6.4	32.1	14.3	19.1	14.4	6.5	11.7	6.6
Work status at interview									
Full time	5,933	16.8	22.7	14.5	16.8	14.4	6.5	10.3	9.1
Part time	1,561	15.5	21.5	8.5	7.3	10.4	3.5	28.9	9.1
Age of child									
5-6 years	2,234	17.0	28.6	16.3	30.1	3.9	0.8	8.4	7.0
7-8 years	2,036	18.1	19.7	17.4	12.2	11.2	2.9	15.1	12.6
9-10 years	1,652	17.1	23.6	11.9	9.9	17.8	2.6	18.7	9.2
11-12 years	1,571	13.1	15.9	5.1	1.6	26.0	20.3	16.7	7.5
Education at interview[2]									
No high school diploma or GED[3]	718	19.6	24.0	11.2	5.9	18.1	2.8	14.7	7.8
High school diploma or GED	3,237	17.3	25.0	11.7	12.7	13.5	5.6	13.4	8.7
Some college, no bachelor's degree	1,968	14.4	21.6	13.7	17.8	16.1	7.5	11.6	9.3
Bachelor's degree or higher	1,553	16.3	17.1	17.1	19.3	8.6	5.8	19.0	10.5
Poverty level income at interview[2]									
0-149 percent	1,207	16.7	29.0	12.6	12.4	14.0	1.8	15.8	4.4
0-99 percent	570	15.4	33.3	11.6	8.0	15.4	1.0	16.6	3.1
150-299 percent	2,911	15.4	24.0	11.6	12.5	14.4	5.7	15.7	8.5
300 percent or higher	3,358	17.5	18.5	15.0	17.6	12.8	7.4	12.3	11.4
Race and Hispanic origin									
Hispanic	735	18.0	32.6	13.5	8.7	10.4	1.8	10.0	10.8
Non-Hispanic white	5,277	18.0	18.9	14.4	16.3	14.9	6.4	14.3	–
Non-Hispanic black	1,189	9.9	27.9	9.1	11.1	10.3	6.0	19.2	8.5
Non-Hispanic other	294	13.4	37.2	9.5	18.6	12.1	5.7	2.9	2.6

[1] Other arrangements include before- or after-school care program, respondent while she was working, and other arrangements not shown separately.
[2] Limited to women 22-44 years of age at time of interview.
[3] GED is general equivalency diploma.
NOTE: Percents may add to more than 100 because some women reported more than one type of child care arrangement.

I1-9 Child Care Arrangements Used by Working Mothers with at Least One Child under Five Years, 1995

Characteristic	Number In thousands	Other parent or stepparent	Grandparent or other relative	Nonrelative	Day care center or preschool	Other arrangement[1]
			Percent			
All women	6,332	13.5	32.0	30.5	28.7	4.7
Marital status						
Never married	1,052	9.7	44.3	22.3	29.9	2.3
Currently married	4,510	15.5	28.4	32.3	28.0	5.3
Formerly married	770	6.6	36.1	31.3	31.3	4.1
Work status at interview						
Full time	5,110	13.0	30.4	31.0	31.0	3.9
Part time	1,222	15.5	38.6	28.6	19.5	7.8
Age of child						
Under I year	1,032	12.4	31.4	38.5	16.2	5.2
1 year	1,450	13.6	39.8	31.8	17.3	5.6
2 years	1,613	14.8	29.5	35.1	27.0	4.1
3 years	1,171	13.5	28.5	25.4	39.2	3.3
4 years	1,066	12.2	29.4	19.7	47.5	19.1
Education at interview[2]						
No high school diploma or GED[3]	455	15.3	42.7	27.4	17.1	5.8
High school diploma or GED	2,480	13.2	34.2	29.8	25.4	4.1
Some college, no bachelor's degree	1,538	12.0	30.1	33.1	30.3	5.2
Bachelor's degree or higher	1,419	13.2	22.0	34.9	38.3	4.6
Poverty level income at interview[2]						
0-149 percent	1,089	14.8	40.0	21.5	21.6	6.7
0-99 percent	523	15.0	43.7	19.7	14.8	8.5
150-299 percent	2,031	16.0	33.8	26.6	28.5	3.9
300 percent or higher	2,772	10.2	25.1	39.5	32.5	4.3
Race and Hispanic origin						
Hispanic	842	15.4	37.3	27.8	16.8	6.6
Non-Hispanic white	4,322	13.3	28.6	34.7	30.4	4.5
Non-Hispanic black	914	10.2	36.3	19.7	36.6	2.5
Non-Hispanic other	254	21.3	66.5	7.8	11.8	8.5

[1] Other arrangements include child's sibling; child cares for self; school (regular hours); before- or after-school care/program; respondent while she was working; and other arrangements not shown separately.

[2] Limited to women 22-44 years of age at time interview.

[3] GED is general equivalency diploma.

NOTE: Percents may add to more than 100 because some women reported more than one type of child care arrangement.

I1-10   Child Care Arrangements Used by Nonworking Women with at Least One Child under Five Years, 1995

Characteristic	Number in thousands	Grandparent or other relative	Nonrelative	Day care center or preschool	None	Other arrangement[1]
				Percent		
All women	7,138	6.1	5.3	7.6	80.0	3.7
Marital status						
Never married	1,541	8.5	4.3	8.3	75.3	4.4
Currently married	4,846	5.3	5.4	7.0	81.7	3.5
Formerly married	751	5.9	7.2	10.3	77.6	3.2
Age of child						
Under 1 year	2,087	5.8	3.7	2.0	86.3	3.1
1 year	1,617	6.1	6.3	4.0	82.0	4.1
2 years	1,556	6.1	5.5	7.8	79.0	2.4
3 years	1,054	6.5	5.6	17.0	69.3	2.6
4 years	823	6.0	6.7	16.4	74.6	8.3
Education at interview[2]						
No high school diploma or GED[3]	1,394	2.6	0.5	2.8	91.7	1.9
High school diploma or GED	2,566	5.7	4.6	8.7	80.4	3.8
Some college, no bachelor's degree	1,243	7.0	6.5	10.1	77.6	3.4
Bachelor's degree or higher	953	3.4	14.5	8.7	73.1	5.6
Poverty level income at interview[2]						
0-149 percent	2,706	4.7	2.9	5.6	86.2	1.6
0-99 percent	1,959	4.6	3.4	6.9	85.1	1.1
150-299 percent	1,704	5.0	2.6	7.8	83.5	2.7
300 percent or higher	1,747	5.2	12.5	10.7	71.4	7.5
Race and Hispanic origin						
Hispanic	1,225	3.8	2.7	3.1	88.4	2.3
Non-Hispanic while	4,480	5.9	6.5	7.9	79.0	4.0
Non-Hispanic black	1,073	7.8	4.4	12.8	72.6	2.9
Non-Hispanic other	359	10.9	2.9	3.8	83.7	7.0

[1] Other arrangements include child's brother/sister; child cares for self, school (regular hours); before- or after-school care/program; respondent while she was working; other parent or stepparent and other arrangements not shown separately.

[2] Limited to women 22-44 years of age at time of interview.

[3] GED is general equivalency diploma.

NOTE: Percents may not add to 100 because some women reported more than one type of child care arrangement.

I1-11   Amount Paid for Child Care by Working Women with at Least One Child under 13 Years, 1995

Characteristic	Number in thousands			Percent with no payment for child care[1]	Mean amount paid (in dollars) per week for child care[1]		
	One child	Two children	Three or more children		One child	Two children	Three or more children
All women[2]	8,691	5,932	2,084	50.7	58	80	82
Marital status							
Never married	1,365	414	142	44.1	59	57	49
Currently married	5,831	4,730	1,603	51.8	61	84	84
Formerly married	1,496	788	340	50.5	46	68	83
Work status at interview							
Full time	6,310	3,987	1,249	43.9	61	87	93
Part time	2,381	1,945	835	65.8	45	58	58
Age of youngest child							
Under 5 years	3,727	2,834	1,425	33.4	66	90	86
5-12 years	4,964	3,098	659	66.4	45	62	68
Education at interview[3]							
No high school diploma or GED[4]	669	477	226	65.3	42	57	60
High school diploma or GED	3,324	2,452	932	54.8	50	69	70
Some college, no bachelor's degree	2,350	1,533	475	48.0	57	79	79
Bachelor's degree or higher	1,853	1,386	432	41.1	75	101	113
Poverty level income at interview[3]							
0-149 percent	1,074	1,132	622	58.8	40	51	55
0-99 percent	494	519	353	64.2	41	45	62
150-299 percent	3,077	2,136	794	57.3	49	61	62
300 percent or higher	4,045	2,580	649	42.1	67	100	115
Race and Hispanic origin							
Hispanic	884	622	335	49.4	49	69	73
Non-Hispanic white	6,233	4,361	1,395	60.1	59	82	85
Non-Hispanic black	1,250	720	277	52.5	54	66	67

[1] Limited to women who reported any payment for child care. Mean amount paid refers to mean of the "typical" weekly payment for child care.
[2] Includes women with missing information on child care payment, and women of other race and origin groups not shown separately.
[3] Limited to women 22-44 years of age at time of interview.
[4] GED is general equivalency diploma.

I1-12   Number of Women Who Have Cared for a Child to Whom They Did Not Give Birth, 1995

Characteristic	Number in thousands	Any child[1]	Stepchild	Child of relative, friend, or partner	Foster child	Adopted child
				Percent		
All women[2]	54,748	11.1	3.3	5.7	0.9	0.9
Age at interview						
18-19 years	3,508	1.9	–	1.6	–	–
20-24 years	9,041	4.3	0.8	2.4	0.1	0.1
25-29 years	9,693	8.2	1.6	5.2	0.8	0.3
30-34 years	11,065	11.1	3.4	6.7	0.6	0.5
35-39 years	11,211	16.0	5.7	7.3	1.7	1.7
40-44 years	10,230	17.5	5.7	7.8	1.2	2.0
Marital status						
Never married	17,300	5.2	0.0	4.1	0.3	0.1
Currently married	29,600	13.5	5.3	5.7	1.1	1.2
Formerly married	7,849	14.9	3.2	9.2	1.1	1.2
Parity						
0 births	19,998	8.0	2.3	4.1	0.3	1.2
1 birth	10,502	12.2	4.9	5.5	0.7	0.6
2 births	13,871	12.9	3.7	6.9	1.1	0.8
3 or more births	10,377	13.5	3.3	7.4	1.7	0.5
Education at interview[3]						
No high school diploma or GED[4]	5,424	14.2	3.2	9.0	1.5	0.7
High school diploma or GED	18,169	14.1	4.3	7.4	0.9	0.9
Some college, no bachelors degree	12,399	13.7	4.3	7.2	1.1	1.1
Bachelor's degree or higher	11,748	7.4	2.8	2.6	0.7	1.1
Poverty level income at interview[3]						
0-149 percent	10,080	12.7	2.7	8.0	1.3	0.4
0-99 percent	5,992	12.8	1.9	9.0	1.4	0.4
150-299 percent	14,932	13.0	4.0	6.9	1.3	0.8
300 percent or higher	22,736	11.8	4.2	5.3	0.6	1.4
Race and Hispanic origin						
Hispanic	6,015	11.5	2.5	6.3	0.8	0.6
Non-Hispanic white	38,987	10.8	3.8	4.9	1.3	0.9
Non-Hispanic black	7,357	12.9	1.9	9.1	0.8	1.0
Non-Hispanic other	2,390	9.3	2.1	6.5	0.4	0.5

– Quantity zero.

0.0 Quantity more than zero but less than 0.05.

[1] Includes children with other relationships not shown separately.

[2] Includes women with missing information on other children raised.

[3] Limited to women 22-44 years of age at time of interview.

[4] GED Is general equivalency diploma.

NOTE: Percents may not add to "Any child" total because some women lived with and cared for more than one child not born to them.

2. FATHERS' PARTICIPATION IN CHILD CARE

I2-1   **Fathers Caring for Their Preschoolers: 1988–1993**

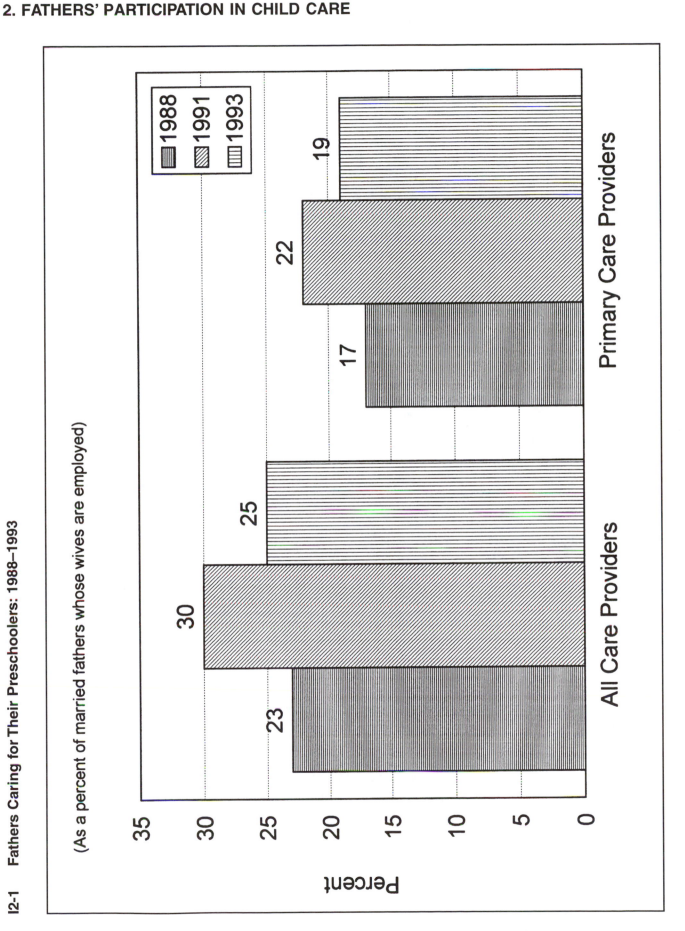

(As a percent of married fathers whose wives are employed)

I2-2   Fathers Providing Care for Preschoolers While Mothers Are Working, by Employment Status of Fathers: 1988–1993

(Numbers in thousands)

Employment status of father	1993		1991		1988	
	Total	Percent Providing	Total	Percent Providing	Total	Percent Providing
All Providers	6,274	24.8	6,274	30.3	6,536	23.3
Employment Status						
Not employed[1]	412	57.6	487	64.1	293	56.9
Employed[2]	5,862	22.5	5,788	27.5	6,242	21.7
Full time	5,428	21.7	5,217	26.4	5,887	21.4
Part time	434	32.3	571	37.0	355	26.9
Type of Work Shift[3]						
Day shift	4,275	18.3	3,981	23.4	4,492	18.7
Nonday shift	1,586	33.6	1,807	36.4	1,751	29.4
Primary Care Providers .	6,274	18.5	6,274	22.4	6,536	16.9
Employment Status						
Not employed[1]	412	50.2	487	52.8	293	46.5
Employed	5,862	16.3	5,788	19.9	6,242	15.6
Full time	5,428	15.4	5,217	19.1	5,887	15.3
Part time	434	27.4	571	27.1	355	20.4
Type of Work Shift						
Day shift	4,275	12.8	3,981	16.2	4,492	12.9
Nonday shift	1,586	25.7	1,807	28.0	1,751	22.3

[1] Includes persons who were unemployed, enrolled in school, or not in the labor force the month prior to the survey.
[2] In the month prior to the survey.
[3] For fathers who were employed in the month prior to the survey.
NOTE: Limited to married fathers whose wives are employed.

I2-3   **Fathers Providing Care for Their Preschoolers, by Employment Status of Fathers: 1988–1993**

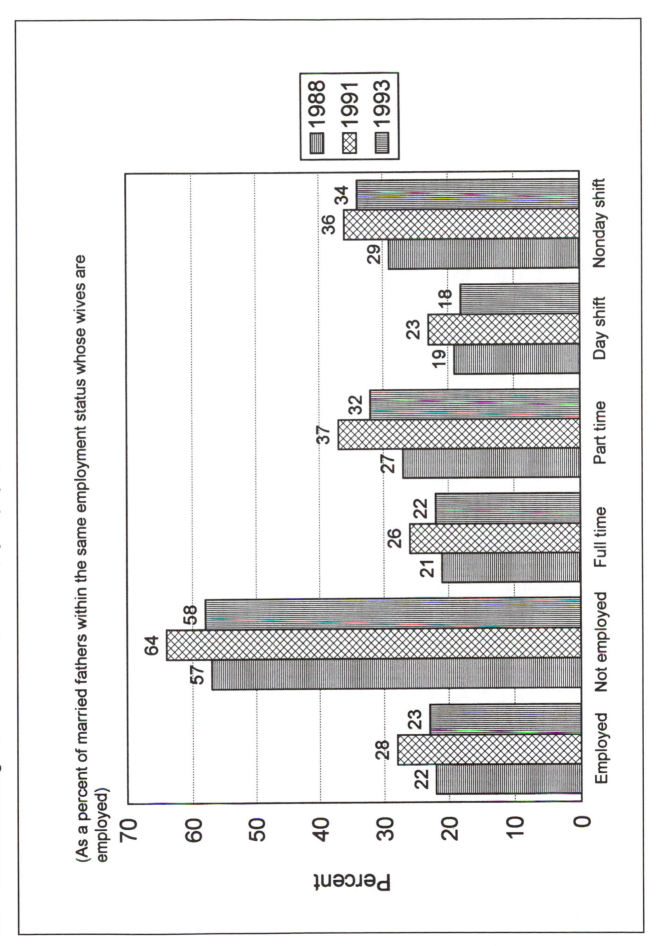

(As a percent of married fathers within the same employment status whose wives are employed)

I2-4   **Fathers Caring for Their Preschoolers, by Hours Available for Care: 1988–1993**

I2-5   Fathers Caring for Their Preschoolers, by Poverty Status: 1988–1993

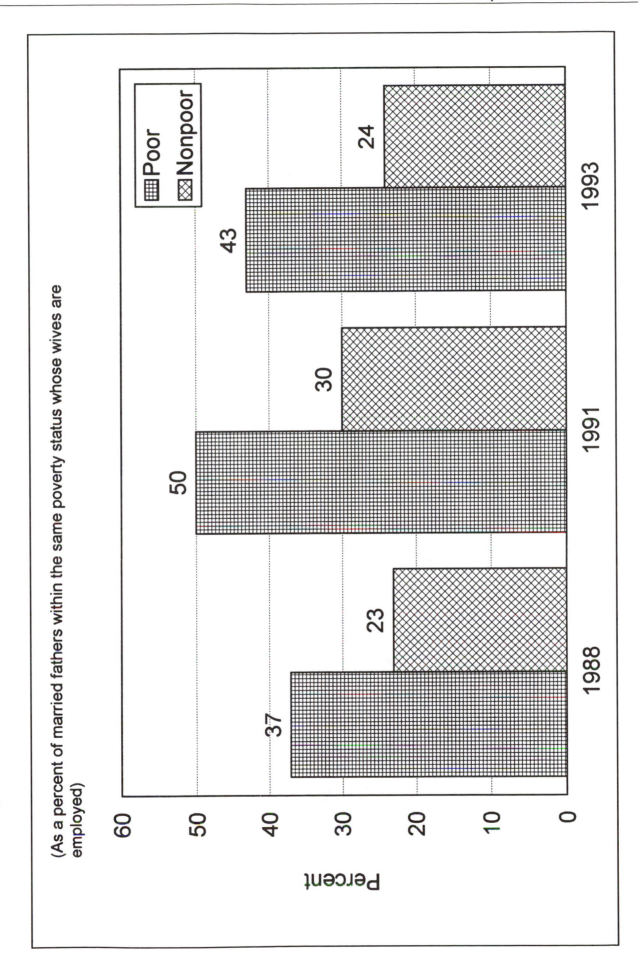

(As a percent of married fathers within the same poverty status whose wives are employed)

I2-6   Fathers Providing Care for Preschoolers While Mothers Are Working, by Various Characteristics: 1988-1993

(Numbers in thousands)

Characteristics	1993			1991			1988		
		Percent providing care			Percent providing care			Percent providing care	
	Number of fathers	All providers	Primary providers	Number of fathers	All providers	Primary providers	Number of fathers	All providers	Primary providers
All Fathers	6,274	24.8	18.5	6,274	30.3	22.4	6,536	23.3	16.9
Race and Hispanic origin:									
White, not Hispanic .	4,908	24.9	18.6	4,948	31.0	22.6	5,184	24.3	18.3
Black, not Hispanic .	475	23.4	16.1	491	24.9	22.1	630	19.2	13.1
Hispanic origin	610	27.2	21.2	521	38.8	28.0	501	21.2	10.7
Other	281	19.8	16.3	314	13.4	11.5	221	15.3	9.9
Father's occupation									
Manager/professional	1,619	18.1	12.9	1,595	23.4	16.4	NA	NA	NA
Technical/sales	1,189	20.1	15.0	1,214	26.9	19.0	NA	NA	NA
Service	508	42.1	29.0	438	47.3	35.5	NA	NA	NA
Other	2,547	22.4	16.6	2,542	26.8	19.7	NA	NA	NA
Not employed last month	412	57.6	50.2	487	64.4	52.8	NA	NA	NA
Number of children under 5:									
One	4,929	22.5	16.3	4,868	27.7	20.4	5,124	21.8	15.7
Two or more	1,346	33.1	26.7	1,407	39.2	29.6	1,411	28.6	21.3
Age of father:									
Less than 25 years ..	402	32.9	25.6	426	31.8	20.7	447	23.2	17.3
25 to 34 years	3,347	24.2	18.2	3,433	30.1	21.4	3,941	24.6	17.4
35 years and over ...	2,526	24.2	17.9	2,416	30.4	24.2	2,147	20.9	15.9
Poverty status[1]:									
Below poverty	286	43.0	36.6	273	49.5	42.1	314	36.9	30.4
Above poverty	5,975	23.9	17.7	5,965	29.5	21.5	6,220	22.6	16.3
Family's monthly income[1]:									
Less than $1,500	407	45.3	40.3	470	39.1	30.6	622	35.6	30.6
$1,500 to $2,999	1,760	30.0	24.9	2,082	37.4	29.4	2,565	26.8	19.3
$3,000 to $4,499	1,856	26.0	18.3	1,910	30.1	22.0	1,985	21.3	14.7
$4,500 and over	2,238	16.1	9.9	1,776	20.0	12.6	1,363	14.0	9.7
Husband's monthly income[2]:									
Less than $1,500	1,619	30.1	25.1	1,930	37.0	29.4	2,060	26.3	19.9
$1,500 to $2,999	2,706	24.6	18.5	2,665	30.9	21.7	3,061	22.6	15.6
$3,000 to $4,499	1,182	19.7	13.1	985	24.8	17.9	883	20.4	13.4
$4,500 and over	651	15.7	10.3	559	12.4	7.5	434	12.6	11.0

NA Data not tabulated for this year.
[1] Omits fathers with no family income. Income in current dollars.
[2] Omits fathers with no income. Income in current dollars.
[3] Receives AFDC, WIC, food stamps, or general assistance.
Note: Limited to married fathers whose wives are employed.

List of Sources

A1-1   No. 145, U.S. Bureau of the Census, *Statistical Abstract of the United States: 1997* (117th Edition). Washington, DC, 1997.

A1-2   No. 145, U.S. Bureau of the Census, *Statistical Abstract of the United States: 1997* (117th Edition). Washington, DC, 1997.

A1-3   No. 146, U.S. Bureau of the Census, *Statistical Abstract of the United States: 1997* (117th Edition). Washington, DC, 1997.

A1-4   No. 152, U.S. Bureau of the Census, *Statistical Abstract of the United States: 1997* (117th Edition). Washington, DC, 1997.

A1-5   No. 148, U.S. Bureau of the Census, *Statistical Abstract of the United States: 1997* (117th Edition). Washington, DC, 1997.

A1-6   No. 150, U.S. Bureau of the Census, *Statistical Abstract of the United States: 1997* (117th Edition). Washington, DC, 1997.

A1-7   No. 147, U.S. Bureau of the Census, *Statistical Abstract of the United States: 1997* (117th Edition). Washington, DC, 1997.

A1-8   No. 148, U.S. Bureau of the Census, *Statistical Abstract of the United States: 1997* (117th Edition). Washington, DC, 1997.

A1-9   No. 147, U.S. Bureau of the Census, *Statistical Abstract of the United States: 1997* (117th Edition). Washington, DC, 1997.

A1-10   No. 62, U.S. Bureau of the Census, *Statistical Abstract of the United States: 1997* (117th Edition). Washington, DC, 1997.

A1-11   No. 61, U.S. Bureau of the Census, *Statistical Abstract of the United States: 1997* (117th Edition). Washington, DC, 1997.

A1-12   No. 62, U.S. Bureau of the Census, *Statistical Abstract of the United States: 1997* (117th Edition). Washington, DC, 1997.

A2-1   No. 58, U.S. Bureau of the Census, *Statistical Abstract of the United States: 1997* (117th Edition). Washington, DC, 1997.

A2-2   No. 58, U.S. Bureau of the Census, *Statistical Abstract of the United States: 1997* (117th Edition). Washington, DC, 1997.

A2-3   No. 58, U.S. Bureau of the Census, *Statistical Abstract of the United States: 1997* (117th Edition). Washington, DC, 1997.

A2-4   No. 58, U.S. Bureau of the Census, *Statistical Abstract of the United States: 1997* (117th Edition). Washington, DC, 1997.

A2-5   No. 58, U.S. Bureau of the Census, *Statistical Abstract of the United States: 1997* (117th Edition). Washington, DC, 1997.

A2-6   No. 59, U.S. Bureau of the Census, *Statistical Abstract of the United States: 1997* (117th Edition). Washington, DC, 1997.

A2-7   No. 60, U.S. Bureau of the Census, *Statistical Abstract of the United States: 1997* (117th Edition). Washington, DC, 1997.

A2-8   U.S. Department of Health and Human Services, *Vital and Health Statistics, Fertility, Family Planning, and Women's Health: New Data from the 1995 National Survey of Family Growth,* Series 23, No. 19. Hyattsville, MD, May 1997.

A3-1   National Survey of Families and Households, 1994. Distributed by the Center for Demography and Ecology, University of Wisconsin-Madison.

A3-2   National Survey of Families and Households, 1994. Distributed by the Center for Demography and Ecology, University of Wisconsin-Madison.

A3-3   National Survey of Families and Households, 1994. Distributed by the Center for Demography and Ecology, University of Wisconsin-Madison.

A3-4   National Survey of Families and Households, 1994. Distributed by the Center for Demography and Ecology, University of Wisconsin-Madison.

B1-1   National Data Program for the Social Sciences, *General Social Surveys, 1972–1996: Cumulative Codebook,* November 1996. National Opinion Research Center, University of Chicago.

B1-2   National Survey of Families and Households, 1994. Distributed by the Center for Demography and Ecology, University of Wisconsin-Madison.

B1-3   National Survey of Families and Households, 1994. Distributed by the Center for Demography and Ecology, University of Wisconsin-Madison.

B1-4   National Survey of Families and Households, 1994. Distributed by the Center for Demography and Ecology, University of Wisconsin-Madison.

B1-5   National Survey of Families and Households, 1994. Distributed by the Center for Demography and Ecology, University of Wisconsin-Madison.

B1-6   National Survey of Families and Households, 1994. Distributed by the Center for Demography and Ecology, University of Wisconsin-Madison.

B1-7   National Survey of Families and Households, 1994. Distributed by the Center for Demography and Ecology, University of Wisconsin-Madison.

B1-8   The Gallup Poll Monthly, October 1993.

B1-9   The Gallup Poll Monthly, October 1993.

B1-10   The Gallup Poll Monthly, March 1997.

B2-1   National Survey of Families and Households, 1994. Distributed by the Center for Demography and Ecology, University of Wisconsin-Madison.

B2-2   National Survey of Families and Households, 1994. Distributed by the Center for Demography and Ecology, University of Wisconsin-Madison.

B2-3   The Gallup Poll Monthly, March 1997.

B2-4   The Gallup Poll Monthly, March 1997.

B2-5   The Gallup Poll Monthly, March 1997.

B2-6   The Gallup Poll Monthly, March 1997.

B2-7   The Gallup Poll Monthly, October 1993.

B2-8   National Survey of Families and Households, 1994. Distributed by the Center for Demography and Ecology, University of Wisconsin-Madison.

B2-9   National Data Program for the Social Sciences, *General Social Surveys, 1972–1996: Cumulative Codebook*, November 1996. National Opinion Research Center, University of Chicago, Chicago IL.

B2-10   National Data Program for the Social Sciences, *General Social Surveys, 1972–1996: Cumulative Codebook*, November 1996. National Opinion Research Center, University of Chicago.

B2-11   National Data Program for the Social Sciences, *General Social Surveys, 1972–1996: Cumulative Codebook*, November 1996. National Opinion Research Center, University of Chicago.

B2-12   The Gallup Poll Monthly, October 1993.

B2-13   The Gallup Poll Monthly, October 1993.

B2-14   The Gallup Poll Monthly, October 1993.

B2-15   The Gallup Poll Monthly, October 1993.

B2-16   The Gallup Poll Monthly, October 1993.

B2-17   The Gallup Poll Monthly, October 1993.

B2-18   The Gallup Poll Monthly, October 1993.

B3-1   National Survey of Families and Households, 1994. Distributed by the Center for Demography and Ecology, University of Wisconsin-Madison.

B3-2   National Survey of Families and Households, 1994. Distributed by the Center for Demography and Ecology, University of Wisconsin-Madison.

C1-1   No. 149, U.S. Bureau of the Census, *Statistical Abstract of the United States: 1997* (117th Edition). Washington, DC, 1997.

C1-2   No. 145, U.S. Bureau of the Census, *Statistical Abstract of the United States: 1997* (117th Edition). Washington, DC, 1997.

C1-3   U.S. Department of Health and Human Services, *Vital and Health Statistics, Fertility, Family Planning, and Women's Health: New Data from the 1995 National Survey of Family Growth*, Series 23, No. 19. Hyattsville, MD, May 1997.

C1-4   U.S. Department of Health and Human Services, *Vital and Health Statistics, Fertility, Family Planning, and Women's Health: New Data from the 1995 National Survey of Family Growth*, Series 23, No. 19. Hyattsville, MD, May 1997.

C1-5   U.S. Department of Health and Human Services, *Vital and Health Statistics, Fertility, Family Planning, and Women's Health: New Data from the 1995 National Survey of Family Growth*, Series 23, No. 19. Hyattsville, MD, May 1997.

C1-6   U.S. Department of Health and Human Services, *Vital and Health Statistics, Fertility, Family Planning, and Women's Health: New Data from the 1995 National Survey of Family Growth*, Series 23, No. 19. Hyattsville, MD, May 1997.

C1-7   National Data Program for the Social Sciences, *General Social Surveys, 1972–1996: Cumulative Codebook*, November 1996. National Opinion Research Center, University of Chicago.

C1-8   No. 150, U.S. Bureau of the Census, *Statistical Abstract of the United States: 1997* (117th Edition). Washington, DC, 1997.

C1-9   No. 151, U.S. Bureau of the Census, *Statistical Abstract of the United States: 1997* (117th Edition). Washington, DC, 1997.

C1-10   National Survey of Families and Households, 1994. Distributed by the Center for Demography and Ecology, University of Wisconsin-Madison.

C2-1   National Survey of Families and Households, 1994. Distributed by the Center for Demography and Ecology, University of Wisconsin-Madison.

C2-2   National Survey of Families and Households, 1994. Distributed by the Center for Demography and Ecology, University of Wisconsin-Madison.

C2-3   National Survey of Families and Households, 1994. Distributed by the Center for Demography and Ecology, University of Wisconsin-Madison.

C2-4   National Survey of Families and Households, 1994. Distributed by the Center for Demography and Ecology, University of Wisconsin-Madison.

C2-5   National Survey of Families and Households, 1994. Distributed by the Center for Demography and Ecology, University of Wisconsin-Madison.

C3-1   National Data Program for the Social Sciences, *General Social Surveys, 1972–1996: Cumulative Codebook*, November 1996. National Opinion Research Center, University of Chicago.

C3-2   National Data Program for the Social Sciences, *General Social Surveys, 1972-1996: Cumulative Codebook*, November 1996. National Opinion Research Center, University of Chicago.

C3-3   National Survey of Families and Households, 1994. Distributed by the Center for Demography and Ecology, University of Wisconsin-Madison.

C4-1   No. 609, U.S. Bureau of the Census, *Statistical Abstract of the United States: 1997* (117th Edition). Washington, DC, 1997.

C4-2   No. 610, U.S. Bureau of the Census, *Statistical Abstract of the United States: 1997* (117th Edition). Washington, DC, 1997.

C4-3   No. 611, U.S. Bureau of the Census, *Statistical Abstract of the United States: 1997* (117th Edition). Washington, DC, 1997.

D1-1   No. 88, U.S. Bureau of the Census, *Statistical Abstract of the United States: 1997* (117th Edition). Washington, DC, 1997.

D1-2   No. 88, U.S. Bureau of the Census, *Statistical Abstract of the United States: 1997* (117th Edition). Washington, DC, 1997.

D1-3   No. 88, U.S. Bureau of the Census, *Statistical Abstract of the United States: 1997* (117th Edition). Washington, DC, 1997.

D1-4   No. 89, U.S. Bureau of the Census, *Statistical Abstract of the United States: 1997* (117th Edition). Washington, DC, 1997.

D1-5   No. 90, U.S. Bureau of the Census, *Statistical Abstract of the United States: 1997* (117th Edition). Washington, DC, 1997.

D1-6   No. 93, U.S. Bureau of the Census, *Statistical Abstract of the United States: 1997* (117th Edition). Washington, DC, 1997.

D1-7   No. 94, U.S. Bureau of the Census, *Statistical Abstract of the United States: 1997* (117th Edition). Washington, DC, 1997.

D1-8   U.S. Department of Health and Human Services, *Vital and Health Statistics, Fertility, Family Planning, and Women's Health: New Data from the 1995 National Survey of Family Growth,* Series 23, No. 19. Hyattsville, MD, May 1997.

D1-9   U.S. Department of Health and Human Services, *Vital and Health Statistics, Fertility, Family Planning, and Women's Health: New Data from the 1995 National Survey of Family Growth,* Series 23, No. 19. Hyattsville, MD, May 1997.

D1-10   U.S. Department of Health and Human Services, *Vital and Health Statistics, Fertility, Family Planning, and Women's Health: New Data from the 1995 National Survey of Family Growth,* Series 23, No. 19. Hyattsville, MD, May 1997.

D1-11   No. 102, U.S. Bureau of the Census, *Statistical Abstract of the United States: 1997* (117th Edition). Washington, DC, 1997.

D1-12   No. 103, U.S. Bureau of the Census, *Statistical Abstract of the United States: 1997* (117th Edition). Washington, DC, 1997.

D1-13   No. 78, U.S. Bureau of the Census, *Statistical Abstract of the United States: 1997* (117th Edition). Washington, DC, 1997.

D1-14   No. 92, U.S. Bureau of the Census, *Statistical Abstract of the United States: 1997* (117th Edition). Washington, DC, 1997.

D1-15   No. 104, U.S. Bureau of the Census, *Statistical Abstract of the United States: 1997* (117th Edition). Washington, DC, 1997.

D1-16   No. 105, U.S. Bureau of the Census, *Statistical Abstract of the United States: 1997* (117th Edition). Washington, DC, 1997.

D1-17   U.S. Department of Health and Human Services, *Vital and Health Statistics, Fertility, Family Planning, and Women's Health: New Data from the 1995 National Survey of Family Growth,* Series 23, No. 19. Hyattsville, MD, May 1997.

D1-18   U.S. Department of Health and Human Services, *Vital and Health Statistics, Fertility, Family Planning, and Women's Health: New Data from the 1995 National Survey of Family Growth,* Series 23, No. 19. Hyattsville, MD, May 1997.

D1-19   No. 97, U.S. Bureau of the Census, *Statistical Abstract of the United States: 1997* (117th Edition). Washington, DC, 1997.

D1-20   No. 97, U.S. Bureau of the Census, *Statistical Abstract of the United States: 1997* (117th Edition). Washington, DC, 1997.

D1-21   No. 97, U.S. Bureau of the Census, *Statistical Abstract of the United States: 1997* (117th Edition). Washington, DC, 1997.

D1-22   No. 98, U.S. Bureau of the Census, *Statistical Abstract of the United States: 1997* (117th Edition). Washington, DC, 1997.

D1-23   U.S. Bureau of the Census, *Statistical Abstract of the United States: 1997* (117th Edition). Washington, DC, 1997.

D1-24   No. 91, U.S. Bureau of the Census, *Statistical Abstract of the United States: 1997* (117th Edition). Washington, DC, 1997.

D1-25   No. 96, U.S. Bureau of the Census, *Statistical Abstract of the United States: 1997* (117th Edition). Washington, DC, 1997.

D1-26   U.S. Department of Health and Human Services, *Vital and Health Statistics, Fertility, Family Planning, and Women's Health: New Data from the 1995 National Survey of Family Growth,* Series 23, No. 19. Hyattsville, MD, May 1997.

D1-27   U.S. Department of Health and Human Services, *Vital and Health Statistics, Fertility, Family Planning, and Women's Health: New Data from the 1995 National Survey of Family Growth,* Series 23, No. 19. Hyattsville, MD, May 1997.

D1-28   U.S. Department of Health and Human Services, *Vital and Health Statistics, Fertility, Family Planning, and Women's Health: New Data from the 1995 National Survey of Family Growth,* Series 23, No. 19. Hyattsville, MD, May 1997.

D1-29   U.S. Department of Health and Human Services, *Vital and Health Statistics, Fertility, Family Planning, and Women's Health: New Data from the 1995 National Survey of Family Growth,* Series 23, No. 19. Hyattsville, MD, May 1997.

D1-30   U.S. Department of Health and Human Services, *Vital and Health Statistics, Fertility, Family Planning, and Women's Health: New Data from the 1995 National Survey of Family Growth,* Series 23, No. 19. Hyattsville, MD, May 1997.

D1-31   U.S. Department of Health and Human Services, *Vital and Health Statistics, Fertility, Family Planning, and Women's Health: New Data from the 1995 National Survey of Family Growth,* Series 23, No. 19. Hyattsville, MD, May 1997.

D1-32   U.S. Department of Health and Human Services, *Vital and Health Statistics, Fertility, Family Planning, and Women's Health: New Data from the 1995 National Survey of Family Growth,* Series 23, No. 19. Hyattsville, MD, May 1997.

D1-33   U.S. Department of Health and Human Services, *Vital and Health Statistics, Fertility, Family Planning, and Women's Health: New Data from the 1995 National Survey of Family Growth,* Series 23, No. 19. Hyattsville, MD, May 1997.

D1-34   U.S. Department of Health and Human Services, *Vital and Health Statistics, Fertility, Family Planning, and Women's Health: New Data from the 1995 National Survey of Family Growth,* Series 23, No. 19. Hyattsville, MD, May 1997.

D1-35   U.S. Department of Health and Human Services, *Vital and Health Statistics, Fertility, Family Planning, and Women's Health: New Data from the 1995 National Survey of Family Growth,* Series 23, No. 19. Hyattsville, MD, May 1997.

D1-36   U.S. Department of Health and Human Services; *Vital and Health Statistics, Fertility, Family Planning, and Women's Health: New Data from the 1995 National Survey of Family Growth,* Series 23, No. 19. Hyattsville, MD, May 1997.

D1-37   U.S. Department of Health and Human Services, *Vital and Health Statistics, Fertility, Family Planning, and Women's Health: New Data from the 1995 National Survey of Family Growth,* Series 23, No. 19. Hyattsville, MD, May 1997.

D2-1   National Survey of Families and Households, 1994. Distributed by the Center for Demography and Ecology, University of Wisconsin-Madison.

D2-2   National Survey of Families and Households, 1994. Distributed by the Center for Demography and Ecology, University of Wisconsin-Madison.

D2-3   National Survey of Families and Households, 1994. Distributed by the Center for Demography and Ecology, University of Wisconsin-Madison.

D2-4   National Survey of Families and Households, 1994. Distributed by the Center for Demography and Ecology, University of Wisconsin-Madison.

D2-5   National Survey of Families and Households, 1994. Distributed by the Center for Demography and Ecology, University of Wisconsin-Madison.

D2-6   National Survey of Families and Households, 1994. Distributed by the Center for Demography and Ecology, University of Wisconsin-Madison.

D2-7   The Gallup Poll Monthly, March 1997.

D2-8   National Survey of Families and Households, 1994. Distributed by the Center for Demography and Ecology, University of Wisconsin-Madison.

D2-9   National Survey of Families and Households, 1994. Distributed by the Center for Demography and Ecology, University of Wisconsin-Madison.

D2-10   National Survey of Families and Households, 1994. Distributed by the Center for Demography and Ecology, University of Wisconsin-Madison.

D2-11   The Gallup Poll Monthly, March 1997.

D2-12   The Gallup Poll Monthly, March 1997.

D3-1   National Survey of Families and Households, 1994. Distributed by the Center for Demography and Ecology, University of Wisconsin-Madison.

D3-2   National Survey of Families and Households, 1994. Distributed by the Center for Demography and Ecology, University of Wisconsin-Madison.

D3-3   National Survey of Families and Households, 1994. Distributed by the Center for Demography and Ecology, University of Wisconsin-Madison.

D3-4   National Survey of Families and Households, 1994. Distributed by the Center for Demography and Ecology, University of Wisconsin-Madison.

D3-5   National Survey of Families and Households, 1994. Distributed by the Center for Demography and Ecology, University of Wisconsin-Madison.

D3-6   National Survey of Families and Households, 1994. Distributed by the Center for Demography and Ecology, University of Wisconsin-Madison.

D3-7   National Survey of Families and Households, 1994. Distributed by the Center for Demography and Ecology, University of Wisconsin-Madison.

D3-8   National Survey of Families and Households, 1994. Distributed by the Center for Demography and Ecology, University of Wisconsin-Madison.

D3-9   National Survey of Families and Households, 1994. Distributed by the Center for Demography and Ecology, University of Wisconsin-Madison.

D3-10   National Survey of Families and Households, 1994. Distributed by the Center for Demography and Ecology, University of Wisconsin-Madison.

D3-11   National Survey of Families and Households, 1994. Distributed by the Center for Demography and Ecology, University of Wisconsin-Madison.

D4-1   National Survey of Families and Households, 1994. Distributed by the Center for Demography and Ecology, University of Wisconsin-Madison.

D4-2   National Survey of Families and Households, 1994. Distributed by the Center for Demography and Ecology, University of Wisconsin-Madison.

D4-3   National Survey of Families and Households, 1994. Distributed by the Center for Demography and Ecology, University of Wisconsin-Madison.

D4-4   National Survey of Families and Households, 1994. Distributed by the Center for Demography and Ecology, University of Wisconsin-Madison.

D4-5   National Survey of Families and Households, 1994. Distributed by the Center for Demography and Ecology, University of Wisconsin-Madison.

D4-6   National Survey of Families and Households, 1994. Distributed by the Center for Demography and Ecology, University of Wisconsin-Madison.

D5-1   The Gallup Poll Monthly, May 1994.

D5-2   National Survey of Families and Households, 1994. Distributed by the Center for Demography and Ecology, University of Wisconsin-Madison.

D5-3   The Gallup Poll Monthly, May 1994.

D5-4   The Gallup Poll Monthly, May 1994.

D5-5   No. 352, U.S. Bureau of the Census, *Statistical Abstract of the United States: 1997* (117th Edition). Washington, DC, 1997.

D5-6   No. 352, U.S. Bureau of the Census, *Statistical Abstract of the United States: 1997* (117th Edition). Washington, DC, 1997.

D5-7   No. 353, U.S. Bureau of the Census, *Statistical Abstract of the United States: 1997* (117th Edition). Washington, DC, 1997.

D5-8   The Gallup Poll Monthly, May 1994.

E1-1   U.S. Department of Health and Human Services, *Vital and Health Statistics, Fertility, Family Planning, and Women's Health: New Data from the 1995 National Survey of Family Growth,* Series 23, No. 19. Hyattsville, MD, May 1997.

E1-2   U.S. Department of Health and Human Services, *Vital and Health Statistics, Fertility, Family Planning, and Women's Health: New Data from the 1995 National Survey of Family Growth,* Series 23, No. 19. Hyattsville, MD, May 1997.

E1-3   U.S. Department of Health and Human Services, *Vital and Health Statistics, Fertility, Family Planning, and Women's Health: New Data from the 1995 National Survey of Family Growth,* Series 23, No. 19. Hyattsville, MD, May 1997.

E1-4   U.S. Department of Health and Human Services, *Vital and Health Statistics, Fertility, Family Planning, and Women's Health: New Data from the 1995 National Survey of Family Growth,* Series 23, No. 19. Hyattsville, MD, May 1997.

E1-5   U.S. Department of Health and Human Services, *Vital and Health Statistics, Fertility, Family Planning, and Women's Health: New Data from the 1995 National Survey of Family Growth,* Series 23, No. 19. Hyattsville, MD, May 1997.

E1-6   U.S. Department of Health and Human Services, *Vital and Health Statistics, Fertility, Family Planning, and Women's Health: New Data from the 1995 National Survey of Family Growth,* Series 23, No. 19. Hyattsville, MD, May 1997.

E1-7   U.S. Department of Health and Human Services, *Vital and Health Statistics, Fertility, Family Planning, and Women's Health: New Data from the 1995 National Survey of Family Growth,* Series 23, No. 19. Hyattsville, MD, May 1997.

E1-8   Michael, Robert T., John H. Gagnon, Edward O. Laumann, and Gina Kolata. *Sex in America: A Definitive Survey.* Little, Brown, and Company, 1994.

E1-9   U.S. Department of Health and Human Services, *Vital and Health Statistics, Fertility, Family Planning, and Women's Health: New Data from the 1995 National Survey of Family Growth,* Series 23, No. 19. Hyattsville, MD, May 1997.

E1-10   U.S. Department of Health and Human Services, *Vital and Health Statistics, Fertility, Family Planning, and Women's Health: New Data from the 1995 National Survey of Family Growth,* Series 23, No. 19. Hyattsville, MD, May 1997.

E1-11   U.S. Department of Health and Human Services, *Vital and Health Statistics, Fertility, Family Planning, and Women's Health: New Data from the 1995 National Survey of Family Growth,* Series 23, No. 19. Hyattsville, MD, May 1997.

E1-12   National Survey of Families and Households, 1994. Distributed by the Center for Demography and Ecology, University of Wisconsin-Madison.

E1-13   U.S. Department of Health and Human Services, *Vital and Health Statistics, Fertility, Family Planning, and Women's Health: New Data from the 1995 National Survey of Family Growth,* Series 23, No. 19. Hyattsville, MD, May 1997.

E1-14   U.S. Department of Health and Human Services, *Vital and Health Statistics, Fertility, Family Planning, and Women's Health: New Data from the 1995 National Survey of Family Growth,* Series 23, No. 19. Hyattsville, MD, May 1997.

E1-15   U.S. Department of Health and Human Services, *Vital and Health Statistics, Fertility, Family Planning, and Women's Health: New Data from the 1995 National Survey of Family Growth,* Series 23, No. 19. Hyattsville, MD, May 1997.

E2-1   National Data Program for the Social Sciences, *General Social Surveys, 1972–1996: Cumulative Codebook,* November 1996. National Opinion Research Center, University of Chicago.

E2-2   National Data Program for the Social Sciences, *General Social Surveys, 1972–1996: Cumulative Codebook,* November 1996. National Opinion Research Center, University of Chicago.

E2-3   National Data Program for the Social Sciences, *General Social Surveys, 1972–1996: Cumulative Codebook*, November 1996. National Opinion Research Center, University of Chicago.

E2-4   National Data Program for the Social Sciences, *General Social Surveys, 1972–1996: Cumulative Codebook*, November 1996. National Opinion Research Center, University of Chicago.

E2-5   National Survey of Families and Households, 1994. Distributed by the Center for Demography and Ecology, University of Wisconsin-Madison.

E2-6   The Gallup Poll Monthly, December 1996.

E2-7   The Gallup Poll Monthly, April 1993.

E2-8   The Gallup Poll Monthly, December 1996.

E2-9   U.S. Department of Health and Human Services, *Vital and Health Statistics, Fertility, Family Planning, and Women's Health: New Data from the 1995 National Survey of Family Growth*, Series 23, No. 19. Hyattsville, MD, May 1997.

E3-1   No. 110, U.S. Bureau of the Census, *Statistical Abstract of the United States: 1997* (117th Edition). Washington, DC, 1997.

E3-2   U.S. Department of Health and Human Services, *Vital and Health Statistics, Fertility, Family Planning, and Women's Health: New Data from the 1995 National Survey of Family Growth*, Series 23, No. 19. Hyattsville, MD, May 1997.

E3-3   U.S. Department of Health and Human Services, *Vital and Health Statistics, Fertility, Family Planning, and Women's Health: New Data from the 1995 National Survey of Family Growth*, Series 23, No. 19. Hyattsville, MD, May 1997.

E3-4   U.S. Department of Health and Human Services, *Vital and Health Statistics, Fertility, Family Planning, and Women's Health: New Data from the 1995 National Survey of Family Growth*, Series 23, No. 19. Hyattsville, MD, May 1997.

E3-5   No. 114, U.S. Bureau of the Census, *Statistical Abstract of the United States: 1997* (117th Edition). Washington, DC, 1997.

E3-6   No. 115, U.S. Bureau of the Census, *Statistical Abstract of the United States: 1997* (117th Edition). Washington, DC, 1997.

E3-7   No. 116, U.S. Bureau of the Census, *Statistical Abstract of the United States: 1997* (117th Edition). Washington, DC, 1997.

E3-8   National Data Program for the Social Sciences, *General Social Surveys, 1972-1996: Cumulative Codebook*, November 1996. National Opinion Research Center, University of Chicago.

E3-9   National Data Program for the Social Sciences, *General Social Surveys, 1972-1996: Cumulative Codebook*, November 1996. National Opinion Research Center, University of Chicago.

E3-10   The Gallup Poll Monthly, April 1993.

E3-11   The Gallup Poll Monthly, March 1993.

E4-1   U.S. Department of Health and Human Services, *Vital and Health Statistics, Fertility, Family Planning, and Women's Health: New Data from the 1995 National Survey of Family Growth*, Series 23, No. 19. Hyattsville, MD, May 1997.

E4-2   U.S. Department of Health and Human Services, *Vital and Health Statistics, Fertility, Family Planning, and Women's Health: New Data from the 1995 National Survey of Family Growth*, Series 23, No. 19. Hyattsville, MD, May 1997.

E4-3   U.S. Department of Health and Human Services, *Vital and Health Statistics, Fertility, Family Planning, and Women's Health: New Data from the 1995 National Survey of Family Growth*, Series 23, No. 19. Hyattsville, MD, May 1997.

E4-4   U.S. Department of Health and Human Services, *Vital and Health Statistics, Fertility, Family Planning, and Women's Health: New Data from the 1995 National Survey of Family Growth*, Series 23, No. 19. Hyattsville, MD, May 1997.

E4-5   U.S. Department of Health and Human Services, *Vital and Health Statistics, Fertility, Family Planning, and Women's Health: New Data from the 1995 National Survey of Family Growth*, Series 23, No. 19. Hyattsville, MD, May 1997.

F1-1   U.S. Bureau of the Census, *Statistical Abstract of the United States: 1997* (117th Edition). Washington, DC, 1997.

F1-2   U.S. Bureau of the Census, *Statistical Abstract of the United States: 1997* (117th Edition). Washington, DC, 1997.

F1-3   No. 66, U.S. Bureau of the Census, *Statistical Abstract of the United States: 1997* (117th Edition). Washington, DC, 1997.

F1-4   *Current Population Reports*, p20–477, Table A, p. vii.

F1-5   No. 64, U.S. Bureau of the Census, *Statistical Abstract of the United States: 1997* (117th Edition). Washington, DC, 1997.

F1-6   No. 65, U.S. Bureau of the Census, *Statistical Abstract of the United States: 1997* (117th Edition). Washington, DC, 1997.

F1-7   No. 66, U.S. Bureau of the Census, *Statistical Abstract of the United States: 1997* (117th Edition). Washington, DC, 1997.

F1-8   No. 67, U.S. Bureau of the Census, *Statistical Abstract of the United States: 1997* (117th Edition). Washington, DC, 1997.

F1-9   No. 68, U.S. Bureau of the Census, *Statistical Abstract of the United States: 1997* (117th Edition). Washington, DC, 1997.

F1-10   No. 69, U.S. Bureau of the Census, *Statistical Abstract of the United States: 1997* (117th Edition). Washington, DC, 1997.

F1-11   No. 73, U.S. Bureau of the Census, *Statistical Abstract of the United States: 1997* (117th Edition). Washington, DC, 1997.

F1-12 No. 74, U.S. Bureau of the Census, *Statistical Abstract of the United States: 1997* (117th Edition). Washington, DC, 1997.

F1-13 No. 75, U.S. Bureau of the Census, *Statistical Abstract of the United States: 1997* (117th Edition). Washington, DC, 1997.

F1-14 No. 75, U.S. Bureau of the Census, *Statistical Abstract of the United States: 1997* (117th Edition). Washington, DC, 1997.

F1-15 No. 75, U.S. Bureau of the Census, *Statistical Abstract of the United States: 1997* (117th Edition). Washington, DC, 1997.

F1-16 No. 75, U.S. Bureau of the Census, *Statistical Abstract of the United States: 1997* (117th Edition). Washington, DC, 1997.

F1-17 *Current Population Reports*, p20–477, Figure 2, p. ix.

F1-18 *Current Population Reports*, p20–477, Table C, p. ix.

F2-1 U.S. Department of Health and Human Services, *Vital and Health Statistics, Fertility, Family Planning, and Women's Health: New Data from the 1995 National Survey of Family Growth*, Series 23, No. 19. Hyattsville, MD, May 1997.

F2-2 U.S. Department of Health and Human Services, *Vital and Health Statistics, Fertility, Family Planning, and Women's Health: New Data from the 1995 National Survey of Family Growth*, Series 23, No. 19. Hyattsville, MD, May 1997.

F2-3 U.S. Department of Health and Human Services, *Vital and Health Statistics, Fertility, Family Planning, and Women's Health: New Data from the 1995 National Survey of Family Growth*, Series 23, No. 19. Hyattsville, MD, May 1997.

F2-4 U.S. Department of Health and Human Services, *Vital and Health Statistics, Fertility, Family Planning, and Women's Health: New Data from the 1995 National Survey of Family Growth*, Series 23, No. 19. Hyattsville, MD, May 1997.

F2-5 U.S. Department of Health and Human Services, *Vital and Health Statistics, Fertility, Family Planning, and Women's Health: New Data from the 1995 National Survey of Family Growth*, Series 23, No. 19. Hyattsville, MD, May 1997.

F2-6 National Survey of Families and Households, 1994. Distributed by the Center for Demography and Ecology, University of Wisconsin-Madison.

F2-7 National Survey of Families and Households, 1994. Distributed by the Center for Demography and Ecology, University of Wisconsin-Madison.

F3-1 National Survey of Families and Households, 1994. Distributed by the Center for Demography and Ecology, University of Wisconsin-Madison.

F3-2 National Survey of Families and Households, 1994. Distributed by the Center for Demography and Ecology, University of Wisconsin-Madison.

F3-3 National Survey of Families and Households, 1994. Distributed by the Center for Demography and Ecology, University of Wisconsin-Madison.

F3-4 National Survey of Families and Households, 1994. Distributed by the Center for Demography and Ecology, University of Wisconsin-Madison.

F3-5 National Survey of Families and Households, 1994. Distributed by the Center for Demography and Ecology, University of Wisconsin-Madison.

F4-1 National Survey of Families and Households, 1994. Distributed by the Center for Demography and Ecology, University of Wisconsin-Madison.

F4-2 National Survey of Families and Households, 1994. Distributed by the Center for Demography and Ecology, University of Wisconsin-Madison.

F4-3 National Survey of Families and Households, 1994. Distributed by the Center for Demography and Ecology, University of Wisconsin-Madison.

F4-4 National Survey of Families and Households, 1994. Distributed by the Center for Demography and Ecology, University of Wisconsin-Madison.

F4-5 National Survey of Families and Households, 1994. Distributed by the Center for Demography and Ecology, University of Wisconsin-Madison.

G1-1 No. 630, U.S. Bureau of the Census, *Statistical Abstract of the United States: 1997* (117th Edition). Washington, DC, 1997.

G1-2 U.S. Bureau of Labor Statistics, Bulletins 2217 and 2340. Washington, DC, 1997.

G1-3 Unpublished results from 1993 *Current Population Survey*.

G1-4 Unpublished results from 1993 *Current Population Survey*.

G1-5 Unpublished results from 1993 *Current Population Survey*.

G1-6 No. 632, U.S. Bureau of the Census, *Statistical Abstract of the United States: 1997* (117th Edition). Washington, DC, 1997.

G1-7 No. 631, U.S. Bureau of the Census, *Statistical Abstract of the United States: 1997* (117th Edition). Washington, DC, 1997.

G1-8 No. 733, U.S. Bureau of the Census, *Statistical Abstract of the United States: 1997* (117th Edition). Washington, DC, 1997.

G1-9 U.S. Bureau of Labor Statistics, Bulletins 2217 and 2340. Washington, DC, 1997.

G1-10 No. 632, U.S. Bureau of the Census, *Statistical Abstract of the United States: 1997* (117th Edition). Washington, DC, 1997.

H1-1 No. 12, U.S. Bureau of the Census, *Statistical Abstract of the United States: 1997* (117th Edition). Washington, DC, 1997.

H1-2 No. 13, U.S. Bureau of the Census, *Statistical Abstract of the United States: 1997* (117th Edition). Washington, DC, 1997.

H1-3   No. 118, U.S. Bureau of the Census, *Statistical Abstract of the United States: 1997* (117th Edition). Washington, DC, 1997.

H1-4   No. 117, U.S. Bureau of the Census, *Statistical Abstract of the United States: 1997* (117th Edition). Washington, DC, 1997.

H1-5   No. 118, U.S. Bureau of the Census, *Statistical Abstract of the United States: 1997* (117th Edition). Washington, DC, 1997.

H1-6   No. 32, U.S. Bureau of the Census, *Statistical Abstract of the United States: 1997* (117th Edition). Washington, DC, 1997.

H1-7   No. 49, U.S. Bureau of the Census, *Statistical Abstract of the United States: 1997* (117th Edition). Washington, DC, 1997.

H1-8   No. 53, U.S. Bureau of the Census, *Statistical Abstract of the United States: 1997* (117th Edition). Washington, DC, 1997.

H2-1   No. 719, U.S. Bureau of the Census, *Statistical Abstract of the United States: 1997* (117th Edition). Washington, DC, 1997.

H2-2   No. 724, U.S. Bureau of the Census, *Statistical Abstract of the United States: 1997* (117th Edition). Washington, DC, 1997.

H2-3   No. 724, U.S. Bureau of the Census, *Statistical Abstract of the United States: 1997* (117th Edition). Washington, DC, 1997.

H2-4   No. 723, U.S. Bureau of the Census, *Statistical Abstract of the United States: 1997* (117th Edition). Washington, DC, 1997.

H2-5   No. 724, U.S. Bureau of the Census, *Statistical Abstract of the United States: 1997* (117th Edition). Washington, DC, 1997.

H2-6   No. 719, U.S. Bureau of the Census, *Statistical Abstract of the United States: 1997* (117th Edition). Washington, DC, 1997.

H2-7   No. 720, U.S. Bureau of the Census, *Statistical Abstract of the United States: 1997* (117th Edition). Washington, DC, 1997.

H2-8   No. 721, U.S. Bureau of the Census, *Statistical Abstract of the United States: 1997* (117th Edition). Washington, DC, 1997.

H2-9   No. 722, U.S. Bureau of the Census, *Statistical Abstract of the United States: 1997* (117th Edition). Washington, DC, 1997.

H2-10   No. 723, U.S. Bureau of the Census, *Statistical Abstract of the United States: 1997* (117th Edition). Washington, DC, 1997.

H2-11   No. 724, U.S. Bureau of the Census, *Statistical Abstract of the United States: 1997* (117th Edition). Washington, DC, 1997.

H2-12   No. 725, U.S. Bureau of the Census, *Statistical Abstract of the United States: 1997* (117th Edition). Washington, DC, 1997.

H2-13   No. 725, U.S. Bureau of the Census, *Statistical Abstract of the United States: 1997* (117th Edition). Washington, DC, 1997.

H2-14   No. 726, U.S. Bureau of the Census, *Statistical Abstract of the United States: 1997* (117th Edition). Washington, DC, 1997.

H2-15   No 747, U.S. Bureau of the Census, *Statistical Abstract of the United States: 1997* (117th Edition). Washington, DC, 1997.

H2-16   No 729, U.S. Bureau of the Census, *Statistical Abstract of the United States: 1997* (117th Edition). Washington, DC, 1997.

H2-17   No. 730, U.S. Bureau of the Census, *Statistical Abstract of the United States: 1997* (117th Edition). Washington, DC, 1997.

H2-18   No. 731, U.S. Bureau of the Census, *Statistical Abstract of the United States: 1997* (117th Edition). Washington, DC, 1997.

H2-19   No. 777, U.S. Bureau of the Census, *Statistical Abstract of the United States: 1997* (117th Edition). Washington, DC, 1997.

H2-20   No. 778, U.S. Bureau of the Census, *Statistical Abstract of the United States: 1997* (117th Edition). Washington, DC, 1997.

H2-21   No. 779, U.S. Bureau of the Census, *Statistical Abstract of the United States: 1997* (117th Edition). Washington, DC, 1997.

H2-22   No. 780, U.S. Bureau of the Census, *Statistical Abstract of the United States: 1997* (117th Edition). Washington, DC, 1997.

H2-23   No. 781, U.S. Bureau of the Census, *Statistical Abstract of the United States: 1997* (117th Edition). Washington, DC, 1997.

H2-24   No. 591, U.S. Bureau of the Census, *Statistical Abstract of the United States: 1997* (117th Edition). Washington, DC, 1997.

H2-25   No. 592, U.S. Bureau of the Census, *Statistical Abstract of the United States: 1997* (117th Edition). Washington, DC, 1997.

H2-26   No. 593, U.S. Bureau of the Census, *Statistical Abstract of the United States: 1997* (117th Edition). Washington, DC, 1997.

H2-27   No. 585, U.S. Bureau of the Census, *Statistical Abstract of the United States: 1997* (117th Edition). Washington, DC, 1997.

H2-28   No. 586, U.S. Bureau of the Census, *Statistical Abstract of the United States: 1997* (117th Edition). Washington, DC, 1997.

H2-29   No. 579, U.S. Bureau of the Census, *Statistical Abstract of the United States: 1997* (117th Edition). Washington, DC, 1997.

H2-30   No. 580, U.S. Bureau of the Census, *Statistical Abstract of the United States: 1997* (117th Edition). Washington, DC, 1997.

H2-31   No. 581, U.S. Bureau of the Census, *Statistical Abstract of the United States: 1997* (117th Edition). Washington, DC, 1997.

H2-32   No. 782, U.S. Bureau of the Census, *Statistical Abstract of the United States: 1997* (117th Edition). Washington, DC, 1997.

H2-33   No. 783, U.S. Bureau of the Census, *Statistical Abstract of the United States: 1997* (117th Edition). Washington, DC, 1997.

H2-34   No. 784, U.S. Bureau of the Census, *Statistical Abstract of the United States: 1997* (117th Edition). Washington, DC, 1997.

H2-35   No. 748, U.S. Bureau of the Census, *Statistical Abstract of the United States: 1997* (117th Edition). Washington, DC, 1997.

H3-1   No. 737, U.S. Bureau of the Census, *Statistical Abstract of the United States: 1997* (117th Edition). Washington, DC, 1997.

H3-2   No. 736, U.S. Bureau of the Census, *Statistical Abstract of the United States: 1997* (117th Edition). Washington, DC, 1997.

H3-3   No. 737, U.S. Bureau of the Census, *Statistical Abstract of the United States: 1997* (117th Edition). Washington, DC, 1997.

H3-4   No. 738, U.S. Bureau of the Census, *Statistical Abstract of the United States: 1997* (117th Edition). Washington, DC, 1997.

H3-5   No. 739, U.S. Bureau of the Census, *Statistical Abstract of the United States: 1997* (117th Edition). Washington, DC, 1997.

H3-6   No. 740, U.S. Bureau of the Census, *Statistical Abstract of the United States: 1997* (117th Edition). Washington, DC, 1997.

H3-7   No. 741, U.S. Bureau of the Census, *Statistical Abstract of the United States: 1997* (117th Edition). Washington, DC, 1997.

H3-8   No. 744, U.S. Bureau of the Census, *Statistical Abstract of the United States: 1997* (117th Edition). Washington, DC, 1997.

H3-9   No. 745, U.S. Bureau of the Census, *Statistical Abstract of the United States: 1997* (117th Edition). Washington, DC, 1997.

H3-10   No. 746, U.S. Bureau of the Census, *Statistical Abstract of the United States: 1997* (117th Edition). Washington, DC, 1997.

H3-11   No. 584, U.S. Bureau of the Census, *Statistical Abstract of the United States: 1997* (117th Edition). Washington, DC, 1997.

H3-12   No. 583, U.S. Bureau of the Census, *Statistical Abstract of the United States: 1997* (117th Edition). Washington, DC, 1997.

H3-13   No. 584, U.S. Bureau of the Census, *Statistical Abstract of the United States: 1997* (117th Edition). Washington, DC, 1997.

H3-14   No. 605, U.S. Bureau of the Census, *Statistical Abstract of the United States: 1997* (117th Edition). Washington, DC, 1997.

H3-15   No. 606, U.S. Bureau of the Census, *Statistical Abstract of the United States: 1997* (117th Edition). Washington, DC, 1997.

H3-16   No. 607, U.S. Bureau of the Census, *Statistical Abstract of the United States: 1997* (117th Edition). Washington, DC, 1997.

H3-17   No. 608, U.S. Bureau of the Census, *Statistical Abstract of the United States: 1997* (117th Edition). Washington, DC, 1997.

H4-1   No. 1200, U.S. Bureau of the Census, *Statistical Abstract of the United States: 1997* (117th Edition). Washington, DC, 1997.

H4-2   No. 1186, U.S. Bureau of the Census, *Statistical Abstract of the United States: 1997* (117th Edition). Washington, DC, 1997.

H4-3   No. 1187, U.S. Bureau of the Census, *Statistical Abstract of the United States: 1997* (117th Edition). Washington, DC, 1997.

H4-4   No. 1188, U.S. Bureau of the Census, *Statistical Abstract of the United States: 1997* (117th Edition). Washington, DC, 1997.

H4-5   No. 1189, U.S. Bureau of the Census, *Statistical Abstract of the United States: 1997* (117th Edition). Washington, DC, 1997.

H4-6   No. 1190, U.S. Bureau of the Census, *Statistical Abstract of the United States: 1997* (117th Edition). Washington, DC, 1997.

H4-7   No. 1195, U.S. Bureau of the Census, *Statistical Abstract of the United States: 1997* (117th Edition). Washington, DC, 1997.

H4-8   No. 1196, U.S. Bureau of the Census, *Statistical Abstract of the United States: 1997* (117th Edition). Washington, DC, 1997.

H4-9   No. 1197, U.S. Bureau of the Census, *Statistical Abstract of the United States: 1997* (117th Edition). Washington, DC, 1997.

H4-10   No. 1200, U.S. Bureau of the Census, *Statistical Abstract of the United States: 1997* (117th Edition). Washington, DC, 1997.

H4-11   No. 1201, U.S. Bureau of the Census, *Statistical Abstract of the United States: 1997* (117th Edition). Washington, DC, 1997.

H4-12   No. 1202, U.S. Bureau of the Census, *Statistical Abstract of the United States: 1997* (117th Edition). Washington, DC, 1997.

H4-13   No. 1203, U.S. Bureau of the Census, *Statistical Abstract of the United States: 1997* (117th Edition). Washington, DC, 1997.

H4-14   No. 1204, U.S. Bureau of the Census, *Statistical Abstract of the United States: 1997* (117th Edition). Washington, DC, 1997.

H4-15   No. 1205, U.S. Bureau of the Census, *Statistical Abstract of the United States: 1997* (117th Edition). Washington, DC, 1997.

H4-16   No. 765, U.S. Bureau of the Census, *Statistical Abstract of the United States: 1997* (117th Edition). Washington, DC, 1997.

H4-17   No. 766, U.S. Bureau of the Census, *Statistical Abstract of the United States: 1997* (117th Edition). Washington, DC, 1997.

H4-18   No. 411, U.S. Bureau of the Census, *Statistical Abstract of the United States: 1997* (117th Edition). Washington, DC, 1997.

H4-19   No. 412, U.S. Bureau of the Census, *Statistical Abstract of the United States: 1997* (117th Edition). Washington, DC, 1997.

H4-20   No. 413, U.S. Bureau of the Census, *Statistical Abstract of the United States: 1997* (117th Edition). Washington, DC, 1997.

H4-21   No. 615, U.S. Bureau of the Census, *Statistical Abstract of the United States: 1997* (117th Edition). Washington, DC, 1997.

H5-1   No. 172, U.S. Bureau of the Census, *Statistical Abstract of the United States: 1997* (117th Edition). Washington, DC, 1997.

H5-2   No. 171, U.S. Bureau of the Census, *Statistical Abstract of the United States: 1997* (117th Edition). Washington, DC, 1997.

H5-3   No. 172, U.S. Bureau of the Census, *Statistical Abstract of the United States: 1997* (117th Edition). Washington, DC, 1997.

H5-4   U.S. Department of Health and Human Services, *Vital and Health Statistics, Fertility, Family Planning, and Women's Health: New Data from the 1995 National Survey of Family Growth,* Series 23, No. 19. Hyattsville, MD, May 1997.

H5-5   U.S. Department of Health and Human Services, *Vital and Health Statistics, Fertility, Family Planning, and Women's Health: New Data from the 1995 National Survey of Family Growth,* Series 23, No. 19. Hyattsville, MD, May 1997.

I1-1   U.S. Bureau of the Census, Current Population Reports, P70–53. Washington, DC, 1995.

I1-2   U.S. Bureau of the Census, Current Population Reports, P70–53. Washington, DC, 1995.

I1-3   U.S. Bureau of the Census, Current Population Reports, P70–53. Washington, DC, 1995.

I1-4   U.S. Bureau of the Census, Current Population Reports, P70–53. Washington, DC, 1995.

I1-5   U.S. Bureau of the Census, Current Population Reports, P70–53. Washington, DC, 1995.

I1-6   U.S. Department of Health and Human Services, *Vital and Health Statistics, Fertility, Family Planning, and Women's Health: New Data from the 1995 National Survey of Family Growth,* Series 23, No. 19. Hyattsville, MD, May 1997.

I1-7   U.S. Department of Health and Human Services, *Vital and Health Statistics, Fertility, Family Planning, and Women's Health: New Data from the 1995 National Survey of Family Growth,* Series 23, No. 19. Hyattsville, MD, May 1997.

I1-8   U.S. Department of Health and Human Services, *Vital and Health Statistics, Fertility, Family Planning, and Women's Health: New Data from the 1995 National Survey of Family Growth,* Series 23, No. 19. Hyattsville, MD, May 1997.

I1-9   U.S. Department of Health and Human Services, *Vital and Health Statistics, Fertility, Family Planning, and Women's Health: New Data from the 1995 National Survey of Family Growth,* Series 23, No. 19. Hyattsville, MD, May 1997.

I1-10   U.S. Department of Health and Human Services, *Vital and Health Statistics, Fertility, Family Planning, and Women's Health: New Data from the 1995 National Survey of Family Growth,* Series 23, No. 19. Hyattsville, MD, May 1997.

I1-11   U.S. Department of Health and Human Services, *Vital and Health Statistics, Fertility, Family Planning, and Women's Health: New Data from the 1995 National Survey of Family Growth,* Series 23, No. 19. Hyattsville, MD, May 1997.

I1-12   U.S. Department of Health and Human Services, *Vital and Health Statistics, Fertility, Family Planning, and Women's Health: New Data from the 1995 National Survey of Family Growth,* Series 23, No. 19. Hyattsville, MD, May 1997.

I2-1   U.S. Bureau of the Census, Current Population Reports, P70–59. Washington, DC, 1995.

I2-2   U.S. Bureau of the Census, Current Population Reports, P70–59. Washington, DC, 1995.

I2-3   U.S. Bureau of the Census, Current Population Reports, P70–59. Washington, DC, 1995.

I2-4   U.S. Bureau of the Census, Current Population Reports, P70–59. Washington, DC, 1995.

I2-5   U.S. Bureau of the Census, Survey of Income and Program Participation (SIPP).

I2-6   U.S. Bureau of the Census, Current Population Reports, P70–59. Washington, DC, 1995.

Index

by Virgil Diodato